Gandhi and King

The Power of Nonviolent Resistance

Michael J. Nojeim

Westport, Connecticut
London

Library of Congress Cataloging-in-Publication Data

Nojeim, Michael J., 1960–
  Gandhi and King : the power of nonviolent resistance / Michael J.
  Nojeim.
    p. cm.
  Includes bibliographical references and index.
  ISBN 0-275-96574-0 (alk. paper)
    1. Nonviolence. 2. Gandhi, Mahatma, 1869–1948. 3. King, Martin
  Luther, Jr., 1929–1968. I. Title.
  HM1281.N63   2004
  303.6'1—dc22   2003068985

British Library Cataloguing in Publication Data is available.

Library of Congress Catalog Card Number: 2003068985
ISBN: 0-275-96574-0

First published in 2004

Praeger Publishers, 88 Post Road West, Westport, CT 06881
An imprint of Greenwood Publishing Group, Inc.
www.praeger.com

Printed in the United States of America

The paper used in this book complies with the
Permanent Paper Standard issued by the National
Information Standards Organization (Z39.48-1984).

10 9 8 7 6 5 4 3 2 1

For Consuelo.
My life, my heart, my teacher.

Contents

Preface

When I set out to write this book, my first thought was that no one would want to read yet another book about Gandhi or King. But, after preliminary research, I realized that there was no single book that gave systematic treatment to both Gandhi and King against the backdrop of nonviolent resistance. This volume seeks to fill that gap in the literature by providing first a summary of the meaning of violence and nonviolence in politics and then a detailed comparative analysis of the life and work of Gandhi and King.

Gandhi and King are inspirations to many people. Holidays, statues, and movies are dedicated to their memory. Conferences, conventions, and colloquia are held even today examining their philosophies and seeking to establish their legacies once and for all. Indeed, I am inspired in this manner. Nevertheless, this book is not simply yet another "praise piece" on two of the most principled public people of the 20th century. While this book examines some of the high-minded, idealistic, perhaps even unrealistic, ideas of both Gandhi and King, it also provides hard-bitten analyses and critiques of both men in order to leave the reader with what I hope is a balanced summation of each man's legacy.

Gandhi and King were not always right. By their own admission, they made some dandy blunders. Neither is nonviolent political resistance always successful. But in both Gandhi's and King's case, they used nonviolence well enough to show the world that there was not only a high-minded alternative to violence, but one that is practical and effective—if done properly.

In writing this book, I have relied on many people for their assistance. I would like to thank in particular my research assistants, Heather Crocker and James Doty, and also my colleagues, Dr. James Casebolt and Dr. Elizabeth Cohn. I would also like to thank our campus dean, Dr. James W. Newton (ret.) and our campus librarians, Patricia Murphy, Brad Cecil, and Donna Capazutto, whose assistance in tracking down source material was invaluable. I would also like to thank my editors: Hilary Claggett for believing in and supporting this project, and Denise Quimby whose editorial brilliance and patience were limitless. Most of all, I wish to thank my wife, Consuelo, who had to convince me again and again that I was actually capable of finishing this project.

Introduction

When the history of the 20th century is written, it shall record that Mohandas Koramchand Gandhi and Martin Luther King, Jr. were at the forefront of that century's most important struggles: the struggle for freedom, the fight for equality, and the battle against violence. Accordingly, this book seeks to make a modest contribution in that regard by examining the nonviolent struggles of both men as they fought for freedom and equality.

Part I will examine the theoretical and conceptual tenets of nonviolence. No discussion of Gandhi and King would be complete without a thorough investigation of the means they so stridently and uncompromisingly advocated. This book is comparative in nature. As such, Chapter 1 illustrates the meaning of nonviolence by comparing it to violence. Not only is this an exercise in establishing what nonviolence is not—it is not intentionally inflicted physical or psychological harm—but this chapter also seeks to demonstrate affirmatively what nonviolence is. For, despite its name, nonviolence is more than a "non"-something. Its meaning, at least insofar as Gandhi and King took it, underscores a positive affirmation of life and spirituality that binds every human. It is the glue holding King's "beloved community" together and the "truth force" through which Gandhi stood nose to nose with the British Empire in South Africa and India.

Chapter 2 compares the two major types of nonviolence, namely philosophical and strategic. Some people believe in and practice nonviolence as a way of life. The Jain religion, for instance, teaches its adherents to adopt nonviolence not just in their actions, but in their words and even their thoughts. Quakers are also committed to adopting nonviolence as a philosophy for life. Alternatively, others, including many in the movements Gandhi and King led, adopt nonviolence as merely a strategy, without necessarily adopting it as a spiritual commitment. For these people, nonviolence is a practical "weapon of resistance." Chapter 2 also examines theoretical explanations for why nonviolent political resistance works, even against an armed opponent. Central to this analysis is the so-called theory of nonconsent. Gandhi said repeatedly that the British could do nothing in India without 300 million Indians first consenting. The theory of nonconsent is a powerful explanatory device that underscores the efficacy of nonviolence. However, it is not without its critics and Chapter 2 will review some of those critiques.

Part II focuses on Gandhi and begins with a brief background to India in order to set the historical stage for Gandhi's nonviolent resistance. Chapter 3 provides a brief biography of Gandhi. Entire books are devoted to tracing Gandhi's life, but this chapter concerns itself with the most influential experiences and events in Gandhi's life that helped set him on the path to becoming the Mahatma ("great soul"). For example, Gandhi said that the humiliation he suffered on a train in South Africa led to the single most creative night of his life and inspired him to resist government policies in South Africa. Chapter 4 addresses Gandhi's major philosophical principles as they pertain to nonviolence. For students to understand Gandhi's nonviolent actions, they must first understand the ideas, concepts, and values that underpin his nonviolent philosophy. Of special importance here is Gandhi's method that he came to call "satyagraha," or truth force. Gandhi's approach is predicated on an unswerving commitment to discovering Truth—and by this knowing God. Chapter Five examines several of Gandhi's critical nonviolent resistance campaigns, beginning in South Africa—where his "real" career started—and finishing in India. Some of Gandhi's nonviolent resistance campaigns were mild successes, some were great successes, and others were dismal failures. I have tried to select a few campaigns that are representative of this spectrum of success and failure.

Part III is devoted to Martin Luther King, Jr. and is organized in the same way as Part II. It begins with a brief introduction to the Civil Rights Movement in the United States, focusing in particular on African Americans' struggle for equality. Chapter 6 focuses on King's milestone events and developmental influences. His family background, for instance, helped mold him into the determined man that he became. Also of particular interest here is King's self-declared "pilgrimage to nonviolence." Chapter 7 focuses on King's major philosophical principles as they pertain to nonviolence. Primary among his ultimate goals was the creation of what he called the "beloved community." In so doing, King relied heavily on his own Christian faith as well as the philosophical underpinnings he picked up while in graduate school, particularly his commitment to a philosophy called "Personalism," which says that everyone's personality (and hence their well-being) matters because God loves all people. Chapter 8 focuses on several of the major nonviolent resistance campaigns King was most involved in. As with Gandhi, this chapter focuses on both successful and failed nonviolent resistance campaigns.

Part IV returns the reader to more comparative analyses. Chapter 9 conducts an in-depth comparative analysis of both the life and the work of Gandhi and King. It compares these two men as leaders, as men singularly devoted to their faiths, as family men, and as heroes. Chapter 10 discusses the legacies of both Gandhi and King for the 21st century. What Gandhi and King accomplished can, in fact, be replicated. Nonviolent direct action does not need an "enlightened" opponent like the British Empire to succeed, nor does it need the constitutional protections found in the United States. Now more than ever, when people all over the world feel threatened by transnational scourges like terrorism, poverty, hunger, and extremism, Gandhi and King can show the world a better way. Perhaps Gandhi and King did not have all the answers, perhaps their techniques were sometimes flawed, perhaps as men they were flawed, and perhaps as leaders they left something to be desired. But their life's work and their ultimate sacrifice—by an assassin's bullet as each tirelessly and steadfastly preached nonviolent reconciliation—point us in the direction that will leave all people with more hope for the new millennium.

PART I

Violence and Nonviolence

CHAPTER 1

Violence and Nonviolence: What's the Difference?

DEFINITIONAL DIFFICULTIES

At the risk of allowing you, the reader, to get bogged down in the quibbling over definitions and semantics, this chapter reviews only a few of the many definitions of nonviolence and violence. Although this exercise may confuse the reader about what is meant by these terms, well, that is precisely the point. There is no general agreement among advocates of violence or nonviolence on what these terms mean. Nevertheless, this chapter sheds light on these terms in order to facilitate a better understanding of the forthcoming chapters on Gandhi and King. Keep in mind the major theme of this section: it is very difficult to separate completely "violent" from "nonviolent" action.

Note some generalizations that will be made here. First, when reference is made to *advocates of nonviolence*, this refers to individuals and groups who choose nonviolence as a matter of principle—either by religious commitment and training or by some form of secular conviction. For instance, the Quaker religion, found mostly in the United States, is based on nonviolent precepts, as is the Jain religion, which is found mostly in India. But not all Quakers, Jains, and other advocates of nonviolence will necessarily agree with the way nonviolence is conceptualized here. In addition, there are secular (nonreligious) groups and individuals who advocate nonviolence out of moral convictions that are not necessarily based on religious doctrines. For example, nonviolent struggles in

Poland and the Philippines during the 1980s were initiated by labor and other secular organizations, not by any religious institutions (although the Catholic Church did play a supporting role in Poland). For many such advocates, there is no compromise on choosing nonviolence: it is an absolute commitment that can admit no exceptions. Others, such as Gene Sharp, approach nonviolence from purely strategic and practical grounds, asserting that nonviolence, regardless of religious or secular convictions, simply works better than violence.

Second, *advocates of violence* refers to those who believe there is merit in sometimes using violent means to achieve goals. Such advocates include military personnel, politicians, diplomats, police officers, political pundits, religious leaders, and even parents who may use corporal punishment to teach their children not to jump on the furniture or play in traffic. Likewise, not all advocates of violence will agree with how violence is described below. The point is to explore in a general way the relative meanings of these terms so the reader is equipped with a thoughtful understanding of social behavior and how changes in society can be elicited through different forms of action.

So, what is nonviolence? What is violence? This chapter introduces some important terms and concepts that will be used and referred to throughout this book. Key terms such as *power, violence, force, coercion, nonviolence, passive resistance*, and *just war* will be explored. Throughout, the focus will be on how these terms relate to action in the sociopolitical sphere. Violence and nonviolence will be examined against the backdrop of politics, rather than, say, in the family setting. After all, both Gandhi and King, although deeply religious men, engaged in nonviolent resistance in the political realm. Gandhi had myriad definitions for nonviolence and for violence. For instance, he saw violence as the willful use of power to force a change in another's behavior in such a way that the opponent is physically or psychologically harmed (Pontara 1965, 199). At other times he said that violence denotes a "moral evil" as when he wrote "[u]nder violence I include corruption, falsehood, hypocrisy, deceit and the like" (Gandhi 1951, 294). In Gandhi's definition, therefore, even lying is a form of violence.

But Gandhi was a man of action, not really an academic or theoretical scholar. So, let's look at how five well-known scholars of nonviolence define these terms. These people are Gene Sharp, Douglas Bond, Johan Galtung, Joan V. Bondurant, and Michael Nagler.

First, consider Gene Sharp, one of the foremost scholars of nonviolent resistance. In his early work (1959), he says there are several meanings associated with nonviolent action. *Generic nonviolence* is characterized by abstaining from physical violence. Not included in this definition is activity by hermits, cowards, and legislators, the latter because such legislation is backed by the threat of state-sanctioned violence. *Pacifists* are people who refuse to kill or participate in wars based on moral, ethical, or religious principles. Then there is *nonviolent resistance* or *nonviolent direct action*, which include acts of commission or omission that defy an opponent but that also reject violence. Acts of omission, for instance, not taking part in political ceremonies, are classified as resistance while acts of commission, for example, purposely breaking the law, are classified as intervention (44–45).

Sharp (1959) lists nine forms of nonviolence, ranging from mild to drastic: nonresistance (reclusive nonparticipation in society), active reconciliation (trying to convince people without nonviolent coercive techniques), moral resistance (evil should be resisted by peaceful and moral means), selective nonviolence (refusing to participate in specific violent conflicts such as international war), passive resistance (conducting nonviolent conflict not for reasons of principle but because one lacks the means of violence or because one knows he would lose in a violent confrontation), peaceful resistance (the same as passive resistance while recognizing the moral superiority of nonviolent struggle), nonviolent direct action (intervention to establish new patterns and institutions in society), satyagraha (attaining truth with the opponent through love and righteous actions), and nonviolent revolution (changing society completely through nonviolent means without the use of the state's apparatus) (46–59). However, Sharp's typology of nonviolence has been criticized as too narrow in that it leaves out nonphysical psychological violence. In general, he defines violence as limited to intentionally causing someone physical injury. If some physical bodily harm occurs, then violence is said to have occurred. Most people, whether they advocate violent or nonviolent means, would likely agree that physically harming someone constitutes violence.

But, two other thorny issues arise in this context, one dealing with damage to property, the other with damage to a person's psyche. Suppose a civilian population destroys the tanks and aircraft of an invading army but kills none of the soldiers. Was that nonviolence? Or suppose that the civilians destroy only their own physical and natural resources—food, water, industrial facilities—in order to deny their use by the invading army. Is that nonviolence? Suppose further that the population begins a campaign of psychological warfare, designed to sow doubt and dissension among the invader's troops, to the point of causing mutiny among them. Is this violence or nonviolence? Consider, for that matter, a civilian spitting on the ground near a soldier and then using a racial slur to insult the soldier. If this hurts the soldier's feelings, was that a type of violence? According to Gene Sharp, the answer to these questions is no. Harm may be done, but it does not rise to the level of violence.

Douglas Bond (1988) sees three meanings for the term nonviolence. The absolute pacifist must endure suffering and sacrifice even until death. However, a completely pacific person like this would be unable to help reduce the suffering of others and therefore, by such acts of omission, would increase the burden to others. Principled pacifists have as their objective mitigating violence to the best of their ability. However problems arise because they have no way of knowing which path is least violent in the long term. Finally, Bond's pragmatic pacifist presents a more instrumental conceptualization because the pacifist is concerned with using nonviolence in pursuit of a specific sociopolitical objective wherein the nonviolent ethic is thus specially utilized as a means to other ends (86–87). Bond's conception of nonviolence must combine a sense of community with an underlying premise of the sanctity of life (refraining from violent behavior): "Sacrifice without a sense of community or unity (between conflicting groups) is but violence for other ends" (87). To many advocates of nonviolence, this sense of sacrifice, especially in the context of building community, is what gives nonviolence its power to transform a conflict and resolve it definitively. Indeed, this is referred to as the "transforming power" of nonviolence because it has the ability to change the structure of a conflict from one of competition to one of cooperation and mutual reconciliation. Robert Woito (1982) sees the ultimate expression of violence—war—in exactly the opposite way:

> War is the denial of community, for it breaks the unity essential to establish non-tyrannical law. . . . [V]iolence also breaks the sense of community because it seeks to end or limit participation in the decision making process. (416–417)

As I will discuss later, developing—not denying—that sense of community was critical to Martin Luther King's desire to use nonviolence.

Johan Galtung (1969), who has written extensively on the nature of violence and nonviolence, asserts that there are many types, or scales, of both. Overall, however, he defines violence as that which causes peoples' *actual* physical and mental realizations or accomplishments to fall short of their *potential* physical and mental realizations (168). Even though he disagrees with it, Galtung asserts that the dominant meaning of nonviolence in the West has come to reflect Sharp's notion of nonviolence, which is one of merely refraining from physically harming others. But Galtung calls this negative nonviolence, and says that it cannot be used to eliminate what he calls structural violence. Structural violence is damage done to people by the very nature of society's composition. The way society's social, political, and economic institutions are constituted and how they interact with people can be forms of violence. As such, structural violence is integrally woven into the fabric of society, it is less easy to identify and is more difficulty to eradicate. Moreover, it may even be seen as natural. Examples of structural violence include poverty, hunger, racism, illiteracy, and inaccessibility to adequate health care. To eradicate these structural forms of violence, Galtung calls for "positive nonviolence," which requires the people to do more than merely refrain from harming others. Positive nonviolence calls for people to take active measures to combat the social ills that are a structural part of society.

Joan V. Bondurant (1998) defines violence as "the willful application of force in such a way that it is *intentionally injurious* to the person or group against whom it is applied" (9; emphasis added). She further defines *force* as the exercise of physical or intangible power to effectuate change (9). Although force can be used in either violent or nonviolent ways, the key distinction for Bondurant is that, with violence, force is used to intentionally harm the opponent. But with nonviolence, force is used to make a change, not to purposefully harm another. If the use of force may lead to harm, then Bondurant says the harm should be inflicted on the person who is also using the force, so she calls for self-suffering through self-sacrifice. Bernard Gert (1966) agrees and says violence is "an unwanted, intentional violation" of several moral rules that forbid killing, disabling, causing pain, and depriving someone of freedom of opportunities or pleasure (616–617). As with Bondurant, notice the role intentions play in this definition. So, nonviolence means more than refraining from breaking moral rules. Rather, it also means doing something to help others to live, to relieve their pain and provide them with opportunities and happiness. This is where the notion of promoting positive construction with others is combined with the moral rules that forbid us from injuring others. This idea is also consistent with Galtung's notion of positive nonviolence.

Finally, David Nagler (1986) says nonviolence is defined as "that force or principle which comes increasingly to motivate a human being as he or she transforms the desire to injure others into its positive counterpart" (72). Again, notice the emphasis on intentions and also on taking positive initiatives. To Nagler, nonviolence connotes more than simply the *absence* of violence, but rather the *presence* "of the positive quality that is its opposite" (72). As David McReynolds (n.d.c) says, "Nonviolence is much deeper than 'not violent.' . . . Nonviolence is much more than the refusal to hit—it is a reaching out to the opponent."

By drawing on the discussion above, nonviolence is here defined as using force to provoke opponents into changing their beliefs and actions, without intentionally harming them, but instead by exercising the transforming power of intentional self-suffering. In turn, violence is using force to deliberately harm, if not destroy, an opponent's physical and psychological well-being in order to compel a change in their behavior. In both cases, intentions are key whether the act is successfully carried out or not. Consider the so-called Shoe Bomber, Richard Reed, who tried to blow up a plane by detonating an explosive device in his shoe. Although he failed in his attempt, his intention to destroy the plane—and kill everyone on board—constitutes violence.[1]

VIOLENCE AND NONVIOLENCE

Notice the similarity in the definitions above, specifically that both violence and nonviolence involve the use of force, which is sometimes referred to as coercion. This can make for confusion when trying to distinguish one form of behavior from the other. The general idea is that violence and nonviolence are contrary terms, diametrically opposed to one another. However, it is not so easy to determine where violence ends and nonviolence begins. This was well expressed by Kirby Page (1963):

> Our difficulty comes, of course, in deciding where ethical coercion ends and unethical violence begins. None of [all the] possible ways

---

[1] I would like to thank Dr. James Casebolt for this example.

of dealing with social injustice can entirely prevent or remove human suffering. . . . The policy of wisdom is to use that method which involves a minimum of suffering and offers a maximum of redemption. (53)

So, the distinction between violence and nonviolence does not have to be crystal clear because "at some point, there is a common-sense dividing line between the two" (Boulding 1962, 323).

Think of both violence and nonviolence as methods of action that exist along a single continuum of political action with "pure" nonviolence at one end of the spectrum and "pure" violence at the other end. Some actions—silent protest, tax resistance, boycotts, or noncooperation—tend toward the nonviolent end of the spectrum while other actions—riots, terrorism, guerrilla war, or nuclear war—tend toward the violent end. The continuum also means, however, that no actions can be totally nonviolent or totally violent. Those are referred to as "ideal types" and exist only in a theoretical sense. If, therefore, it is better to look at violence and nonviolence as separate, but related, actions along a single spectrum, then it follows that people can only conduct themselves more or less violently, or more or less nonviolently. Gandhi would agree with this assessment because he argued that the line between violence and nonviolence was not the same for everyone and because the term nonviolence was too vague for him (Pontara 1965, 199). Gandhi asserted that "strictly speaking, no activity and no industry is possible without a certain amount of violence, no matter how little" (Pontara 1978, 29). Hence, there is no clear-cut boundary between violence and nonviolence. Accordingly, we can never be certain where violence ends and nonviolence begins. Therefore, people can never hope to be absolutely nonviolent. More precisely, nonviolence can never be completely bereft of all harmfulness. Violence and nonviolence, although contrary to each other, exist and occur in the same processes of human interaction.

Violence and nonviolence differ from one another in significant ways. Foremost among these differences is the split over intentions. With violence, the aim is to deliberately harm the opponent in order to compel the opponent's defeat or destruction. Harm is usually inflicted by destroying something. Destruction is a key element of violence and usually occurs in three ways: destruction of property, destruction of peoples' bodies, and destruction of peoples' psyches. In using violence, people seek to "solve" a conflict by targeting and conquering the opponent. During the Persian Gulf War in 1991, then-Chairman of the Joint Chiefs of

Staff General Colin Powell said the U.S. military's objective was clear: to locate the enemy "and kill it." While the soldier in combat makes great sacrifices and takes great risks, the soldier's object is not to invite suffering on self, but rather to inflict more pain and suffering on the opponent. The soldier's objective is to make the opponent's suffering so severe that it either destroys the opponent or renders the opponent unable to continue fighting. This does not necessarily solve the conflict in any genuine way, but only alters its structure. For instance, who could say that using military force against Iraq in 1991 actually solved the conflict in the Persian Gulf? In fact, it only moved it onto a different plane, on a different level. Only 10 years after the military "victory," the second President George Bush was drawing up plans for yet another military operation which culminated in the 2003 U.S. invasion and occupation of Iraq.

With violence, therefore, the intention is to inflict more pain and suffering on the opponent than the opponent can absorb while, at the same time, limiting one's own absorption of pain and suffering. But with nonviolence, the object is to use methods of self-sacrifice that are designed to melt the hardest of hearts in the opponent and convert the opponent to your way of thinking. Again, this transforming power seeks to completely alter the structure of the conflictual relationship by winning the hearts and minds of the opponent, not by destroying them. Examples include courting arrest, standing unarmed in front of a column of advancing tanks, conducting a fast, and openly breaking a law and accepting the punishment. Nonviolent activists also try to limit the suffering their actions inflict on the opponent. They take active measures to avoid causing harm to the opponent. In Gandhi's case, he called off a major nonviolent resistance campaign when he learned that the protests had turned violent and some protestors killed some police officers. According to Bondurant (1988), the idea is not to avoid the exercise of power, but to use power—and coercion—in such a way as to effectuate change without injuring the opponent, or, in the least, by inflicting as little harm on the opponent as possible (9).

To be sure, this is difficult to achieve because some injury of some sort will in fact be visited upon an opponent in any conflict. This is especially true in the case of using economic coercion as a method in a conflict. Are labor strikes, boycotts, or government-imposed economic trade sanctions forms of violence or nonviolence? It is here where the distinctions between violence and nonviolence become blurry and difficult to differentiate along the political action continuum.

Consider a teachers' strike, usually thought of as a time-honored method of nonviolent action to effectuate change. Assuming no one is being killed, tortured, or beaten, there is no physical harm occurring. But what about the potential psychological harm that occurs throughout the community? Are not the children, innocents to be sure, harmed by this strike? Or consider a grocery store that is subjected to an economic boycott by customers because it refuses to hire women. The financial boycott results in the store going bankrupt and all its employees being left without jobs. Surely many of the store's employees (the newly hired cashier, the maintenance worker, or the cleaning crew) are not to blame for the store's wrongdoing. Yet they will all suffer, they will all be harmed in some way. Even though strikes and boycotts are normally considered nonviolent resistance they are not totally devoid of causing some harm.

But when this action is viewed against the context of alternative methods (firebombing the store? assassinating its owner?) and against the differentiating idea of intentions, there exists a significant difference between these forms of nonviolence and other forms of violence:

> Withholding of services or profits may cause a very real discomfiture to the opponent and he may interpret this as serious injury—but compared with physical destruction and deliberate undermining of morale, possibly coupled with extreme distortion of truth (as in the use of certain types of psychological warfare) the contrast is significant. (Bondurant 1988, 9–10)

The point is that, although some harm is being done, the intention is not to destroy the opponent, which is contrary to violence, as was made clear by General Powell during the 1991 Persian Gulf War.

Now consider a far more serious example from current history. As part of containing Iraqi aggression, the United States led the effort to impose economic sanctions on Iraq throughout the 1990s. These sanctions prohibited any significant international trade with Iraq until the United Nations verified that the Iraqi government had completely destroyed its ability to make weapons of mass destruction. Such sanctions ostensibly target the military regime in Baghdad, but they had an indirect impact on Iraq's civilian population, particularly its most vulnerable, the aged and the young. Consequently, according to the United Nations (which officially supported the sanctions), the sanctions have contributed to the death of more than 500,000 Iraqi children from maladies such as malnutrition, disease, and poisoned drinking water.

Assuming that the United States does not intend to kill innocent Iraqis, are these sanctions really similar to the teachers' strike or the grocery store boycott? Are international trade sanctions on the same point of the violence/nonviolence political action continuum as a strike or boycott? Probably not, because economic trade sanctions, used as a type of force by one government against another, are only just short of military warfare and are typically backed by the threat of war. They can have the same devastating effects on a population that bombing them can have. As such, trade sanctions imposed in this manner are closer to the violence end of the continuum than are the strikes and boycotts mentioned above, which tend toward the nonviolent end of the spectrum.

Finally, consider a hypothetical conflict scenario (Pontara 1978, 24). Suppose two countries find themselves bound in an increasingly tense dispute over a piece of land, which is believed to be rich in natural resources. As both prepare for war, scientists in one of the countries discover and release a gas that causes residents in the other country to feel nothing but extreme euphoria. At the same time, this gas limits their ability to think independently, hence rendering them susceptible to suggestions. The conflict is thus resolved by virtue of the first country "suggesting" that the "gassed" country give up its claim to the land, which the latter all too happily agrees to. So, where on the violence/nonviolence continuum would this action belong? The gassed country suffered no fatalities and, in fact, the residents there are happier now than they have ever been. The situation was resolved in a bloodless and painless manner (nothing but happy emotions were emitted). But did violence occur? Arguably it did, at the level of psychological destruction, because the conflict was resolved only at the expense of killing the opponent's ability to think independently. But where on the continuum would this action be placed?

Another important difference between violence and nonviolence is how their advocates view the role of ends and means. For many advocates of violence, using the means of violence can be justified if the ends sought are just. For instance, using violence against Iraq's Saddam Hussein is justified because containing or destroying his military dictatorship will produce a greater good since so many other countries and people in the region will be protected from his aggressive adventurism. In what is referred to as a utilitarian analysis, violent means are used to justify preventing even greater violence in the world. Of course, this example of utilititarianism must confront the age-old cliché "two wrongs do not make a right."

However, does "might make right?" When then-U.S. Ambassador to the United Nations Madeleine Albright was asked in a television interview if imposing the trade sanctions on Iraq was worth the price of so many dead Iraqi children she answered that "the price is worth it." For at least some advocates of violence, the ends can, in fact, be used to justify the means, even if those means are indirectly responsible for the deaths of hundreds of thousands of children. Of course, terrorists such as Osama bin Laden also defend their use of violence as a just method to achieve just goals. Hence, the attack on the World Trade Center and the Pentagon, which killed thousands of innocent civilians, is justified—and glorified—as a noble act, striking at the heart of American power and might.

By contrast, advocates of nonviolence recoil at the use of such violent means, no matter how "justified" or "noble" the ends are purported to be. To the nonviolent activist, the ends can never justify the means. As will be shown in the later chapters on Gandhi and King, advocates of nonviolence believe that impure means can never lead to pure ends. They believe that the *way* a conflict is conducted dictates whether it will be truly resolved in a just and fair manner. In fact, to them, the road that one chooses (the means) is far more important than the destination (the ends) one is aiming for. Using violent means will not resolve the conflict, but using nonviolent means will help create the conditions for meaningful conflict resolution. Consequently, in attempting to better manage political disputes, advocates of nonviolent political action have long called for a new paradigm in thinking. Such a new paradigm emphasizes the importance of pursuing means rather than ends in both the conduct and resolution of conflicts, domestic or international. What happens, then, is that discovering and practicing pure means becomes as much a goal of the nonviolent activist as are the stated political objectives. This is based on the recognition that the instances in political history when nonviolent struggles have been used show it to be at least as successful as actions employing the threat or use of violence.

To continue with examples from the Middle East, it is axiomatic that no major conflict in the region has been resolved by using violent means. When violence is used in the Middle East, such as in the U.S.–Iraq conflict or in the Palestinian–Israeli dispute, the conflict's ultimate resolution is never accomplished. It is only postponed. Sometimes it appears to have been resolved, but in fact all the violence has done is drive the conflict deeper from which it only rises again with more fury and destruction. Despite U.S. success in ousting Iraq from Kuwait, the circumstances that originally contributed to the conflict remain, thus setting the stage for many more military skirmishes and yet another war. Similarly for the Palestinians, their use of military force as well as their use of terror have not regained for them a single parcel of land they claim as their own. Palestinian use of violence has surely postponed their long-held dream of independence. For the Israelis, their disproportionate military reprisals, including tank and gunship bombings of residential neighborhoods, assassinations, and military occupation, have not brought them any closer to their goal of national security.

Another significant difference between violence and nonviolence is how the notion of 'power' is conceived. A common definition of power is the ability to get someone to do something he or she would otherwise not do. Although advocates of both violence and nonviolence recognize the importance of possessing power and properly wielding it in order to achieve their objectives, they differ significantly as to the sources of power and how power is acquired. Advocates of violence view power relations in a conventional manner: power exists in a hierarchical structure, flowing from the top down. In this conception of power, a general gives orders to a colonel who then gives orders to a major who in turn gives orders to a captain and so on. The general is seen as inherently possessing power, which gives him the authority to issue orders down the chain of command. To advocates of nonviolence, however, the general's power does not exist inherently, but only because the bottom of the chain of command agrees to obey. Power is vested in the masses, the people who convey authority to leaders by virtue of their willingness to obey.

Yet another difference between violence and nonviolence is in how each is viewed by society and in how language is used in conjunction with describing both methods. Most cultures express confidence in the ability of violence to solve problems despite the flourish of rhetoric that says "violence doesn't solve anything." Even schoolchildren are taught from an early age about the military exploits of Hannibal, Caesar, and Napoleon. Few children learn about the nonviolent exploits of A. J. Muste, John Woolman, or even Gandhi and King for that matter. Inculcated in their minds at a very early age is a glorified idea of violence. Of course, mainstream Hollywood contributes to this perception with its "shoot-'em-up" movies.

There is little acceptance of nonviolence as a legitimate form of political action warranting its serious consideration in the social sciences (much less its treatment as entertainment value in Hollywood). Its advocates are considered naïve idealists more interested in flaky intellectual pursuits than in the serious contemplation typically associated with the military sciences. Studies in the military sciences are quite advanced compared to studies in the "science" of nonviolent resistance. If one form of violence is ineffective—say, a machine gun up against a tank—few people would argue that violence itself is ineffective. Rather, they argue that a new, more improved form of violence needs to be discovered and employed against the tank. However, and contrary to that notion, if a form of nonviolence—say, a boycott—fails to achieve its goals, the entire idea of nonviolent resistance is indicted as ineffective and, hence, the entire notion of nonviolent resistance is discarded. Few insist on finding new, more improved forms of nonviolence: instead, it is not the particular method that is flawed, but the very idea of nonviolence itself is flawed and should therefore be whisked away to the trash heap. Accordingly, nonviolence suffers from a sort of unequal treatment in society.

But there is more to it than that, for even in language, the terms start out inherently unequal. Language is the container of all knowledge and all perspectives. Examining linguistic styles and usages can give insight into a society's values and preferences regarding violence and nonviolence. For illustrative purposes consider the terms *war* and *peace*, terms that represent contrary concepts similar to violence and nonviolence. English-language speakers can say "there are two nations *warring*" or there are "two nations *waging* war," but they cannot say "there are two nations *peacing*" or "*waging* peace" (Cox 1986, 9). This suggests the former is somehow a more normal or even correct form of behavior. An explanation for the disparity in phraseology has to do with the notion of violence being sanctioned as a normal and acceptable form of social behavior, whereas nonviolence is considered "out there."

Next, consider the word nonviolence itself. Practitioners and scholars alike have labored for years to find a replacement for this term because nonviolence is taken to mean only that it is a "non"-something, the absence of violence. Nonviolence then becomes only a reactive word with a negative connotation. This serves to afford violence an element of normalcy and legitimacy at the expense of nonviolence. Nonviolence loses its ability to imply something more such as a proactive program for positive social change because the term only implies what the method is not. In the Arabic language, the term used for nonviolence, *la 'unf*, carries an even more negative connotation because its translation is more akin to "no violence," as if to say "do nothing." As will be shown later, even Gandhi was so frustrated by his inability to find a suitable term, in any language, for the method of resistance he was pioneering, that he simply made up a new word for it. In fact, many advocates of nonviolence today have taken to using the terms from Sanskrit, an ancient Indian tongue, which were originally coined by Gandhi. Examples include satyagraha, a term that combines truth and force, or truthforce, as an alternative to describe nonviolent resistance. Also, Gandhi used *ahimsa. Himsa* means violence and the "a" prefix negates it. However, as will be shown in greater detail in Chapter 4, ahimsa is more than a simple negation of violence: its meaning also carries with it a charge to do good deeds. Thus, many scholars prefer ahimsa and satyagraha because nonviolence in English does not usually carry with it the positive, constructive undertones that the Sanskrit alternatives connotate.

As demonstrated by the way it is used in language, violence becomes not only an acceptable form of sanction, indeed the most profound expression of conviction, but also a norm of political behavior around which peoples' expectations converge and from which predictable patterns of social behavior emerge. Perhaps this is why the theory and practice of military science is so much more developed than is the science of nonviolence. Writers on nonviolence acknowledge this when they appropriate the terms and concepts from the more "evolved" lexicon of warfare. As a field of study, nonviolence has relied to a great extent on its moral, yet more sophisticated, opposite for much of its vocabulary. Gandhi, Gene Sharp, Richard Gregg, and Anders Boserup and Andrew Mack describe people who engage in nonviolence as "soldiers of peace" who need to be "trained" in order to wage a nonviolent "war." Boserup and Mack (1975, 148) base their analysis of civilian-based nonviolent defense on "classical strategic theory" using Carl von Clausewitz's 19th-century classic *On War*, which is required reading for serious students of the military sciences. Also Richard B. Gregg (1934), another scholar of nonviolence and peace studies, asserts that "[s]ince war is the most highly understood mode of mass struggle, we will find our explanation [for how nonviolence works] first from authorities on the science and art of war" (88).

Now, consider how violence and nonviolence are similar to one another. First and foremost among the shared elements between violence and nonviolence is that both are active methods of resistance. Advocates of both types of resistance seek to create justice by agitating for change. This is an especially important point to be made for nonviolence because, contrary to many popular misconceptions, there is nothing passive about nonviolent resistance. Nonviolent direct action is not to be confused with passive resistance, which is an inactive method people adopt as a way of enduring injustice, not confronting it. The idea behind passive resistance is to tolerate an injustice instead of confronting it, since confronting it, might end up creating even more suffering and harm in the world. The passive resister feels it is better to withdraw from society than to participate in it and get sucked up in its evil ways. With passive resistance, pacifists consider that the best alternative to mitigating the harm and hurt in the world is by not participating in it. They withdraw from active participation in social and political behavior for two reasons:

1. To avoid contributing to the harm done to others in a dangerous world; and
2. To avoid being victimized by the harmful actions of others.

It is a submissive form of nonresistance. It is different from nonviolence, which rejects submission and instead refuses to comply. In some ways, the Amish people living in Ohio and Pennsylvania fit this description: they are against violence but also avoid significant contact with the "world outside."

Those practicing passivism do not conduct nonviolent resistance and those practicing nonviolent resistance are not passive (Lakey 1987, 57). Those adhering to nonviolence ask why a violent situation arose in the first place and what society or the individual can do in order to prevent such events. The passivist is less inclined to ask these questions, more content to remain on the sideline. Not so advocates of nonviolent resistance. Like violence, nonviolence is a dynamic technique that seizes the initiative and tries to hold it with active, creative methods. Neither Gandhi nor King would countenance passive nonresistance. Both were men of action who considered it their duty to fight for justice and against human degradation.

Accordingly, nonviolence is for the social activist who not only wants to participate in the social community but also feels a duty to help positively transform it. With nonviolence, active resistance is offered, but without causing harm to others, without trying to conquer them, and without seeking their destruction. So, nonviolence is not about passive resistance to evil; rather, it is resistance that is active, creative, and dynamic but not violent in its implementation. In this way, advocates of both violent and nonviolent action share the same approach to conflict, whereby action is preferred to inaction. The difference between violence and nonviolence, therefore, is smaller than the difference between action and inaction, or between passive acquiescence and active agitation.

Another feature inherent to both violent and nonviolent political action, and largely absent from passivism, is coercion. Coercion, compelling someone to do something by exercising power, can be either violent or nonviolent. With violent coercion, force is used to cause injury and suffering to the "coercee" in order to compel certain types of desired behavior. By contrast, nonviolent coercion "denotes those attempts to limit or destroy freedom of choice which do not involve the threat or use of physical force, whether directed against persons or property" (Crespigny n.d.).

Advocates of nonviolent action do not see the world through rose-colored glasses. Like those who advocate violence, they are not pie-in-the-sky idealists who believe in the ultimate perfectibility of humanity. They see that human relations are messy, rife with conflict and clashes. They believe in the ubiquitous nature of conflict and assume conflict is inevitable (McReynolds n.d.a). There are two separate types of conflict to consider. First, there is Conflict (with a capital "C"), which refers to the clash of values that exist between individuals and groups. This type of Conflict herein is defined as a "property of an action system when two or more incompatible or mutually exclusive values are pursued" (Galtung 1959, 67). If we assume that humans will continue to pursue different and competing values, then "we must concede the inevitability of conflict" (Bondurant 1971, 13). That is to say, advocates of violence and nonviolence agree that this type of conflict—Conflict as a condition or property of human affairs—cannot be eradicated as long as people interact in social groups whose values differ. There is no vaccination that can inoculate the world against this type of conflict.

The question then is not really how to eliminate Conflict as a phenomenon. Rather, the question is how best to conduct, manage, and resolve the second type of conflict discussed here. This is called "conflict" (with a lowercase "c"), to distinguish it from the type of Conflict described above. This second type of conflict refers to the individual and specific antagonisms and hostilities that exist between separate groups and individuals. By conflict of this sort, the emphasis is on those particular disputes that arise over the clash of values. There is, for instance, a conflict between Republican and Democratic politicians over how to boost the economy. There is a conflict between husband and wife over whether to spend money on a vacation or on home renovations. There is a conflict between two siblings who tussle over the last remaining piece of candy. Or perhaps there is a conflict between two countries over the boundary line.

These are all examples of specific conflicts or conflicts as an event and they can all be resolved in one way or another. While advocates of both violence and nonviolence agree on the presence of these conflicts, they differ over how to resolve them. Does the married couple resolve their conflict by violence or by nonviolence? Do the countries resolve their dispute over the boundary line using warfare or peaceful means? Do the siblings fight it out for the candy or do they reach a peaceful agreement over sharing? Here is where the nonviolent activist privileges means of conduct over ends.

To sum up, advocates of violence and nonviolence agree that Conflict will recur throughout the course of human interaction. Where they differ, however, is in the choice of means to treat individual conflicts that arise between groups and individuals. Perhaps it might help to think of it this way: sibling rivalry in general is a Conflict (because it exists as a property of human affairs) and cannot be totally eliminated from the human condition. But a specific conflict between brother Billy and sister Suzy over the Halloween candy can be resolved (until next Halloween at least). The ultimate question, therefore, is how they will resolve this particular dispute. Billy and Suzy can knock heads in a fight or they can use nonviolent alternatives to resolve the candy dispute—Billy can cut the candy into two pieces while Suzy gets first pick.

Finally, one other very important element shared by advocates of both nonviolence and violence must be pointed out and that is the need for proper training and preparation before wading into any conflict. Perhaps it is too obvious to mention that one of the most important elements in the success of any military mission is for the soldiers to train, train, and then train some more. No soldier can hope to survive on the battlefield without proper training. They need to train constantly in order to succeed in the face of myriad scenarios. They need to learn all about the different tools of violence and how best to employ them. They need to learn about different military strategies and tactics and about command, control, and communications. They need to study their opponents' strengths and weaknesses to learn how to match up better against them. They need to train their minds as well as their bodies, so they can endure the rigors of combat. Practice and preparation are absolutely vital for the success of any military operation.

And so it is with nonviolent direct action campaigns. In fact, there is a common misconception about nonviolent resistance: that it is easy to conduct and easy to sustain. On the contrary, nonviolent direct action campaigns are very difficult to organize and even more difficult to sustain. They need to be planned out systematically, paying attention to every little detail in the same fashion as military planners. Nonviolent campaigns involve organizing, training, and disciplining large masses of people. As with combat soldiers, nonviolent peace activists must also be housed, fed, and clothed. They must be trained and practice their operations over and over. For instance, in the 1960s blacks planned a nonviolent direct action campaign aimed at integrating the interstate bus transportation system. The participants prepared by attending training seminars that included, among other things, repeated role play exercises, where racial taunts and epithets were screamed into their ears, much like they would expect to have happen to them in a real-life scenario aboard the buses. Again, like military training, this kind of repetitive training can help prepare nonviolent activists for the difficulties and risks to come.

JUST WAR

Do countries have just wars or do countries just have wars?[2] For centuries, Western scholars and philosophers have grappled with the question of violence. They have especially struggled with the concept of war and whether going to war violates the main tenets of Christianity, the West's dominant faith. Christ's mes-

---

[2] I would like to thank Dr. Elizabeth Cohn for this clever insight.

sage in the New Testament centers more on love, forgiveness, and turning the other cheek than it does on punishment and vengeance. A convincing case can therefore be made that Christ's teachings dovetail nicely with nonviolence: Christ was an early practitioner of nonviolence.

However, by the fourth century, Christianity had changed from being a heretical faith to being officially recognized by the Roman Empire. Christians began assuming administrative roles as official leaders and politicians in the Roman Empire and later in Christian kingdoms. Since the empire and Christian Europe was built in part on the use of force in war, Christians had to wrestle with the idea of using violence, for instance, going off to battle "for King and Country." Is it ever acceptable for a Christian to kill? Under what circumstances? When is war ever justified? What type of war could be used? Against whom could one go to war? Above all, how can engaging in warfare be justified in light of Christ's teachings?

By the Middle Ages, religious scholars, especially St. Thomas Aquinas and St. Augustine, hashed out a sophisticated theory of warfare that Christians used in deciding whether they could use violence and go to war. Theologians tried to devise a way to resolve the conflict Christians faced between Christ's teachings—such as love and nonviolence—and their own warlike kingdoms. They needed to find a solution that would allow Christians to use impure means (violence) to ostensibly achieve pure ends (peace). This became known as Just War Theory and is composed of two main elements. First, in order for Christians to rightfully go to war, there must be what Aquinas called *jus ad bellum*, or justice of war. That is to say, there must be a righteous reason for even deciding to go to war. According to Just War Theory, you cannot kill without a just cause. Although determining what a "just" cause is can be highly subjective, self-defense is considered a minimum requirement for a just cause. In addition, before a just war can be launched, the action must be sanctioned by a legitimate authority. For example, before going to war against Iraq in 1991 President Bush cited the United Nations Security Council resolution authorizing the use of "any means necessary" as proper authority to attack Iraq. By contrast, his son, President George W. Bush, has been criticized for launching an unjust war against Iraq in 2003 since he failed to obtain UN support. Next, a just war cannot be waged unless there is a reasonable chance of success; the idea behind this provision is that the soldiers should not be made to sacrifice themselves in a fruitless slaughter. Finally, before war can be declared, every attempt must be made at reaching a peaceful resolution to the conflict. Again, critics of the 2003 Iraq War claim President Bush failed to exhaust all peaceful means before attacking Iraq.

In general therefore, the jus ad bellum requirement is met when war is undertaken as a defensive action and only as a last resort. For instance, it is normally considered jus ad bellum when a country resorts to war to repel an invading aggressor. The idea of a just war sounds simple, but it is not so easy to determine what exactly a righteous cause is for which one may kill another. Was the Nazi attack on the Soviet Union justified? Was the U.S. war in Vietnam a "righteous cause"? Was the American invasion of Grenada in 1983 in the service of a just cause? Was the U.S. attack on Panama in 1988 an act of self-defense? And did the United States go to war in Panama as a last resort? In other words, were all peaceful alternatives to resolve the conflict exhausted? To be sure, it is difficult for all observers to agree on these questions.

The second requirement that must be met in Just War Theory is *jus in bello*, which means justice in war. Once the first requirement is met and a country decides to go to war, it then must choose how it shall conduct itself during the war. Just War Theory provides several important guidelines for ensuring jus in bello, the first of which is the treatment of prisoners in times of war. Nearly all the world's sovereign countries have signed several international treaties and conventions stipulating the proper treatment of prisoners of war (POWs). These agreements prohibit countries from executing their prisoners without due process, forbid countries from physically or psychologically torturing their POWs, and bar them from forcing prisoners to conduct slave labor. The treaties also require countries to allow POWs visits by independent groups, most notably the International Committee for the Red Cross. Despite the clearly laid out provisions on the treatment of POWs, many countries, including the United States, have violated these conventions at one time or another. The United States is criticized for violating POW conventions with its treatment of Taliban and Al Qaeda inmates housed at Guantánamo Bay.

A second element of jus in bello is the principle of proportionality, which states that a country under attack can only respond with comparatively the same level and type of force used against it. Proportionality means that a relative balance in the lethality and destructive firepower must be met between combatants. For instance, assume that a country uses small arms fire to launch a limited hit-and-run attack on another country's military outpost. If the attacked country responds to this limited assault on an isolated part of its territory by using nuclear weapons against the aggressor country, it would be in violation of the principle of proportionality. Similarly, if one army uses conventional tanks and artillery in a battle and the enemy responds by deploying weapons of mass destruction—chemical or biological agents—that too is a violation of the principle of proportionality. This may sound odd because the idea in warfare is to engage the enemy using superior firepower so that the enemy is either decisively destroyed or surrenders. However, the principle of proportionality is designed to prevent massive retaliations in the face of a minor provocation and to also help set the stage for an honorable conclusion to the war, thus reducing the danger of never-ending tit-for-tat retaliations.

A third component of jus in bello is the prohibition against killing noncombatants. For there to be justice in war, combatants may only kill other combatants. Innocent civilians are not supposed to be targeted. However, even with its highly sophisticated "smart" bombs that supposedly strike with surgical precision, the United States has killed innocent civilians in its wars in Afghanistan and Iraq. Moreover, it is difficult to determine with complete confidence who is a "combatant" and who is a "civilian." In Vietnam, American soldiers were confounded in their attempt to determine if peasants in the villages were also part-time soldiers: after a while, nearly all Vietnamese—in uniform or in civilian attire—began to appear suspicious and hostile to American troop patrols. Additionally, is a combatant confined only to the soldiers on the actual field of battle? Or is launching an assault on an army's rear echelon—where supplies are stored and distributed— also a fair target? For that matter, is attacking the factory where old men and women are making the tanks and bombs a fair target? Or how about the farmer and his acres of grain that he is growing to feed the soldiers?

Before answering, consider these historical examples: was it jus in bello for the United States to carpet bomb the city of Dresden, Germany, during World War II, literally incinerating thousands of Germans in a horrible firebomb that engulfed the city? Did the United States avoid noncombatant casualties in that case? Did Hitler avoid noncombatants when he launched the German Luftwaffe's aerial assault on London? Did Japan violate the principle during its brutal occupation of China, Korea, and the Philippines? Did the United States avoid noncombatants when it dropped nuclear bombs on Hiroshima and Nagasaki in Japan?

Just War Theory is designed to produce a kind of "rules of the game" for the ultimate form of human violence, warfare. Nevertheless, advocates of nonviolence reject Just War Theory as a sophisticated attempt to rationalize the use of extreme violent means. First, critics of Just War Theory argue that it is impossible to ever achieve a just end by mass killing in warfare. Given the nature of modern warfare—which targets civilian population centers as well as the field of battle—and given the incredibly lethal and destructive firepower of modern weaponry, it is increasingly difficult, if not virtually impossible, for a country to meet all the requirements for a just war. Innocent noncombatants will be killed and proportionality of response will rarely be followed. Second, critics argue that the theory cannot be defended by relying on anything Jesus Christ had to say about violence and war. Rather, Just War Theory's origins are found in the rather twisted interpretations of early Christian scholars trying to use scripture to rationalize and justify their violent acts after their occurrence. In fact,

> [t]he ethics of the just war [theory] have virtually nothing to do with Jesus. . . . No one [from among the just war theorists] argues that Jesus meant to speak of just wars and it is clear that St. Augustine was forced to draw heavily on Greek and Roman sources in creating the earliest definitive version of the idea. (Smith-Christopher 1998, 155)

Accordingly, critics of Just War Theory insist it is impossible to apply to modern conflicts and hence should be discarded. Instead, they call for developing forms of nonviolence that are better suited to permanently resolving conflicts.

CHAPTER 2

Philosophical and Strategic Nonviolence

PHILOSOPHICAL NONVIOLENCE

This chapter examines how strategies of nonviolent resistance are supposed to work. As with any form of social and political action, successful nonviolent resisters must have a well-laid-out plan with sound methods and strategies. The methods and strategies of nonviolent resistance are quite diverse. In addition, the chapter will emphasize the alternative approach nonviolence takes to, first, defining goals and, second, to defining success.

Before getting to the specifics of a nonviolent strategy, however, let's first discuss the difference between the two major types of nonviolence, which are nonviolence as a philosophy and nonviolence as merely a strategy. In the first instance, those who commit to nonviolence as a philosophy commit their entire lives to it. Philosophical nonviolence is practiced as a way of life. Its adherents seek to internalize nonviolence in all that they do. Theirs is a devotion based on a total commitment, a life-encompassing doctrine. Philosophical devotees of nonviolence apply every fiber of their being to behaving nonviolently, not just in political conflicts where political resistance is offered, but in every aspect of their lives. This includes their day-to-day conduct and their interactions with people, animals, and their environment.

A philosophical commitment to nonviolence commands a total undertaking in every way. Although it is not a prerequisite, the philosophically committed usually have a faith-based, even

dogmatic, commitment. Philosophical adherents to nonviolence
are found among all the major world faiths, Christianity, Islam,
Judaism, Hinduism, and Buddhism. Nonviolence for these people
is not just a matter of choice, it is an undeniable and inviolable
way of life that springs directly from their religious beliefs. It is
their covenant. Jainism, for instance, is a religion originating in
India that has about four million adherents in India and several
hundred thousand more in the rest of the world (Chapple 1998,
13). Jainism espouses a complete philosophical commitment to
nonviolence. Jain beliefs are broad-based and complex: Jains may
not commit violence in thought, word, or deed toward any sentient
life form. Of course, Jain nonviolence also demands strict vegetarianism and Jains must restrict themselves to occupations that
minimize harm to humans and animals, such as law, financial
services, and certain types of manufacturing (Chapple 1998, 17).
You will not find Jain farmers in India. Many Jains sponsor and
run clinics in India that care for and protect animals. The most devout Jains wear small cotton face masks that filter their inhala-
tions in order to prevent them from ingesting—and thereby
killing—even the smallest of airborne organisms. They also carry
large, soft brushes that are used to gently sweep the area they are
about to sit or lay down on. Some Jain monks even refuse to cook
for themselves for fear of killing organisms during the cooking
process: they only eat once a day (if that) and only if others will do
the cooking for them. Those doing the cooking believe they are, in
fact, being less than perfectly nonviolent, so they seek blessings
and absolution from the revered Jain monks for whom they are
doing the cooking thus forming a symbiotic relationship between
Jain monk and layperson. Many Jain monks take vows of celibacy
and some even take a vow of nudity as they seek total disengage-
ment from worldly possessions and desires.

But a total commitment to nonviolence is not limited to eastern religions like Jainism. Important Christian denominations,
such as the Society of Friends (often called Quakers) and the Mennonites, also possess a philosophical commitment to nonviolence.
As with the Jains, being nonviolent does not occur for one hour
each week during religious services: nonviolence is a way of life, a
belief system that permeates all action. Quakers believe that divine revelation comes from within and that there exists an "inner
light" in all people that can be used to touch God. Early Quakers
were very influential in the American colonies: they founded Pennsylvania and also had a significant influence on the formation of

the American penal system insofar as it emphasized rehabilitation. Quakers were also some of the earliest people to resist slavery and the oppression of Native Americans. Mennonites, which include the Amish people in the United States, live simple, austere lives and are strict pacifists.

Gandhi and King both possessed a philosophical commitment to nonviolence. For Gandhi nonviolence was based on religious influences that came out of the Hindu and Jain traditions (see Chapter 4). King's philosophical commitment was grounded in his deeply held Christian beliefs (see Chapter 7). For each, nonviolence was a way of life, a set of rules by which all aspects of their lives must be guided. Of course, as with any religious commitment, the practice thereof often falls short of the doctrine of beliefs. Nevertheless, practitioners strive to attain the ideal goal, that is the guiding principle that informs one's actions.

STRATEGIC NONVIOLENCE

By contrast, strategic nonviolence does not necessarily involve a way-of-life commitment. Those who choose to use nonviolence as a strategy do so out of a rational calculation that nonviolent methods and tactics are the most pragmatic form of resistance they can offer in order to achieve their goals. Those who use nonviolence only as a strategy see it as a wise policy choice or as an expedient to help achieve their goals. For instance, the union workers who launch a labor strike have adopted a nonviolent strategy (the strike), but they may not have internalized nonviolence as a personal way of life. They may, in fact, still harbor the desire—and the inclination—to use violence if they wish, say against a scab or a fellow worker who crosses the picket line.

It is important to note here that those who adopt nonviolent strategies may or may not also have a philosophical commitment to nonviolence as a way of life. This was the case for Gandhi and King, both of whom used all manner of nonviolent tactics and strategies while at the same time adhering to nonviolence as their commitment, in conjunction with their religious beliefs. But not all those who adopt a nonviolent strategy necessarily share Gandhi or King's philosophical commitment to the notion. In fact, both Gandhi and King acknowledged that most of their followers practiced nonviolence, not as a philosophy, but rather only as a strategic tool to meet the goals of the present circumstances.

Practitioners of both types of nonviolence have been criticized. Philosophical types are criticized for trying to adhere to an overly rigid, unrealistic, even naïve set of values, which could make them more vulnerable to the world's predators. Those who use nonviolence only as a strategy are criticized for not being genuinely committed to nonviolence. Since they lack this total commitment, their critics assert that they therefore must also be prepared to resort to violence if the situation suits them. Critics argue that this makes their use of nonviolence suspect.

THEORETICAL EXPLANATION FOR HOW NONVIOLENCE WORKS

Power and the Theory of Nonconsent

For nonviolence to work, its practitioners must properly exercise power. In nonviolence, power in general is seen as the capacity to change the environment, and social power in particular is the capacity to control the behavior of others (Albert 1985, 14). Advocates of nonviolence believe that people have the agency to effect change and that they have many ways of doing this. Power, therefore, can be seen as a group's "totality of influences" giving it the relative ability to control a situation (Sharp 1990, 2–3). Power in nonviolence flows from the bottom up, from the subjects to the ruler. For Gandhi, the British could not do anything in India without the Indians allowing it. Therefore, according to the theory of nonconsent, a ruler's power is completely dependent on the acquiescence of the ruled, namely, the masses. If the masses withdraw consent to be ruled, this renders the ruler impotent. Power, therefore, is devised by virtue of the masses' willingness to obey. Without this consent, a ruler is, indeed, powerless.

But, why do people obey in the first place? There are several explanations:

1. They genuinely identify with and support the leader;
2. They may be rewarded for their obedience;
3. They may be punished for their disobedience;
4. They have been conditioned to obey ("obey your parents," or "obey you teacher," or "obey the police");
5. They lack confidence to do otherwise; and
6. They do not care enough to do otherwise. (Sharp 1973a, 18–24)

Rulers depend on the voluntary submission of the ruled for their power. But the ruled can nonviolently withdraw their consent by refusing to cooperate with the rulers, by purposefully disobeying the rulers, and by refusing to submit to the rulers' decrees. If this nonviolent resistance, which is based on the theory of nonconsent, can be sustained, it will strip rulers of their authority and expose their utter dependence on their subjects (Sharp 1973a, 34). This is how power is exercised in nonviolence.

Power is not determined by agents of the state, elected or otherwise. Rather, power originates from the masses who have given their consent, for whatever reason(s), to be ruled. The people, by virtue of their consent, possess the power to convey authority to their leaders. In other words, the ruled are actually the cause of power, the rulers the effect. Put another way, the people are the source of power while the government and all its institutions, such as the military, are the result of that power being exercised and deployed. Advocates of nonviolence believe nonviolent resistance is more efficient than violence because nonviolence works at the sources of power rather than at the outcomes of power (Albert 1985, 14).

In nonviolence, power is a resource used to achieve goals. Acquiring power does not become an end in itself but is rather a tool to be wielded nonviolently. In fact, the people possess latent power that can be harnessed, through their nonconsent, to influence the ruler. Alternatively, those who see utility in violence argue that power is intrinsic to the ruler and cannot be significantly altered (Sharp 1973a, 4, 8). This view holds that power has its roots in the capacity for violence, especially the military or police violence of the state. In violence, power is used to injure intentionally or to destroy the opponent and extract submission, usually a humiliating unconditional surrender, against the opponent's will. However, according to the theory of nonconsent, violence is not central to power but "the will to defy and the capacity to resist is" (Sharp 1990, 6).

However, there are some critiques of the theory of nonconsent. Michael Howard (1997) asserts that the world of power based on military might remains "stubbornly autonomous" from the "suzerainty of ethics" (364–376). What this implies is that advocates of nonviolence may appear as easy targets to the military strongman unconstrained by ethics. Yet this ignores the rich historical record documenting successful nonviolent campaigns even in the face of Howard's so-called stubborn military might. Consider the nonviolent revolt by Norwegian schoolteachers who successfully resisted the Nazis' attempt to force them to adopt Nazi school curricula. Or Corazon Aquino's nonviolent "people power" revolt against Ferdinand Marcos's violently oppressive regime in the Philippines. Or the successful nonviolent revolt by Solidarity against the Soviet-backed communist government in Poland. In the Polish case, the Solidarity Movement succeeded even after its initial suppression by the Soviet-backed regime:

> [I]t is now a matter of record that by far the most effective movement ever launched [against] a totalitarian regime was completely nonviolent. Nonviolent action, far from being helpless in the face of totalitarianism, turns out to be especially well-suited to fighting it. (Schell 1985, xxxvi)

Another criticism asserts that the theory of nonconsent relies too much on the concept of collective obedience. Such compliance is not always crucial for the rulers to attain their objectives (Lipsitz and Kritzer 1975, 727–728). For example, in cases where the conqueror's goal is the expulsion of the local population, the ruler cares little about, and depends little on, the population's obedience. The ruler merely ejects the indigenous population by force and perhaps can even make an easier time of it knowing they will not violently resist. In other words, granting or withdrawing consent becomes a futile exercise because a belligerent who is completely violent and bent on depopulating the region is highly unlikely to become a recipient of, or responsive to, nonviolent action.

Similarly, refusing to obey may not work against an opponent who has the specific aim of wiping out an entire population like in Nazi Germany's case vis-à-vis the Jews, or in 1970s Cambodia with the murderous Khmer Rouge regime. Indeed, the idea of power as consent is rendered meaningless in this case because the ruler, with no interest in obtaining consent from the people, carries out a campaign of mass expulsion or extermination. Nonconsent in this context rings hollow. However,

> it is important to note that no known violent defense methods offer any guarantee against genocide [either]. Nonviolent defense is therefore likewise relieved of any necessity of guaranteeing a successful defense against genocidal attack. (Salmon 1988, 77)

Finally, the notion of power as consent has been criticized as too simplistic, since it ignores different structural elements that may make it hard to withdraw consent for any length of time. For example, Kate McGuinness (1993) argues that, given the still patriarchal structure of modern society, "power in gender relations is not based on consent" (112). In a male-dominated society, women have difficulty finding the resources needed to sustain their non-consent for an extended period. Additionally, economic structures may co-opt potential strikers by promising them economic favors, thereby precluding unity in, say, a workers strike. Neocapitalist structures, such as the modern-day welfare system, may serve to co-opt many potential strikers from participating in the strike (Martin 1989, 216).

The Ability to Transform

Advocates of nonviolence argue that it works not only because of how it sees and uses power but also because it has the ability to transform conflicting sides in a dispute. First, nonviolence can transform those who wield it through its insistence on self-purification and reform. Both Gandhi and King emphasized self-purification in training their followers in nonviolence. They stressed personal cleanliness, self-discipline, and proper conduct in the face of provocation. Gandhi used nonviolent resistance as a great symbolic gesture to help increase Indians' self-awareness, raise their pride and unity, and give all of them a chance to participate in the national resistance effort (Brown 1989, 56). Aside from Gandhi and King, the historical record is replete with other examples of people around the world who were oppressed and downtrodden but rose up to throw off their chains of repression and challenged their oppressors through nonviolent resistance. Their backs straightened, their pride restored, the people are transformed into a courageous force of resistance and steadfastness.

Nonviolence helps arm and prepare an entire population for resistance: unlike the military, where only a small number of highly trained warriors operate multimillion dollar equipment, nonviolence can be utilized by any and all in the population. Women, children, and the elderly can join with the able and disabled in utilizing nonviolent resistance techniques such as noncooperation and civil disobedience (these terms will be discussed in more detail later in this chapter). If done properly, nonviolence can transform and empower an entire population.

Second, nonviolent resistance also has the power to transform the opponent against whom the struggle is directed. Nonviolence views and treats the opponent much differently than violence since practitioners of nonviolence acknowledge their own selves in others and seek not to hurt the opponent but to treat them instead with respect. By doing so, they avoid dehumanizing the opponent. Their actions change the structure of the conflict, heretofore defined as "you versus me," into simply "we."

By contrast, for someone to be trained to kill others, they have to be trained to dehumanize their target in order to help make killing them more psychologically palatable. When people do this, they fail to see any part of themselves in the other. With this comes the inclination to see the other as nonhuman and somehow inferior. Consequently, the chance for violence increases markedly because killing one's enemies "becomes not a regrettable necessity, but a glorious affirmation of group identity" (Lipsitz and Kritzer 1975, 723).

Advocates of nonviolence decry the process of dehumanizing the "enemy" that a soldier must undertake; instead, they strive to establish connection with all people, especially their opponent. For real conflict resolution to occur, advocates of nonviolence call for reducing the social and psychological space that separates the self from the other. The efficacy of nonviolence rests on the idea of recognizing the human being in the other and appealing to that human being. If a process of dehumanization has taken place between self and other, then the degree to which this is embedded will have a direct impact on the ability to resolve the conflict (Galtung 1989, 14).

Nonviolent resistance transforms the other by virtue of how its practitioners insist on treating the other. Nonviolence insists on seeing the self in the other; on loving, understanding, and respecting the other; and on not hitting the other back when provoked. Based on a combination of bold kindness and firmness, nonviolence reaches out to the opponents and has an effect on them in ways violence never can. Nonviolent resistance can even work to shame opponents into changing their ways. Nonviolence is predicated on the idea that no person can long abuse another person, who meets that abuse with a forgiving love, "without beginning to feel in himself at least some dull answering stir of discomfort" (Frady 2002, 39). As King said, "You are shaming them into decency" (Frady 2002, 39).

If victims of violence respond with violence of their own, that reinforces the violence in the original attacker and validates the attacker's choice of methods. The attacker can provoke the victim to respond in a certain way, thus validating the attacker's claim to the use of violence in the first place (Gregg 1934, 43). However, if a victim responds to a violent provocation by not hitting back but instead responds with courageous self-control and steadfast adherence to nonviolent resistance, assailants will increasingly replace their anger, hatred, and scornfulness with surprise, wonder, and curiosity. Eventually they will "lose their moral balance" with each successive blow (Gregg 1934, 44). They become confused when the opponent refuses to hit back or obey. This method of using the opponent's capacity for violence to rebound against it by refraining from responding in kind is called nonviolent political jujitsu (Sharp 1973b, 677–704; 1990, 13–14).

The aggressors' extreme capacity for violence is rendered useless. King believed this type of resistance confronted his opponents with morally perplexing questions that are difficult to reconcile. They become divided between their aggressive instincts and their mercy instincts; they lose their poise, especially if there are onlookers observing the brutal assault. By a willingness to incur suffering, the victim seizes the moral initiative while the assailants lose self-respect (Gregg 1934, 47). Competing self-images, that of righteous and peaceable official combined with that of brutal oppressor, begin to take their toll as the stress of cognitive dissonance sets in.

Third, nonviolence seeks to transform the conflict onto a plane of interaction entirely alternative to how the military might view it. With nonviolence, the object is not to seek victory over the opponent, but rather conquest over the conflict itself that separates people from one another. "In nonviolent struggle," says one author, "the objective is *not to have a victory* but to change the situation itself—a radically different concept" (McReynolds n.d.b). In this regard, *success* is defined quite differently in nonviolence. Success in nonviolence is not determined by how and whether the opponent is defeated or somehow brought to submission. Nor is success determined by comparing body counts as was the case with the U.S. military during the Vietnam War. Rather, nonviolence succeeds when the social conditions that gave rise to the conflict are changed. That is to say, nonviolence does not succeed when people are forced to bend against their will. Rather, nonviolence succeeds when the agitation leads to changes that not only resolve the conflict but also transform the relations between the opponents.

Recall from Chapter 1 the emphasis nonviolence places on privileging means over ends. This gives nonviolent political resistance, unlike violent political resistance, a greater chance of changing political, social, and economic relations in ways that can be mutually beneficial to both sides in a conflict. This implies a direct linkage, or interdependence, between the behavior of the conflicting parties and changes in the way success is viewed. Success hinges in part on avoiding or reducing suffering to the opponent as much as possible and incurring self-suffering (Bondurant 1988, 26–27). Concern is with nonviolence designed to reduce the relative amount of suffering between opponents. Nonviolence launches a process of cross-group identification and provides a greater chance for tearing asunder the boundaries that separate the conflicting groups.

In this way, nonviolent resistance distinguishes itself from, say, realism because nonviolence rejects zero-sum alternatives where there is typically a victor and a vanquished. It is worth mentioning that, given the scenarios that have played out in war—winner–loser, loser–loser, stalemate–loser, stalemate–stalemate—there is no record of a war having winner–winner as its end result. Nonviolence rejects the utility of war on the grounds of the use of impure means that result in there usually being one loser and one winner:

> In fact the categories "win" and "lose," "us versus them" lose their hypnotic significance; conflict becomes a stage on a scale of interaction nodes in which all participants can gain, not the least by achieving a closer integration with one another, which is part of the overall purpose of life. (Nagler 1986, 75)

APPROACHES TO USING NONVIOLENCE

There are generally three ways nonviolence can be utilized to create change: nonviolent coercion, nonviolent accommodation, and nonviolent conversion (McCarthy 1990, 116–117).

Coercion

Recall from Chapter 1 that nonviolent coercion involves compelling the opponent to do something against his or her will while at the same time limiting the physical and psychological damage incurred. Objectives are obtained against the will of the opponent. In this case, the opponent recognizes that his or her ability to maintain a privileged position within the status quo has not only been severely hampered but threatened altogether (Albert 1985, 37). With coercion, the opponent essentially capitulates before suffering any further erosion in its position. It gives in on a variety of issues without entirely sacrificing its position. However, if the opponent continues to resist in the face of a strong, nonviolent coercive force, it runs the risk of disintegrating altogether. In this case, the opponent's authority is so severely stripped, as a result of the activities of the nonviolent resisters, it ceases to exist as a viable entity (Sharp 1990, 15–16). In his classic three-part series, Sharp does not mention disintegration as a way success may be achieved (Sharp 1973b, 705–776). For example, despite the rising tide of a nonviolent "people power" revolt against Filipino leader Ferdinand Marcos in the 1980s, the dictator refused to compromise. As a result, Marcos's governing regime was toppled with nary a shot fired in anger. Marcos's rival, Corazon Aquino, who was widowed by Marcos's death squads, led the mass nonviolent uprising that resulted in Marcos's overthrow. Shah Reza Pahlavi's regime in Iran also disintegrated because of a largely, but not entirely, nonviolent revolution. Both the Shah of Iran and Ferdinand Marcos were ultimately defeated.

Accommodation

Accommodation is the most common approach advocates of nonviolent resistance take (Albert 1985, 38). Nonviolent accommodation occurs when the opponent becomes willing to accede to the demands of the nonviolent activists but not because the opponent believes in the righteousness of the nonviolent campaign. Rather, it is because the nonviolent campaign has changed the social structure of the conflict such that it becomes more in the opponent's interest to accede rather than to continue fighting. Continuation of the situation might result in an outcome even worse than that which prevails.

Opponents accommodate because they engage in damage control, calculating that acceding to the nonviolent resisters' demands is the least destructive path to take. In nonviolent accommodation, therefore, the opponent undertakes a cost-benefit analysis and concludes that the costs of continuing to fight the nonviolent activists exceed the benefits. In the 1960s, for example, the willingness of white businessmen in Atlanta to accede to demands of nonviolent boycotters resulted from their fear of losing even more sales revenue as the Christmas shopping season approached and not because they had a change of heart about supporting black civil rights (Albert 1985, 38). Similarly, when management, seeking to end the costly effects of a workers' strike, accedes to most of the strikers' demands, it is doing so to cut its losses: it is accommodating.

Conversion

In nonviolent conversion, the opponent has truly changed his or her beliefs concerning the conflict situation. It is the clearest case where both sides of the conflict merge into a single group, with differences no longer existing between self and other. There is only "us" now, all of us. With conversion, the nonviolent activists have succeeded in changing the value structure of the opponent (Sharp 1990, 14). The opponent has undergone an internal transformation in which core values are no longer in competition with the other: conflict changes to harmony. This approach to nonviolence is the hardest to achieve, the least frequently occurring, takes the longest time and requires the most discipline (Albert 1985, 37–42). However, conversion has the longest lasting and most profound effects.

Conversion is what Gandhi tried to practice most. This logically follows from the fact he adhered to nonviolence as a philosophical commitment and not just a strategy. He sought to convert his opponents by being truthful and trustful; by refraining from violence and hostility; by maintaining personal contact with them; by refraining from humiliating them; by making visible sacrifices for his own cause; by carrying on constructive work in the community; and by developing and displaying empathy, goodwill, and patience toward the opponent (Albert 1985, 43–44). King also sought conversion, especially since it was consistent with his desire to create a beloved community. However, he also employed coercion as when he sought to defeat Bull Connor in Alabama (see Chapter 8).

DEVISING A NONVIOLENT RESISTANCE CAMPAIGN STRATEGY

Setting Goals

Devising a proper strategy of nonviolent resistance requires that its practitioners be clear about what their goals are. Types of goals are often listed in chronological order: short-term goals precede long-term goals and are essentially seen as prerequisites for achieving long-term goals. But this often reveals little regarding the importance of goals and the different relationships various goals have to each other. Time alone is not a very good organizing principle, although discussing goals in terms of the short-term and long-term may be useful. There is a more instrumental way of considering goals, namely, distinguishing the types of goals one wishes to achieve in such a way as to illustrate the progressive nature of nonviolent resistance. These are process, achievement, and ultimate goals. Process goals focus on the group's internal dynamics while achievement and ultimate goals target people outside the group.

Process Goals. These goals involve procedural activities that must be accomplished in order to create a movement that will have a reasonable chance of success (McCarthy 1990, 116). Before it can do anything else, a group must get its own house in order. Process goals, therefore, are directed at activities that must be accomplished within the group before any agitation and confrontation directed at targets outside the group can occur. With process goals, the group must decide on, prepare, and then perform a variety of tasks, duties, and responsibilities that are designed to create and sustain the organization. For instance, a group must first coalesce into some kind of cohesive entity with a higher purpose. To do this, a group must succeed in actually convening meetings, selecting leaders, and setting an agenda.

A labor union, for example, meets a process goal by virtue of its existence. That it has formed and organized is an accomplished process goal. It achieves other process goals by recruiting additional members, by choosing leaders from among those members, by collecting membership dues, and by holding meetings at which important issues are discussed and decisions are made. The union's continued existence and operation is evidence of process goals being continually met. Without constantly accomplishing them, a group risks losing its members and resources and will eventually dissolve.

Achievement Goals. Once a group has been formed, its members convened, and its leaders chosen, it then must accomplish achievement goals: transitional objectives aimed at publicizing the group's grievances and demonstrating its resolve (McCarthy 1990, 116). Achievement goals are transitional because they involve action that is of greater magnitude than process goals, but that fall short of the final objective. Through nonviolent action, achievement goals link the group to external targets, including the opponent, the media, and neutral observers who might be sympathetic to its cause. Reaching out to neutral observers is critical because they can be converted into active adherents or members of the group.

Let's return to the labor union example. After the union meets with its own members and decides among itself what it wishes management to do, it presents its demands to management (all process goals). These demands could be for safer work conditions, higher pay, a more equitable seniority system, an expanded health care package, or an improved profit-sharing plan. If management does not accede to the labor union, then the union can utilize the tools of nonviolence at its disposal. The union will most likely attempt to conduct some form of strike, such as a sit-down, a go-slow, a sick-out, or a picket line. While the final objective of the strike may be higher pay, the actual occurrence of the strike itself is an example of successfully accomplishing an achievement goal: it is a transitional objective directed at the opponent. Holding the strike also empowers the nonviolent actors regardless of whether management grants the concessions ultimately sought after.

Ultimate Goals. Process and achievement goals are necessary but insufficient accomplishments. Ultimate goals involve the final changes one seeks to effectuate (McCarthy 1990, 116). These changes involve a reordering of the dominant social, political, and economic structures in any given conflict situation. In the striking labor union example, if the union's strike results in the pay hike originally sought, the nonviolent campaign accomplished its ultimate goal. To sum up the illustration, when the workers actually get together and form their union, they have accomplished a process goal; when they go on strike to compel management to make changes, they have met an achievement goal; and when the strike actually leads to a change sought after in management's behavior, that is an ultimate goal.

Now, apply this discussion of goals to King's statement of goals for his organization, the Southern Christian Leadership Conference (or SCLC). King said that the SCLC had five main goals:

1. Disseminating information on the philosophy and technique of nonviolence through local area workshops (building and training a membership is a process goal);

2. Stimulating nonviolent direct mass action in order to expose and remove barriers of racism and segregation (publicizing grievances is an achievement goal);
3. Securing the ballot (right to vote), unhampered, for every citizen (a transitional objective for change is an achievement goal);
4. Decreasing the cultural lag through citizenship training programs (achievement goal); and
5. Achieving full citizenship rights and total integration of blacks in all aspects of American life (ultimate goal). (Washington 1986, 350)

Turning to Gandhi for an example, he met a process goal when he recruited and trained volunteers for his famous Salt March. He met an achievement goal when he launched and completed the march, which lasted nearly a month. He met an ultimate goal when the British viceroy agreed to lift the tax on household salt purchases.

Stages of Nonviolent Resistance

Given the goals of nonviolent resistance, a properly devised strategy will progress through different stages, ranging from moderate tactics, which rely on negotiation, to much more radical methods, which employ more aggressive forms of nonviolent action. The discussion here will cover a few different approaches, beginning with those of Gandhi and King. Despite the difference in detail of their approaches, notice that each approach is oriented toward turning up the pressure on the opponent by using increasingly provocative nonviolent tactics with each successive stage.

The phases of Gandhi's nonviolent resistance campaigns can be summarized as follows:

1. Negotiation;
2. Agitation for redress;
3. Self-purification;
4. Issuing an ultimatum;
5. Noncooperation; and
6. Civil disobedience.

In the negotiation phase, Gandhi seeks to establish certain ground rules for actually managing or conducting the conflict. In this phase, Gandhi sought to demonstrate goodwill and mutual understanding. He sought to establish mutual respect with the opponent because he knew this would go a long way toward a mutually satisfactory resolution of the conflict. The agitation phase ensues if negotiations alone do not solve the conflict. Agitation involves drawing public attention to a grievance, usually by way of mass meetings (recall that this would be an achievement goal). Agitation activities are also designed to lift the morale of the aggrieved as well as to shake the opponent out of his or her complacency. Next comes self-purification, which involves prayer and fasting conducted in both private and public. Self-purification also means practicing self-discipline in right beliefs, right speech, and right conduct. Gandhi wanted to reform and improve the lives of Indians even more than he wanted to end British rule. He said that if Indians wanted freedom and equality, they must prove worthy of it. Next comes issuing an ultimatum to the opponent. Gandhi believed that all people—even the likes of Hitler or Stalin—were capable of reform and change. Consequently, he always held out hope that the opponent would come round to his way of thinking. But, if not, he would issue an ultimatum by writing a very personal letter to the opponent. Gandhi would appeal to the opponent's own highest ideals and plead with him to see his way to changing. He would ask his opponent for help in preventing Gandhi from taking more drastic measures. This type of ultimatum actually puts the onus on the opponent but must also involve another chance for reaching agreement and saving face.

If the ultimatum did not work, then Gandhi would switch to the most aggressive stages of nonviolence, namely, noncooperation and then civil disobedience, with the latter a much more provocative, challenging form of confrontation. Nonviolent noncooperation is defined as refusing to take part in the activities or institutions of value to the opponent. This involves boycotting the opponent's economic, political, social, and educational institutions. Gandhi's boycott of British-made clothing is an example of noncooperation. Noncooperation includes a full range of activities, among them:

1. Boycotting government functions (diplomatic receptions, national holiday celebrations);
2. Refusing to accept—or returning—government awards (medals and grants);
3. Resigning from government jobs; and
4. Launching general strikes (workers, bankers, and teachers).

Noncooperation is a serious challenge to an opponent. If it is widespread and sustained, it can seriously undermine an opponent's ability to continue functioning. But if noncooperation fails to coerce or convert the opponent, then even more drastic nonviolent tactics are available in the form of civil disobedience. In noncooperation, no laws are broken, but with civil disobedience, certain laws are deliberately broken. Civil disobedience involves deliberately breaking some, but not all, laws. Civil disobedience is defined as a "public, nonviolent, conscientious yet political act contrary to law usually done with the aim of bringing about a change in the law or policies of the government" (Rawls 1971, 364). Civil disobedience is an act usually directed against the majority of society and is guided by political principles. Civil disobedience, like other tactics of nonviolent resistance, can be used to alter government policies, to change the law, or even to destroy the state. John Rawls (1971) asserts that civil disobedience is considered nonviolent for two reasons. First, it is done publicly, not covertly. "Civil disobedients" do not seek to get away with violating the law. Instead, the public act of defiance is designed to warn and admonish and to draw publicity to an unjust law, all without the threat of violence. Second, civil disobedience

> expresses *disobedience to law within fidelity to law*, although it is at the outer edge thereof. The law is broken, but the fidelity to law is expressed by the public and nonviolent nature of the act, [and] *by the willingness to accept the legal consequences of one's conduct.* (366; emphasis added)

Civil disobedience differs from criminal behavior. While both entail lawbreaking, a civil disobedient openly and publicly breaks the law and willingly accepts the punishment. By contrast, the criminal covertly breaks the law, almost always for personal gain, and does so while trying to escape detection and capture. Civil disobedience must only be undertaken "with deep respect for the law. Indeed, it is voluntary submission to the due penalty of the law that discourages frivolous violations" (Wink 1987, 59).

Like noncooperation, civil disobedience includes a broad range of activities. As long as it complies with the description above, breaking virtually any law can qualify as civil disobedience. Some specific examples include:

1. Indians defying British law and making their own salt (1930s);

2. Blacks defying various state laws and eating at segregated lunch counters (1960s);
3. South Africans defying government-imposed curfews (1970s);
4. Americans refusing to pay taxes during the Vietnam War (1960s–1970s); and
5. Palestinians establishing alternative government institutions and refusing to pay taxes to the Israeli authorities (1980s). (Grant 1980, 65)

Indian and black civil disobedience campaigns will be discussed at length in the following chapters so, for now, this section will only examine nonviolent tax resistance. When Americans cheat on their taxes and try to conceal their actions, they are not civil disobedients: they are criminals committing tax fraud. But when Americans openly refuse to pay all or a part of their taxes as a symbol of protest and not for personal gain and then willingly accept the punishment, they are committing an act of civil disobedience. One of America's most famous tax resisters is the author Henry David Thoreau, who spent a short time in prison for his tax refusal. His essay *Civil Disobedience* (1849) is a classic statement of principled nonviolent resistance.

Tax resistance is done for a variety of reasons: some Americans object to paying taxes that might fund clinics that provide abortion services; some object to paying taxes that support the U.S. military; and some object to U.S. aid to foreign countries and withhold that portion of their taxes they calculate is going overseas. In any case, tax resistance is a very aggressive form of civil disobedience. If engineered on a mass level, this type of civil disobedience can destroy a government.

One last point about Gandhi's strategy: each succeeding phase presents an increasingly provocative challenge to the opponent insofar as each additional challenge and provocation increasingly interrupts the operation of the government. The ultimate form of civil disobedience—establishing parallel government institutions—is a direct threat to the government's continued existence because the resistance seeks to establish alternative institutions that will replace the government and hence make its existence irrelevant. It is a very serious challenge and, hence, should not be undertaken until the proper preparation and training are completed.

Turning to King, his four basic steps, or stages, for nonviolent resistance are as follows:

1. Collection of facts to determine if injustice exists;
2. Negotiation;
3. Self-purification; and
4. Direct action. (King 1964b, 79)

In stage one, accurate, unbiased information must be gathered. Without reliable and objective information, one injustice might be compounded by another. In addition, both sides in any conflict must be wary of the potential negative impact of propaganda. If the information gathering reveals an injustice, then stage two calls for discussions with the opponent in order to try to convince them to make the necessary changes to correct the injustice. These talks must take place in an open, sincere environment, with all points of view expressed in a frank yet respectful setting. If these negotiations fail to accomplish the ultimate goal(s), then stage three calls on the people to prepare for active resistance, including purification of the self and the spirit. This stage also calls for proper planning and training. Nonviolent resisters are not born, they are created. Nonviolent resisters must constantly plan and train, just like soldiers. In essence, this stage has an internal focus and concentrates on meeting process goals. King's stage four provides the menu for active nonviolent resistance along the lines of noncooperation and civil disobedience described above.

Gene Sharp (1973a) presents a strategy similar to Gandhi's and King's, but he focuses on just three main elements:

1. Nonviolent protest and persuasion;
2. Noncooperation; and
3. Intervention.

Protest and persuasion includes formal statements (public speeches and declarations), mass communications (radio, television, slogans, and banners), pressures on individuals (vigils), symbolic public acts (displaying a defiant symbol such as a flag), processions (marches and pilgrimages), public gatherings (assemblies and protests), and renunciation (renouncing honors). Noncooperation can be either social (ostracism, boycotts of social affairs, and institutions), economic (boycotts by workers and consumers, strikes, shop closings), or political (refusing allegiance, election boycotts). Intervention can be psychological (harassment, hunger strikes), physical (obstruction, occupation), social (establishing new and independent social patterns), economic (land seizure, alternative markets, and institutions), and political (civil disobedience, parallel government institutions, and functions).

Like Gandhi and King, Sharp's stages depict an increasingly serious challenge to authority. He also emphasizes the importance of clear, articulated goals that are pursued after the proper amount of training and preparation are undertaken. Preparation includes gathering the proper resources. The object here is for the resisters to prepare for using the resources at their disposal so as to create a mismatch between their strengths and their opponents' strengths.

Training involves practice in the art of nonviolent resistance and building up a tolerance for suffering, thus ensuring the best possible safety for participants (Satha-Anand 1986, 19) and knowing how to organize and implement the actions listed above using the resources at one's disposal. As the chapters on Gandhi's and King's nonviolent resistance campaigns will illustrate, learning the proper timing is very important during training because engaging in certain methods of nonviolent political action at certain times or stages in a struggle can be premature and prove detrimental to success.

An important difference between Sharp and Gandhi involves their attitude toward the opponent. Gandhi tried to unite the opposing groups in his process of "mutual conversion" such that there was not victory of one group over another, but victory over a conflict situation. For Gandhi, the opponent is a potential ally to be convinced through firmness and self-suffering as illustrated by such actions as hunger strikes, jail-going and self-denial (Hettne 1976, 229). In short, recall that Gandhi most sought conversion. By contrast, Sharp's focus on the opponent is based on a divide and conquer strategy. Nonviolent political action for him serves to divide and weaken the opponent in order to better thwart the opponent's intentions. Gandhi's concern for emphasizing means over ends is deeper than Sharp's. Sharp's approach is likely to emphasize nonviolent coercion over conversion.

In contrast to the more linear approach taken by Gandhi and Sharp, Souad Dajani (1991) sees only two phases of a nonviolent strategy; there is nothing inherently sequential about them. In her offensive phase, activity is directed against the opponent, for instance, by appealing to the conscience of the citizens or agents of the state. In the defensive phase, focus is directed internally, toward the group in an effort to secure "weak links" among the members, to develop an independent community structure, and to sustain consensus (9–12). The advantage to this type of categorization is the flexibility it affords nonviolent actors who can alternate between offensive and defensive phases of resistance in accordance with circumstances prevailing in the environment. They could be engaged in offensive and defensive phases simultaneously as well.

PART II

Gandhi

Introduction:
A Brief Background of India

THE BRITISH RAJ: INDIA AS A BRITISH COLONY

To better understand Gandhi, the social and political setting in which Gandhi found himself must first be discussed. Upon his birth in 1869, India was considered the "Jewel in the Crown" of Britain's vast empire. Given its massive size and rich resource base, India was Britain's prized colonial possession. The land was exploited for its silk, gold, and other precious resources. Moreover, with its teeming millions, India provided a sizable market for Britain's exports, such as textiles. More important, India provided an excellent source of cheap labor, which was used in all manner of Britain's imperial economic enterprises. Indians were employed as indentured servants throughout the British Empire, from the cane fields of the Caribbean Islands to the gold mines of South Africa, where Gandhi lived and practiced law for more than 20 years.

Despite being members of the empire, Indians usually did not enjoy the same rights and privileges as European, or white, citizens of the empire. This was especially so for those working in South Africa, whose white government imposed particularly harsh restrictions on nonwhites (Asian immigrants and indigenous black Africans), all of whom were referred to disparagingly as "kafirs," "coons," or "samis." Despite the fact that Gandhi had attended law school in London, where he was treated as an equal, he and other Indians in South Africa were denigrated and denied basic rights enjoyed by their white counterparts. Gandhi first conducted his creative nonviolent resistance campaigns while living in South Africa.

A British viceroy and his British staff headed Britain's colonial administration in India, known as the British Raj (rule). But British government in India depended to a great extent on the cooperation of Indians working in the Indian Civil Service (ICS) to carry out the day-to-day operations of the government. Indians in the ICS worked as low ranking civil servants such as policemen and trash collectors. By virtue of steady work for steady, albeit marginal, wages in the ICS, many Indians were co-opted into working for their British colonial masters. While some Indians worked for Britain's colonial administration and hence colluded in creating their own inferior status, many Indians chafed under British rule and wished to throw off the yoke of British colonialism. This was a source of tension between Indians working for the Raj and those working against it, including Gandhi, who frequently called on members of the ICS to resign from their posts in order to cripple the Raj.

Ironically, the British contributed to Indian disenchantment with the British Raj. Since the British controlled the educational system, Indians learned about British and European history and philosophy. As they learned about European concepts of freedom, liberty, and equality, Indians also became aware that these hallowed ideals seemed to apply only to the resented British and other Europeans. Moreover, Indians became increasingly "infected" with another European idea, namely, nationalism. Nationalists believe that a group of like-minded people who share a common language, history, and ethnicity should be able to govern themselves and determine their own future. And, while nationalism originated in Europe, the Europeans brought the idea to their colonies, thus planting the seeds for Indian nationalism and Indian nationalists' resistance to the Raj. Gandhi was an ardent Indian nationalist.

Some Indian nationalists resisted the British using violence and rebellion, the most famous of which was the Sepoy Rebellion (or War) in 1857 that ended in disaster for the Indians. Indian soldiers (sepoys)—conscripted by the British to help maintain control of Britain's expanding empire in Asia—rose up against their British officers. The sepoys had numerous grievances against British rule, which they considered oppressive, discriminatory, and an affront to their religious views. The yearlong uprising was eventually put down by the British and Indian soldiers who remained loyal to the Crown. Ultimately, this uprising, which cost thousands of lives on both sides, did not win Indians their independence. In fact, it resulted in direct British rule over much of southern Asia for nearly a century more.

Others chose to resist the British by fighting within the system. Using lawful means, they would petition the British viceroy and his minions to change the statutes and policies to give Indians more control over their own affairs. Toward that end, some influential Indians formed the Indian National Congress Party in 1885, which grew to dominate Indian politics both before and after Indian independence.

Gandhi offered yet a third alternative for resisting the British Raj. He called this alternative satyagraha, which means truth force or soul force or the strength that comes from adhering to the truth. Satyagraha, in essence, was Gandhi's version of nonviolent resistance, in which he refused to cooperate with the British and also willfully and openly disobeyed laws while doing so without using violence.

Gandhi remained convinced of the ultimate power of satyagraha and sought to perfect it as a weapon of the courageous, yet nonviolent, resister. Upon his return to India after more than 20 years in South Africa, Gandhi sought to fashion the Congress Party's resistance to the Raj along the same lines he resisted the government in South Africa, using satyagraha. But satyagraha is really much more than nonviolent resistance to the British; it shall be explored at great length in Chapters 4 and 5.

INDIA AFTER INDEPENDENCE

India obtained its independence from Britain on August 15, 1947, just six months before Gandhi died. The Congress Party dominated Indian national politics from independence until the late 1990s. All but two of independent India's prime ministers have come from the Congress Party. Despite its dominance, however, the Congress Party never succeeded in fulfilling its claim to representing all Indians. On the eve of independence, many Muslim Indians, who comprised a significant minority on the Asian subcontinent, did not identify with the Congress Party. They feared that the Congress Party was just a tool for instituting the majority Hindu religion as dominant over India. Rather, by the late 1940s, many Muslims in India gave their loyalty to the Muslim League, headed by Mohammed Ali Jinnah, one of Gandhi's archrivals.

As the British Raj ended, Jinnah and the Muslim League argued for partitioning the subcontinent into two independent countries,

India for the Hindus and Pakistan for the Muslims. Jinnah and the Muslim League claimed an independent Pakistan for Muslims was the only way to protect Muslims from becoming second-class citizens in a single, unified India, a country that would be dominated by a substantially larger Hindu majority. Although millions of Hindus and Muslims lived together peacefully for generations throughout India's thousands of villages, Pakistan proclaimed its independence at the same time as India.

When this happened, Gandhi wept because two—not one— countries emerged: an independent India occupying most of the Asian subcontinent's peninsula and an independent Pakistan that consisted of two separate chunks of land, one on India's north-western flank and one on its northeastern flank. So, Pakistan actually consisted of West Pakistan and East Pakistan, which were separated by several hundred miles of Indian territory. As an *Indian* nationalist, Gandhi believed that all of ancient India should remain united, under one flag, in communal harmony between all its diverse religious groups. However, many Muslims—who were fast becoming *Pakistani* nationalists—felt such a scenario for them meant only that the mastery of the British would be replaced by the mastery of the Hindus. When the interests of these groups clashed—and frequently the conflicts had more to do with land ownership and other economic issues than with doctrinal or religious differences—violence often erupted.

Most countries are born of blood and India and Pakistan are no exceptions. Even before formal independence was declared on August 15, 1947, Hindu and Muslim fighting left thousands dead. As these two infant countries hoisted their separate flags, one of the 20th century's worst communal disasters occurred, with the slaughter of more than one million Hindus and Muslims during the horrifying Hindu–Muslim transmigration. Hindus who found themselves in what was now called Pakistan fled to Hindu-dominated India and Muslims fled India to Muslim Pakistan. During this violent and mangled border crossing, millions of people were uprooted from their ancestral homes and forced into the wretched life of refugees while they struggled to find new homes in their adopted country. For Gandhi, what he called the "vivisection of India" was a horrifying experience, a crushing blow to one who spent his life not only dreaming of, but also preaching and working for, communal harmony between Hindus and Muslims.

India and Pakistan have fought three wars since their independence, plus a slew of violent border clashes. The main dispute is over a region inside India called Kashmir, which both countries claim (Kashmir is India's only region with a Muslim majority). Pakistan and India continue to engage each other in a low-intensity conflict over Kashmir that has cost hundreds of lives and over which they almost waged another all-out war against each other in 2002.

The last major war India and Pakistan fought actually involved Pakistan's own dismemberment in 1971. Recall that when Pakistan first became independent, it consisted of two separate chunks of land, East Pakistan (what is now independent Bangladesh) and West Pakistan (what is now referred to as just Pakistan). Even though East Pakistan was the most populous part of Pakistan, East Pakistanis were upset because Pakistan's politics and economics were dominated and controlled by West Pakistanis. Differences between East and West Pakistan eventually led to war between both wings. By providing East Pakistan with considerable military assistance, India helped East Pakistan defeat West Pakistan and proclaim its independence as Bangladesh. As a result, where Gandhi wanted only one independent country, there were now three: India, Pakistan, and Bangladesh, all born of blood.

INDIAN SOCIETY TODAY

Today, India is the world's largest democracy. With a population hovering near one billion, India's population is almost three times larger than it was when Gandhi died. India is the second most populous country on Earth, after the People's Republic of China, its neighbor and regional rival. In addition to its wars and border clashes with Pakistan, India has also skirmished with China over border disputes. India now has two significant regional rivals, China and Pakistan. All three countries possess nuclear weapons. China has had nuclear weapons for decades, but India and Pakistan officially and openly declared themselves nuclear powers in 1998. Only days after India "went nuclear" with an atomic blast, Pakistan did likewise. With outstanding, and violent, border conflicts between India and Pakistan and between India and China, combined with the fact that all three countries are nuclear armed, southern Asia is a politically unstable and volatile region. Neither the nuclear armaments, nor the continuing border disputes India has with its neighbors, are a legacy of Gandhi's influence and certainly are not what he envisioned for his beloved Mother India.

India has an incredibly diverse population: it has more than one dozen major languages and hundreds of dialects and many different accompanying racial and ethnic groupings. In fact, many Indians cannot even communicate with each other, particularly the millions of uneducated and illiterate Indians who live in extreme poverty (India's average per capita income in 2001 was about $2,200; per capita income in the United States was 15 times greater than that). All these factors together make it difficult for India to weave together a stable national consensus on what it means to be an Indian.

However, India's diversity is best understood when considered against the backdrop of the many different religious currents crisscrossing the country. Much of Indian society—its social, economic, and political institutions—are in large measure a product of India's incredibly rich religious and spiritual history. Ancient India is the birthplace of the two major eastern faiths, Hinduism and Buddhism, as well as the smaller yet significant religion known as Jainism. India is also home to many other important different religious communities including Muslims, Sikhs, and Parsis. Hinduism, Jainism, and to a lesser extent Buddhism are generally referred to as polytheistic faiths since their adherents believe in multiple deities (this is not always the case with Buddhists). The three most prominent gods in Hinduism are Brahma, the creator of the universe; Vishnu, the preserver of the universe; and Shiva, the god of destruction and reproduction. Additionally, each of these gods is married to a powerful goddess: Brahma is married to Saraswati, Vishnu is married to Laxmi, and Shiva is married to Parvati. Although Gandhi was a devout Hindu, his exposure to other faiths, especially Jainism and Christianity, had a profound influence on his philosophical beliefs, as will be discussed in Chapter 3.

India is also home to sizable communities of Muslims and Christians, which are considered two of the three great monotheistic faiths (the third is Judaism). They are monotheistic because their adherents believe in and worship only one—and the same—god. Monotheistic faiths, like Christianity, are linear insofar as people are born, they live, they die, and, then, depending on how sinful or virtuous they lived, their souls go either to heaven or hell where they remain for eternity (the Catholic concept of purgatory notwithstanding). Hence, the fear of burning in hell presents a powerful incentive to Christians, Muslims, and Jews to live a virtuous life.

Unlike monotheistic faiths, Hinduism, Buddhism, and Jainism are circular, or cyclical, faiths. In cyclical faiths, when people die, their souls are reborn, or reincarnated, in another living being. Even gods can be reincarnated: the God Vishnu has been reincarnated as Rama and Krishna. For Hindus, this cycle repeats itself in accordance with the law of karma. The law of karma says that a Hindu's soul must keep experiencing what are essentially many different and painful rebirths until the soul corrects for improper deeds committed in past lives. So long as Hindus do not correct for past karma they will continue to be reborn: in other words, the more improper deeds one commits that go uncorrected, the more rebirths the soul must endure. If someone is said to have bad karma, it means that the difficult life he or she currently faces is a sort of payback for bad deeds committed in a previous life. Hence, the law of karma presents a powerful incentive to Hindus to live a pious life, lest they be punished with a more miserable next life.

Many Hindus believe that the source of bad karma comes from people's uncontrollable urges, their desires, or cravings. So, if people can conquer or detach themselves from their desires, they will no longer be tempted to commit wrongful deeds. By detaching themselves from earthly cravings, Hindus will attain a state of desirelessness, which will free their soul from the painful reincarnation process once and for all. A state of complete desirelessness is called *moksha* and involves freeing the soul from desiring things, such as cars and televisions, as well as freeing it from passions, such as those for sex and food. When Hindus achieve moksha, their souls' journey is complete: the painful process of death and rebirth ceases. Moksha is the ultimate goal of devout Hindus: attaining moksha preoccupied Gandhi's public and private life.

As India's majority religion, Hinduism exerts a considerable influence on the pulse of Indian society. For instance, Hinduism imposes on India a rigid hierarchical structure, known as the caste system. Think of the caste system as a ladder. On each rung of the ladder sit people of different castes. The top rung is the highest caste—the Brahmin (or priestly caste), which enjoys the highest status and most privilege. Below the Brahmin caste is the Kshatriya caste, India's traditional rulers and soldiers. On the next rung below sits the Vaisya, or merchant, caste, which was Gandhi's caste (the name *Gandhi* means grocer). Fourth sat the working class, the Sudras. On the bottom rung, actually below the ladder altogether, are the so-called outcastes or Untouchables, a poor and disparaged group of people whom all other castes are forbidden to even touch and who are expected to do India's dirty work such as sweep the streets and clean toilets. By traditional belief, Hindus are born into a certain caste as a consequence of their karma. Once born into a caste, Hindus remain there for the duration of their life and hope, upon death, to be reborn into a higher caste until they reach the goal of moksha, or heavenly desirelessness. Traditional Hindu belief holds that social, family, and even economic relations should be conducted strictly with members of the same caste but this has broken down considerably in contemporary India.

Gandhi challenged some of these conventions. Although his views on the caste system evolved considerably, he basically supported the concept of a caste system for India because he believed, like many other Hindus, that the caste system provided Hindus with a structured system of interaction that not only provided social order, but also even explained each Hindu's existence in life. However, Gandhi harshly criticized the way the caste system had evolved, with its many subcastes within castes that were designed more for social exclusion than for spiritual purity. Instead, Gandhi espoused a modified version of the caste system whereby there would be no Untouchables and only four major castes, each equal to the other. But even later in his life, Gandhi changed his mind again and argued in a published newspaper editorial that the caste system must be abolished altogether.

Few of Gandhi's fellow Hindus supported this vision: even though Indian law now forbids discriminating against so-called Untouchables, they still comprise India's lowest class. Nevertheless, as he did with all his ideas, Gandhi put his new vision of the caste system into practice in the communal farm homes, or ashrams, he founded in South Africa and India. On these ashrams, Gandhi prohibited caste distinctions. In fact, everyone, even a Brahmin, was expected to take his or her turn cleaning the ashram's toilets. Gandhi also advocated intercaste marriages, which was considered heresy by orthodox Hindus. At one point, intercaste marriages were the only ones permitted in Gandhi's ashram. Moreover, Gandhi renamed the Untouchables the Harijan, or Children of God. He also named one of his newspapers Harijan. In that newspaper and elsewhere Gandhi encouraged upper-caste Hindus to welcome the Harijan into their temples and homes, again a jaw-dropping heresy among orthodox Hindus. As will be shown in the coming chapters, removing the blight of untouchability was a hallmark of Gandhi's work in South Africa and India.

With the Indian Ambulance Corps during the Boer War in South Africa, 1899–1900. Gandhi, fifth from the left in the middle row, was transformed by the violence he observed in the Boer War and Zulu Rebellion in South Africa. (© Vithalbhai Jhaveri/GandhiServe)

Mahatma and Kasturbai Gandhi shortly after their return to India, 1915. While in South Africa, Gandhi shed his western garments and began dressing more like the Indian masses in order to better identify with them. (© Vithalbhai Jhaveri/GandhiServe)

In a characteristic pose, 1924. Gandhi's struggle to attain desirelessness led to vows of celibacy and poverty. Beyond the simple loincloth he's pictured wearing here, Gandhi's worldly possessions consisted of only a few personal items such as sandals, reading glasses, a bowl, and some writing utensils. (© Vithalbhai Jhaveri/GandhiServe)

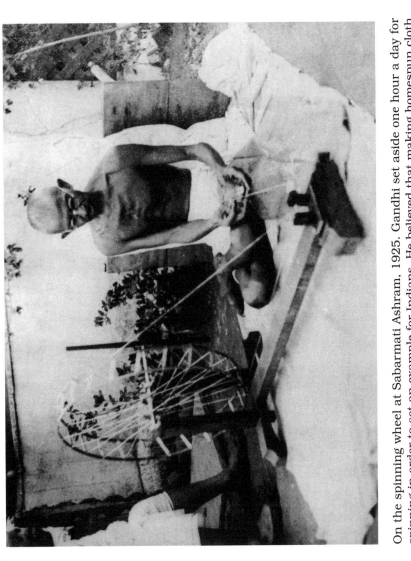

On the spinning wheel at Sabarmati Ashram, 1925. Gandhi set aside one hour a day for spinning in order to set an example for Indians. He believed that making homespun cloth was the key to uplifting India and reviving self-sufficiency in its thousands of villages. (© Vithalbhai Jhaveri/GandhiServe)

Salt March in progress, March 12, 1930. The Salt March was the pinnacle of Gandhi's career in the practice of satyagraha and demonstrated his masterful ability to merge broad-based political action with high-minded principles. (© Vithalbhai Jhaveri/GandhiServe)

A rare studio photograph of Gandhi taken in London at the request of Lord Irwin, 1931. Although Irwin was Gandhi's main opponent during the Salt March, the two deeply religious men held each other in mutual respect and esteem. (© Vithalbhai Jhaveri/GandhiServe)

Walking in Naokhali (East Bangal), November 1946. Gandhi picked up the habit of walking everywhere while he was a student in London. Not only was it good for his health, it also kept him in close contact with India's adoring masses. (© Vithalbhai Jhaveri/GandhiServe)

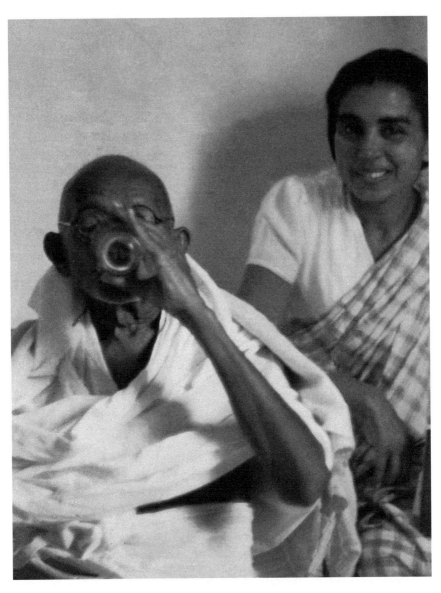

Breaking his last fast in Birla House, Delhi, January 18, 1948. Gandhi's fasts had a remarkably calming effect on Hindu–Muslim riots. They succeeded where police and military troops failed. (© Vithalbhai Jhaveri/ GandhiServe)

CHAPTER 3

From "Moniya" to the Mahatma

The fact that I recollect nothing more of those days than having learnt, in company with other boys, to call our teacher all kinds of names, would strongly suggest that my intellect must have bee sluggish and my memory raw.
—Mohandas K. Gandhi, recalling his childhood, in his autobiography, 1957

What makes someone great? What happens in the life of a person to indicate that, one day, that person will do great things, far beyond what average men or women have ever done? More important, who were the people and what were the events in Gandhi's youth that played a role in molding him into what his people came to lovingly call him the Mahatma, or great soul?

Gandhi's was not an extraordinary upbringing. He was in many ways a typical boy. He was not very religious; he was a borderline atheist for much of his youth. Nor was he very studious; he was an average student of less than impressive intellect. As a small, almost enfeebled boy, he did not take well to athletics either, although as a young law student and even as the elderly Mahatma, he would display remarkable strength and stamina by walking miles each day.

By his own reckoning, Gandhi was an unremarkable boy with no more than average intelligence. His early experiences do not really set him apart from others, nor do they give us much of an inkling of the man he would become. Nevertheless, we must explore some singular events that helped to shape Gandhi. Although we cannot get the full measure of someone merely by looking at a few events or people that stand out in their background, this chapter shall examine some of the most important milestones that influenced and shaped Gandhi's life.

As such, I will explore who Gandhi was, where he came from, and the paths he took that led him to become the Mahatma. I will discuss the most important familial, educational, and professional experiences of Gandhi's early life, again focusing on those experiences that had profound and lasting influences on his personal and professional development. Although far more space—and time—could be devoted to this subject, attention here will focus on the important milestones or "peak experiences" in Gandhi's life that left a lasting impression on his personality. A peak experience is a self-transforming encounter that leaves an enduring imprint on a person who later describes the event as a "religious" or "supernatural" moment of clarity (Herman 1998, 182–183). Gandhi had several critical peak experiences. Peak experiences often happen suddenly and unexpectedly. Sometimes their effects are felt immediately and sometimes their more profound influences materialize over time. In either case, A. L. Herman (1998) argues, such peak experiences are a necessary precondition for a person like Gandhi (or King) to become filled with an insatiable passion for changing the world and for improving the community in which they lived (186).

AN UNREMARKABLE BOY IN INDIA (1869–1888)

Gandhi was born in a small seafront town called Porbandar on October 2, 1869. For point of reference, consider that he was born only four short years after the American Civil War ended and Abraham Lincoln was assassinated. Porbandar, which is located along the coast of the Arabian Sea in the Kathiawar peninsula, had a significant influence on Gandhi, in particular contributing to his renowned reputation for tolerating, even encouraging and including, various religious expressions. Because it was a seafront town, Porbandar was home to traders and merchants from all over the world and from all different types of religions and racial backgrounds. At an early age, therefore, Gandhi was exposed to an incredibly diverse array of Indians and foreigners, some of whose unfamiliar behavior must surely have appeared strange to the young boy.

Gandhi was a fortunate child of India, born to a loving mother who was a devout Hindu and a father of no small influence in local government. Gandhi's father, Karamchand Gandhi, married his fourth wife Putlibai after each of his first three wives died. Karamchand was 47 years old and Putlibai was only 25 when she gave birth to their youngest son, Mohandas, who was affectionately called Moniya as a boy (Erikson 1969, 103). Karamchand, like his father, was a respected high-ranking government official, known for his loyalty, character, and ability (Tendulkar 1951, 1:24). Under the British Empire, India was dotted with "Princely States," principalities of varying sizes run by local "princes," or monarchs or clans, under the supervision of the British administration. Gandhi's family played an important role in the politics of Porbandar: first his grandfather and then his father became the prime ministers in Porbandar. Although Karamchand was not formally educated, he rose to a position of considerable power in the local government and was known for his loyalty and deep identification with the state. Consequently, Gandhi grew up accustomed to political issues and interacting with government officials. Moreover, it was assumed that one day someone from Gandhi's generation—most likely his eldest brother, Laxmidas—would continue the family's "business" and become the third Gandhi in as many generations to achieve the rank of prime minister.

Neither was Gandhi's family poor, as were so many of India's teeming masses. Gandhi's family was well fed, lived in a nice home with servants, and Karamchand Gandhi ensured that his children had modern, Western-style educations (Brown 1989, 17). On that score, Gandhi was an adequate, if unremarkable, student. He showed little passion or interest in his studies and his mediocre academic record reflects that. Nor did Gandhi show much interest in or deep love of reading books (Brown 1989, 17), although that changed dramatically as he matured and especially when he spent lengthy spells in jail.

Gandhi's mother, Putlibai, was very religious. She said prayers before every meal, went to temple every day, and fasted frequently during Hindu holy periods. During one such fasting period, she vowed not to eat unless she saw the sun shine through the clouds (she declared the fast during India's four-month rainy season). Mohandas, with his older sister and two older brothers, would stare impatiently at the sky, hoping and praying for a ray of sun to break through. When they saw the sun, they would run to their mother, proclaiming that she could end her fast and eat something. However, by the time Putlibai came to see for herself, the sun had gone back behind the clouds, so she would continue her fast. But her spirit never faltered; she happily informed her children that God did not want her to eat that day (Fischer 1950, 16).

This anecdote shows the example of devotion, commitment, and strength of character that Gandhi grew up with. And while his father and grandfather also displayed such strong characteristics, particularly in their honesty and loyalty toward the local government and princely court, it was Putlibai, more than any other person, who played a significant role in forming the character of young Mohandas, including the intense religious outlook that he later developed (Tendulkar 1951, 1:24) as well as his well-known stubborn streak. Putlibai's "daily prayers and visits to Temples, and her rigorous fasting . . . [left] the most lasting impressions he had of her" (Brown 1989, 21) although they would not really start to show until much later in Gandhi's life. Perhaps Gandhi's own incredible capacity to fast and the stubbornness with which he refused to give up his fasts until others had fully committed to do his bidding were legacies his mother left him.

In keeping with Hindu tradition, Gandhi's parents arranged for him to be married at the age of 13 to Kasturbai ("Ba"), the daughter of a local merchant, who was herself still an adolescent. Actually, Gandhi had been engaged twice previously, most likely while still a toddler, but both girls to whom he was unknowingly betrothed had died (Fischer 1950, 16). Although Gandhi would spend much of his adult life condemning child marriages as "preposterous" and calling for legislation banning them, he loved Ba and remained married to her until she died in 1944, after more than 60 years of marriage. But at the time of their marriage, which was celebrated along with two other siblings in order to save expenses, the wedding ceremony for the 13-year-old boy was little more than a curiosity, a chance to play with friends, including his new bride.

To ease their transition into married life, young Gandhi and Kasturbai did not live together at great length immediately after they were married. They would spend months at a time apart. When they were together, Gandhi asserted himself as an "active sexual partner" and also as Kasturbai's companion and reformer who tried to teach her how to write (Brown 1989, 19). However, Gandhi reveals in his autobiography, aptly titled *The Story of My Experiments with Truth* (1957), that he failed repeatedly in his attempts to educate Kasturbai, saying she was a reluctant student, but primarily blaming himself and his lust for her as a distraction getting in the way of teaching her.

Although Gandhi was a terribly shy and reticent boy, he displayed no such meekness toward his young wife. At nearly every opportunity, Gandhi was an authoritarian in the marriage, attempting to dictate and mold Kasturbai into the traditional, submissive Hindu wife. This Kasturbai resisted, for she had a strong personality. In fact, throughout their marriage, Kasturbai would vehemently resist some of Gandhi's more unusual practices and social experiments, such as when he made it a rule that everyone in the ashram must clean the toilets. This rule was a great source of tension between Gandhi and Kasturbai, the latter initially refusing, claiming it was work so dirty that it was suitable only for Untouchables. Nevertheless, Gandhi usually prevailed in these disputes.

In both his Porbandar home and the Hindu temple where his family worshipped, people from all different religious walks of life were welcomed and made to feel at home. The cleric in Gandhi's temple would read from both the Hindu holy scriptures like the Bhagavad Gita (or Gita) and the Muslim holy book, the Koran. So, even from an early age, Gandhi was no stranger to religious diversity. Perhaps this helps explain why Gandhi later became so self-confident about his own religious convictions and also so tolerant of and receptive to the convictions of others. Gandhi was fond of saying that he considered himself a Hindu and a Christian and a Muslim insofar as he believed that all religions spoke truthfully about God. But he saw no reason to submit to his Christian friends' exhortations to convert to Christianity, nor did he try to convert others to Hinduism, although thousands would have if he had only asked. Instead, he urged Hindus to become better Hindus, Muslims to become better Muslims, and Christians to become better Christians. He said, "Let each keep his own religion and become better within it" (Kanithar and Cole 1995, 189). He thought this was the best way individuals could get closer to God.

As a young boy, however, and despite the fact that he was exposed to and *tolerated* religious diversity, Gandhi was not a very religious—much less spiritual—child. Not only was he disinterested in Hindu teachings, he was downright hostile to religion. He did not even read the Hindu Gita until he was 20 years old. He was ashamed to admit that he had to read an English translation of it because he could not read Sanskrit, the ancient Indian tongue of the Hindu holy scriptures.

In addition to the strong Hindu presence in his hometown, Gandhi was also exposed to a similar faith while growing up in Porbandar. In Gujarat, the region of India where Porbandar is located, the Jain faith was particularly strong. Recall from Part I that Jainism is an ancient religion whose several million worldwide adherents, found mostly in India, believe very strongly in ahimsa. Jainism is similar to the Quaker faith in that both Jains and Quakers believe that, although conflict exists in the world, it is each person's duty to find a peaceful, nonviolent alternative resolution to differences among people. Neither Jains nor Quakers believe in withdrawing from society to a life of hermitage. Both believe in the kind of social activism that involves the practice of nonviolence for improving the social condition of humanity. For Jains, there is little difference between the person who only thinks hateful and violent thoughts and the person who acts on those thoughts. True Jain devotees should be able to purge violent impulses from their hearts as well as their hands. Jainism's presence in Gandhi's childhood was a "significant determinant of his ultimate convictions as to the nature of truth, of his personal tolerance and high estimation of all major faiths . . . and of his supreme dedication to nonviolence" (Brown 1989, 18). As I shall discuss later in this chapter, one of Gandhi's closest friends as a young man was a young, devout Jain who had a profound influence on him.

Gandhi's boyhood playmates came from different religious backgrounds as well. One boy in particular, an older Muslim friend named Sheik Mehtab, left a lasting impression on Gandhi. Although Gandhi was raised to be a vegetarian, in accordance with his mother's devout faith, Mehtab would periodically try to convince Gandhi to eat meat. Mehtab was bigger and stronger than Gandhi was and he tried to convince Gandhi that his more impressive physique was because he ate meat. He argued that a few big and strong Englishmen could rule over so many diminutive Indians because the English ate meat. So, if Gandhi wanted a hand in ending English domination of India, he too would have to eat meat in order to confront the English colonialists on an even playing field. Indians even sang a song about it:

> Behold the mighty Englishman,
> He rules the Indian small,
> Because he is a meat-eater
> He is five cubits tall. (Fischer 1950, 11)

Never mind that the herbivorous elephant, a "vegetarian," is the largest, strongest land animal on Earth. Eventually Gandhi relented and ate meat, convincing himself that he if did not tell his parents of the deed, it would not be "a departure from the truth" (Gandhi 1957, 22). But Hindus—even those who are not vegetarians—have strict prohibitions not only against eating beef, but also against mistreating cows in any way because cattle are considered sacred animals to Hindus. Moreover, Muslims (and Jews for that matter) are prohibited from eating pork, because they consider swine a dirty animal, unfit for human consumption. Consequently, since beef was forbidden to Gandhi and pork was off limits to Gandhi's Muslim friend, the conspirators settled on eating goat. Gandhi's account (1957) of the incident is truly a treasure:

> I had a very bad night afterwards. A horrible nightmare haunted me. Every time I dropped off to sleep, it would seem as though a live goat were bleating inside me, and I would jump up, full of remorse. (22)

Gandhi was riddled with guilt about deceiving his parents and breaking with his own religious tradition, but he resolved to keep eating meat, considering it his "duty" if he wished to stand up to the British. However, the guilt, not only of violating his Hindu vegetarian tenets, but also of lying to his parents, compelled Gandhi to give up this secret habit after a year. According to Gandhi (1957), the guilt gnawed at his heart: he wrote that "deceiving and lying to one's father and mother is worse than not eating meat" (23). So Gandhi pledged not to eat meat again until after his parents died. Actually, Gandhi would never again eat meat, despite this earlier vow to resume eating meat upon his parents' deaths.

This incident reveals some important things about Gandhi. First, it shows that, even from a young age, Gandhi was inculcated with the idea that the British were colonial masters in another's home and that they were to be resisted so that one day the British could be tossed from India and Indians would rule themselves. Second, it reveals Gandhi's highly developed sense of conscience, even at a young age. Gandhi's conscience and, perhaps, his overdeveloped sense of guilt and responsibility, had an impact on his behavior and the development of his principles and values.

To be sure, Gandhi's conscience would lead him to another peak experience during his boyhood, this time with his father. Gandhi had at least two such notable experiences with his father, one when he was 15 years old and the other when he was 16. The first occurred when Gandhi, overcome by guilt, confessed to his father that he had stolen some money from his brother, Laxmidas. Again, the incident occurred with a twist of irony. Laxmidas had an extravagant lifestyle and would accrue considerable debt since he often lived beyond his means. Gandhi, in his attempt to help relieve his brother of the debt, stole some gold trinkets from Laxmidas in order to pay off the debt. Gandhi had actually taken to thievery before: a few years earlier, he and a friend would steal copper pieces from the servants' pockets in order to steal away and smoke cigarettes.

But this theft from his brother at the age of 15 weighed heavily on Gandhi. Even though he stole from his brother to pay off his brother's debts, Gandhi became so guilt-ridden that he confessed his sin to his father but only in a handwritten note since he was too frightened and choked up to speak it aloud. He even requested from his father the proper punishment (Gandhi 1957, 27). At that time, Gandhi saw his father as aloof and stern (Brown 1989, 20) and he expected that, upon confessing his thievery to his father, Karamchand would give him a beating as punishment, since his father was not normally one to be so forgiving. Instead, Gandhi was surprised to see that his truthful and heartfelt confession brought his father to tears. Karamchand was so overcome by the boy's confession that he could not speak. Instead, he ripped up the confession note and tearfully embraced his son, who was also weeping by that time.

This incident tells us some important things about Gandhi. First, the relationship with his father attained a new level of understanding. Gandhi realized how much his father loved him and how passionate his father was about truth and honesty. Second, Gandhi learned firsthand how telling the truth, perhaps when it is least expected and when it can get the truth teller in a heap of trouble, can have a transformational and redemptive influence on an event. Third, this incident foreshadows one of the Mahatma's most famous and unequivocal philosophies, namely, that impure means cannot be justified while striving for pure ends. Even for young Gandhi, stealing from his brother to pay off that same brother's debt was something he could not bear. Perhaps Gandhi put it best when he wrote of the incident that it was pure ahimsa for him: "When such *ahimsa* becomes all-embracing, it transforms everything it touches. There is no limit to its power" (Gandhi 1957, 28).

The second milestone Gandhi experienced in relation to his father occurred with Karamchand's death, when Gandhi was just 16 years old and before he had ever had the chance most sons have to relate to his father as a fully mature and equal adult male. Although Gandhi the adult would take a solemn vow of celibacy in his mid-thirties, Gandhi the teenager had a normal teen's sexual libido and he frequently satisfied his sexual urges with Kasturbai. As Karamchand grew seriously ill, Gandhi became his chief nurse, massaging his sore legs and tending to him. One time, while nursing his father, Gandhi's thoughts turned to his wife and their bed. When his uncle relieved him from his nursing duties, Gandhi went to his wife, who was already pregnant, seeking to satisfy his sexual urges "at a time when religion, medical science and common sense alike forbade sexual intercourse" (Gandhi 1957, 29). While in bed with his wife a servant arrived to inform him that his father had passed away. Gandhi's guilt over this incident was compounded by the fact that the child Kasturbai gave birth to died after only several days. Gandhi later referred to his father's and the infant's deaths as his "double shame."

This event left Gandhi extremely guilt-ridden, for he was supposed to be nursing his father, not shamelessly and selfishly satisfying his carnal desires. If not for his lustfulness, Gandhi said, he would have had the "honor" of being at his father's bedside at the moment of his passing. Many observers assert that this event colored Gandhi's attitude toward sex in his later years. Gandhi came to believe that sexual intercourse should only be for procreation and not for satisfying fleshly desires. Moreover, Gandhi came to believe that if a man succumbs to the temptations of the flesh, then his mind would be too cluttered to seek truth in God. Rather, his mind would be captivated by the desires of the flesh. Some 40 years later, still guilt-ridden and ruminating on the event, Gandhi said, "If animal passion had not blinded me, I should have been spared the torture of separation from my father during his last moments" and "the shame of my carnal desire even at the critical moment of my father's death . . . is a blot I have never been able to efface or forget" (Gandhi 1957, 30–31). Clearly, Gandhi's guilt over this incident carried well into his adult life. Surely, his several attempts at declaring *brahmacharya*, or celibacy, are connected to this experience. When he was in his mid-thirties, he finally succeeded in forever keeping his vow of chastity. Although many Hindus declare brahmacharya, few undertake it at such a young age.

A NAÏVE LAW STUDENT IN LONDON (1888–1891)

Upon Karamchand's death, the family needed to find new means of support. Although Gandhi was a fairly unimpressive student, he was selected by the family to be the main provider (Brown 1989, 22). After Gandhi graduated from high school in 1887, he passed his matriculation exams and went off to Samaldas College in Bhavnagar.

However, since he failed his first set of exams, he returned home to Porbandar a college dropout after only one term. After his failure in Bhavnagar, a family friend advised that Gandhi should go to law school in London as a shorter, more assured route to success. So, in 1888, Gandhi, who had never before traveled overseas, set sail for London—a shy, naïve young man—to one of the world's most cosmopolitan and unforgiving cities. His departure heralded a dramatic change not only for him, but for his family as well. At that time, no one from his caste had ever gone abroad and many, including his mother, opposed him studying in London, fearing that the influences of Western culture might lead Gandhi to eat meat, drink alcohol, or go with women who were not his wife. But after making a solemn vow of three promises to his mother—under the supervision of a Jain monk—that he would not eat meat, or drink alcohol, or go with women, his mother relented. Others in his caste remained opposed to his traveling abroad and declared him an outcaste and imposed a fine on anyone who saw him off (Tendulkar 1951, 1:28–32).

Gandhi was undeterred. Showing some of that stubbornness for which he would become renowned, Gandhi arranged to leave for London. So, despite many in his family and caste opposing him, despite being cast out, despite the fact that he had never traveled even so far as Bombay and despite the fact that he was painfully shy and spoke very little English, Gandhi set sail for London in September 1888. He left behind a young bride and an infant son.

Gandhi's nearly three years in London were a time of great educational, intellectual, and spiritual discovery for him. At first, he naïvely threw himself into Westernization. He dressed in the finest, albeit uncomfortable, Western-style suits. He studied French, Latin, European dance, and the violin. He even took elocution lessons in order to improve his English diction. Gandhi, whose father grew up extremely loyal to the state, was himself a firm supporter of the British Empire at this time and sought to become a proper English gentleman. He tried to emulate what he considered the best aspects of Western civilization while never once breaking any of the promises he made to his mother. His stubborn adherence to his vows gives us an indication of the moral seriousness with which Gandhi was possessed.

At first, Gandhi's adjustment to life in London was troublesome. He did not have a lot of money and his strict vegetarianism made it exceedingly difficult to find suitable cuisine, either at home or in restaurants. Moreover, since he was unaccustomed to the local cuisine, Gandhi found it difficult to prepare meals suitable to his tastes, especially since he was not much of a cook. However, he became an active member in London's vegetarian societies and clubs and even helped issue a vegetarian newsletter. These contacts encouraged him and made his striving for a vegetarian diet easier. Moreover, when Gandhi read Henry Salt's *A Plea for Vegetarianism* (1886), he had another milestone experience because, from that moment on, vegetarianism for Gandhi was no longer an obligation or duty that he must stubbornly and rigidly fulfill in accordance with the promise he made to his mother (Herman 1999, 183). Rather, Salt's book so convinced Gandhi that vegetarianism was the proper form of diet for people that his vegetarianism thereafter became a passionate commitment, a choice he made freely and not out of a sense of obedience to his mother or an obligation he felt from his earlier promise. Accordingly, and despite his childhood vow to resume eating meat once his parents died, Gandhi never again considered eating meat after reading Salt's *Plea*.

The young law student's need to economize proved a boon to Gandhi in his later years. To save money, he walked everywhere, usually 8 to 10 miles each day. He also kept scrupulous financial accounts. Both of these habits, which were developed in England, proved to be good training for Gandhi as he founded the self-sufficient communal-type ashrams, as he entered public life, and as he worked among the masses. Although the Indian peasantry had to walk just about everywhere, Indian leaders thought it was beneath them to walk anywhere. To Gandhi, this attitude meant that Indian leaders thought the peasants were beneath them (Brown 1989, 24). By contrast, Gandhi wanted to be and live among the masses, so he would walk, literally for hundreds of miles from village to village, preaching nonviolence and reaching out directly to the masses who were elated to see him in this manner. Accordingly, other Indian leaders could not capture the hearts and minds of the masses the way Gandhi could as he walked everywhere to learn about the peoples' problems and difficulties, to become one with them in sharing their hopes and dreams and joys and sadness.

Where previously he showed little interest in books, Gandhi also became a voracious reader while in London. He read books on philosophy, religion, and history. During his second year in London, he read for the first time the Hindu holy book, the Bhagavad Gita, which had a profound influence on him. As mentioned earlier, Gandhi was somewhat hostile to his and other religions, specifically expressing antipathy toward Christianity: "Surely, thought I, a religion that compelled one to eat beef, drink liquor and change one's clothes did not deserve the name!" (Tendulkar 1951, 1:1, 1:27).

Nevertheless, his hostility to religion began to change in London. He was more fully exposed to Hinduism, Christianity, and other faiths in a way that left him permanently changed in his attitude toward religion, faith, and God. Particularly influential on him during his legal studies in London were readings from the Gita and the New Testament, both of which left indelible marks on him. According to the Gita, "The man who sheds all longing and moves without concern, free from the sense of 'I' and 'Mine'—he attains peace" (Fischer 1950, 34). Gandhi became enraptured by the Gita, which he read every day of his adult life, declaring "I regard it today as the book *par excellence* for the knowledge of Truth" (Gandhi 1957, 67). Gandhi became the Mahatma, not by study, research, or force of intellect, but by being a doer and since the Gita was Hinduism's holy scripture that glorified doing, it became a natural fit for Gandhi (Fischer 1950, 29–37). The Gita, a lengthy religious poem or song of profound significance to Hindus, became the supreme authority in Gandhi's daily life because he was so inspired by its teaching of nonpossession, tranquility of the mind, and fair-minded treatment of all (Brown 1989, 77). The Gita became Gandhi's "dictionary of daily reference" (Gandhi 1957, 265).

But the Gita is, at least on one level, a story of an epic battle between good and evil, a story about violence and war. This presented a significant challenge to Gandhi, the devout votary of nonviolence. Gandhi was convinced that the Gita's vivid battle scenes were really allegories for depicting the enduring conflict in the hearts of people. For Gandhi, the battlefield in the Gita was actually the human soul where the struggle is waged over whether to use violence (the lower impulse) or nonviolence (the higher impulse) (Fischer 1950, 32).

But Gandhi did not just read Hindu holy texts while he was studying in London. He read about the Buddha, whose teachings about nonpossession resonated with his previous exposure to Jainism and helped him crystallize his germinating views on nonviolence, nonpossession, compassion, and vegetarianism (Brown 1989, 26). He also read about Islam and theosophy, which is an eclectic form of religious thought claiming mystical insights into the divine nature. And while Gandhi said the Old Testament put him to sleep—he found it difficult to read and its blood vengeance themes even more difficult to accept—the New Testament spoke deeply to him. In particular, Jesus Christ's Sermon on the Mount set him afire. Gandhi was deeply moved by the message of nonviolence, forgiveness, and redemptive love Christ urged his followers to obey in the Sermon on the Mount. Gandhi saw similarities between this sermon and the Gita's emphasis on compassion for all life, self-renunciation, forgiveness, and nonviolence (Brown 1989, 26). Although Gandhi accepted much of Christ's teachings as sacred truths in pursuit of God, he remained a devout Hindu, satisfied that he could find his true path to God within the confines of his own religion. Finally, while in London, Gandhi was exposed to a different type of Christian than what he saw in India. In London, Gandhi met more Christians of genuine piety and not the self-righteous, moralizing street preachers he saw in India (Brown 1989, 26).

Unlike during his high school and college career, Gandhi turned out to be a diligent law student, having passed his bar exams—on the second try—in Latin. Having been admitted to the bar—and hence becoming an attorney—Gandhi returned to India in June 1891. Upon his arrival, Gandhi was shocked to hear that his mother had died while he was in London. Knowing how close Putlibai and her youngest son were and how hard Gandhi would take news of her passing, his family kept Putlibai's death a secret from him because they knew that he would be overcome with grief, yet unable to make the trip home for her funeral. Like the death of his father, Gandhi was not with his mother when she died and he felt guilty about that too. People have speculated that much of Gandhi's adult behavior—his celibacy, his strict vegetarianism, his fasting rituals, his quirky dietetic habits, and so on—reveals his attempt to come to terms with the immense guilt he felt over the circumstances surrounding his parents' deaths, his father's while he was in bed with his wife and his mother's while he was away at law school. According to Judith Brown (1989), Gandhi's strong identification with women—doing "women's" work, such as spinning cotton for cloth—as well as his withdrawal from male sexual activity "may well reflect in part the still powerful mother figure" who, in death gripped Gandhi even more powerfully than in life (27).

London helped Gandhi blossom. After nearly three years, Gandhi returned to India having made "immense strides in self-knowledge and growth in personal identity" (Brown 1989, 26). According to Louis Fischer (1954), Gandhi's life actually began after he returned from London. He was more self-confident than ever before. Not only did he possess an excellent command of the English language, but he could also speak French and Latin. Yet he was still shy and reluctant—characteristics unsuitable for an attorney.

Gandhi did not acquit himself well as an attorney once he returned to India. On one occasion, he was publicly humiliated by a low-ranking British official whose brief acquaintance Gandhi had made while in London. Gandhi used this connection to approach the official on behalf of his brother, Laxmidas, who asked Gandhi to help him make a favorable application to the official. The British official was unreceptive but Gandhi persisted with his case only to provoke the official into having one of his minions physically throw Gandhi out of his office. According to his autobiography, the shock of this incident changed the entire course of Gandhi's life. He became disgusted with the idea of having to play palace politics and sucking up to officials in order to get ahead; he sought to escape this type of environment, with its petty intrigues and snobbery (Fischer 1954, 20–21). On another occasion, Gandhi again proved a dismal failure, this time in a courtroom. Having become so embarrassed and tongue-tied before the judge and other attorneys, Gandhi could not even speak. He turned and fled the courthouse, turning the case over to a colleague.

After that fiasco, Gandhi did not go to court again. Instead, he took to drafting legal briefs for colleagues, at which he turned out to be quite good. Gandhi spent about a year in Bombay writing legal briefs. While he was there, he befriended a Jain named Rajchandra Ravjibhai Mehta, who went by the name Raychandbhai. Raychandbhai was a jeweler and poet about the same age as Gandhi, but so devout and impassioned about his faith that he left a lifelong impression on Gandhi. Even after Gandhi moved to South Africa, he would correspond with Raychandbhai, seeking his counsel on important matters of family and work.

Raychandbhai's intense idealism and intellectual gifts greatly influenced Gandhi. In later years while reflecting on those who influenced him the most, Gandhi said that he considered Raychandbhai to be "higher than Tolstoy in religious perception" (Tendulkar 1951, 1:35). While the writings of Leo Tolstoy and John Ruskin had profound influences on Gandhi, it was Raychandbhai's living example that Gandhi gives preeminence to as a major influence. Raychandbhai was like a mentor to Gandhi who could answer Gandhi's probing, searching questions about God and about living a life of compassion for others. Raychandbhai's passion, intellect, and deep faith provided Gandhi with a living example for how a man caught up in modern society could still seek God. In Raychandbhai, Gandhi saw that a man could combine active involvement in day-to-day commercial ventures with religious devotion and a quest for virtue and detachment from earthly desires (Brown 1989, 76–77).

From Raychandbhai, Gandhi took the example of ceaselessly striving for self-knowledge and of being open to the truths contained in all religions. From Raychandbhai, Gandhi came to believe that all religions were, at their essence, both perfect and imperfect, but that each provided its own way to the truth about God and worship. Gandhi also became convinced, through Raychandbhai's influence, that anyone from any faith could find the true path to God and salvation within their own religious traditions and teachings. Gandhi also learned from his young Jain "teacher" that truth was a "many-sided" phenomenon and therefore people must be tolerant, open, and accepting of other peoples' views of what the truth is. This became a keystone of Gandhi's living philosophy, along with his passionate commitment to nonviolence, which Raychandbhai also had a hand in influencing (Brown 1989, 76–77).

But despite his friendship with Raychandbhai, Gandhi's legal practice of writing attorneys' briefs did not provide enough compensation to support his family. A family friend recommended him for a one-year position as legal counsel to some Indian Muslim traders and merchants in South Africa. While Gandhi would have to spend a year away from his wife and family in South Africa, the position was too good to pass up. He wanted to be out of Porbandar, out of India, and to have new experiences. So, in April 1893, Gandhi set sail for South Africa, initially planning to stay for only one year. Little did he, or anyone else for that matter, expect that he would end up staying in South Africa for more than two decades, where his journey toward becoming the Mahatma would crystallize.

A TRANSFORMATION IN SOUTH AFRICA (1893–1915)

While in South Africa, Gandhi changed dramatically. According to Brown (1989):

> When the mature Gandhi's relations with Europeans are compared with those of the diffident student in London with his hosts and hostesses, it is clear what a watershed South Africa was for his personal development. (61)

A series of peak experiences, together with an increasingly insatiable intellect that compelled him to seek out new ideas through friends and literature, cast Gandhi into a new mold, one that never fully hardened because Gandhi was always changing, always experimenting with new ideas and new practices. Sometimes, as when he experimented with all forms of diet and nutrition, these experiences left him emotionally adrift, groping for answers and meaning. At other times, such as when he became fully committed to nonviolence, Gandhi was a freight train whose direction and path could not be altered by the strongest of forces.

Overall, Gandhi was transformed in South Africa from a mild, meek, and less-than-adequate lawyer into a famous and successful attorney, a man devoted to nonviolence, possessed of incredible courage in the face of overwhelming odds, and committed to a life of public service. As his time in South Africa progressed, Gandhi experienced a transformation so profound and so complete that every aspect of his life—his style of dress, the food he ate, the way he cared for and raised his family, the way he practiced law, and the methods he used to confront the South African government— would change radically. Moreover, through his legal work, through his newspapers, through his communal lifestyle at the ashrams, and most of all through his total commitment to a life of service to others, Gandhi transformed not only himself, but also all those around him—Indians, Africans, and Europeans.

Perhaps the most significant transformation Gandhi underwent in South Africa was his commitment to ahimsa. This transformation occurred slowly, across a range of experiences and activities.

How the Experience of Bigotry and Racism Transformed Gandhi

While he was studying in London, Gandhi had little occasion to taste the bitter pill of white, European racism. London was the capital of the British Empire, a cosmopolitan city, whose population was quite sure of itself, its identity, and its role in the world. Although London was predominantly white (or perhaps because of this), Londoners of different races related to and mixed with each other better than elsewhere in the empire. Whites in London showed relatively little racism towards people of color.

Gandhi sought to portray himself as the proper English gentleman in South Africa, a carryover from his student days in London. He dressed himself and his family in expensive Western-style suits. Many Indians, including Gandhi's toddler boys, found Western clothing cumbersome to wear, especially the stockings, which caused Gandhi's sons' legs to sweat and smell. He used Western-style eating utensils, again an inconvenient and impractical way for Indians to eat because they were accustomed to eating with their fingers. But these attempts to imitate all things Western did not protect him from the bigotry and racial superiority he was subjected to upon his arrival in South Africa, where the minority whites dominated but also felt threatened.

Perhaps because of their minority status in South Africa, whites severely restricted the rights of nonwhites, especially the Indians there who had a flare for business and commerce: the whites wanted to prevent the Indians from becoming their commercial rivals in South Africa. Unlike in India or London, Indians in South Africa were subjected to many humiliating social constraints and racial insults, not only by Europeans living in South Africa, but also by the South African government. Government laws, ordinances, and policies placed restrictions on Indians' rights, preventing them from trading freely, limiting their voting rights and other civil liberties, and even restricting their movements about the country. Indians, for instance, were not allowed outdoors after nine o'clock in the evening and even when they were allowed outside, they could not walk on the public footpaths, which were reserved for Europeans.

Gandhi was in South Africa for about a week when he got his first real taste of European racial arrogance. This bitter experience actually turned out to be one of Gandhi's most important peak experiences because it set him on a path of action he had not previously contemplated or imagined for himself. Gandhi purchased a first-class train ticket for a lengthy ride through South Africa to the city of Johannesburg, his final destination where he would begin his legal practice. While riding in the well-appointed first-class car—and dressed in his finest European attire—a white passenger, offended at the presence of a "colored" or "sami" riding in a first-class car, complained to the conductor who then ordered Gandhi out of first class. In his stubbornness, Gandhi refused both on principle and on the grounds that he had paid for a first-class ticket and therefore was entitled to a first-class seat.

At the next train stop, Gandhi and his luggage were forcibly thrown off the train. It was a dirty, unpleasant train station, late at night, cold and dark, but Gandhi remained there the whole night, miserable, wounded, and brooding, wondering what he should do about such an injustice. Here was a citizen of the empire, a graduate of London University, a member of the High Court, and impeccably dressed to boot, yet he could not take a first-class train ride in South Africa simply because of his skin color—something that he could not change. Gandhi later said that the night he spent at the train station was the most creative moment of his life. As he shivered all night in the cold and dank train station, he pondered his options. He felt he could remain silent and accept this humiliating racial discrimination, he could refuse to accept such treatment and return to India, or he could stay in South Africa and fight against racial discrimination. Gandhi chose the latter. This peak experience was perhaps the single most important event that put Gandhi on the path to the type of man he would become because it changed the course of his life:

> What was my duty, I asked myself. Should I go back to India, or should I go forward, with God as my helper, and face whatever was in store for me? I decided to stay and suffer. My active nonviolence began from that date. (Tendulkar 1951, 1:37–38)

The incident seemed to spark a hidden resolve in him. Where it would ultimately take him he was not entirely certain. But in the meantime, he would at least secure his right to ride on a train. Gandhi actually examined the railway policies and regulations and concluded that they could not deny him a first-class seat. He wrote to the authorities, threatening legal action if he was denied his right to a first-class seat. On his next trip, he was allowed to purchase a first-class ticket and ride in a first-class compartment, despite the objections of a railway official (an English passenger stood up in his defense).

Thus began Gandhi's lifelong practice of public agitation to fight social injustice. He began to organize fellow Indians, he formed clubs and associations, he gave speeches, he organized nonviolent resistance campaigns, he established contacts with the press, he founded his own newspaper, and he even kept in constant contact with his adversaries in the South African government. Ironically, and despite his train-ride humiliation, as Gandhi's South African experience further transformed him, he would eventually refuse to ride first class, preferring instead to ride third class in order to be closer to the Indian masses, the peasants with whom he most identified.

How the Experience of War Transformed Gandhi

Repeated racial insults, as well as having to endure strict legislation restricting the rights and movements of Indians in South Africa, increasingly chipped away at Gandhi's admiration for the West. He went from being the dutiful Indian loyalist—supportive of the British Crown and the British Empire—to one of its harshest critics. Until then, Gandhi remained a staunch and loyal supporter of the British Empire. By the early 1900s, however, he began criticizing not just the British Empire, but Western civilization as a whole. And by 1920, Gandhi's faith in the British system of justice had all but crumbled. After his repeated appeals to the British government regarding an issue of great importance to India's Muslims went unheeded,[1] Gandhi concluded that Hindus and Muslims together had "lost faith in British justice and honor. . . . I can no longer retain affection for a Government so evilly manned as it is nowadays" (Tendulkar 1951, 1:296, 1:301).

But Gandhi's attitudes toward the British were anything but simple; they were very complex, as evidenced by his staunch and vocal support for the British in three separate wars: the Boer War (1899–1902) and the Zulu Rebellion (1906) in South Africa and World War I (1914–1918). A major theme of this book is that Gandhi was a man of action, a doer, more than a theorist or philosophizer. Before his views of the British Empire turned sour, Gandhi considered himself a loyal and supportive citizen of the empire and, since he wished to enjoy its privileges, he felt compelled to rise to its defense in time of need; he felt he must do something. His participation in the Boer War and the Zulu Rebellion contributed to the significant transformation he would experience while in South Africa.

But how did Gandhi, an Indian immigrant to South Africa, become involved in the British Empire's military conflicts? Gandhi had long been pondering how to be of service to others; he longed to do humanitarian work. His desire to be of service intensified at the outset of the Boer War in October 1899, which pitted independence-minded Dutch settlers against the British Empire in South Africa. Despite his own sympathies for the Boers and despite past humiliations at the hands of the British, Gandhi stayed loyal to the

---

[1]Muslims in India and around the world were angry over the dissolution of the Islamic Caliphate—the main Islamic center of authority—in Turkey as the European powers, led by Britain, dismantled the Ottoman Empire.

British Empire: he remained convinced of its superiority and sought to contribute to its splendor. He saw the Boer War as a triple opportunity: first, he could be of service to others; second, he could do his part to prop up the British Empire; and third, he could show the British that Indians had courage and ability and could make a contribution to the empire's defense and therefore should be treated as equals and not as "coolies," or manual laborers.

Accordingly, Gandhi sought to form an all-Indian ambulance corps to help aid the wounded and dying during the war. At first the British authorities rejected Gandhi's request to form the corps, given their racist belief that he and other Indians were incapable of such a gruesome task. However, this time Gandhi's stubbornness paid off and through his struggles with the British administration, he was able to field an ambulance corps of some 1,100 volunteer Indians.

Indians in the ambulance corps worked tirelessly, bearing wounded soldiers in the midst of battle, sometimes walking more than 20 miles a day. Gandhi and the others did such praiseworthy work they received medals for their part in Britain's victorious, albeit bloody, conflict with the Boers. Gandhi was proud of his experience, gratified and satisfied by the contribution he had made to the empire. But he was also impressed by the courage he saw displayed by the outmanned and outgunned Boers who stood up and defied the British, despite impossible odds. These acts of courage and resistance, albeit using violence, nevertheless left their mark on Gandhi (Tendulkar 1951, 1:54). He even wrote an enthusiastic review of the Boers' martial prowess: "Every Boer is a good fighter. . . . [A]ll get ready and fight as one man" (Erikson 1969, 183).

Yet another bloody war the British Empire fought in South Africa left its mark on Gandhi, but this time in a different way. In 1906, the Black African Zulus rose up in rebellion against the British. Again Gandhi formed an ambulance corps, this time much smaller and again he acquitted himself and his corps honorably during the six-week conflict. Ironically, Gandhi's corps treated mostly Zulu casualties because British medics and nurses, in their racism and bigotry, refused to treat them. Like the Boers, the Zulus were outmanned and woefully outgunned, pitting their crude weapons, such as spears, against the might of the modern world's most impressive military machine. Gandhi watched, horrified, as British soldiers literally cut the Zulus to pieces and whipped captives so severely that bits of flesh would fly from their bodies. He was also sickened by the bloodlust of many British soldiers. He began to question the assumptions he held about the empire's virtues. And again, the bravery and courage with which the Zulus approached the war and accepted their suffering impressed Gandhi. Although Gandhi's ambulance corps acquitted itself admirably in both wars and although its efforts did increase the prestige of Indians in South Africa, it did little to alleviate the racist and restrictive legislation Indians were subjected to.

Gandhi's participation in the Zulu War also led to a most remarkable peak experience, which dramatically transformed him. While working in the ambulance corps, Gandhi had a sort of epiphany: he concluded that if a man is going to be truly devoted to a life of service toward others, he must lead a life of purity, free from desires and cravings. Such cravings and desires would interrupt Gandhi's hope of being totally committed to serving others. Consequently, Gandhi took his famous vow of brahmacharya and vowed to live a life of voluntary poverty (Tendulkar 1951, 1:76). He had tried and failed to adhere to the vow at least twice before, but this time, his determination was unwavering. In accordance with this vow, Gandhi's diet also changed because he saw the first step toward celibacy as control of the palate: "A mind consciously unclean cannot be cleansed by fasting. . . . But there is an intimate connection between the mind and the body, and the carnal mind always lusts for delicacies and luxuries. To obviate this tendency, dietetic restrictions and fasting would appear to be necessary" (Gandhi 1957, 329).

Consequently, food "had to be limited, simple, spiceless and, if possible, uncooked" (Gandhi 1957, 209). Moreover, Gandhi came to believe that periodic fasting was necessary to keep the senses from being overwhelmed: "*brahmacharya* means control of the senses in thought, word and deed" (Gandhi 1957, 210). Gandhi's emphasis on controlling thoughts, words, and deeds reflects the Jain influence on his intellectual and philosophical heritage. In this regard, he began to see that vows, such as brahmacharya and fasting, open the door to real spiritual freedom and that without such vows, people are destined to suffer from doubt and failure. Moreover, such vows are necessary before a life of service to others can commence. For Gandhi, a person cannot live life pursuing pleasures of the flesh simultaneously with spiritual enrichment. True brahmacharya comes from total surrender to God, which means mental as well as bodily restraint, including in one's dreams (late in life, Gandhi had an involuntary discharge while sleeping and this troubled him greatly because he thought he had, by that time, overcome his fleshly desires).

The final war experience Gandhi had that is worth mentioning at this point involves his commitment to help the British in their fight against Germany in World War I. After the war broke out, Gandhi traveled from South Africa to London to take a first-aid course in order to treat injured soldiers. Since he was unable to complete the course, due to ill health, Gandhi returned to India and spoke and wrote about India's duty to support the British war effort. By then, Gandhi was already well-known for his commitment to nonviolence, having become world renowned for waging successful nonviolent resistance campaigns against the South African government (see Chapter 5). But back in India, Gandhi became the poster boy for British army recruitment, urging his fellow countrymen to volunteer for service, all the while proclaiming that he still loved the English nation: "I wish to evoke in every Indian the loyalty of Englishmen" (Tendulkar 1951, 1:229). He explained his reasons for not only supporting the British but for recruiting Indians:

> If we want to learn the use of arms . . . it is our duty to enlist. . . .
> There can be no friendship between the brave and effeminate. We
> [Indians] are regarded as a cowardly people. If we want to become
> free from the reproach, we should learn the use of arms. The easiest and straightest way, therefore to win [independence] is to participate in the defense of the Empire. (Tendulkar 1951, 1:230)

Such comments confused Indians: on their face, Gandhi's exhortations seemed to contradict his concepts of satyagraha and ahimsa, which he so strongly espoused. Here was an apostle of peace, a vocal proponent of nonviolent resistance, using macho language, carrying on like a brute, and actively recruiting soldiers for the British war effort. Since his childhood days as a meek little boy, Gandhi appears to have had a complex about being viewed a coward. Gandhi felt strongly about being brave. He insisted that nonviolence was not for the weak or cowardly. Gandhi despised cowardice even to the point of considering it sinful. He said that, if faced with only the (hypothetical) choice between violence and cowardice, he would choose violence:

> [I]f one uses nonviolence to disguise one's weakness or through
> helplessness, it makes a coward of one. Such a person is defeated
> . . . and cannot live like a man. . . . It is a thousand times better

that we die trying to acquire the strength of the arm. Using physical force with courage is far superior to cowardice. At least we would have attempted to act like men. (Gandhi 1990, 54)

But Gandhi's point was not so much to illustrate exceptions to his philosophical commitment to ahimsa, rather it was to emphasize the importance of courage over cowardice, for only the courageous—who actually had access to the tools of violence—could renounce violence and practice real ahimsa. It is also important to note, however, that Gandhi refused to accept the hypothetical condition that only two choices—violence and cowardice—were all that existed. He refused to believe that social and political action could be reduced to only those two choices: if he was pure, strong, and courageous, he could always come up with a creative nonviolent alternative to either cowardice or violence. Nevertheless, the comment does indicate his intense disdain for cowardice, which to this man of action was the worst form of inaction.

Few heeded Gandhi's call to arms, but he saw his role as an active recruiter for the British as consistent with his views on nonviolence. He argued that the root of nonviolence is the unity of all life and that nonviolence comes with a duty to stop war. So, the British would need as much help as they could get in order to stop the war as fast as possible. His other option would have been to resist the war through nonviolent protest, but since he still had feelings of loyalty toward the British, he felt resistance at this time would be traitorous because it might have undermined London's ability to prosecute the war.

How the Exposure to New Ideas Transformed Gandhi

Most of Gandhi's transformation in South Africa can be accounted for by virtue of the experiences he had: his train-ride humiliation, his participation in military conflicts, his legal practice, founding and living in the ashrams, nonviolent resistance, going to jail, and so on. However, Gandhi's transformation was also a product of the intellectual growth he experienced. While in South Africa, Gandhi's appetite for books seemed insatiable. Although he read many authors on many subjects, including communism, theosophy, and Christianity, by his own account, two books stand out as the most important and influential in helping to transform him into the Mahatma: Count Leo Tolstoy's *The Kingdom of God Is Within*

You (1894) and John Ruskin's *Unto This Last* (1860). Tolstoy literally took Christ's admonition to "resist not evil." His refusal to meet violence with violence was manifest in his vocal condemnation of just about any institution—government, church, schools—that he believed aided the ability of the rich and powerful to inflict a "tyranny of force" over the poor (Gifford 1982, 56).

Interestingly, Gandhi had much in common with the famous Russian writer. They both practiced nonviolence. They both believed in the idea of "bread-labor," or manual work. They both admired and worked on behalf of the rural peasant, whose simplicity and commonsense wisdom attracted them. Like Gandhi, Tolstoy asked a lot from humanity. He called on people to obey the Ten Commandments without exception. Like Gandhi, Tolstoy's expectations were probably too high for the "average" person. However, and this is also like Gandhi, Tolstoy placed the toughest demands on himself, above all others (Gifford 1982, 61). Could this be why Gandhi admired him so much? Perhaps the most remarkable trait Gandhi shares with Tolstoy is a fundamental essence that boils down to fearlessness and truth. Both were determined to expose the truth and then to boldly act on it. Like Gandhi, "for Tolstoy, when truth is at issue, no other authority can be tolerated" (Gifford 1982, 79).

Gandhi said Tolstoy's *The Kingdom of God Is Within You* "overwhelmed me" (Gandhi 1957, 37). Although most people know Tolstoy as the famous novelist who wrote *War and Peace* (1886) and *Anna Karenina* (1877), Tolstoy was also a devout Christian who took Christ's teachings seriously and literally. Given his intense devotion, Tolstoy was nicknamed the "Thirteenth Apostle." For Tolstoy, war and violence was not admissible under any circumstances. In *The Kingdom of God Is Within You*, Tolstoy condemned the modern nation-state as the single greatest purveyor of violence in history. The modern state, with its emphasis on nationalism, patriotism, and love of country, creates in peoples' minds a false sense of worship, which is to say that the state compels us to worship a country and its flag, at the expense of the proper target of worship, namely, God. Tolstoy argued that the modern state, with its singular and obsessive goal of survival at any cost, is aggressive and violence prone and therefore no real Christian could support the state or its agents. He said that there was no such thing as a "Christian State" since the term contradicts itself. Tolstoy urged his readers not to take part in the state's activities and functions, counseling his readers that the true "Kingdom" was to be found in our own hearts, transformed by truth and love. Tolstoy wrote that God's Kingdom is achieved only by "sacrificing outward circumstances for the sake of truth" (Fischer 1950, 97). These words resonated deeply with Gandhi.

For Gandhi, the book's influence was so profound that it demolished any lingering faith he might have had in violence: "from the moment of reading that book in the first year of South Africa, he gained an enduring faith in the efficacy of nonviolence" (Brown 1989, 78). This was a time of great religious ferment for Gandhi, and Tolstoy's book seemed to confirm for him thoughts and ideas that were already germinating in his mind as a result of his own searching and the influence his Jain friend, Raychandbhai, was having over him. Ever the doer, Gandhi took Tolstoy's teachings and put them into practice: he admonished Indians to return good for evil and to work in agriculture and not industry (Brown 1989, 78).

Gandhi was so struck by Tolstoy's book that, years after he read Tolstoy, he initiated a correspondence with the count. The two became pen pals of a sort. On a 1909 trip to London, Gandhi wrote his first letter to Tolstoy who responded with a letter of his own, supporting and encouraging the upstart activist, referring to Indians as "our dear brothers and workers in the Transvaal" area of South Africa (Tendulkar 1951, 1:104). For his part, Tolstoy thought Gandhi's nonviolent resistance in South Africa and his communal lifestyle at the ashram were profoundly important examples Gandhi was setting for all humanity. Indeed, Tolstoy became a great admirer of Gandhi; he even read one of the early biographies of Gandhi's life. When Tolstoy died in 1910, Gandhi's newspaper in South Africa, *Indian Opinion*, published an obituary that spoke reverently of him.

The other book that profoundly transformed Gandhi was Ruskin's *Unto This Last*, which Gandhi first read in 1904, when he was on a train ride in South Africa. Ruskin was an English essayist and art critic. According to Gandhi, Ruskin's book gripped him tightly and kept him up all night. He said the book marked a turning point in his life: "I determined to change my life in accordance with the ideals of the book. . . . [The book] brought about an instantaneous and practical transformation in my life" (Gandhi 1957, 298–299). Gandhi was so seized by Ruskin that he translated *Unto This Last* into Gujarati, his native tongue. In Ruskin, Gandhi discovered and confirmed some of his deepest feelings. From Ruskin, Gandhi took three fundamental principles:

1. That the good of individuals is contained in the good of all. Ruskin argued that what one person owns another cannot—this idea of collectivized property sharing resonated with Gandhi, who was struggling to overcome his own (and his family's) cravings for material possessions;
2. That everyone, regardless of occupation, has a right to earn a livelihood from their work and that a lawyer's work is equal to the work of anyone else's, such as a barber; and
3. That a life of manual labor, such as tilling the soil or handicrafts, is the life most worth living. (Gandhi 1957, 299)

Gandhi was so influenced by Ruskin's call to the simple life of labor that he founded an ashram, which he named Phoenix Settlement. He even relocated his 18-month-old newspaper, *Indian Opinion*, to the ashram, where it was published from then on. Gandhi's ashram was designed to be as self-sufficient as possible. Material possessions were minimal, in keeping with Gandhi's increasing desire to detach himself from possessions. Members of the ashram would be treated as equals, regardless of caste or socioeconomic status. Gandhi's quarters were basically identical to everyone else's, only slightly larger. In the hot, dry season, Gandhi would sleep on the roof. Members of the ashram would take turns doing the chores, which ranged from latrine duty to kitchen duty. They would also grow and cook their own food, make their own clothes, build their own homes, operate their own schools, and so on (Tendulkar 1951, 1:66–68). Many of these practices would have horrified upper caste, orthodox Hindus back in India.

Operating on a financial shoestring, Gandhi received donations—often unsolicited—from wealthy donors from all over South Africa and even from Europe. Perhaps his greatest benefactor at this time was an industrialist named Herman Kallenbach, a wealthy German Jew who donated more than just his considerable fortunes; he also came to live at Phoenix Settlement. The ashram and its inhabitants became Gandhi's "family of choice" as opposed to his "family of origin," those kin to whom he was bound by blood. Gandhi felt stronger ties to his "family of choice" because they voluntarily shared in his vision for improving the world through a simple life of labor and service toward others.

Phoenix Settlement was only the first of Gandhi's four major "experiments" with ashramic life. He later founded another ashram in South Africa, aptly named Tolstoy Farm, and then two more after his return to India. Like any close-knit community, these ashrams experienced their trials and tribulations. For instance, petty jealousies would emerge between one personality and another and members would occasionally steal from each other, or from the ashram's budget. All this pained Gandhi, but it did not alter his belief in the correctness of ashramic life, rather it only strengthened his conviction that his example of nonviolence and satyagraha must be even more profound. As will be shown in Chapter 5, Gandhi often resorted to fasting as a way of cleansing himself of his and others' sins.

Of course, Gandhi was not immune to behaving high-handedly at times. Early in Gandhi's South African experience, his wife refused to take her turn at cleaning out the latrine, arguing vehemently that it was dirty work suitable only for the Untouchables. In his fury at his own wife, Gandhi dragged Ba to the compound's entrance, attempting to forcibly expel her. After her screams and pleas finally reached an enraged Gandhi, he calmed down and allowed her back in. On another occasion, while conducting a lesson for school-age residents of the ashram, Gandhi once used a ruler to hit a child who was misbehaving. He felt guilty and ashamed of this act and he repented for years afterward for having hit the boy out of anger and a desire to punish (Gandhi 1957, 339). Clearly, Gandhi was no saint, which was something he constantly reminded his admirers.

Ruskin and Tolstoy helped convince Gandhi to refuse compensation for work he considered in the public service. Moreover, he also gave up receiving gifts, such as jewelry and trinkets, likening adults to children whenever they became transfixed by glossy charms and ornaments. Gandhi had an ongoing dispute with Ba about owning jewelry. Like American and other cultures, Indian custom encourages women to adorn themselves with pieces of jewelry; that is how Ba was raised and that is what Ba believed. When Gandhi tried to dispossess the family's jewels and turn them over to charity in trust, Ba was adamantly opposed. She argued that Gandhi could do what he wished with his material possessions, but that she fully intended to keep her own jewelry and that of the children in order to prepare them for marriage. Gandhi was adamant and eventually won out, compelling Ba to give up her jewelry.

Gandhi's exposure to the ideas found in Tolstoy and Ruskin also influenced the way he conducted his law practice. By its general nature, the legal profession is based on adversarial relations between competing parties with one side usually the victor and the other side the vanquished. For Gandhi, however, practicing law did not have to conform to this zero-sum game. In his growing law practice in South Africa, Gandhi sought repeatedly and successfully to settle cases based on mutual gain. Arguing that attorney's fees could be avoided, he convinced a major client—a Muslim merchant named Abdullah—and Abdullah's opponent—his cousin named Tyeb—to submit their case to arbitration. When Abdullah won the arbitration, Gandhi convinced him to allow Tyeb to pay off the debt in installments so as to avoid bankruptcy (Gandhi 1957, 133). Although this technique might have cost Gandhi some profits, he nevertheless became popular among Indians in South Africa, who actually sent him more and more legal business as his reputation for fairness grew. Gandhi's 20-year legal practice in South Africa grew so well that, at one point, he was earning upward of $30,000 a year, a veritable fortune in those days.

The American writer Henry David Thoreau, especially his essay on *Civil Disobedience* (1849), also had a strong influence on Gandhi. Gandhi liked to quote from Thoreau's famous essay in which Thoreau said he was no lover of government and that he firmly believed that "government is best which governs least, or not at all" (Thoreau 1990, 29). Thoreau condemned U.S. policy toward the Native Americans and the U.S. war with Mexico. Thoreau was jailed for refusing to pay taxes to a government whose policies he could not, in good conscience, support. Thoreau was content, even satisfied, to be a guest of the warden for refusing to pay his taxes. What better place for a man who sees virtue in his open defiance of an unjust government? According to Thoreau, "Under a government which imprisons any unjustly, the true place for a just man is also a prison" (34). Thoreau even had a chuckle at his jailer's expense: they thought by denying his body freedom, they had denied him his freedom when in fact, Thoreau remained free by virtue of his open defiance of the government:

> I could not help being struck with the foolishness of that institution which treated me as if I were mere flesh and blood and bones, to be locked up. . . . [T]hey thought that my chief desire was to stand [on] the other side of that stone wall. I could not but smile to see how industriously they locked the door on my meditations. . . . As they could not reach me, they had resolved to punish my body, just as boys. (36)

Ironically, Gandhi had not read *Civil Disobedience* until he was jailed for committing that very offense. But, like Thoreau,

Gandhi came to believe that jail-going not only served an important political purpose, but it also helped nourish and cleanse the spirit. Gandhi liked to quote Thoreau in explaining his principles on nonviolent noncooperation. According to Thoreau, "[P]ossession of power and riches is a crime under an unjust government; poverty in that case is a virtue" (Tendulkar 1951, 1:294). To be sure, Thoreau's ideas were not entirely new to Gandhi; he had already begun to think similarly. However, in reading Thoreau, especially from the confines of his jail cell, Thoreau's words resonated with Gandhi and confirmed and reinforced values he was already forming. Gandhi referred to Thoreau's *Civil Disobedience* as a "masterful treatise" that "left a deep impression on me" (Fischer, 1954, 38).

How the Experience of Jail Transformed Gandhi

Going to jail proved to be yet another transformative experience for Gandhi. Gandhi's first experience in prison was in South Africa in 1906. Not only did Gandhi's courting jail time transform him, it also transformed the way imprisonment was viewed by others, not least of whom were his fellow Indians. Ordinarily, going to jail was supposed to be a shameful, peril-riddled experience that no self-respecting Hindu, and surely not one from Gandhi's social status, could ever imagine or countenance. But Gandhi changed all that because he was able to convince other Indians that going to jail while fighting for a just cause could be a point of honor and even prestige. He made going to jail "the hallmark of integrity and national commitment rather than an experience of degradation and public shame" (Brown 1989, 117). Moreover, Indians having served time in jail for taking principled, nonviolent stances often increased their political stock among their nationalist brethren, which added to their qualifications to become high-ranking members of the Indian Congress Party (Brown 1989, 56).

Going to jail also influenced Gandhi in other ways. South Africa's prison rules forbade Indian and African prisoners from drinking tea and all meals had to be finished by sunset. Although these rigors were alien to Gandhi, he actually came to appreciate them and even adopted both these practices after his release. Moreover, Gandhi's repeated incarcerations in South Africa (in 1908, 1909, and 1913) for conducting civil disobedience campaigns provided an excellent training ground for other reasons. He learned to court and face prison sentences with pride and resilience and for the sake of conscience. He also took advantage of the time in confinement to read, write, and meditate. Later in his life—with the incredible demands on his time and person—Gandhi actually welcomed his jail sentences because it was the only place where he could be left alone for awhile to recuperate from an exhausting schedule. In jail Gandhi could read the Gita, the Koran, Tolstoy, Ruskin, Thoreau, and many others. He could write letters, articles, and pamphlets. He could meditate. Perhaps most important, he could rest and recuperate from the extreme physical and psychological stresses of being the Mahatma who defied the British Empire. One time while imprisoned, Gandhi even made a pair of sandals for his chief South African rival, General Jan C. Smuts, the powerful defense minister against whom Gandhi matched wits. Although surprised to receive the gift from his former foe, Smuts actually kept the sandals and wore them frequently. That is a fine statement about the respect Gandhi won from even his most ardent foes.

Other Transformations in South Africa

Even though Gandhi was a lawyer by training, his transformation in South Africa led him to develop many more vocations—and avocations. Professionally, Gandhi became more than just a well-known and well-paid barrister. He trained and then volunteered as a nurse and later experimented with alternative health care techniques, such as nature cures, thus transforming himself into his family's (and many friends') primary medical provider. He even wrote articles on how to give a proper enema. He experimented with alternative foods, thus becoming his family's chief cook and dietician. Through his work in the ashram, he became an agronomist, accountant, carpenter, educator, and janitor. As a politically active Indian who sought to be of service to other Indians in South Africa, he became a politician, a labor organizer, a newspaper publisher, an author, and a speech maker. With each new endeavor, he experienced setbacks and failures. Gandhi was initially a horrible public speaker, but he became an accomplished orator along the way. But most of all, Gandhi became an avowed satyagrahi, one who practices satyagraha.

Gandhi's transformation in South Africa also involved an evolving relationship with his immediate family and other kin. This transformation was a product of the many different experiences he was having in addition to the new ideas he was exposed to. By the early 1900s, Gandhi was adamant about showing no favoritism or special treatment to family members, including his sons, one of whom, Harilal, chafed under the pressure of being the son of a famous man. Harilal had great difficulty living up to his father's expectations, which were no less than the stringent expectations Gandhi had for himself and which Gandhi placed on others, especially those living in the ashrams. Whether out of weakness or open revolt, Harilal fell into a life of debauchery, becoming an alcoholic and frequenter of brothels. At one point, Harilal published an open letter in a newspaper criticizing his father's treatment of him. Moreover, and perhaps to spite his father, Harilal announced his plans to wed a Muslim woman, which Gandhi opposed. The relationship between Gandhi and Harilal degenerated to the point that Gandhi effectively disowned him as a son.

In India, there is a play, *Gandhi vs. the Mahatma*, that explores this sad relationship between "Gandhi" (that is, the son) and the "Mahatma." Despite its sensitive subject matter, the play, which takes place in the afterlife where Harilal and Gandhi meet and try to iron out their differences, was very well received in India. It even had a popular run in the United States, playing in New York City, Cleveland, Ohio, and elsewhere across the country. The play depicts the harsh and austere life Gandhi imposed on his ashramites. Several times in the play, Harilal is heartbroken and disappointed when his father does not select him to receive a special scholarship or to travel abroad, choosing another young man instead. Despite Harilal's pleas to his father as Gandhi's son, the Mahatma refuses to give him any special privileges and, arguably, actually treats him more severely than others in the ashram.

Gandhi's role as a family man is a sensitive subject for many Indians to explore, since the revered Mahatma was not a "good" father or husband in the conventional sense. In addition to his vow of celibacy and his insistence on giving up material possessions such as jewelry, Gandhi increasingly neglected what most consider customary and traditional familial obligations as he became more and more committed to a simple life of existence and to public service in South Africa. In 1906, Gandhi wrote a letter to his older brother, Laxmidas, reproaching Laxmidas for asking him for money. Gandhi refused to send Laxmidas any money, arguing that, since he was now dedicated to a life of public service, his money went for public use. He told Laxmidas that if he, or any other relation, devoted themselves to a similar life of public service, they could have what he had. Gandhi also told Laxmidas about his attitude toward Harilal:

> I have never said that I have done much for brothers or other relations. . . . [But] rest assured that I will cheerfully assume the burden of supporting the family in case you pass away before me. . . . It is well if Harilal is married; it is also well if he is not. For the present at any rate, I have ceased to think of him as a son. . . . I like those who are pure in heart. . . . Young Kalyandas [a member of his ashram] is therefore dearer to me than one who is a son because so born. (Tendulkar 1951, 1:77)

Make no mistake, Gandhi loved his family—he just refused to treat them any differently because they were born of the same blood as he. For Gandhi, the ties that bind are not those born of blood, but those born of a common sense of humanity and love toward all. Of course, practicing this belief often made Gandhi appear to be a bad father, husband, or brother. When he sailed from South Africa for India in 1914, he was looking forward to seeing his brother Laxmidas. But, Laxmidas had died long before Gandhi arrived in India and Gandhi was grief-stricken. However, he began to view his grief as a form of selfishness, which he sought to overcome. In so doing, he also conquered his fear of his own death (Tendulkar 1951, 1:150).

And, of course, Gandhi loved his wife, but his commitment to be of service to a broader community of Indians often conflicted with what most people regard as the traditional duties of a husband. For instance, when Gandhi was in jail in 1908, Kasturbai became seriously ill. Gandhi could have paid a fine and been released from jail and, therefore, come to Ba's aid, but he refused to pay the fine on principle (he thought it would be an admission of guilt). He wrote her a letter, saying he was heartbroken that he could not come look after her, but also explained his reasons why: "I have sacrificed all in the *satyagraha* struggle. I love you so much that even if you are dead, you will always be alive to me. . . . I shall never marry again" (Tendulkar 1951, 1:97). By the time Gandhi was finally released from prison, Ba's condition had worsened. Angry that the hospital in which she was being treated had fed her beef-flavored liquids, Gandhi removed his wife from the hospital and cared for her himself at Phoenix Settlement, using unorthodox nursing techniques. He never left her side and, according to one author, Kasturbai made a miraculous recovery (Tendulkar 1951, 1:98).

This chapter has already provided an inkling to some of Gandhi's values, such as vegetarianism, celibacy, and, of course, nonviolence. Chapter 4 discusses those and other ideas more fully in order to better understand who the Mahatma was.

CHAPTER 4

Gandhian Principles of Nonviolence

Nonviolence is the law of our species as violence is the law
of the brute. Nonviolence in its dynamic condition means
conscious suffering. It does not mean meek submission to
the will of the evil-doer, but it means the putting of one's
whole soul against the will of the tyrant.

—Mohandas K. Gandhi, from an article
in his newspaper, *Young India*, 1920

If someone were to ask, What two major principles rank highest
among Gandhi's philosophical approach to social relations? the answer would consist of just two words: ahimsa and satyagraha—
nonviolence and truth force. Satyagraha translates as soul force or
truth force but Gandhi said it also means the strength that comes
from adhering to the truth. Seeking after the truth was of para-
mount concern for Gandhi because he believed "a truthful person
cannot long remain violent." "Indeed," he said, "lying is the mother
of violence" (Gandhi 1990, 56). His idea of satyagraha illustrated
just how central the pursuit of and adherence to the truth was in
his operational code. Truth was so important to Gandhi that he
ranked truthfulness higher in importance than peacefulness.

To be sure, ahimsa and satyagraha are related concepts. If people believe in and practice satyagraha, they must always be open to
finding the truth, which may actually reside more in their opponent's perspective than in their own. As such, people cannot dis-
cern the ultimate, absolute truth: that is something only God can

do. While Gandhi believed that there is *the* truth, he could not be certain he was right. Therefore, Gandhi insisted, if a person cannot know the absolute truth, then he or she is unqualified to inflict punishment on others and so must remain nonviolent in the conflict. Moreover, Gandhi believed strongly that "Truth is God," and that there is no way to find Truth (God) except through nonviolence (Bondurant 1988, 18). Since violence is a product of deceit, dishonesty, and falsehood, it can never be relied on to bring people closer to God. He said the "more truthful we are, the nearer we are to God" (Bondurant 1988, 19).

Gandhi was neither a theorist nor a philosopher. Nor was he trained as such. As his autobiography indicates, he was an "experimenter." Trained as a lawyer, he was a man of action who pursued such action in accordance with strict adherence to deeply held beliefs and principles. Yet he also exasperated both advocates and opponents because he often contradicted himself and changed his mind about issues. He was often confusing and inconsistent in his positions, which opened him to ridicule and criticism. Gandhi's frequent changes, combined with his imposing high moral standards on his followers, often cost him support among those who loved him the most. This made it easier for his followers to accept him as a saint than to try to comprehend him and live out the challenges he posed by his demanding beliefs and standards (Dalton 1993, 34).

Nevertheless, Gandhi insisted that if he changed his mind or seemed to contradict an earlier position or statement, it was always in regard to his relentless pursuit of the truth. On that score, Gandhi never wavered. If Gandhi later discovered that a position he held from his early years was no longer consistent with his understanding of what the truth was, he would not hesitate to change his position to align it with what he then thought was the truth. Recall from the last chapter, for instance, that Gandhi changed his mind about the British Empire and the caste system. Consequently, although his positions might not have been consistent, adherence to his principles—ahimsa and satyagraha—never wavered. In response to his critics, Gandhi said, "[M]y aim is not to be consistent with my earlier statements on a given question, but to be consistent with truth as it may present itself to me at a given moment" (Brown 1989, 283). Gandhi's quest for the truth was inextricably bound up in his search to know God face to face. He said that changing and shifting attitudes were a hallmark of one who is singularly devoted to uncovering the truth and saw this as a sign of growth because, he reasoned, humanity is not spiritually static (Brown 1989, 191) in its quest to know God.

Gandhi was a prolific writer. For decades, he expressed his ideas on a wide variety of subjects in the newspapers he published in South Africa and India, in the books he wrote, and in the many articles and pamphlets he wrote. Gandhi produced shelves of opinions and perspectives on a wide range of issues, from how to conduct a proper nonviolent campaign to how to prepare a nourishing vegetarian meal. It is beyond the scope of this book to explore all of Gandhi's philosophies and views on all the subjects he wrote about. Rather, discussion here shall be confined to discussing his philosophical views as they pertain to nonviolence.

Gandhi also approached life from the position of the eternal optimist. Judith Brown even titled her famous biography of Gandhi *Prisoner of Hope* (1989) to make the point that Gandhi, for all the sin and evil he had witnessed, never wavered in his belief that all people had good in them, that all people were redeemable and that all people could accomplish what he had.

Although Gandhi was a shrewd politician, capable of masterful strategic and tactical thinking in the political realm, he was, first and foremost, a religious man devoted to spiritual growth and the search for God. Gandhi said that "politics cannot be divorced from religion" and that politics divorced from religion was like a corpse only fit to be buried (Tendulkar 1951, 1:185). Gandhi insisted that he entered politics because he was so deeply religious and sought to spiritualize political life and political institutions (Tendulkar 1951, 1:166). He even said that, although he could live without food, he could not live without prayer, because prayer purified his heart each day (Brown 1989, 198).

However, Gandhi's devotion was India's danger because the more he popularized religion in politics, the more Indian Muslims felt threatened. Even though Gandhi accepted and considered all religions as essential truths, he was a devout Hindu. His emphasis on integrating religion and politics was taken by many Muslims as an attempt to impose his own faith on the Muslim minority. Although Gandhi went to great lengths to assuage these concerns, his emphasis on mixing religion and politics helped inflame the fears of India's religious minorities who were alarmed at such public displays of Hindu worship in Indian politics. No matter that Gandhi also led public prayers from other religions: many Indians were just too fearful and ignorant of his religious approach to politics.

THE MAIN PRINCIPLES OF GANDHI'S NONVIOLENT PHILOSOPHY

Satyagraha

There is an interesting story behind the origins of the term satya-graha. During a 1906 resistance campaign against the South African government, Gandhi realized that the new type of struggle he was fa-thering needed a special name because the old terms were unsatis-factory for describing what was emerging. He could not think of a proper word in any Indian language to describe what he was trying to accomplish. Nor was he content using the English term *passive resistance*, because people considered passive resistance a method for the weak and powerless, which Gandhi did not condone. Moreover, passive resistance contradicted the very active nature of the tech-nique he was developing. At a loss, he decided to hold a contest through his newspaper, *Indian Opinion*, and offered a prize to who-ever came up with a term that would accurately describe the method of resistance being developed in South Africa. The award went to a Gujarati-speaking Indian who suggested the term *sadagraha*, which meant firmness in a good cause (Bondurant 1988, 8). Although Gandhi liked this term, he refined it to satyagraha, a term which more accurately reflected the technique he was developing. Gandhi translated satyagraha to mean "the Force which is born of Truth and Love" (Bondurant 1988, 8). Since, according to Gandhi, "truth is the very substance of the soul," satyagraha can also be seen as pure soul force (Gandhi, 1990, 52). A satyagrahi, therefore, uses soul force, or truth force, as a method of resistance in conflict situations.

But satyagraha is more than a method of resistance. It also works to heal rifts and resolve conflict in society. Satyagraha seeks not to defeat adversaries, but rather to win them over through a lov-ing, yet firm and uncompromising, adherence to the truth. Satya-graha also calls for adhering to pure means, which must be founded on an open pursuit of the truth. Gandhi never claimed that he, or anyone else, had complete knowledge of the absolute truth and, therefore, he insisted that since no one could know the absolute truth, everyone had to remain open to the viewpoints of those who might differ with them (Bondurant 1988, 16). Gandhi said, "to find Truth completely is to realize oneself and one's destiny, that is to become perfect" (Bondurant 1988, 17), something which he felt only God was capable of. Discovering the truth was more important to Gandhi than "winning" any political battle. Even as a young lawyer in South Africa, Gandhi was adamant about being truthful. He learned to become an expert cross-examiner who could break down a dishonest witness on the stand. Moreover, if Gandhi learned that one of his clients had deceived him or the court, he immediately resigned as the attorney on the case (Tendulkar 1951, 1:70).

A satyagrahi does not use physical force, nor does he or she seek to inflict pain on the adversary (Gandhi 1990, 52). Not only does the satyagrahi avoid the violence associated with, say, firearms, but also the violence associated with ill will. Such violence only serves to drive conflicts deeper. Neither weapons nor ill will can perform the healing function that satyagraha can. According to Gandhi (1990), a satyagrahi

> does not wish the destruction of his antagonist; he does not vent anger on him; but has only compassion for him. . . . A *satyagrahi* cannot perpetrate tyranny on anyone . . . he does not strike at anyone. [Moreover,] we do not bear malice towards the government. When we set its fears at rest, when we do not desire to make armed assaults on the administrators, nor to unseat them from power, but only to get rid of their injustice, they will at once be subdued to our will. (53)

Satyagraha is not intended to prevail over an opponent, but to prevail over the conflict that separates people, to transform the conflict in such a way that all parties are uplifted and brought closer together in a greater sense of community and common interest (Dalton 1993, 96). Satyagraha is not a selfish, zero-sum technique where one person's victory is another person's defeat. Satyagrahis must conduct themselves on the highest moral plane. They must show more concern for their adversary than even for themselves. Gandhi said that satyagraha "is the vindication of truth not by infliction of suffering on the opponent but on one's self" (Fischer, 1954, 35). The ultimate goal of the satyagrahi is not victory over the adversary, not a decisive triumph, but a transformation of the conflict so that it is really resolved, not merely postponed to a later time (Dalton 1993, 43).

Satyagraha must not be practiced when the opponent has been weakened by circumstances unrelated to the conflict situation. In South Africa, for instance, Gandhi called a halt to a satyagraha campaign protesting discrimination against Indians after white rail workers went on strike, paralyzing much of the transportation and commerce in the region. According to Gandhi, a satyagrahi does not take advantage of an opponent's weaknesses; rather, he or she hopes to convert the heart and soul of the opponent by virtue of adhering to the truth, enduring self-suffering, remaining sincere and chivalrous and by avoiding hurting, humbling, or embittering the opponent (Fischer, 1954, 47).

Satyagraha rejects the age-old adage "an eye for an eye" and instead advocates returning good for evil until the person inflicting the evil tires of the conduct and is transformed by the incredible response of the satyagrahi. By patiently and steadfastly adhering to the truth and by willingly suffering the consequences, satyagraha holds that the differences between opponents will eventually melt away and real conflict resolution, true reconciliation, can commence.

Nor does a satyagrahi have any fear, including fear for his or her own body. Gandhi was a strong advocate of developing fearlessness among Indians and sought to infuse satyagrahis with the same spirit of courage and strength that a soldier in the military might be called on to demonstrate. Satyagrahis, therefore, must be possessed of strength and fortitude. They are not cowed by threats; instead, they are willing to risk their lives in the cause of truth. Nor does a satyagrahi fear the punishment that is surely to come once laws have been broken. Punishment is not only welcomed, but also demanded, for the act of punishing a truthful person for disobeying an unjust law has redemptive powers, powers that can transform adversaries into allies and conflicts into compassion. Trust is a corollary of satyagraha's emphasis on adhering to the truth. According to Gandhi, since a true satyagrahi has learned not to fear anything, not even death (since life is temporary and death is inevitable, why fear the fact?), he is therefore never afraid to trust the opponent because "an implicit trust in human nature is the very essence of his creed" (Fischer, 1954, 36).

According to Joan Bondurant (1998), "[S]atyagraha allows for several stages of winning over an opponent" (11). First, a satyagrahi will use persuasion in an attempt to reason with an opponent to get him or her to agree with the satyagrahi. If that does not work, the satyagrahi will escalate resistance to the point of self-suffering in hopes of dramatizing the issue at stake and of convincing the opponent to come around to the satyagrahi's way of thinking. Finally, if that does not work, then the satyagrahi escalates the resistance even further, to include coercive actions aimed at confronting and provoking the adversary. At this level, a satyagrahi engages in the two major forms of nonviolent resistance discussed in Chapter 2: noncooperation and civil disobedience.

Recall that noncooperation means refusing to participate in institutions of value to the opponent. Social and economic boycotts, as well as labor strikes, are examples. Recall also that civil disobedience calls on the resister to refuse to comply with laws considered unjust. After being convinced that a particular law is unjust, a satyagrahi is duty bound to disobey that law. That is not to say that the satyagrahi is an anarchist interested in promoting chaos by disobeying all laws and resisting government at all turns. On the contrary, a satyagrahi must obey all the laws except those considered unjust. Gandhi called for "a willing and respectful obedience to state laws" and said that

> a *satyagrahi* obeys the laws of society intelligently and of his own free will, because he considers it to be his sacred duty to do so. It is only when a person has thus obeyed the laws of society scrupulously that he is in a position to judge as to which particular rules are just and which unjust and iniquitous. (Gandhi 1990, 51)

For Gandhi, a commitment to truth demands that one's life be held open for the world to see. As such, his defiance of unjust laws must be done openly, honestly, and in goodwill. Before he actually engaged in civil disobedience, Gandhi would not only publicize his intentions to break the law in his newspaper, but he would also write a letter directly to the British authorities, pleading with them to help him find a way to avert the confrontation.

Gandhi's commitment to the truth also meant that he would banish all distinctions between his public and his private life. He held no secrets and shared his personal life with everyone to the extent that one could scarcely tell where Gandhi's personal life ended and his public life began. For instance, Gandhi published editorials confessing the disappointment and pain he felt regarding his wayward son. On another occasion, extremist Hindus accused Gandhi of being a "secret Christian." Gandhi said he considered that both a "libel and a compliment—a libel because there are men who believe me to be capable of being secretly anything" and a compliment because it was a "reluctant acknowledgement of my capacity for appreciating the beauties of Christianity" (Fischer 1950, 333). As will be shown, other attempts to be open and truthful caused quite a stir among his supporters.

Of course, Gandhi's use of noncooperation and civil disobedience as the keystones of satyagraha required a total commitment to ahimsa, or nonviolence. According to Gandhi, a satyagrahi could never use violence "because man is not capable of knowing the absolute truth and therefore [is] not competent to punish" (Dalton

1993, 10–11). This demonstrates how truth became the vital link between Gandhi's ideas of ahimsa and satyagraha. His singular devotion to the truth compelled him not only to resist dishonesty and injustice by refusing to comply with its wishes, but to do so by using noninjurious, nonharmful means because this was the only way truth could be uncovered. Only nonviolence could safeguard the truth. Violence could never hope to bring out the truth, but only to drive dishonesty even deeper. He considered truthfulness and openness a sign of courage and believed it could empower people. By contrast, he believed that dishonesty, deceit, and distrust were signs of weakness.

Ahimsa

Himsa is a Sanskrit term that means harm, injury, or violence. By placing an "a" in front of himsa, the term becomes negated (just like in English when the "non" in nonviolence negates the term violence). Ahimsa, thus, means nonharm, noninjury, or nonviolence. But ahimsa to Gandhi really translates into something more than just refraining from committing harm or violence. Rather, ahimsa carries with it a positive, life-affirming connotation that calls for action based not just on the refusal to do harm, but also on the notion of doing good, even to an evildoer (Bondurant 1988, 23–24). Ahimsa involves conduct based on the renunciation of the will to hurt or to damage and also on action that uplifts and benefits others through loving and peaceful works. Ahimsa, therefore, is more than the absence of violence. It is the affirmative presence of peace, love, and justice:

> *Ahimsa* is an antidote to . . . violence. But there is far more to *ahimsa* than merely non-hurting or non-killing. It includes giving up concepts of "otherness," "separateness," "selfishness," and "self-centerdness" and identifying oneself with all other beings. (Shashtri and Shastri 1998, 67)

Moreover, according to Gandhi,

> Not to hurt any living thing is no doubt part of *ahimsa*. But [this] is its least expression. The principle of *ahimsa* is hurt by every evil thought, by undue haste, by lying, by hatred, by wishing ill to anybody. . . . [Ahimsa] is not merely a negative state of harmlessness but it is a positive state of love, of doing good even to the evildoer.

> But it does not mean helping the evildoer to continue the wrong or tolerating it by passive acquiescence. On the contrary, love, the active state of *ahimsa*, requires you to resist the wrongdoer. (Bondurant 1988, 24)

Gandhi contended that we do not practice ahimsa if we love only those who love us (Ansbro 1982, 5). He also said that it is not enough merely to avoid killing any living being and urged that a true disciple of nonviolence may not even show anger toward an unjust opponent, much less try to harm the opponent. He urged people to confront tyrants by showing love for them (Tendulkar 1951, 1:170). Moreover, real ahimsa means that you cannot even harbor an "uncharitable thought," even toward one you might consider an enemy. Harboring feelings of resentment, hatred, or ill will is a departure from the doctrine of ahimsa (Bondurant 1988, 26). The object, according to Gandhi, was not to seek a triumphant victory over the opponent, but rather to use ahimsa to conquer the tyrant's inner demons.

Gandhi's idea of ahimsa came from fusing traditional Jain and Hindu concepts with ideas he found in Tolstoy and also in Christ's Sermon on the Mount. He was deeply moved by Christ's exhortation to his followers to turn the other cheek. The result was a "principle that evoked rich religious symbolism and contributed to a dynamic method of action unique in Indian history" (Dalton 1993, 14). This is especially important when considered against the backdrop of Hindu religious tradition, which is not known for social activism (King 2001, 155). In a 1915 speech to university students, Gandhi insisted that violence, terrorism, and assassination were foreign imports, not native to Indian soil and hence could not take root in India. He urged the students to fight against and resist tyranny, but not by using violence because "that's not what is taught by our religion. Our religion is based on *ahimsa*," which is love in action, not only toward friends but "even to those who may be our enemies" (Tendulkar 1951, 1:165).

Gandhi combined these sentiments with his interpretation of the Christian doctrine of turning the other cheek, which he felt meant that someone resisting injustice must be willing to show courage and absorb repeated violent blows—neither striking back in kind nor giving in—to the point when this self-suffering has a positive and wondrously transformative effect on the person inflicting the blows. Suffering injury to one's self is the essence of ahimsa, said Gandhi. The ancient Sanskrit word for self-suffering is *tapasya*, which is part of the doctrinal beliefs in Hinduism and Jainism. Gandhi believed that tapasya by throngs of people would weaken a violent opponent's resolve, soften his heart, and eventually compel the opponent to cease his violent behavior (Nakhre 1982, 17). By contrast, inflicting suffering on others is the essence of violence and does not require the positive type of courage that tapasya calls for:

> The votary of [ahimsa] has to cultivate the capacity for sacrifice of the highest type in order to be free from fear. . . . He who has not overcome fear cannot practice *ahimsa* to perfection. . . . He who trembles or takes to his heels the moment he sees two people fighting is not nonviolent, but a coward. A nonviolent person will lay down his life in preventing such quarrels. The bravery of the non-violent is vastly superior to that of the violent. (Gandhi 1990, 55)

Gandhi believed that tapasya was a necessary condition of progress (Ansbro 1982, 5) and that self-sacrifice in the form of non-violent resistance was morally, as well as practically, superior to vi-olence because the force contained in the emotions of love and compassion was stronger than those contained in hate and vengeance (Dalton 1993, 37). Note that this did not mean submit-ting to humiliation. Gandhi insisted that a nonviolent resister must always refuse to do anything that the conscience opposes, even if that refusal to submit means death.

Gandhi warned that violence can be effective in suppressing evil only for a time, but that evil will then resurface, with more vigor than before (Ansbro 1982, 6). Unprovoked suffering, however, experienced silently and with dignity and humility, is the surest way to fix a wrong (Brown 1989, 179). The idea of self-suffering is something that Westerners have difficulty understanding or accepting. However,

> [s]uch sacrifice may well provide the ultimate means of realizing that characteristic so eminent in western moral philosophy: the dignity of the individual. (Bondurant 1988, 29)

One of the characteristics about Gandhi that distinguished him from so many other activists was his firm belief in the use of only nonviolent means in the pursuit of political objectives. Gandhi ex-alted means over ends since he was actually more concerned about living a life devoted to the philosophy of nonviolence and less con-cerned about political goals. Gandhi's ultimate goal was not to achieve Indian independence, but rather to have Indians behave nonviolently toward themselves and the world. For Gandhi, the means *were* the ends and pursuing purity of means in all endeavors, including India's independence struggle, was critical. Means and ends became interchangeable and convertible for Gandhi. Put another way, Gandhi was more concerned about how he arrived at a place than where he might be going. He wanted no part of political action that sought its objectives by using the impure means of violence, dishonesty, deceit, and hate. Gandhi said:

> Nonviolence for me is not a mere experiment. It is part of my life and the whole creed of *satyagraha*, noncooperation, civil disobedience and the like are necessary deductions from the fundamental proposition that nonviolence is the law of life for human beings. For me, *it is both a means and an end*. (Brown 1989, 271; emphasis added)

Gandhi insisted on right, or pure, means to a right, or pure, end. Intentions of the satyagrahi are key; if a person using nonviolent resistance wants only to achieve victory over his or her opponent, then this is not true satyagraha. On the contrary, Gandhi advocated nonviolence as a philosophy of life and not just as an expedient. He felt that those who adopt nonviolence only for pragmatic reasons still possess violence in spirit. Unless nonviolent means were pursued as a matter of deep philosophical belief, the door would always be left open for resorting to violence. This, Gandhi said, was the nonviolence of the weak and fearful, not the nonviolence of the strong and courageous. Gandhi felt that most of his fellow Congress Party members saw nonviolence only as an expedient and not the way he did, as a creed or philosophy. And in 1947, when the Indian subcontinent degenerated into bloody communal violence between Hindus and Muslims, Gandhi blamed the horror on the fact that very few Indians had actually adhered to nonviolence the way he had, as a total commitment (Dalton 1993, 42).

Gandhi's views on using pure, nonviolent means in the fight for independence can be illustrated by examining *Hind Swaraj* (Indian Home Rule), which is a short book he wrote on a return trip to India from London in 1909. In *Hind Swaraj* Gandhi expressed his views about Indian independence, nonviolence, colonialism, and Western civilization. He wrote the book in just 10 days, including about 50 pages written with his left hand because his right hand was exhausted (Tendulkar 1951, 1:105). Gandhi was 40 years old when he wrote *Hind Swaraj* and he stood by the main principles and arguments presented therein decades later. Using the Socratic technique, *Hind Swaraj* presents a question-and-answer format between the "Editor" and the "Reader." The Reader represents the impatient, youthful Indian who wants to use any means necessary, including violence, to gain independence. The Editor is essentially Gandhi expressing his own views. The Reader is skeptical and poses challenging questions and statements to the Editor about the nature of swaraj, nonviolence and modern society. Gandhi then uses the Editor's answers as a technique to present his views and principles. He convinces the Reader that using soul force and not brute force is the only way India can attain true swaraj:

> Let us first take the argument that we are justified in gaining our end by using brute force . . . [that] is the same as saying that we can get a rose by planting a noxious weed. . . . The means may be likened to a seed, the end to a tree; and there is just the same inviolable connection between the means and the end as there is between the seed and the tree. (Gandhi, 1922, 62)

The Editor provides an excellent allegory illustrating how different means contribute to different ends:

> If I want to deprive you of your watch, I shall certainly have to fight for it; if I want to buy your watch, I shall have to pay you for it; and, if I want a gift, I shall have to plead for it; and, *according to the means I employ, the watch is a stolen property, my own property, or a donation.* Thus we see three different results from three different means. (Gandhi, 1922, 63)

Gandhi's idea of swaraj, or independence, was not really about kicking the British out of India, but about reforming Indian society in ways that reject Western civilization and adopt Indian traditions. He said that "India is being ground down, not under the English heel, but under that of modern civilization" (Gandhi 1922, 28.) As the Editor, Gandhi condemns the trappings of modern civilization—railways, doctors, lawyers, modern medicine, and machinery—as evil because they have turned Indians away from God and toward the West, which has lost its spiritual way because it "takes note neither of morality nor of religion" (Gandhi 1922, 22–23). *Hind Swaraj* represents the culmination of a process of his disillusionment with Western civilization in general and the British Empire in particular. Gandhi argued that the British were held hostage by a lifestyle obsessed with acquiring material wealth and power at the expense of more important pursuits, namely, spirituality. By 1908, Gandhi warned that Western civilization had reduced Westerners to a state of cultural anarchy (Brown 1989, 66, 87). Over and over, the Editor in *Hind Swaraj* refutes the Reader's contentions about the greatness of Western and British civilization. He argues instead that Indian civilization is superior:

> The tendency of Indian civilization is to elevate the moral being, that of the Western civilization is to propagate immorality. The latter is godless, the former is based on a belief in God. So . . . it behoves [sic] every lover of India to cling to the old Indian civilization. (Gandhi 1922, 53)

He was so convinced of the inferiority of Western civilization he said that "one has only to be patient and it will be self-destroyed" (Gandhi 1922, 22).

Gandhi insisted that true swaraj lay in individuals being able to govern themselves first. According to the Editor, "It is *swaraj* when we learn to rule ourselves" (Gandhi 1922, 55). This meant that Indians not only had to defy the British, but also to reform themselves and control their impure impulses. Gandhi constantly preached about a wide variety of issues on which he sought reform, including improved cleanliness and hygiene, ending untouchability, ensuring Hindu–Muslim unity, uplifting women, and creating economic self-sufficiency in the villages. Indians had often spoken of these types of reforms but "Gandhi's contribution was that he linked them as integral to *swaraj*" (Dalton 1993, 27).

Gandhi contrasted his notion of swaraj with Western notions of freedom and independence. Whereas the West's idea of freedom meant the absence of restraints on individual pursuits and an exclusivist notion of individual behavior, Gandhi's notion was of an inclusive universalism that acted affirmatively in uniting the individual with the society (Dalton 1993, 4–5). Swaraj, to Gandhi, consisted of four main elements: truth, nonviolence, political freedom, and economic freedom (Dalton 1993, 23). Until his death, Gandhi argued that swaraj would be meaningless for India unless people could achieve these four goals. Gandhi's point was that Indians had to gain sovereignty over themselves and how they behaved in their own lives before they could gain real sovereignty over their country. This could only be accomplished through purity of means. The Hindu–Muslim rioting and civil war that ensued during India and Pakistan's creation in 1947 was proof that India had not achieved the true swaraj Gandhi sought, even after the British colonialists departed. Real freedom meant control over one's most bestial instincts and Hindu–Muslim violence showed Gandhi that Indians had not yet achieved sovereignty over themselves (Dalton 1993, 24).

Gandhi believed that humans, if they are to act and live in society, cannot hope to totally avoid committing himsa. The very fact
of a person's living—eating, drinking, and moving about—brings
with it repeated acts of himsa. This troubled Gandhi, who said:

> We have to recognize that there are many things in the world
> which we do although we may be against doing them. . . . Posses-
> sion of a body, like every other possession, necessitates violence,
> be it ever so little. The fact is that the path of duty is not always
> easy to discern amidst claims seeming to conflict one with the
> other. (Tendulkar 1951, 1:233–234)

But he also held that people can remain true to the faith of
ahimsa if they shun, to the best of their ability, the destruction
of even the tiniest creatures and instead actively try to save them
while at the same time ensuring that all their actions stem from a
position of compassion for and service to others (Gandhi 1957,
349). By living thusly, the practitioner of ahimsa will be "constantly growing in self-restraint and compassion, [even though]
he can never become entirely free from outward *himsa*" (Gandhi
1957, 349).

This shows that Gandhi's optimism was not naïve. Rather, people should do their best in an imperfect world. Moreover, despite
the incredible acts of cruelty he witnessed, Gandhi was convinced
that nonviolence is the law of human nature and the only way for
people to behave if they truly wish to be human (Brown 1989, 291).
He argued that even if people can never hope to be entirely nonviolent in their thoughts, words, and deeds, they must retain nonviolence as their ultimate goal and strive to make steady progress
toward that end (Gandhi 1990, 56). This is reminiscent of the
violence–nonviolence continuum presented in Chapter 1.

Although Gandhi was vehement in his philosophical commitment to ahimsa, there were times when it seemed that he contradicted his own views. For instance, Gandhi's recruitment of Indians
in World War I seemed to contradict his views of ahimsa. This confounded his supporters and fueled his critics' charges against him.
To be sure, a devotee of ahimsa must not countenance war. However, Gandhi asserted that sometimes the acute moral dilemmas
posed by human existence means that violence, on occasion, can be
part of ahimsa. Gandhi said, "I was opposed to war, but had no status for offering effective nonviolent resistance" (Tendulkar 1951,
1:233). He further defended his position by arguing that only those

who can really use violence can renounce it (Dalton 1993, 126). This is consistent with what many Hindus believe from their ancient scripture, namely, that "sometimes war is necessary" (Shashtri and Shastri 1998, 82).

He also tried to explain his position as one totally committed to seeking the truth. During World War I, Gandhi felt that he could best serve the cause of swaraj if he supported the British war effort. He also saw the war as a chance to teach Indians about courage and fearlessness, something that Gandhi felt was a critical component of ahimsa. Many were unimpressed with Gandhi's efforts and even ridiculed the logic by which he tried to reconcile his position on the war with his belief in ahimsa. Gandhi later said that, during the war, he was a supporter of the empire and not the "nonviolent rebel" he later became. If he had been, he would not have helped the empire and instead would have used every effort of nonviolence to defeat the empire's purpose (Tendulkar 1951, 1:233). Despite what amounts to some as inconsistency, Gandhi was an outspoken critic against war. Just before he died, he wrote that

> if war cannot be abolished, there is absolutely no hope for the future of the human race, as sooner or later society is bound to annihilate itself. . . . If war is not soon avoided or abolished, a conflict will arise in which entire nations and races will be completely blotted out of existence and even vast continents will be reduced to impotency and dissolution. One thing is clear, therefore; war must be abolished at all costs if civilization is to survive. (Shashtri and Shastri 1998, 83)

Although he was an idealist, Gandhi's views were not dreamy, pie-in-the-sky stuff. Gandhi's idealism ran more toward practical action than toward unrealistic hope and inaction. Gandhi recognized that even if the perfect form of ahimsa cannot be attained, people's actions should be guided by that ideal, toward which they must continually strive (Dalton 1993, 189). Gandhi saw that the exercise of power in social and political relations is unavoidable, so it comes down to how that power will be exercised. Should power be exercised by using violence or nonviolence? Of course Gandhi preferred nonviolence. Will power be exercised for self-interested gain or for selfless giving toward others? Gandhi preferred power to be exercised by people who had freed themselves of "the tyranny of self-interest" (Dalton 1993, 190–191).

The Relationship between Ahimsa and Satyagraha

Gandhi's notion of truth was relativistic in nature, since he did not believe anyone can know the absolute truth. Gandhi acknowledged the possibility of equally correct versions of the truth. Gandhi's opponents, including fundamentalist Hindus, Christians, and Muslims, criticized this approach as contrary to what they saw as the absolute truth of their own religions. They argued that Gandhi's views on relative truths could lead to moral relativism, which could be used to justify all sorts of bad behavior. In answer to his critics and aware that competing, relativistic versions of the truth could prove dangerous, Gandhi said, "[T]hat is why the nonviolence part was a necessary corollary" to the principle of satygraha (Bondurant 1988, 20). People with conflicting views of the truth can never hope to resolve their conflict by resorting to violence. Accordingly, ahimsa and satyagraha are inextricable concepts.

Gandhi's commitments to satyagraha and ahimsa combined to forge a powerful method of social action. Gandhi often equated ahimsa with love and satyagraha with truth. He considered these concepts inseparable in social action:

> Without *ahimsa* it is not possible to seek and find Truth. *Ahimsa* and Truth are so intertwined that it is practically impossible to disentangle and separate them. They are like two sides of a coin. . . . Nevertheless, *ahimsa* is the means, Truth is the end. (Bondurant 1988, 24)

The only way to obtain the truth is by strict adherence to ahimsa. Truth, in contrast, cannot but be destroyed by the use of violence and without truth the path to God is blocked and unattainable.

When a satyagrahi claims to have the truth and this truth differs from other versions of the truth, conflict emerges. To resolve the conflict, the satyagrahi must be prepared for two outcomes: First, he or she must try to convert the opponent, using ahimsa, to his or her version of the truth. Second, the satyagrahi must be prepared to be converted to the opponent's version of the truth, since the satyagrahi must "reexamine continuously his own position—for his opponent may be closer to the truth than he" (Bondurant 1988, 33). In this, Gandhi acknowledged a deep debt to Jainism, which teaches that the truth has many different sides and therefore pursuit of the truth required its pursuers to be tolerant of others, especially if they do not share the same idea of truth (Brown 1989, 196). Satyagraha means steadfastly holding onto the truth wherever it is found, whether in the satyagrahi or in the opponent. Either way, the discovery of truth is the main pursuit, since adhering to the truth is the ultimate goal of the satyagrahi.

GANDHI'S PRINCIPLES PUT INTO PRACTICE

In practice, Gandhi's principles demand an austere, disciplined lifestyle dedicated to the service of others. A satyagrahi on the path to truth must remove all obstacles along the way, such as envy, hate, and lust. A truth seeker must:

1. Live a pure life, free from desires and passions;
2. Live a life dedicated to promoting the welfare of all, but especially the neediest; and
3. Live a simple life.

Before discussing these practices in depth, consider just one anecdote that illustrates the dedication with which Gandhi put his principles into practice. To quiet his mind, Gandhi observed total silence for one day each week. He held this practice for decades, even in the midst of important discussions with Indian and British dignitaries. One time, as he was negotiating India's independence with the viceroy, he came to a meeting with his fingers over his lips to indicate that he would not be talking that day. Exasperated, the viceroy could do little except sigh in disbelief and disparage one of the Mahatma's silent days. They communicated somewhat by passing notes back and forth, but that is no substitute for oral discussion.

Desirelessness

To remain faithful to his quest for discovering truth and growing nearer to God and to maintain his commitment to ahimsa, Gandhi sought to overcome earthly desires. Like many Hindus (and others), Gandhi believed one of his highest spiritual imperatives was to conquer his desires. If he did not conquer his cravings, he would forever be distracted and weakened by them, since his energies would be devoted to satisfying his cravings rather than fulfilling his spiritual mission. He also believed that if people could not conquer their desires, then that would lead to an irresistible temptation to use whatever means were necessary to achieve their desires, which in turn leads to violence:

> He who is ever brooding over result often loses nerve in the performance of duty. He becomes impatient and then gives vent to doing unworthy things; he jumps from action to action, never remaining faithful to any. He who broods over results is like a man given to the objects of senses; he is ever distracted, he says goodbye to all scruples . . . and he therefore resorts to means fair and foul to attain his end. (Fischer 1954, 18)

Accordingly, Gandhi set out on a strict and rigid campaign to rid himself of all earthly desires. Renunciation of material and fleshly desires would free Gandhi's mind, spirit, and body and empower him with the energy and devotion he needed to see God. This renunciation included nonpossession of material items, control of the palate, and sexual control. Desirelessness meant controlling all the senses at all places, at all times, and in all thoughts, words, and deeds. It meant restraint in diet, emotions, and speech (Fischer, 1954, 33). According to Gandhi, the practice of ahimsa and devotion to satyagraha demanded nothing less.

Nonpossession

Gandhi referred to peoples' desires to own more and more property and more and more things as the "disease of materialism." In keeping with his objective of reaching a state of complete desirelessness, Gandhi sought to own as little as possible. He insisted that it was not enough merely to limit one's property and possessions. He argued that it was sinful to keep anything that was not absolutely necessary for bodily needs. Gandhi urged people to strive to simplify their lives by dispossessing themselves of material things. To possess a thing means also being possessed by it.

Gandhi condemned stealing as a violation of ahimsa and satyagraha. But it is not enough merely to refrain from stealing what is clearly considered another's property. Theft, for Gandhi, is also in using articles and materials that are not truly needed.

Controlling the Palate

Craving food, especially the flesh of animals, also has to be conquered. Like the desire for nice things, the desire for food distracts the truth seeker and leads to the suffering of others. Gandhi had a very strict diet, governed by three things:

1. Eating as simply as possible (Gandhi's nutritional experiments included a stint of eating only uncooked vegetables and unleavened bread);
2. Eating as little as possible (this involved consuming tiny portions, skipping meals, and fasting); and
3. Vegetarianism.

Gandhi's vegetarianism was inflexible. One time his son Manilal came down with a severe case of typhoid, complicated by pneumonia. A doctor recommended chicken broth and eggs, but these violated Gandhi's strict vegetarianism:

> To my mind it is only on such occasions that a man's faith is truly tested. Rightly or wrongly it is part of my religious conviction that man may not eat meat, eggs, and the like. . . . Even for life itself we may not do certain things. (Gandhi 1957, 246)

Refusing the doctor's advice, Gandhi assumed care for his son. Similarly, Gandhi withdrew his wife from hospital after he discovered that she was being treated with medicines derived in part from animals. Due to his strict vegetarianism, Gandhi embarked on a lifelong quest in which he experimented with all different kinds of home remedies and folk-style medicinal practices. He was constantly experimenting with his diet and wrote lengthy exposés on a proper vegetarian diet.

Celibacy

Sexual cravings are distractions that must be overcome if a devotee of satyagraha and ahimsa wished ultimately to be successful. Succumbing to sexual relations clouds the mind. Gandhi wanted his mind to be free from such preoccupations in order to devote the full range of his energies to truth and nonviolence. Gandhi thought people should control their "animal" passions, in their thoughts as well as in their deeds. Even married couples, after reproduction is complete, must reach the point where husband and wife establish a close lifelong friendship absent not only of the act of sex, but the desire for it as well (Tendulkar 1951, 1:170).

Recall that Gandhi tried to maintain a vow of celibacy several times. His wife, Kasturbai, agreed with this. They began sleeping in separate beds and Gandhi never went to bed until he was physically drained (Fischer 1954, 32). However, it took Gandhi until his third try when, in 1906 and at the age of 37, he took a solemn vow of celibacy (Brown 1989, 41), which he never broke. Gandhi also saw this vow as a way of relinquishing a desire for wealth and children. There is some uncertainty about Gandhi's motives for declaring celibacy at this time. At one point, he said it was a response to the call to public service. At another he said his main objective was to escape having more children; perhaps he felt four sons were enough. Some observers have speculated that Gandhi forever felt guilty about sexual intercourse because of the incident involving his father's death. Or perhaps it was because he did not want to endanger his wife, who was anemic, with another pregnancy (Fischer 1954, 33).

Ultimately, through Gandhi's quest for desirelessness, his concern with self became almost nonexistent. As Gandhi relinquished concern for himself, there was an almost total unawareness of self in his actions and words (Fischer 1954, 31). The more Gandhi mastered his senses, the less self-centered he became, which enabled him to devote his energies to serving others. This type of renunciation not only created admiration for Gandhi, but it raised his reputation as a politician who could be trusted to do what he thought was right for others and not what he thought might enrich himself.

Service toward Others: *Sarvodaya*

Gandhi's commitment to ahimsa and satyagraha increasingly led him to believe that serving others, especially the poor and downtrodden, was key to discovering the truth and, hence, growing nearer to God. He called these efforts *sarvodaya*, which means uplift, or welfare for all. One of his most famous quotes dealt with helping others:

> I will give you a Talisman. Recall in the face of the poorest and most helpless person who you may have seen and ask yourself if

the step you contemplate is going to be of any use to him. Will he gain anything by it? Will it restore him to control over his life and destiny? In other words, will it lead to *swaraj*, self-rule, for the hungry and the spiritually starved of our countrymen? (Kanithar and Cole 1995, 183)

During his time in South Africa, he grew increasingly dedicated to the idea of sarvodaya and decreasingly concerned with helping himself and also with helping his relatives solely because they had kinship ties with him (Brown 1989, 35). He became convinced that a life devoted to sarvodaya could not be accomplished as long as he allowed traditional familial obligations to take precedence. Gandhi's relationship with many of his relatives grew strained as he seemingly neglected them while he sought to be of service to people whom he thought needed his assistance more.

Gandhi developed a strong sense of inclusiveness, which reflected this abiding desire to help others. Toward that end, Gandhi had a social reform program that targeted the sectors of Indian society that he felt needed his services the most. Gandhi's program of sarvodaya and inclusiveness was aimed at:

1. Creating Hindu–Muslim unity;
2. Helping the poor by relieving their poverty, disease, and illiteracy;
3. Ending untouchability; and
4. Uplifting women.

Hindu–Muslim Unity

Gandhi wanted to ensure inclusion of India's Muslim minority in the country's future as it gained independence. He recognized the communal tensions that existed between Hindus and Muslims and constantly preached Hindu–Muslim unity wherever he went. Although Islam and Hinduism differed in fundamental ways, Gandhi liked to use his own childhood in Porbandar as an example of how Hindus and Muslims could live together harmoniously while worshipping God through different faiths. He liked to tell the story of how the Hindu cleric in his temple would read from the Islamic as well as Hindu scriptures. He also lobbied the British government in London on behalf of Muslim interests throughout Asia. Ironically, both Hindus and Muslims viewed

Gandhi's efforts suspiciously, questioning the sincerity of his motives. It pained Gandhi to be accused of deception, but he never ceased preaching Hindu–Muslim unity.

However, attaining Hindu–Muslim unity was the least successful element of his social reform program. Despite his own tireless efforts, he could not stop the disintegration of his beloved India. Gandhi adamantly opposed India's partition in 1947, seeing it as a bold-faced rejection of his program of inclusion. He wept when the Indian subcontinent was divided into two separate countries and when the civil war left hundreds of thousands of Hindus and Muslims dead. Twice before Hindu extremists tried to kill him. In the end, he was assassinated while in the midst of efforts to repair the schism between southern Asia's Hindu and Muslim populations. His assassins were Hindu extremists who opposed his efforts and even accused him of causing a decline in Hinduism.

Helping the Poor: *Swadeshi* and *Khadi*

Gandhi was devoted to uplifting India's poverty-stricken masses, specifically the illiterate peasants scattered throughout India's hundreds of thousands of villages. Long ago, India's villages were self-sufficient in food and clothing and Gandhi wanted to revive the villagers' basic cottage skills in order to help them regain their self-sufficiency. Toward this end, Gandhi preached the twin ideas of *swadeshi* and *khadi*. Swadeshi means consuming only those products that are locally produced. Gandhi wanted each village in India to be able to support its needs without outside help or interference. He sought to revive the traditional skills of villagers as a way to help them gain the type of economic and social independence he sought for all of India. Each Indian village should rely on only the resources available in the village's immediate surroundings.

Khadi means producing and wearing only homespun cloth made by hand with the help of the spinning wheel. Gandhi abhorred the idea of obtaining cloth from large clothing mills where garments were mass-produced, which he believed caused the villagers' poverty. He also said it was inconsistent with truth because there was always the possibility of deception and exploitation occurring in the mass production of these products (Tendulkar 1951, 1:170). Gandhi asserted that British-made cloth in particular caused India's poverty. The only way to safeguard against this was to produce one's own clothing. Gandhi urged the production of khadi because it was cheaper than imports, it helped create jobs, and it loosened Britain's economic grip on India (Chadha 1997, 216). In 1915, Gandhi urged all Indians to make and wear khadi and to restrict consumption of goods and services to those that were available in their immediate surroundings. He said khadi and swadeshi were doctrines consistent with the law of humanity and love (Tendulkar 1951, 1:187). To set an example, Gandhi devoted himself to spinning his own clothes. Even with the incredible demands on his time, Gandhi set aside an hour each day for spinning. He said that with each thread of yarn Indians spun, they were brought that much closer to real swaraj. He also said that spinning helped him understand the daily toils of India's masses. Spinning was so vital an element of Gandhi's reform program that he used his influence to have the spinning wheel incorporated into India's national flag.

Gandhi did not want swaraj for India to be won if it meant that the poverty-stricken masses on the bottom rungs of society would be supporting the elites at the top. Some misinterpreted this idea as one that called for socialist policies. But this was wrong because Gandhi's ideas of sarvodaya, khadi, and swadeshi did not call on the government to own and operate industries and agriculture. Nor did he advocate government being the main employer of the workers. Nor did he advocate a super strong central government that would dictate to the masses. He preferred decentralized authority because he felt it was more democratic and because he was convinced that decentralized power centers were more appropriate for promoting uplift in all India's villages. He wanted each resident of each village linked in concentric, expanding circles, with each village in each circle giving strength and support to all the others (Dalton 1993, 21). Gandhi's concern for the downtrodden, his preference for living among the ignorant rural masses, and his constant fight against social injustice may have intersected with the concerns of some socialists and, incidentally, with Christian missionaries too. But that made him neither socialist nor Christian. Gandhi did not care for the socialists because they advocated using violence. Moreover, Gandhi stressed individual efforts as opposed to the collective workers' mentality that socialists espoused (Brown 1989, 292).

Gandhi condemned what he saw as an increasing addiction for machinery among Indians. Many observers have misinterpreted Gandhi's attitude toward machines, wrongly asserting that he was openly hostile toward modern inventions and all things mechanical. What concerned Gandhi about India's increased industrialization and mechanization was that it was robbing the local villages of their cottage skills, which helped keep them self-sufficient for so many centuries. Moreover, Gandhi opposed industrialization only if such processes enriched a few at the expense of so many and if it displaced useful labor (Brown 1989, 300). Gandhi's ideas regarding khadi and swadeshi were meant to revive and improve the local villagers' basic skills in order for each village to support itself and contribute to the welfare of all (sarvodaya). It was not machinery per se that Gandhi condemned, rather it was the craze for machinery. To be sure, Gandhi did not condemn all machinery; he just wanted limits on how machines influenced peoples' lives. For instance, Gandhi admired the Singer sewing machine and felt it was a good machine because it could be used to help produce khadi in the villages. He also recognized the need for heavy machinery in the public utility sector and he did want these to be state owned and operated. Some of Gandhi's closest friends disagreed with his emphasis on homespun and local production. They did not believe that these were realistic answers to India's problems in the 20th century. But, khadi was Gandhi's way of

> [b]ringing political consciousness to the people of India. The wearing of *khadi* was the only visible and tangible tie that bound educated Indians to the masses. The spinning wheel was thus the bond of brotherhood that united all Indians; *khadi* became the uniform of the national movement. (Chadha, 1997, 217)

Ending the Caste System and Untouchability

Recall that Gandhi's vision for Indian society involved more than simply gaining independence from British colonial rule. That was only a part of his overall program in India. In addition, as a devout Hindu, he sought to reform customs he felt contradicted Hindu philosophy. This is especially so regarding Hinduism's caste system. Hinduism has four major castes and several subcastes within each of the four. Traditional Hindus practiced and observed the caste system in a hierarchical fashion, with members of the Brahmin caste considered the most superior, sitting atop the social and religious ladder, while the Untouchables were considered so inferior and so low that they were not even seen as part of the caste system: they were outcastes.

Gandhi's attitude toward the caste system evolved over time. From 1916 until 1926, he defended the caste system, although he only advocated the four major castes and wished to eliminate all the subcastes. He supported the caste system's practice of prohibiting intercaste marriage and dining, asserting that such social structures and restrictions would foster self-control, create discipline, and provide "wonderful powers of organization" to India's complex and vast country. Even though he supported the four major castes and the intercaste prohibitions against social interaction at this time, he did not support what he referred to as the "hypocritical distinctions between high and low" castes (Dalton 1993, 49). Gandhi opposed the idea that one caste was superior to another; he wanted them all to behave as equals toward each other.

By 1926, however, Gandhi began to openly call for dramatic change to the caste system. He called for an end to the prohibitions on interdining and intermarrying (Dalton 1993, 51). He issued several radical critiques of the caste system. He condemned the idea of inherited superiority, which said a Brahmin was better than a Vaisya or Sudra simply by virtue of his birth. By 1935, Gandhi's denunciation of the entire caste system was complete; he authored an article entitled "Caste Has to Go" and declared that "untouchability is a crime against humanity" (Kanithar and Cole 1995, 189). By 1946, Gandhi sanctioned only intercaste marriages in his ashrams (Dalton 1993, 52–53). If Gandhi believed that "caste has to go," a surefire way of doing this would be to condone only intercaste marrying, which would naturally dilute caste distinctions as intercaste children were born.

If Gandhi's attitudes toward the caste system evolved over time, his views on India's so-called Untouchables remained consistent: he always opposed the Hindu practice of ostracizing India's outcastes. Outcastes were badly treated in India. They were discriminated against in education, employment, and housing. Most were politically disenfranchised and toiled at the bottom of India's social and economic stratum. It was forbidden for other Hindus to even touch them, much less welcome them into their homes. Untouchables usually lived in the crowded, poorest, and most desolate quarter of a city, amid its waste and filth. They were the ones expected to perform what many Indians consider the dirtiest of jobs: handling corpses, picking up trash, and disposing of human waste.

Gandhi believed that untouchability was a terrible blight on the Hindu faith and that it was not a true part of Hinduism. He believed that the concept of untouchability had been artificially grafted onto Hinduism long ago and remained there as part of an atavistic tradition. Gandhi believed that the practice contradicted basic Hindu beliefs (Brown 1989, 206). Whereas he sought unity and inclusivity, untouchability perpetuated division and exclusivity. Ridding India of the scourge of untouchability was one of Gandhi's lifelong goals. Even though many of his compatriots in the Congress Party disagreed with him, Gandhi believed that ending untouchability was integral to achieving swaraj, if for no other reason than because its practice could ultimately lead to violent rebellion. On this he never wavered.

Accordingly, Gandhi—who always practiced what he preached—began a decades-long campaign to remove untouchability from Hindu society. He began referring to the Untouchables as Harijan, or children of God. He even named one of his newspaper publications *Harijan* to honor them and bring more attention to their plight. In 1932, he went on a fast to force the nation out of its complacent attitude toward the evils of untouchability (Dalton 1993, 57). He traveled throughout India's rural countryside and urban centers lecturing—sometimes to very hostile crowds of upper-caste Hindus—against the practice of untouchability. He also targeted the Untouchables for reform. To them, he preached the importance of sanitation, cleanliness, and abstaining from consuming meat or alcohol (Brown 1989, 207). He welcomed them as valued and equal members of his ashrams and insisted that all other members of the ashrams treat them as equals. This meant that everyone in the ashram, regardless of caste, had to take their turn cleaning out the toilets. Anyone who wanted to become a member of Gandhi's ashram had to agree to this rule (among others). Although this practice scandalized some orthodox Hindus, who believed that contact with Untouchables causes contamination, many of Gandhi's followers supported his efforts at reforming India's attitudes and practices. To be sure, many Hindus, especially orthodox Hindus but even some prominent Untouchables, opposed Gandhi's reformist program. But once Gandhi was convinced of the truth of an issue, he would not budge from his viewpoint. He was most stubborn in this fashion. He cared less about rankling the sensibilities of his traditional-minded countryfolk than he did about discovering, and then acting upon, what he considered the truth.

Gandhi's efforts at ending untouchability were more success-ful than his attempts at achieving Hindu–Muslim unity. One of his greatest legacies in India is efforts the Indian government has taken on behalf of the Untouchables. Discrimination against them has been outlawed and programs have been passed throughout the years designed to improve their social and economic condi-tions. Nevertheless, change comes hard to any society and India is no exception. Even though it is now illegal, many Indians still ob-serve prohibitions against interacting with Untouchables and still discriminate against them. Moreover, in a few of India's isolated rural areas, there have been acts of violence against entire villages of Untouchables.

Uplifting Women

Like many other traditional societies, women's identities in India were tied almost exclusively to the relationship they had with the dominant male in their family, for instance, as daughter, wife, child bearer, and child rearer. Women in India were—and in many cases remain—uneducated and "staggeringly" overworked, especially in the most poverty-stricken homes (Brown 1989, 208). Political oppression and economic poverty characterize life for women in India, as elsewhere in most of the world. In India, this was especially the case for widows. Ancient Hindu tradition looks down on widows, who often lose everything, including ties to their families, once their husbands die. One particularly harsh prac-tice—outlawed today but still not unheard of—involves a widow being hurled on her husband's funeral pyre. Many traditional Hindus frown on widows remarrying, even though it is acceptable for men who have lost their wives to do so. Even today in India, despite laws granting widows the right to remarry and despite a reduction in the social stigma of being a widow, a widow's life can be especially harsh, particularly in some rural areas. Some Hin-dus even see widows as bad luck, blaming them for their hus-band's death.

Unlike typical men in India, Gandhi empathized with women. Perhaps this was because he was more in touch with his feminine side than most males and thus more willing to express sentiments that were traditionally characteristic of women. Or perhaps it was because of the close personal relationship he had with his mother, particularly since his father died when he was still quite young.

Regardless, Gandhi saw the empowerment and uplifting of women as a crucial component of his reform program.

By today's standards, Gandhi's ideas about the role of women in Indian society may not seem too revolutionary or progressive. However, considering that Gandhi was born in 1869, his efforts on behalf of women were way ahead of his own time. Gandhi saw that since women played such a large role in raising Indian children, women were critical to achieving swaraj. In 1918, he said, "[M]any of our movements stop half way because of the condition of our women" (Tendulkar 1951, 1:226). Gandhi lamented the fact that even ignorant and worthless men enjoyed positions of superiority over women they surely did not deserve. He argued that women have the same mental capacities as men and therefore should have the same right to participate in all men's activities, enjoying the same rights, freedoms, and liberties as men (Tendulkar 1951, 1:226). He said that if women were to be treated as equals to men, then the attitudes of both men and women must change (Brown 1989, 209). These may seem like commonplace ideas today, but consider that many of Gandhi's male contemporaries in western Europe as well as the United States (not to mention traditional Hindus in India) did not believe women were or could be equal to men and were openly hostile to efforts on behalf of women's rights.

Although he remained supportive of the traditional arranged marriage, Gandhi did condemn the practice of arranged child marriages. Moreover, he argued that the woman should have the final say regarding whether she will marry a man selected for her. Gandhi wanted women liberated, but in a traditional sense. Gandhi's main achievement regarding the condition of women in Indian society was to enable them to perform certain roles in public that they had never performed before and also to make public discussion of women's role in society a legitimate and essential component of the overall movement for India's freedom and independence (Brown 1989, 213).

Women in India today still remain comparatively worse off than their male counterparts in most social and economic areas, such as income, education, and health. Of course, this remains true for women in virtually every country. In India, however, there exists an innovative program designed to bring Indian women, particularly lower-caste women, into important decision-making positions throughout India's more than 500,000 villages. A 1993 amendment to India's constitution set aside one-third of all council seats in

India's villages for lower-caste women. In many villages, where women—especially lower-caste women—have long been expected to submit to the men, women are now challenging centuries-old traditions of caste and gender (Dugger 1999). Although this recent constitutional amendment is not a direct result of Gandhi's efforts a half century earlier, India's affirmative action tradition on behalf of its oppressed groups such as Untouchables and women has been around since India's birth and that is a result, in part, of Gandhi's program of sarvodaya.

Ashramic Life

Gandhi put all these principles and practices to work in his celebrated ashrams. He founded four ashrams, two in South Africa and two in India. Ashrams served as a refuge for many, including satyagrahis who were in and out of jail for their nonviolent resistance. The main objective of Gandhi's ashram was service to the nearby community.

Ashramic life was not without its difficulties and trials. Members of the ashrams had to abide by strict rules, including vows of ahimsa, celibacy, nonstealing, and truthfulness. Each ashramite had to spin a quota of cloth and everyone had to share in all the chores. Not everyone could always follow these rules. Gandhi struggled with this. He was often dejected by the troubles he experienced in the ashrams because he reasoned that if he could not uphold these principles in a small community of devotees, how could he possibly bring those values to bear on all of India?

Gandhi established his first ashram, which he called Phoenix Settlement, in South Africa in 1904. Phoenix Settlement reflected the deep influence Ruskin's *Unto This Last* had on Gandhi's thinking at that time (Brown 1989, 43). Ruskin's writings inspired Gandhi to adopt a life of simplicity and Phoenix Settlement was the vehicle for that. Using funds from his lucrative law practice, Gandhi purchased 100 acres of farmland in South Africa's Natal Province. He sought to create an austere life where everyone at Phoenix Settlement would contribute equally, live simply, and dedicate themselves to serving others. Gandhi and the others (members of his family and some close friends) lived a frugal existence, eschewing material comforts, even sleeping out in the open on just a thin cloth (Fischer 1954, 38). Phoenix Settlement was also the place where Gandhi took his vow of celibacy.

After Phoenix Settlement, Gandhi founded Tolstoy Farm in 1910, also in South Africa. This ashram was founded as much out of political necessity as from principled ideals. It was politically necessary because it served as a haven for the many Indians who were literally on "jail rotation" for their resistance to South African laws that discriminated against Indians and also for the family members of Indians who were jailed for their civil disobedience. The population of the farm varied, depending on the number of civil resisters in jail at any one time. Sometimes there were more than 100 members participating on the farm. Like Phoenix Settlement, Tolstoy Farm was an attempt to build a community based on self-abnegation and away from the materialistic civilization of which Gandhi had grown so critical (Brown 1989, 89). Gandhi said that Tolstoy Farm was something like a commune with him acting as "father." Although Tolstoy Farm was similar to Phoenix Settlement, the former was much more intense than the latter to the extent that members of the ashram were expected to take part equally in all forms of labor, cleaning, cooking, fasting, praying, and especially in being of service to others (Herman 1998, 85).

Tolstoy Farm was made possible by the generosity of Herman Kallenbach who bought 1,100 acres of land about 21 miles outside of Johannesburg, South Africa, and donated it entirely to Gandhi and the Indian civil resisters (Fischer 1954, 41). At Tolstoy Farm, Gandhi's experiments in simple living expanded: he learned to bake bread, make coffee, preserve oranges, mend clothing, make furniture, teach the children, and a host of other activities. He was so devoted to living an austere life that when he had occasion to go into Johannesburg on a legal case, he would walk the entire distance— 42 miles there and back—in the same day (Fischer 1954, 42).

In 1915, the same year Gandhi returned to India from South Africa for good, he founded his first ashram on Indian soil, Sabarmati Ashram. Sabarmati focused on the same general principles of renunciation and service as the previous two ashrams. But Sabarmati added a new component, namely, the political objective of liberating India from colonial rule. Ironically, nearby textile and shipping industrialists donated the funds to help establish the ashram. Except for his periods of imprisonment and travel, Gandhi spent more than 16 years at Sabarmati.

The last ashram Gandhi founded was in Sevagram (population about 600) in 1933. With the founding of the ashram in Sevagram, Gandhi sought to demonstrate how India's social and economic problems in rural villages could be addressed. Sevagram was small, isolated, disease-ridden, and populated mostly by Harijan. The village had no shops or post office and a dirt road was all that linked it to the outside world (Chadha 1997, 342). Gandhi thought it the perfect place to rededicate his efforts at reforming all of Indian society by starting with the most downtrodden masses in small villages.

In each ashram, Gandhi worked diligently to put into practice his principles and beliefs, especially regarding satyagraha and ahimsa. Whenever rules were violated Gandhi was pained. Sometimes he would launch a fast in response to these transgressions. He undertook these fasts in part because he blamed himself for the others' transgressions and also in part because he knew that his suffering would help transform members of the ashram into more observant devotees, which would pave the way for the rest of India.

CHAPTER 5

Gandhi's Nonviolent Resistance Campaigns

A votary of *ahimsa* therefore remains true to his faith if the spring of all his actions is compassion, if he shuns to the best of his ability the destruction of the tiniest creature, tries to save it, and thus incessantly strives to be free from the deadly coil of *himsa*.

—Mohandas K. Gandhi, from his autobiography, 1957

NONVIOLENT RESISTANCE CAMPAIGN DEFINED

A nonviolent resistance campaign is defined as an organized, purposeful action designed to use nonviolence to accomplish process, achievement, and ultimate goals. Nonviolent resistance campaigns are usually organized on a geographic- or issue-oriented basis. Gandhi often launched his campaigns against untouchability. His Salt March focused on a singular issue also, namely, challenging the British over whether Indians had the right to make their own salt. Similarly, Gandhi's fasts, which were designed to pressure Indians (not the British) into changing their ways, were also issue-oriented campaigns. But his nonviolent resistance campaigns in Champaran and Bardoli, India, were restricted to those geographic regions. King's Montgomery Bus Boycott was organized on geographic lines. That nonviolent resistance occurred only in Montgomery, Alabama, and focused only on Montgomery's city buses.

Consider the American presidential elections as a way of illustrating the idea of a campaign. In an election year, some candidates run for office, focusing their efforts on a geographically centered strategy, such as winning the votes in the South and the West or appealing to voters' interests in the Northeast and the Mid-Atlantic states. Accordingly, they will confine most of their speeches, appearances, and other campaign resources to the geographic region in which they hope to win the most votes. For instance, in the 1960s, George Wallace campaigned for president by focusing his strategy on southern states. In the 2000 election, George W. Bush's campaign ignored California because it did not want to spend money and time in a state it knew it had no chance of winning. Other candidates focus their campaign on a single issue and hope that their appeal on this issue will be enough to achieve victory. Steve Forbes's 2000 campaign message focused almost single-mindedly on passing a flat tax, Ralph Nader's 2000 Green Party campaign focused mostly on the environment, and Ross Perot's 1992 campaign focused almost exclusively on the budget.

Examples of nonviolent resistance campaigns can be found throughout history and all over the world. They include organized and sustained efforts of tax refusal, economic boycotts, shop strikes, sit-ins, hunger strikes, demonstrations, flag waving, and creating parallel institutions of government. Witness, for example, the nonviolent resistance of the early Christians, who were sacrificed to the lions for their refusal to comply with the Roman Empire. Or consider the nonviolent campaigns undertaken in the Palestinian–Israeli conflict by Mubarak Awad. Awad's activists launched a campaign of planting olive trees on disputed land. Olive trees symbolize peace and reconciliation and Awad wanted to use them as a dual symbol: first, to plant "the seeds of peace" between Palestinians and Israelis, hoping that peaceful means of conflict resolution would take root in the area; and second, the olive trees symbolized Palestinian determination to remain firmly planted on the land.

Some of Gandhi's nonviolent campaigns were focused on a local issue, such as the campaign in Champaran that sought to document and uncover abuses by landlords against the local peasantry. Others had a national focus, involving all the masses. Gandhi's "Quit India" campaign toward the end of World War II in the 1940s galvanized nearly the entire Indian population in defying the British Empire. He gave his people a mantra, "Do or Die!" proclaiming that Indians were determined to use nonviolence to get Britain to leave India or die in the attempt. His day of fasting and prayer, to protest oppressive legislation, became a nationwide strike that paralyzed the country and cut it off from the world for a short time. Sometimes these mass-oriented campaigns were successful, like the Salt March, and sometimes they were failures, like the Rowlatt Campaign (both campaigns will be discussed in detail later in this chapter). In addition, some of Gandhi's campaigns involved only Gandhi himself—the lone activist—engaging in a solo campaign of satyagraha. For instance, he declared a fast, which single-handedly put an end to Hindu–Muslim violence in Delhi and Calcutta.

To assess whether a nonviolent campaign was a success or failure, it must be measured against the goals it hopes to achieve. Goals depend on the specific context surrounding the nonviolent campaign. Gandhi pursued multiple goals with his nonviolent resistance campaigns, among them:

1. Reforming Indian society (see the discussion of his reform program in Chapter 4);
2. Creating for Indians a sense of empowerment and control over their own lives;
3. Getting the British to "quit India"; and
4. Establishing the foundations and institutions for an independent India committed to ahimsa and satyagraha.

Notice that for many of these goals, such as reforming Indian society, Gandhi's nonviolent campaigns targeted his Indian compatriots and not the British. His greatest goals were in improving Indian society; Gandhi actually saw independence from British rule as a by-product of his efforts to reform and revive Indian society.

It is difficult to assess whether a specific campaign was a success or failure for several reasons. First, a campaign's goals are sometimes poorly articulated. A campaign's success cannot be assessed accurately if it is not clear from the beginning what its intentions are. Not only are campaign objectives sometimes poorly articulated, but they can change in midstream too, which also makes it hard to assess their success. Second, it is difficult to isolate the effects of a nonviolent campaign from all other variables that may or may not influence outcomes. For example, in the midst of King's 13-month bus boycott to end segregation on public transportation, a fortuitous U.S. Supreme Court ruling declared bus segregation unconstitutional. Although King's Montgomery Bus Boycott is given a lot of credit for ending segregation, the Supreme Court's ruling surely had a contributory impact. Third, unlike an election campaign, which usually has a definitive end date—election day—many of Gandhi's nonviolent campaigns, especially in South Africa, did not have clear-cut endings or beginnings. Nor are there anything like election returns to give quantitative or definitive measures of whether a nonviolent campaign was a success.

In this chapter, several of Gandhi's nonviolent resistance campaigns will be examined. His professional career lasted about half a century so this chapter cannot cover all of his campaigns. Instead, the discussion will focus on some of Gandhi's earlier efforts in South Africa and then conclude by examining a few of his key campaigns in India. The campaigns included here were chosen to contrast different aspects of Gandhi's nonviolent resistance: some of the campaigns discussed were successes, some were failures; some of the campaigns involved a mass movement of people while others involved only Gandhi; finally, some campaigns were chosen because they are examples of nonviolent noncooperation and others because they exemplify civil disobedience.

GANDHI'S NONVIOLENT RESISTANCE CAMPAIGNS IN SOUTH AFRICA

During the late 18th–early 19th centuries, South Africa consisted of four British colonies: Orange Free State, Transvaal, Natal, and Capetown. Each was under the suzerainty of the British Crown, although to different degrees. South Africa's minority white population was composed primarily of descendants of Dutch (called Boers) and English immigrants. The Dutch established colonies in South Africa more than 200 years before Britain's arrival and capture of the Cape in 1805. Since the Africans refused to work on the European plantations (Chadha 1997, 50), the British shipped in Indian peasants to work the sugar, tea, and coffee fields and also to work in the gold and diamond mines. Although the British referred to them as "contracted laborers," they were really indentured servants.

Gandhi's nonviolent resistance germinated in South Africa on behalf of these ragged Indian laborers. As a young man in South Africa, Gandhi came to hone not only his ideals, but also his techniques. His actions and beliefs in South Africa were continually evolving, with nonviolent campaigns blending into one another. As such, Gandhi's nonviolent resistance in South Africa does not easily divide into distinctive beginnings and endings like the many he conducted in India. The specific issues on which Gandhi and other

Indians fought in South Africa were varied, but they all focused on a central theme: achieving racial equality for Indians. Accordingly, the lengthy nonviolent resistance Gandhi conducted in South Africa will be considered as one long campaign, characterized by periods of quiet and then punctuated by periods of fitful agitation. Moreover, although Gandhi arrived in South Africa in 1893, discussion here will be confined to his nonviolent resistance during the period 1906 to 1914 because this period represents a time of great growth for Gandhi, because it marks the birth of satyagraha, and because this period saw the most intensive activity for Indian rights.

Gandhi arrived in South Africa dedicated to behaving like a model British citizen. However, his ideas about Britain and the empire began to change as he learned of the harsh treatment of Indians in South Africa who were confronted by an increasingly racist and oppressive white regime. It turned out that vaunted European notions of equality and private enterprise applied only to Europeans in South Africa. Once an indentured servant worked off his contract—usually after five years—he was able to become a free workingman. He could obtain a small parcel of land to farm or open a small business. Soon, these former Indian servants developed agricultural and merchant skills that rivaled or surpassed their European counterparts (Chadha 1997, 51). Threatened by Indian competition, the white-dominated government sought to control Indian successes by imposing punishing taxes on Indians, by restricting their travel, and by imposing crippling regulations on their business.

By 1906, Gandhi positioned himself in direct opposition to these policies of South Africa's governing authorities, for it was in that year that the infamous Black Act was passed. A major objective of this legislation was to restrict "Black" immigration (at that time, Europeans called all nonwhites in South Africa blacks) to make South Africa "a white man's country," in the words of General J. C. Smuts, the leading minister in South Africa (Tendulkar 1951, 1:84). According to the Transvaal Asiatic Registration Act, Indians, Arabs, and Turks ("Asiatics") over eight years old, who wished to reside in South Africa's Transvaal, were required to obtain a pass by registering with the government. The law required Asiatics to not only give their fingerprints but also to submit to a personal inspection to find any identifying body marks. Failure to comply with this ordinance would result in being deported from the Transvaal, imprisoned, and/or fined up to 100 British pounds, an exorbitant sum (Tendulkar 1951, 1:78).

Indians found this legislation offensive and humiliating for several reasons. First, it discriminated against Indians and other immigrants of color since no European immigrant was required to possess the pass. Second, it was an affront to Indian cultural sensibilities because it required Indian women to submit to intrusive body inspections. Third, it treated Indians as if they were all common criminals whose movements had to be tracked and recorded. Fourth, the registration card had to be proffered whenever and wherever a police officer demanded and police were allowed to enter private homes, with or without permission, to inspect the inhabitants' certificates. Last, without the card, Indians would not be allowed to trade in the Transvaal colony, which had more lucrative business prospects than Natal, the colony where most Indians resided.

Gandhi went to London to argue his case against the law before what turned out to be a sympathetic British government, which declared that the bill's provisions would not be enacted. However, by 1907, when the South African government had obtained a measure of autonomy from London, the Transvaal government was able to still pass the law (Tendulkar 1951, 1:82–83). Gandhi then embarked on what became an incipient form of satyagraha (Dalton 1993, 14). It was during this movement that Gandhi coined the term satyagraha.

By the thousands, Indians conducted civil disobedience, refusing to register. Only about 500 out of more than 13,000 Transvaal Indians submitted to the law (Herman 1998, 79–80). Moreover, Indians deliberately marched into the Transvaal without a pass card, courting jail sentences in order to draw attention to their cause. Gandhi was among those imprisoned.

Amid this resistance, General Smuts and Gandhi reached a negotiated compromise. Gandhi believed this agreement called for Indians to voluntarily register as long as the Black Act was formally rescinded. Once Gandhi made this agreement with Smuts, he was released from prison and immediately became the lead organizer of voluntary registration (Tendulkar 1951, 1:94). Many Indians were incredulous with Gandhi. How could they now agree to register after so many had given up so much for their refusal to register? Further, how would voluntarily registering address other concerns about Indian freedoms and equality? Gandhi responded by saying that to register voluntarily and not under orders was an honorable thing. Besides, in keeping with his ideals regarding truth and nonviolence, Gandhi insisted that he trusted Smuts to keep his word. A satyagrahi bids good-bye to fear, he said, and says hello to trust. Many Indians were nonplussed and one rather powerfully built Indian even threatened to attack anyone who registered. Gandhi was undaunted by such threats, proclaiming that to die by the hand of a countryman in service of a good cause was a high honor. Gandhi was the first to register and true to his word the large Indian attacked him, smacking him over the head with a heavy instrument. Despite this attack, Gandhi refused to press charges against the man.

Despite Gandhi's faith in the general, Smuts claimed that he never agreed to repeal the Black Act, so it remained on the books. Moreover, the legislature added another discriminatory law, which actually strengthened the original Black Act. The new provision stated that non-Europeans could not immigrate unless they were familiar with a European tongue (Brown 1989, 45).

In response to what most considered Smuts's broken promise, Gandhi resumed satyagraha, organizing his first *hartal*, which is a form of noncooperation. Hartal means strike, and in this case, Gandhi organized a business strike, calling on shopkeepers and merchants to close their doors in sympathy with all those who had gone to jail for violating the Black Act. Gandhi also organized what came to be the first of many bonfires, which was used to burn the registration cards and to call media attention to the cause. One British journalist likened the bonfire to the American Revolutionaries' Boston Tea Party (Tendulkar 1951, 1:96).

Amid this agitation, Gandhi and Smuts again reached agreement. But this also proved short-lived because a 1913 South African court ruling on immigration laws essentially rendered all non-Christian marriages illegal. That meant that all Hindu, Muslim, and Sikh marriages were null and void. It also implied, as Gandhi informed his horrified wife, Kasturbai, that they were living in sin and that their children were bastards. Outraged by such an affront to Indian customs and beliefs, Gandhi's satyagraha came into full swing with a much more aggressive and provocative act. Gandhi organized what he called the "Great March," whereby men, women, and even children, would undertake a days-long march from Natal into the forbidden Transvaal in order to protest this oppressive legislation, to assert Indian self-respect and dignity, and to provoke the authorities into arresting them en masse. The Great March lasted five days and consisted of 2,037 men, 127 women, and 57 children (Dalton 1993, 101).

However, Gandhi postponed the plans for the march when he realized that the government was under heavy pressure from a general strike of European railway workers. A true satyagrahi, said Gandhi, did not try to exploit the weaknesses and vulnerabilities

of his opponent. Despite the goodwill and respect this earned
Gandhi among many of his British opponents, when the Great
March resumed, Gandhi was immediately arrested, thus depriving
the marchers of their leader. But the government could not find
enough evidence to prosecute its case against Gandhi. So, in keeping with his principles of truth and nonviolence, Gandhi furnished
the witnesses needed to convict him.

Meanwhile, Gandhi fretted about what to do with the unwieldy
crowd of marchers, many of whom were poorly trained in satyagraha. He appealed to the authorities to see them safely deposited
in jail once they illegally crossed into Transvaal, but the authorities
refused to cooperate. Moreover, the march received little publicity
(Dalton 1993, 102) and the marchers ultimately went home, having
achieved little in terms of ultimate goals.

The nonviolent resistance movement did score some successes,
not least of which was in the area of winning public opinion. Even
the British press ultimately praised the march as one of history's
most remarkable nonviolent resistance campaigns (Tendulkar
1951, 1:145). And as the South African government resorted to increasingly extreme and heavy-handed tactics to oppress the resisters, it created a backlash against the government: not only were
Indians in India outraged at the news, but whites in India as well
as England were also upset by the oppression in South Africa. This
is exactly what nonviolent resistance is supposed to achieve. Outrage in India and England over South Africa's oppression of the
satyagrahis forced the South African government to agree to form a
commission to investigate Indians' complaints. Even though this
commission was stacked heavily against Indian interests, it recommended compliance with all of the Indians' demands. In response,
the government passed the Indians' Relief Bill in 1914, which abolished many of the oppressive measures against which the Indians
had been fighting for so long. The bill recognized non-Christian
marriages as legal again, repealed a prohibitive tax on Indian immigrants, and settled most of the other outstanding problems for
Indians (Brown 1989, 146; Tendulkar 1951, 1:149). It was the first
South African law to specifically address Indian grievances and it
finally brought an end to the satyagraha campaign there.

With the passage of this bill, Gandhi set sail for India that same
year, but without having achieved his ultimate goal of attaining
permanent equality for South Africa's Indians. To be sure, he had
accomplished many goals in South Africa: he and his fellow Indians
learned to stand up to the white Europeans and fight for their

rights, they learned how to organize, to petition, and to keep regular financial accounts. Additionally, they won several concessions from a government that was initially determined to put an end to the Asiatic presence in South Africa. Finally, they succeeded in getting repealed the most egregious provisions of the laws that discriminated against them.

However, "what Gandhi did to South Africa was less important than what South Africa did to Gandhi" (Dalton 1993, 15), for South Africa provided the training ground upon which Gandhi forged his ideals about truth, love, and nonviolence. South Africa was where Gandhi shaped his philosophies and crafted satyagraha. South Africa taught Gandhi lessons that would serve him well during his decades-long struggle against the British Empire in India. For instance, Gandhi's experience during the Transvaal campaign taught him the importance of appealing not just to Indians in South Africa, but to a much wider audience, including Indians back in India and whites in Europe and North America (Brown 1989, 51). It taught him the importance of planning and training for lengthy satyagraha campaigns. He learned, for instance, that a campaign must be prepared to have secondary leaders take over when primary leaders are imprisoned. Moreover, Gandhi learned that it was critical to unite all diverse groups of Indians, Hindus, Muslims, Sikhs, and Parsis who often did not speak the same language and whose interests were often at odds. But attempts at achieving unity back in India proved much more difficult for Gandhi. Gandhi's failure to achieve Hindu–Muslim unity in India led him to despair that decades of work "have come to an inglorious end."

GANDHI'S NONVIOLENT RESISTANCE CAMPAIGNS IN INDIA

When Gandhi returned to India in 1915, it was virtually an alien land to him. Notwithstanding occasional visits and a brief, failed attempt as a young barrister, Gandhi lived outside India for nearly three decades. Despite the respected national reputation Gandhi earned by virtue of his work in South Africa, he did not wade into Indian politics immediately. Instead, he spent several months traveling around the country and reacquainting himself with India and Indians, particularly the rural, poor Indian peasant. Indian peasants held Gandhi in high esteem, in part because so few other national figures would even consider visiting and living

among them. For his part, Gandhi seemed totally at home and relaxed with India's peasantry. He regarded rural Indians as noble, if
ignorant, people who toiled too hard for far too little.

The Champaran Campaign, 1917

Compared to subsequent nonviolent resistance campaigns, the
one Gandhi launched in Champaran was small in scale and limited
in duration. Nevertheless, Champaran was a very important campaign and must be discussed before moving on to others. Champaran is significant for two reasons. First, it is the first place
Gandhi conducted satyagraha upon his return to India. Although
Champaran was a small, isolated community, Gandhi's defiant actions there stirred the whole country. Second, Champaran's problems were local in nature. Gandhi was still relatively new to India
and Champaran offered a good opportunity to ease into Indian politics on a small scale. Champaran enabled Gandhi to conduct this
campaign with a narrow focus, something familiar to him from his
South Africa days. Although Gandhi was an outsider to Cham-
parans and did not speak their local tongue (Brown 1989, 109), he
was so well-known among them that his train's imminent arrival
energized the citizens.

Champaran's economy centered on agriculture where the land
from large estates was controlled mostly by British planters who
leased the land to Indian peasants. This gave the planters control
over the tenants' lives as well as the land (Brown 1989, 110). Tenants were cheated, cajoled, and coerced into growing indigo plants
(from which indigo, a blue dye, is made) for the planters (Tendulkar
1951, 1:200). But when German manufacturers began producing
cheaper, synthetic alternatives to indigo, the price of indigo plummeted. To make up for a loss in profits, the planters raised the rent
they charged the Indian tenants, who found themselves in a desperate situation. On the one hand, tenants were required by the
planters to grow indigo plants, a product whose profitability had
plummeted; on the other hand, the planters kept raising the tenants' rent to make up for decreased indigo sales. Feeling trapped
and hemmed in, tenant grievances sometimes erupted into violent
demonstrations against the planters. It was this situation into
which Gandhi stepped.

In April 1917, Gandhi visited Champaran at the behest of a
local elder who implored him for help (although Gandhi kept telling

the elder he could not make it to Champaran, the elder's dogged persistence so impressed Gandhi that he changed his mind). Gandhi informed the secretary of the Planters' Association that he intended to launch a fact-finding investigation to see for himself whether the Indian tenants' grievances were legitimate. Although Gandhi was denounced as an outsider who had no business inter-posing himself between the planters and the tenants, Gandhi nevertheless began recording statements of abuse by the tenants, thousands of whom came forward (Tendulkar 1951, 1:201–204), not only to lodge their complaints, but to get a look at Gandhi. Amid this activity, the local magistrate, fearing that Gandhi's fact-finding mission might cause trouble, ordered Gandhi out of Champaran. Gandhi refused, saying his refusal was "not for want of respect for lawful authority, but in obedience to a higher law of our being, the voice of conscience" (Tendulkar 1951, 1:204). Before this act of defiance, Gandhi's fact-finding mission could hardly be considered nonviolent resistance.

However, by defying the British judge's order, Gandhi launched his first act of civil disobedience since returning to India. Confounded by Gandhi's defiance, the magistrate postponed his judgment and ultimately let Gandhi stay in Champaran to investigate the situation (Brown 1989, 110). As Gandhi investigated and documented the injustices visited on the tenants by the planters, he caused an amazing stir in the district. His image grew: rarely had a politician of Gandhi's stature ever waded so deeply into poor, rural India. Wherever he went, he called for the formation of a commission of inquiry. Amid this pressure, the government conceded to such a commission and Gandhi was even given a seat on it. The commission's findings confirmed Gandhi's investigation and it issued recommendations, most of which were incorporated into new legislation that was passed on behalf of the tenants (Tendulkar 1951, 1:213). The legislation abolished the system under which tenants were required to cultivate indigo plants and also curtailed the planters' abuses (Brown 1989, 111).

Although the new legislation represented a success stemming from Gandhi's efforts on behalf of the tenants, he did not consider his work in Champaran finished. First, he wanted more than a new law passed that compelled changes in the planters' behavior. He wanted true, honorable reconciliation between the tenants and the planters based on principles of satyagraha and ahimsa. But relations between the two remained strained (Brown 1989, 111). Second, in typical fashion, Gandhi believed that not only must the planters change their ways, but so too must the tenants. He sought to reform the tenants' habits in many areas, including hygiene and education. He enlisted volunteers to open a school, then a second and then a third (Tendulkar 1951, 1:211). Angry planters resisted these efforts and even burned down one of the schools, but the tenants rebuilt it immediately.

Champaran was a critical stepping-stone for Gandhi and helped set the stage for his confrontation with the British Raj on a national scale. Champaran showed Gandhi the power of satyagraha: his steadfast refusal to obey the magistrate's expulsion order was based on a stubborn adherence to the truth he was discovering in Champaran. Despite the fact that this satyagraha campaign was limited primarily to one individual—Gandhi—it showed him how this weapon could be wielded to help make India free and to reform Indians' practices. It also showed Gandhi that there were different points through which government could be influenced: although the local government resisted Gandhi's efforts in Champaran, higher levels of government pressured Champaran authorities to settle the matter (Brown 1989, 112). Champaran also introduced Gandhi to India's rural poor on deeply intimate terms. He saw firsthand how they suffered from abuse, inequality, poverty, disease, and ignorance (Brown 1989, 111).

Champaran demonstrated Gandhi's good intentions by virtue of his openness and willingness to talk to his opponents from the beginning of the conflict. This shows Gandhi's constant attempts to seek converts and not conquests. Champaran revealed Gandhi's potential to be extremely stubborn on principles, especially when he saw that truth was involved. This stubbornness exasperated allies and adversaries alike throughout Gandhi's lengthy career. Champaran showed Gandhi how important it was to keep meticulous records of events and finances. Members of Gandhi's ashrams would not have been surprised to hear of his precise document keeping, given the detailed accounting records he insisted on at the ashrams. Champaran also showed Indians Gandhi's knack for attracting donations from wealthy sympathizers. Throughout his career, Gandhi had a flare for convincing wealthy people to literally strip themselves of the jewelry they were wearing and donate it to his many causes. He objected to receiving personal gifts, so he donated them to charities. He even auctioned off the garlands he received as welcoming gifts and gave the proceeds to the poor. Finally, Champaran illustrates Gandhi's practice of working closely with trusted locals. This enabled Gandhi to establish a deeper connection with the people, build huge reserves of trust, and also contribute to his efforts to train and reform the locals.

The Rowlatt Act and a "Himalayan Miscalculation," 1919

During World War I, Britain instituted a series of tough measures in India designed to help its war effort by suppressing any challenges to its rule there. Traditional freedoms regarding speech, the press, and association were severely curtailed. Although Gandhi and many other prominent Indians supported the British war effort, they opposed the new restrictions. Some, such as the highly regarded and immensely popular Lokamanya Tilak and Annie Besant, spoke out fiercely against the British and demanded home rule for India. Both were imprisoned. Secret tribunals had been set up throughout India and were sentencing many Indians to jail during the war (Fischer 1950, 174).

Shortly after the war ended in November 1918, many expected that the tough measures would be rescinded. They were encouraged for several reasons. First, Tilak and Besant were released from prison (although Tilak was later rearrested). Second, many Indians had fought and died for the empire during the war and thus expected some kind of political payoff in the area of enhanced Indian self-determination. Third, a statement made by the British secretary of state for India toward the war's end seemed to indicate that the British government was preparing itself and India for significantly greater Indian self-rule.

However, contrary to expectations and the hopeful signs discussed above, the government published a proposed bill, which would, in effect, continue the harsh wartime measures. Known as the Rowlatt Bills, after Sir Sidney Rowlatt who chaired a committee investigating the administration of justice in India, the two proposed bills sought to muzzle outspoken Indians who would challenge British suzerainty. Rowlatt's committee issued a report warning of "revolutionary conspiracies" in India and urged harsh measures to counter them (Brown 1989, 128). The bills had provisions for special trials and imprisoning suspects. Although designed ostensibly to counter terrorist acts by Indian militants, the legislation raised serious doubts about due process of law for all Indians because it made it a crime, punishable by imprisonment, to possess, with the intention to circulate, any "seditious" document.

Specifically mentioned were several of Gandhi's writings, including *Hind Swaraj*, which was written 10 years earlier.

Indians were outraged by this legislation. Gandhi wrote that the bills reflected an "unmistakable symptom of a deep-seated disease in the governing body" (Tendulkar 1951, 1:241). He called the legislation "unjust, subversive of the principle of liberty and destructive of the elementary rights of individuals" (Fischer 1950, 176). Ironically, the Rowlatt Bills actually provided Gandhi with a great opportunity to launch, for the first time since his return from South Africa, a mass-oriented campaign against the British government in India. The government unwittingly provided Gandhi with a nearly foolproof cause, around which virtually the whole country could rally. World War I had just ended and many Indians had endured great sacrifice on behalf of the empire. Many peasants were being crushed by the steep increases in prices during wartime. Further, the Rowlatt Bills sought to muzzle basic freedoms that European members of the British Empire enjoyed without consideration.

But what resistance would they offer? Gandhi, whose star was fast rising in Indian politics, suggested conducting a hartal. The idea, he said, came to him in a dream one night and from it he saw a clear path to forming a potent resistance campaign against the Rowlatt Bills. In March 1919, just after one of the bills became law, Gandhi issued a statement calling for a nationwide hartal, a daylong strike involving fasting and prayer. Gandhi used the term hartal deliberately, for it meant more than just a work stoppage along the lines of what many unionists conduct when they launch a strike. Hartal denoted a religious exercise, often employed during times of mourning. Gandhi thus called on Indians to conduct a religiously inspired act of political defiance, something the masses found inherently appealing. He also called on Indians to purify themselves during the hartal by, for instance, renouncing violence and by giving up alcohol. Gandhi, ever persistent in his reform efforts, meant to use the hartal not only as a nonviolent tactic to confront the British, but also to reflect his philosophy of nonviolence to admonish Indians to change their behavior.

When a thing becomes forbidden, it also becomes irresistible. And so it was with the literature proscribed in the Rowlatt Bills. In conjunction with the daylong hartal, the Rowlatt Bills also gave Indians a perfect opportunity to practice mass civil disobedience by simply possessing and disseminating some of the banned literature. Gandhi wanted to ensure an orderly mass civil disobedience campaign, so he encouraged people to disobey only those aspects of the new law that could be done so by individuals and that would cause as little disruption as possible. He therefore selected largely his own writings from among the list of banned material for "illegal" possession and dissemination. *Hind Swaraj* was at the top of his list. Here was a short book, which not only condemned British rule and Western civilization but also contained a strong attack on Indians who would do violence against the British. *Hind Swaraj* made a strong case for using nonviolence. So, when the British banned this work, Gandhi seized on the blunder as an ingenious way to give all Indians the chance to stand up to the British and an opportunity to further publicize and disseminate his arguments and ideas about satyagraha.

Although in ill health (Gandhi's personal secretary, Mahadev Desai, often had to read his speeches during this campaign), Gandhi traveled all over the country calling on people to sign a satyagraha pledge to civilly disobey the new legislation. He proclaimed,

> The bills require to be resisted not only because they are in themselves bad, but also because Government who are responsible for their introduction have seen fit practically to ignore the public opinion and some of its members have made it a boast that they can so ignore that opinion. . . . I have . . . pledged myself to offer *satyagraha* against these bills and invited all men and women who think and feel with me to do likewise. (Tendulkar 1951, 1:245)

Since this was the first time Gandhi launched a South African–style mass satyagraha campaign against the British government in India, he sought to propagate the nature of this technique. He explained, in his writings and speeches, that satyagraha was truth expressed as love. This meant that hatred could not be returned with hatred, that only good could be returned for evil. He said that Indians could reform the country by introducing religion and spirituality into politics and by incurring self-suffering, instead of imposing suffering on others: "*Satyagraha* . . . is a religious movement. It seeks . . . redress of grievances by self-suffering" (Tendulkar 1951, 1:246–247).

Nearly the whole country was energized. The hartal severely disrupted commerce in many of India's cities and towns (Fischer 1950, 177). In some parts of India, such as Bombay, the hartal went off successfully, with widespread adherence. Gandhi joined others who went out to sell copies of *Hind Swaraj*, insisting that participants write their names and addresses in the books so that the government could easily locate them for arrest and prosecution (Tendulkar 1951, 1:249). This is reminiscent of the time in South Africa when Gandhi furnished the witnesses on behalf of the government in its case against him. A properly trained satyagrahi does not do anything in secret, nor does he or she break the law with the intention of getting away with it.

However, in other parts of India, like Delhi and Ahmedabad, some people were energized to the point of spontaneous and uncontrollable combustion. Tempers frayed and stones flew. Many Indians, who took to rioting instead of self-purifying, were clearly ill prepared for conducting a disciplined, nonviolent civil disobedience campaign. For its part, the government helped fan the fire with its oppressive and brutal countermeasures and also by detaining and arresting Gandhi, the news of which incensed people. The violence that broke out in some areas was so severe that it led to the beating deaths of several Englishmen.

Horrified and hurt by the violence, Gandhi reproached his countrymen. On April 18, he called for a temporary suspension of the campaign and announced that he would conduct a 72-hour fast as penance for his own role in inflaming such passions among the people. He also called on people to join him in the fast, but only for 24 hours. As would happen so many more times in the future, Gandhi's personal efforts—frequently in the form of a fast—to quell the unrest had an immediate impact: disturbances in Ahmedabad came to an end (Tendulkar 1951, 1:256). Gandhi had to launch a personal satyagraha campaign to put a stop to the mass satyagraha campaign. He realized that he had committed a grave error when he, prematurely, called on the people to participate in a campaign for which they were poorly trained: "I had called upon the people to launch upon civil disobedience before they had thus qualified themselves for it and this mistake of mine seemed to me to be of a Himalayan magnitude" (Tendulkar 1951, 1:260). In calling for a suspension to the campaign, Gandhi also called on people to assist the authorities in restoring law and order, a tall task since just before this declaration many were engaged in the exact opposite behavior.

Although the campaign was a failure insofar as the Rowlatt Bills remained in force, the campaign solidified Gandhi's status as a powerful, nationwide figure (Brown 1989, 134). And Gandhi's faith in satyagraha never wavered. It was clear to Gandhi that he had much more work to do in spreading his message of truth and nonviolence before another mass civil disobedience campaign could commence. It was not the method, but rather the weaknesses and limitations of people (he most of all) in inappropriately applying the method that led to the "Himalayan miscalculation," so named by Gandhi to indicate the magnitude of his error.

Nonviolent Resistance in the 1920s

A note on this decade is in order since it was a time when Gandhi's influence in Indian politics rose and fell along with his brand of resistance. This was due, in part, to the lengthy period he spent in jail during this time. By the 1920s, the Congress Party, recognizing Gandhi's indispensable role in the national independence movement, made Gandhian-style resistance the cornerstone of its platform. Nonviolent resistance was adopted as the Congress Party's official policy. For his part, Gandhi was no longer the loyal British subject. Instead, he spoke of the British Raj as "satanic" and refused to cooperate with government authorities and institutions. He told his compatriots to do likewise, encouraging students and teachers to quit public schools and calling on civil servants in the courts to resign their posts. As a symbol of his break with the British, he also returned the war medals and other commendations he earned while serving in South Africa (Brown 1989, 148), which is a form of nonviolent noncooperation.

Although Gandhi had been promising that nonviolence would bring the Raj to a grinding halt, this did not occur. Taxes were collected and the government continued to function despite the obstacles that satyagrahis placed in its way. So, although swaraj, an ultimate goal, was not attained, plenty of process goals, such as fund-raising, recruiting volunteers, and training multitudes in satyagraha, were successfully accomplished. Many achievement goals were accomplished as well, such as boycotts of British imports, public school closures, and resignations by Indian civil servants from their government posts. The promotion of local Indian industries, such as swadeshi, also had a significant impact. Throughout the 1920s, Gandhi made speech after speech imploring people to sign khadi and swadeshi pledges.

However, these victories were only temporary, as, for instance, school enrollment and sales of British cloth increased to nearly preboycott levels (Brown 1989, 163). Moreover, at one point in the early 1920s, Gandhi called a halt to the campaigns because in some areas across the country they had degenerated into violence.

In calling off the campaign, Gandhi said, "If I can have nothing to do with the organized violence of the government, I can have less to do with the unorganized violence of the people" (Brown 1989, 166). Despite his calling a halt to the campaign, the government arrested him in March 1922 and sentenced him to six years in jail.

Still, something new was happening in the Indian countryside and in the cities. People began to understand that they could effect change in their own lives if they were strong, disciplined, united, and fearless. It is in these areas where significant, long-term successes can be counted. It was also as a result of these successes that Gandhi chose to "turn the screw a little tighter" as the next decade began.

The Salt March, 1930

By most accounts, the Salt March was Gandhi's greatest triumph in politics. His masterful manipulation of Indian national symbols, combined with a well-organized mass civil disobedience campaign, demonstrated just how potent nonviolent resistance could be. In marching hundreds of miles to the sea while gathering thousands of followers along the way, Gandhi's simple, yet potent, act of defiance in illegally making salt galvanized the Indian populace. The beauty of the Salt March was that virtually any Indian— male or female, rich or poor, young or old—could participate.

It is important to note that the Salt March did not occur in a vacuum. Rather, it occurred amid an ongoing, generalized nonviolent resistance movement that Gandhi and others designed with several key goals in mind. First, the campaign was devised to give the Indian masses a method for standing up to the British and to give them hope of ridding the subcontinent of colonial rule. Nonviolent resistance—not unlike conventional military confrontations— waxed and waned through periods of high intensity and quiet lulls. Both major forms of nonviolent resistance marked this period: civil disobedience, such as illegally making salt, and noncooperation, such as boycotting foreign-made cloth.

Second, Gandhi and other leaders of the Indian National Congress sought to solidify the Congress's hold on the independence movement. Congress leaders wanted to make sure that the British could not ignore the Congress Party when it came time to discuss India's future. Gandhi's Salt March ensured the Congress Party's supremacy in Indian national politics.

Third, and most important, the satyagraha Gandhi sought to offer in India at this time was directed as much at reforming Indians as it was toward defying the British. Gandhi frequently lamented that so few British could dominate so many Indians, not by dint of weapons or force, but rather by virtue of the Indians' acquiescence in their own subjugation. Gandhi felt that the British could only accomplish things in India as long as Indians let them. And as has been discussed in earlier chapters, the key to understanding how nonviolent resistance works is in uncovering why people obey authority figures, because this obedience is what gives authority its power. Part of that power came from the many Indians who held government positions, which buttressed the British Imperial regime. Therefore, in each village Gandhi visited during the march, he encouraged officials to resign their posts; many did.

If the reasons for Indian obedience to British rule could be undermined, then so could the Raj. Gandhi, therefore, sought to strip the British of both their willing and unwitting accomplices in the Indian population by fostering a struggle within Indian society that would strengthen and unify it as it confronted the British. Gandhi emphasized that Indians must first succeed in their own inner struggle for Indian unity and strength in order to succeed in their outer struggle for swaraj against the British.

The Salt March, which covered more than 240 miles and lasted nearly one month, proved an irresistible phenomenon, made all the more remarkable by virtue of Gandhi's age: he was 61 years old and in ill health. People marveled at his physical stamina during the march. Gandhi marched so deliberately that many of the other marchers had difficulty keeping up with him. His troupe arrived at the sea a day earlier than expected. All along the way, Gandhi made stops in the villages to draw attention to the desperate situation of India's rural poor. At each stop, Gandhi would lead the locals in prayer and request that they sign pledges of nonviolence. He would contact the media and give it time to catch up to him so journalists could file their stories, thereby publicizing his crusade. Most of all, he would ceaselessly push his message of reform, preaching the benefits of khadi, swadeshi, Hindu–Muslim unity, ending untouchability, ending child marriages, personal hygiene and household cleanliness, and abstaining from drugs and alcohol. For Gandhi, these were the real keys to swaraj, for if these reforms took hold, no force in the world, including the mighty British Empire, could hold sway against the people.

But, why, of all things, did Gandhi choose to march hundreds of miles just to make salt? Even though it was against the law to make salt without government sanction, Gandhi's simple act would not deny the government's treasury of any significant revenues. Even if thousands of Indians made salt for their own personal consumption, government coffers would barely feel the strain. Gandhi's choice of salt making showed his genius for being able to illustrate high-minded principles—ahimsa, satyagraha, and swaraj—with concrete, observable, and dramatic action that would cause a worldwide stir.

But the idea did not just appear to him out of thin air. Gandhi's decision to make salt was influenced in part by a small tax resistance effort in the Bardoli District two years earlier. Refusing to pay taxes is an old form of nonviolent resistance and the tax refusal efforts in Bardoli received extensive, positive press coverage. Sardar Patel, a close friend and disciple of Gandhi and a high-ranking Congress Party official, led the satyagraha campaign, which protested an increase in government land taxes. The Bardoli campaign struck a deep blow to the government's authority and credibility (Dalton 1993, 92–93). The Bardoli tax resistance inspired Gandhi because it portrayed the moral drama of an oppressed peasantry using nonviolence against an unjust government and because it illustrated how impotent the government was in the face of mass nonviolent resistance, in this case tax refusal. Gandhi even staged the Salt March in the same district, drawing on the courage and experience the residents previously demonstrated (Dalton 1993, 95). Bardoli showed that Indians of diverse backgrounds could unite on an important issue and fight to undermine the government on a sustained, mass level. To Gandhi, Bardoli was more a victory for truth and nonviolence than it was for political independence (Brown 1989, 221).

But Gandhi also chose salt because of its deep symbolic importance to Indians. India has oppressive weather conditions, with temperatures frequently rising above 100 degrees Fahrenheit and made worse by a sticky, drenching humidity. Salt held special significance in India because it was essential not only to help prevent dehydration, but also as a preservative in foods. Nothing, including germs, can grow in salt, so in order to protect foods from spoiling, salt was used. Salt, therefore, was as vital to Indians as water was.

Ever since the India Salt Act of 1882, the British maintained a royal monopoly on the production, sale, and taxation of salt, which gave them an excellent means of controlling the population. Indians complained bitterly about the government monopoly, arguing that it was used more as a means of oppression than for anything else. By calling on Indians to make their own salt, Gandhi demonstrated how nearly everyone in the country could play an active role in defying the British and breaking the monopoly. Moreover, to do so using nonviolent civil disobedience would again demonstrate the power of ahimsa. In one masterful stroke, Gandhi was able to accomplish several goals simultaneously.

First, since the march took nearly a month to complete, it gave Gandhi and his fellow marchers plenty of time to publicize their grievances. The Salt March focused attention on one of the most oppressive policies the colonial administration enforced in India. As Gandhi marched closer and closer to the sea, the crowds grew larger, the anticipation mounted, and the media coverage reached a crescendo. Salt was a necessity, Gandhi said, not a luxury or privilege, like tea or land (Dalton 1993, 101). For the government to tax salt and control its production was like stealing something that rightfully belonged to the people. Gandhi called the policy "inhuman," "beastly," and "satanic" (Dalton 1993, 112). Since the government's salt monopoly had a direct negative impact on nearly all Indians, the citizenry was relatively united in resisting it and the Salt March gave expression to their grievances.

Second, since salt was fairly easy to make, Gandhi provided the masses with an excellent method of resistance. It also gave everyone, including the poor and the uneducated, a tangible way to not only confront the British, but to do something economically beneficial for themselves as well. Soon, thousands and thousands of ordinary Indians were joining Gandhi, enthusiastically doing their part in defying the British Raj, simply by making salt and being arrested and jailed for the offense.

Gandhi's simple act empowered millions of Indians, especially women. This proved yet another masterful stroke of Gandhi's. Since women were the primary householders in Indian society, they knew firsthand the burden the salt monopoly placed on home economics. Making salt provided a mutually reinforcing component to the movement. On the one hand, this form of nonviolent resistance appealed to women who mobilized in large numbers to make their own salt. On the other hand, women's participation gave the civil disobedience movement a significant boost. Not only did Gandhi strengthen the movement by politicizing and mobilizing women, but he also was able to use the Salt March to goad Indian society toward reform regarding the role and status of women. Unfortunately, only a few Muslims took part in the campaign (Dalton 1993, 119).

Third, the Salt March demonstrated the impotence of British Imperial might in the face of mass, nonviolent civil disobedience. This proved a huge symbolic defeat for the British. At first, the British were paralyzed over what to do. Despite declaring its intention to arrest Gandhi immediately if he broke the Salt Laws, the government was reluctant because it did not want to alienate the support of moderate Indians (Dalton 1993, 125). Nor was the government able to fashion a proper response to the throngs of women who were now breaking the law. This placed Gandhi in a win–win situation. If the government did arrest him and the others, it risked igniting the whole of India in protest. If it did not arrest him, it would signify defeat and encourage others to join in the campaign. Interestingly, Gandhi was not arrested until a month after his arrival at the seacoast at Dandi, and for reasons unrelated to his salt making: rather, he was arrested to demonstrate that the government could still assert its strong hand (Brown 1989, 237–238).

Gandhi's campaign target was the British Raj

> whose determination to enforce law and order was thrown off balance by the moral thrust of Gandhi's leadership. The peculiar moral force and religious thrust of Gandhi's example prompted [British Viceroy Lord] Irwin to pause and reflect deeply on his government's purpose. (Dalton 1993, 131–132)

This contributed to the government's ambivalent and hesitant reaction to the Salt March and also to an expansion of the salt-making campaign as Indians felt more confident to stand up to the government. Even British officials, including police officers, expressed ambivalence and reluctance about arresting salt satya-grahis (Dalton 1993, 133).

By the time the government did react, it was too late. Despite arresting thousands and thousands of Indians, including Gandhi and virtually all of Congress's major leaders, salt making continued nationwide for more than a year and so, therefore, did Britain's humiliation from its inability to stop it. In Bombay, for instance, salt makers were surrounded by rings of Congress Party volunteers, linked arm in arm. This provided a protective shield through which the police could not penetrate without resorting to force, which prompted precisely the sort of moral outrage toward the government for which Congress hoped (Brown 1989, 240). Nonviolent raids on government-run salt manufactories also provoked a violent government reaction, which further diminished British moral sway in India and strengthened the forces for independence. Ultimately, the government was compelled to negotiate with Gandhi and the pact Gandhi signed with Viceroy Lord Irwin brought an end to the campaign.

Gandhi's arrival at the sea in Dandi on April 5 and his breaking the salt law the next day was the result of a painstakingly planned campaign, which demonstrates Gandhi's strategic genius. Part of this strategy revolved around Gandhi's desire to be truthful. As was his custom, Gandhi wrote a letter informing the viceroy of his intentions and his plan to start a civil disobedience campaign on March 12, 1930. Interestingly, the letter was hand delivered by a sympathetic young Britain who supported nonviolence and India's independence. Gandhi's openness toward his opponents was legendary. His letters to the viceroy would combine elements of vulnerability with an ultimatum. Typically, he would express support and admiration for the viceroy, but condemn the system under which the viceroy operated. Then, he would plea for the viceroy's assistance in helping him avert a confrontation. Failing that, he would, regrettably, have no choice but to launch a satyagraha campaign, thus giving the impression that it was the viceroy's fault (Dalton 1993, 106).

Of course, being open was part of Gandhi's philosophical commitment to truthfulness. However, such openness had strategic advantages as well. Not only did it help Gandhi seize the moral high ground, but it also placed the onus on the government to act. If the government did not act, then it would be seen as either coldhearted or weak: coldhearted for ignoring Gandhi's pleas and weak for being unable to control him. If the government did react, however, say by arresting Gandhi, then it would spark condemnations and protests.

Another part of Gandhi's strategy involved carefully selecting the right people to join the march. Gandhi planned the march using only trusted, disciplined followers chosen directly from his ashram, not from Congress's ranks. He wanted to ensure control over the marchers' behavior and he knew his followers at the ashram were more likely to adhere to his strict conditions for joining the march. Choosing marchers from among the ashramites, not from the upper echelons of Congress's leadership, also dramatized the plight of a "weak" group of simple farmers who confronted a mighty empire but who only wished to control their own resources and control their own future (Brown 1989, 236). So, on March 12, 1930, Gandhi and about 78 handpicked men set out from Sabarmati Ashram to march 240 miles to the sea. The march lasted 24 days and covered between 10 and 15 miles each day, a distance and pace that proved to be too much for some marchers, but not the indomitable Gandhi.

Gandhi's strategy also involved manipulation of the media and nationalist symbols. The very act of a frail 61-year-old man marching hundreds of miles to the sea to make salt captured the world's imagination. Gandhi had a gift for dramatic action and the Salt March proved to be the pinnacle of this gift. Since Gandhi arrived at the coast a day earlier than expected, he used the extra day to contact the media, spread the word, and build the suspense of his impending defiance. Moreover, Gandhi timed his action at the sea to coincide with the beginning of National Week, which was established more than a decade earlier to commemorate Indians' nationalist resistance to the British.

Ultimately, although the Salt March and the resulting civil disobedience campaign did not end the British monopoly on salt nor harm the government's revenues, it did lead to some achievement successes. First, the campaign contributed to the so-called Gandhi–Irwin pact, which allowed people to make salt for home use. Additionally, a year later, the Salt Law was repealed in part because of the salt campaign's effect. Second, the Salt March galvanized thousands of Indians in their active resistance to the Raj. It showed that the Indians could mount and sustain a countrywide nonviolent challenge to the British. Third, Gandhi also succeeded in integrating different groups into Congress's plans, especially women and youths. However, he was not able to mobilize Muslims, whose participation in the Salt campaign was "paltry" (Brown 1989, 242).

Britain's oppressive reaction to the Salt March was not the only incident that eroded its moral position in India. At Amritsar, in 1919, the infamous General Dyer ordered his troops to open fire on an unarmed, peaceful gathering of protesting Indians, who were unaware that their gathering was a violation of Dyer's orders. Dyer had issued a no-meetings notice only the previous day, but the notice was issued in English only and not widely disseminated, so few Indians even knew of the order's existence. As Dyer's troops cut down the protesters—who were trapped in an enclosed space—Dyer directed his men to fire at the thickest part of the crowd. For 10 minutes, the massacre continued, ceasing only after the troops spent their last round of ammunition. In all, some 1,650 rounds were fired, leaving 379 dead and about 1,137 wounded, including old men, women, and children (Fischer 1954, 66). After ceasing fire, Dyer refused to offer assistance to the wounded. This outrageous act convinced many that the British Empire was not as "civilized" as it claimed to be. A little more than a decade later, the government's harsh crackdown on Indians just for making salt further eroded its moral legitimacy in India. Ever the master at manipulating symbols, Gandhi timed the Salt March so that he would reach the sea on the anniversary of the massacre.

Nonviolent Resistance in the 1930s

Simultaneous to the Salt March, other forms of nonviolent resistance played a huge part in India's nationalist movement against the British during the 1930s. Gandhi and the Indian National Congress Party were at the forefront of these campaigns as well, even as Gandhi and many Congress leaders were imprisoned. Nonviolent resistance during this time included not only the civil disobedience associated with salt making, but also Indians boycotting British cloth imports.

Much as the Salt March generated a countrywide civil disobedience campaign, it also helped generate a countrywide noncooperation program. In 1930, the combined mass efforts of nonviolent satyagrahis seriously challenged British authority in much of India. Foreign cloth imports plummeted markedly in 1930, down between one-fourth and one-third of the previous year's levels, and 16 British-owned mills in Bombay alone closed (Tendulkar 1951, 3:44).

Nonviolent resistance during this period was not an unmitigated success, however. First, by 1931, sales of imported cloth had rebounded because the Gandhi–Irwin Pact had called for an end to "aggressive" forms of boycott. Second, although Gandhi's efforts at integrating generations of Indians into Congress succeeded, he did not succeed well in uniting Hindus and Muslims, or in securing broad Muslim participation in the campaign.

Fasts: Self-Suffering Sacrifice or Controversial Coercion?

Gandhi's use of the fast as a political weapon deserves special treatment. Fasts are a unique form of resistance for three reasons. First, Gandhi insisted that fasts were to be used only as a last resort. Fasts are not to be engaged in on a whim, but only after careful deliberation and only after all other nonviolent alternatives have been attempted. A fast is a very serious and obviously life-threatening form of resistance. In addition, Gandhi recognized that his fasts contained both coercive and manipulative elements, both of which seemed contrary to his views regarding satyagraha. As such, he did not enter into a fast casually or without careful deliberation. He said he would suspend the fast if he believed that his fast was changing peoples' behavior due to coercion and not conversion.

Second, unlike other forms of satyagraha, fasts are a limited weapon because not everyone can use them. Few people command the moral stature and respect that is required for a fast to receive great attention and to be effective. Even Sardar Patel remarked that hardly anyone would notice or even care if *he* undertook a fast. Patel reportedly once said to Gandhi, "If I fast, they will let me die. If you fast, they will go to no end of trouble to keep you alive" (Chadha 1997, 323). Many British officials—including the viceroy and Winston Churchill—and even some vocal Muslim opponents, would have sat idly by while Gandhi starved himself to death. But other, perhaps cooler, heads in the British government recognized that allowing that to happen would produce a "solution" far more catastrophic than the "problem." This had the effect of putting the British in a very awkward position when it came to Gandhi's fasts, especially those he declared were fasts "unto death" if his demands were not met.

Fasts are also a limited weapon because few people have the qualities it takes to sustain a fast. Fasting requires great stamina, discipline, courage, and a complete fearlessness from death. Several times, when Gandhi was near death due to one of his fasts (the body's vital organs malfunction and even shut down from lack of nutrition), his weight dropped to less than 100 pounds, he suffered from fever and nausea, and he began hallucinating. Gandhi recognized that many of his supporters were not suited to conducting fasts so he often discouraged the public from joining him in "sympathy" fasts (although this still did happen, even among some police officers).

Third, fasts tend to work best when their target audience loves or reveres the faster. If a man as beloved as Gandhi announces that he will inflict great suffering on himself for the misdeeds of others, then those who love him will surely do what they can to keep him alive. After all, who among the Indian population (or the British for that matter) wanted to be held responsible for the premature death of the beloved Mahatma?

Gandhi's first public fast occurred during a millworkers' strike when the workers' resolve began to disintegrate. As more and more workers faltered and quit the strike, Gandhi declared that he would not touch any food unless the strikers rallied and reached a settlement. According to Gandhi's own account of the incident,

> [t]he labourers were thunderstruck. Tears began to pour down [their faces]. The labourers broke out: "Not you, but we shall fast. It would be monstrous if you were to fast. Please forgive us our lapse, we shall now remain faithful to our pledge to the end." (Chadha 1997, 227)

This account gives a vivid illustration of the force of the fast, as long as it is conducted by such a revered man as Gandhi and is aimed at those who so revere him. For how could the millworkers, on whose behalf Gandhi was fighting, not be moved by this cherished man, who undertook to punish himself for their misdeeds?

Gandhi conducted no less than 10 public fasts. He also conducted many private fasts as a way to compel wayward members of his ashrams to mend their ways. Both opponents and supporters criticized Gandhi for conducting the fasts, arguing that they amounted to nothing more than moral extortion or political stunts. But Gandhi was usually impervious to such attacks. Once he was convinced of the rightness of his actions, there was no dissuading him.

Gandhi's fasts sometimes lasted for days, sometimes for weeks. Frequently, he was near death, which was why the fasts were so often successful. Sometimes he took only water, while at other times he laced the water with some fruit juice. Most of Gandhi's public fasts were aimed at reforming Indian society, particularly in the two areas of great importance to him: ending untouchability and achieving Hindu–Muslim unity. He had more success with the former than with the latter.

In 1932, Gandhi launched a fast to dramatize his opposition to plans for establishing separate electorates, one for caste Hindus and one for the outcastes. Even though many Untouchables supported the separate electorate system as a way to guarantee them at least some representation in a future Indian parliament, Gandhi adamantly opposed the idea. He could not support a plan to statutorily separate electorates because he had worked all his life to create a single, united India, not an India of separate classes and castes. He said separate electorates would "vivisect and disrupt Hinduism" and so, while he was in jail, Gandhi pledged to resist the idea "with all my life" by conducting a fast unto death (Chadha 1997, 323). His fast led to the signing of the Yeravda Pact (named for the prison in which Gandhi was staying at the time), a compromise agreement that satisfied Gandhi, especially since his major principle of ending untouchability was upheld. According to Yogesh Chadha (1997),

> The fast had focused caste Hindu attention on the Untouchables to such an extent that all across the country Hindus opened their temple doors to the *Harijans*, allowed them to use village water wells, and, in some cases, even touched them and broke bread with them. (329–330)

However, much of these changes did not last, so Gandhi actually launched other fasts in a continual effort to reform Hindu society in its treatment of the Harijan.

Another famous fast occurred in Calcutta in 1947 after Indian independence and amid bloody communal riots between Hindus and Muslims. Gandhi opposed the partition of India because he felt that Hindus and Muslims were the left and right hands of "mother India." Nevertheless, his efforts at achieving Hindu–Muslim unity were often met with tepid response at his prayer meetings around the country. As independence neared, long-simmering rivalries and hatred overflowed into the "Great Calcutta Killing" of August 1946 in which some 4,000 Hindus and Muslims were slaughtered (Dalton 1993, 146). This hastened the advent of the civil war between Hindus and Muslims, which began before independence and lasted through the partition process and the bloody transmigration of Hindus from Pakistan into India and Muslims from India into Pakistan.

Amid this madness, Gandhi arrived in Calcutta in August 1947. Showing his characteristic fearlessness, he moved into a deserted Muslim home in one of the worst affected quarters of Calcutta. Angry Hindu rioters burst into the residence, smashing up the place and even threatening Gandhi, who confronted them and calmed them down (Dalton 1993, 152). On the first day of Gandhi's fast to the death, looting and rioting continued unabated; some mobs were even heard yelling "Death to Gandhi!" However, by the fast's second day, the rioting subsided and the attention of both Hindus and Muslims turned increasingly toward the Mahatma's bed. Even though many believed the fast would not touch the hearts of the Muslims or the hardened Hindu goons and therefore lead to Gandhi's death, the result of this fast was miraculous. Soon, Hindus and Muslims launched joint peace demonstrations, embracing one another in public. Even the police, which consisted of Indian and European officers, commenced a 24-hour sympathy fast, including officers who were still on duty (Dalton 1993, 155). Gangs of Hindus and Muslims turned in large supplies of weapons. But Gandhi agreed to end his fast, which lasted about 73 hours, only after Calcutta's leaders—Hindus, Muslims, and Sikhs—openly pledged to give their lives to stop the violence if it resumed. This fast was an incredible success: violence did not return to Calcutta even as other parts of India erupted in communal slaughter during the independence period. This is an excellent example of how a fast by someone of Gandhi's stature can work: though Gandhi did not take part in any of the violence, it was he who was suffering as a result of this madness. His unearned suffering had a mollifying effect on virtually the whole of Calcutta.

On only one occasion, in 1943 during World War II, does it appear that Gandhi conducted a fast aimed specifically at the British and not his fellow Indians. This was also the time when Gandhi offered his famous Do or Die! mantra during the Quit India campaign, imploring his people to do all that they could to nonviolently win independence, or die trying. Gandhi was in prison for making his Do or Die! statements and also for speaking out against helping the British in the war. Many Congress leaders were in jail at this time, which contributed to violent acts by leaderless, undisciplined crowds. Gandhi blamed the British for the violence, saying it was due to the government's brutal crackdown on Indians for their civil disobedience and noncooperation during the Quit India campaign. However, the British government blamed Gandhi for the violence, claiming it had secret evidence that showed the violence was a result of orders given by Congress leaders.

This hurt Gandhi so much that he wrote to the viceroy announcing that he would "crucify the flesh" by fasting for 21 days (Chadha 1997, 386). This was not to be a fast unto death but only a means of convincing the viceroy of Gandhi's innocence in the violence. Secret government documents revealed that the viceroy was in favor of letting Gandhi starve himself to death (Chadha 1997, 388). However, perhaps the last thing the British wanted was for Gandhi to die in jail while fasting over a personal dispute with the British viceroy, so the viceroy offered to release Gandhi, but Gandhi refused. Despite the predicament this put the government in, Gandhi survived the fast, but no positive, concrete results seem to have emerged from the ordeal (Brown 1989, 343).

INDIAN INDEPENDENCE AND GANDHI'S ULTIMATE FAILURE

"In the India [of today] there is no room for me."
"I am a spent bullet."
"Who listens to me today?"
"[I live] in a fool's paradise."
"I have given up hope of living 125 years."
"Why are they celebrating [independence]?"

These are just a few of the declarations of despair that Gandhi expressed as India was partitioned. Gandhi's ultimate goal was not ousting the British, nor was it even a united India. Gandhi's ultimate goal was to see God through his pursuit of the truth. But since Gandhi was convinced of the truth of a united India, a two-state partition would be a sin or a "blasphemy" as he put it. Although many of his supporters in Congress, such as Patel and Nehru, believed Gandhi was right in his opposition to partition, they nevertheless went along with partition plans in the hopes of averting a civil war (which occurred anyway) and in preserving their own power. Alas, Gandhi's efforts against partition failed and the subcontinent was plunged into a horrific bloodletting.

As India and Pakistan formally declared independence on August 15, 1947, Gandhi announced that he could not participate in the celebrations and instead spent the day at his spinning wheel, preaching Hindu–Muslim unity. During the partition, hundreds of thousands lost their lives and millions were uprooted and left homeless. The bloody partition left a subcontinent severely scarred to this day, a region that remains engulfed in nationalistic bitterness. India and Pakistan are two of the poorest countries on earth, yet both devote scarce economic resources to arming themselves with nuclear weapons.

Yet, despite the violence, despite his failure to keep India together, and despite his open despair, Gandhi remained forever hopeful: he never gave up his faith in God, in his ability to become an even better satyagrahi, or even in reforming Indians. This is yet another of those strange contradictions of the Mahatma: it took great courage and fearlessness for Gandhi to continue working amid "the wreckage of a lifetime's labor" (Fischer 1954, 175). He was assassinated while still pursuing the dream of a united India. While the "world he had built lay partly in ruins," Gandhi's "faith never left him" as he laid plans to fight the violence and hatred that partition had wrought (Fischer 1954, 175–177).

PART III

King

Introduction:
A Brief Background of the
Civil Rights Movement in
the United States

THE STRUGGLE FOR EQUALITY IN THE UNITED STATES

Here begins my investigation of Martin Luther King, Jr., his life, his beliefs, and principles and the nonviolent resistance campaigns he conducted during his short tenure as "the moral leader" of the United States. Much as was done with Part II on Gandhi, Part III on King briefly sets the stage for King's entry into American politics in the mid-1950s. This section will provide a brief background on the Civil Rights Movement in the United States up to the time of King's arrival on the stage.

Civil rights are obligations imposed on government to take positive (or affirmative) action to guarantee equal treatment of all its citizens under the law. Equality is therefore a hallmark of civil rights. *Equality* itself is a controversial term because it has different meanings to different people. For some, equality means that everyone has equal material possessions; this is often called "equality of result," but few Americans share this notion of equality. For most Americans, equality means that every individual, regardless of race, religion, gender, and so forth, should have the same chance, or opportunity, to realize his or her full potential, without unfair obstacles placed before them, either by government or private institutions.

Civil rights advocates fight to ensure that individuals are treated equally, no matter what group they belong to. If a woman is denied a promotion because she is a female, then her civil rights have been violated and she is entitled to just compensation. Of course, the same goes for individual members of other groups such as blacks, Latinos, Native Americans, and the disabled.

To protect Americans' civil rights, the U.S. government, since the 1960s, has implemented programs to ensure that individuals who suffered past discrimination are brought in to valued roles in society. For instance, women have been excluded from occupying positions of leadership in corporate America and blacks and other racial minorities have been excluded from valued positions in higher education. As a whole, programs designed to rectify these inequalities are referred to as "affirmative action."

Civil rights are not to be confused with *civil liberties*, which are constitutional protections against what government can do to its citizens. Think of civil rights as government "dos," that is, what government must actively do in order to guarantee individuals their equal rights. So, if the Equal Employment Opportunity Commission files a lawsuit against a company for discriminating against women in the workplace, then that is government assuming its role in ensuring citizens' civil rights. By contrast, think of civil liberties as government "don'ts," that is, what government is prohibited from doing to its citizens so they can remain free. For instance, the U.S. Constitution forbids government or its agents (such as the police) from prohibiting the free exercise of religion, the curtailment of free speech, or limits on the press. Most civil liberties are contained in the U.S. Constitution's first 10 amendments, its Bill of Rights.

Throughout its history, the United States has struggled with the notion of equal rights. Despite its claims to being a country dedicated to equality and freedom, the U.S. record on civil rights is spotty, especially given its treatment of blacks. Although many groups have fought for equal treatment, concern here is with the struggle of blacks because their struggle set so many precedents for other groups' struggles and because, of course, it was the group from which Martin Luther King, Jr. came. The black struggle for civil rights is divided into three separate periods: slavery, segregation and Reconstruction, and the Civil Rights Movement. Each period can be characterized by a significant political thrust of its time represented by a landmark Supreme Court case, which set the tone for that era.

SLAVERY: EARLY 1600s–1865

From the 1600s until the Civil War's end in 1865, most blacks essentially did not have any civil rights because they were slaves and treated as no more than chattel, or property. To be sure, many Americans opposed slavery and wished to abolish the institution. Recall that Henry David Thoreau went to jail over his opposition to slavery. But many Americans, especially in the South, either actively supported slavery or acquiesced to the institution. Even the framers of the U.S. Constitution implicitly sanctioned slavery as an indelible American institution when they agreed to count each slave as three-fifths of a person in determining a state's population and, hence, its level of representation in the U.S. House of Representatives.

Of course, slavery was vital to the South; in 1787, when the Constitution was being written, 90 percent of all slaves resided in Georgia, Maryland, Virginia, and North and South Carolina, which equaled about 30 percent of the entire population of those states. The South's economy was mostly agrarian-based, dependent on large, labor-intensive sugar and cotton plantations. Slaves thus provided a cheap source of labor, which was crucial to the South's economic growth. Many white southerners saw attempts to abolish slavery as a direct attack not only on the lifeblood of the South's economy but also on their way of life. During this era, government policies favored and accommodated the property interests of slaveholders. Slavery was not only allowed but slaveholders were given special treatment in some business areas.

Nevertheless, there were many who opposed slavery and they tried—unsuccessfully—to use legal means to abolish the institution. The most famous Supreme Court case regarding slavery during this period was *Dred Scott v. Sandford* (1857). Born into slavery, Scott found himself first in Illinois and later in Wisconsin Territory, both of which prohibited slavery. With the help of his original owners, Scott sued for his freedom on the grounds that since he was in a free state, he should be a free man. However, the Supreme Court ruled, seven to two, that Scott was not a citizen and therefore not a free man. Further, the Court held that slaves "were never thought of or spoken of as anything except property." So, how could "property" possess a right to freedom? Scott remained a slave and slavery remained a steadfast institution. Ironically, Scott's owners freed him anyway (that was their right, not his), but he died a year later, from tuberculosis.

Dred Scott represents the Supreme Court's boldest defense of the institution of slavery. Political scientists like to point out that this ruling exposed a profound paradox of the U.S. Constitution: it upheld the idea of liberty, "that all men are created equal," yet it also affirmed the idea of owning human beings as property and slaves. But even the framers acknowledged the paradox. Thomas

Jefferson famously said that freedom and slavery, as opposite as heaven and hell, were both codified in the U.S. Constitution. This ruling, by a very conservative Court, also held that Congress had no power to ban slavery in the western territories, which is where Scott found himself and thus it severely restricted what the national government could do regarding slavery. Most important, many historians believe this ruling unintentionally hastened the Civil War (1861–1865), which marks the beginning of the second period of struggle for black civil rights.

SEGREGATION AND RECONSTRUCTION: 1865–1954

With the North's victory in the Civil War, not only was slavery abolished as a legal institution, but also three constitutional amendments were passed to ensure equality for the former slaves and their progeny. These are called the Civil War Era Amendments. The 13th Amendment (1865) abolished slavery, the 14th Amendment (1868) gave former slaves full citizenship rights and "equal protection of the laws," and the 15th Amendment (1870) gave former slaves (male only) the right to vote regardless of "race, color or previous condition of servitude." (Interestingly, nearly half a century passed before the Constitution was amended again, in 1913, when the 16th Amendment gave Congress the right to collect income taxes.) Although the Civil War Era Amendments guaranteed former slaves freedom and civil rights—at least on paper—blacks were still very far from achieving equality in reality. After all, slavery lasted hundreds of years and left a legacy of deep scars that are still healing today.

Immediately after the Civil War, freed slaves actually enjoyed some power. Many were elected to public office and government agencies, such as the Freedman's Bureau, were created by Congress to help former slaves adjust to their newfound freedom. Nevertheless, the starting line for former slaves was certainly not equal to that of whites. For instance, slavery—and its abolishment—created a new, instant class of Americans who were uneducated, poorly skilled, and politically disenfranchised. Moreover, policies and laws in the postwar South indicated that many southerners intended to keep blacks in a permanent state of servitude and second-class status. According to Lerone Bennett (1968), the whites' post-Reconstruction reaction to the Civil War pushed blacks back toward slavery (12).

As southern states were reconstructed and readmitted to the Union, white voters there became increasingly important in electoral politics. For instance, presidential candidate Rutherford B. Hayes promised to pull federal troops out of the South in exchange for voter support in his presidential campaign. White southerners used this newly acquired political clout to enact a code of "Jim Crow" Laws that required blacks to use separate public facilities such as restaurants, buses, hotels, and schools. Named after a character in a minstrel show, Jim Crow Laws thus instituted the system of segregation in the South that legally and forcibly kept blacks from exercising their full rights to equality and prohibited them from participating in the full range of American opportunity. Segregation was also common in the North, but the South required it by law. Jim Crow Laws essentially reversed many of the gains blacks had won in the immediate aftermath of the Civil War.

Segregation laws had a devastating and humiliating effect on the lives of blacks. Without having participated in forming the laws and policies that created their societal exclusion, blacks were forced to use separate schools, buses, restaurants, hotels, libraries, bathrooms, and even drinking fountains. Consider, for instance, the difficulty blacks had while traveling long distances using interstate busing companies. Frequently, a busload of white and black passengers would stop at a whites-only restaurant, at which point whites could disembark and enjoy a hot meal while blacks had to remain on the bus. Or consider blacks who might be traveling in their own vehicles. If they wanted to stop for rest and refreshment, they had to find restaurants and hotels that would serve them. Too often, however, black travelers would be forced to pull off the road and eat and sleep in their cars, having found no restaurant or hotel that would serve "their kind." Imagine the sense of fear and insecurity a black family must have felt while passing through a strange place, exposed and vulnerable while spending the night in their own vehicle.

Besides segregating blacks, Jim Crow Laws also prevented blacks from voting or otherwise taking an active role in politics. For instance, southern states instituted a poll tax, which was a fee people had to pay if they wanted to vote. What made this law especially pernicious for blacks was the fact that most of them were so poor, they could not afford to pay the tax, which in effect prevented them from exercising their right to vote. Moreover, the poll tax came due when most blacks had little money. Back then many blacks, including King's paternal grandfather, were sharecroppers (farming for and on someone else's land) and thus were paid seasonally, usually after the harvest in the fall. So, blacks had little money left over come springtime when the poll tax came due.

Even if blacks could afford to pay the poll tax, they faced yet another obstacle: the literacy or voter registration test. Many southern state legislatures reasoned that, in order for people to be judged worthy of the right to vote, they had to be able to read, say, a newspaper, in order to learn about the candidates and the issues. But since it was a crime to educate slaves, few former slaves and their children could read. Moreover, the questions on the literacy tests were so difficult and obscure, many literate blacks could not have passed the exam. But many whites could not have passed the exam either, so to shield illiterate whites from having to take the literacy test, the law said anyone whose grandfather had voted in previous elections was exempt from having to take the literacy test. But, for nearly all blacks, the grandfather clause did not help them, since all their grandfathers were slaves who did not have the right to vote.

Southern states also sponsored whites-only primary elections in order to exclude blacks from participating in the political process. Primary elections occur before the general election and are an important part of the U.S. democratic electoral process. However, many southern states argued that political parties—and the primary elections that were held to elect their candidates—were private institutions and thus could exclude anyone they wanted.

Segregation and Reconstruction were marked by a series of Supreme Court rulings that essentially gutted the provisions of the Civil War Era Amendments. Ultimately, these rulings, together with the Jim Crow Laws, effectively denied the freedom and equality that blacks thought they had won after the Civil War and with passage of the 13th, 14th, and 15th Amendments. The most important Supreme Court case during segregation and Reconstruction was called *Plessy v. Ferguson* (1896). Plessy was a black man who challenged Louisiana's segregation policy on the grounds that it violated his 14th Amendment right to equal protection under the law. However, the Supreme Court ruled that a state could require its black citizens to use separate facilities, as long as the black and white facilities were equal. The Court—again, it was a conservative one—said that using race as a criterion of exclusion in public matters was *not* unconstitutional. This ruling codified the infamous separate but equal policies of southern states.

Plessy upheld and extended the infamous segregation period, based on the flawed principle of establishing separate but equal facilities for blacks and whites. Enforcement of the "separate-but-equal" doctrine resulted in inhumane treatment for blacks, as in the many cases when sick blacks, in need of emergency medical care, were denied treatment at a nearby hospital because the hospital was for whites only. Moreover, the doctrine's practice resulted in more "separate" than "equal" facilities for blacks; black schools, colleges, and medical facilities were of a much lower standard than their white counterparts. Although this period did see blacks make some progress in the first half of the 20th century, for example, the U.S. Army was integrated, it was not until the third period that blacks finally saw some significant victories in gaining true equality.

THE CIVIL RIGHTS MOVEMENT: 1954–PRESENT

The third period is called the Civil Rights Movement and began with the landmark Supreme Court case *Brown v. Board of Education, Topeka, Kansas* (1954). With this unanimous ruling, the Supreme Court relied on its interpretation of the 14th Amendment to overturn the *Plessy* ruling of 1896. No longer were separate-but-equal educational facilities considered constitutional. According to the chief justice,

> Our decision cannot turn on merely a comparison of . . . tangible factors in the Negro and White schools . . . we must look to the *effect* of segregation itself on public education. . . . To separate them from others of similar age and qualifications solely because of their race generates a feeling of inferiority as to their status in the community that may affect their hearts and minds in a way unlikely to ever be undone. . . . We conclude that in public education the doctrine of separate but equal has no place.

The ruling not only outlawed segregation in public schools, but it also opened the door to decisions that dismantled segregation in other areas, such as public transportation and restaurants. But despite this ruling, blacks discovered that their long, hard battle for civil rights was far from over. Although the Court said public schools must be desegregated "with all deliberate speed," few schools actually were desegregated even 10 years after the ruling.

Blacks came to believe that increased public agitation was their only recourse. This agitation found expression in the nonviolent resistance of Dr. Martin Luther King, Jr. and the more bellicose resistance of black nationalists like Malcolm X, a so-called Black

Muslim nationalist, who preached an eye for an eye. While King fought for an end to segregation and eventual black–white integration in all aspects of American society, Malcolm X sought to achieve separation, which was a self-imposed isolation from whites. Whereas King sought creation of a beloved community (see Chapter 7), in which blacks and whites chose to live and work together harmoniously, Malcolm X sought to detach the black community from whites and to shield blacks from what he considered the corrupting influences of white society, such as alcohol, drugs, and sexual licentiousness.

King's nonviolent resistance exposed the brutality and violence of white segregationists in the South, including high-ranking officials such as Alabama Governor George Wallace. This compelled Congress to pass landmark civil rights legislation. In 1964, Congress passed, and President Lyndon B. Johnson signed into law, the Civil Rights Act, despite a lengthy filibuster by southern senators attempting to derail its passage. The Civil Rights Act outlawed discrimination in public accommodations and employment on the grounds of race, color, religion, national origin, or sex (interestingly, the act did not prohibit discrimination in housing until it was renewed in 1968). The act not only helped guarantee equal rights for blacks in education, employment, and voting, it also led to creation of affirmative action programs for minorities and women who suffer from discrimination. Additionally, in 1965, Congress passed the Voting Rights Act to guarantee equal voting rights for blacks.

The Civil Rights Movement reached its heyday during a tumultuous period in American history. Besides the black struggle for equality, many other important struggles were waged. Inspired by the successes they observed in the black community, women, Native Americans, and Latinos began organizing and demonstrating for equality. Some groups became radical and violent. Black nationalists, Puerto Rican nationalists, and Native American nationalists formed groups that were not afraid to use violence and terrorism in pursuit of their goals.

In addition to the civil rights issues that tore at the country's fabric, this era was marked by controversial American policies in Southeast Asia that also divided the country. American military involvement in Vietnam (1965–1973) split the United States and left scars on the country's collective psyche that remain today. More than 55,000 servicemen and women died in a futile attempt to prevent South Vietnam from being united with North Vietnam under communist rule. When the U.S. media began uncovering government conspiracies and deceptions regarding U.S. conduct in the war, American public opinion turned against U.S. involvement in Vietnam. Young men burned their draft cards and fled to Canada rather than risk being sent to Vietnam. Protests on university campuses and across the country sometimes turned violent.

It was against this backdrop that Martin Luther King, Jr. found himself. In 1954, when he arrived in Montgomery, Alabama, as the newly hired minister at Dexter Avenue Baptist Church, King had no idea what the future held for him. He was a 25-year-old newlywed finishing his Ph.D. dissertation and planning a family. Whether he wished it or not, King soon got swept up by what he called the *zeitgeist* (a German word for the nature of the times). The zeitgeist grabbed hold of him, swept him up in its current, and really took control of his life. King did not ask for, and certainly did not go searching for, the eye of this hurricane. Instead, it appeared to seek him out purposefully and thrust him into its maelstrom and then ruthlessly spit him out.

King and his wife, Coretta Scott King, center wearing sari, in New Delhi, India, on March 10, 1959. While in India visiting with Gandhi's followers, King remarked that although others may travel to India as tourists, he came as a pilgrim. To Coretta's right is Acharya J. B. Kripalani, considered one of the best interpreters of Gandhi's teachings on nonviolence. (AP/Wide World Photos)

King is escorted from the Atlanta, GA, jail by two unidentified officers as he is taken to neighboring DeKalb County courthouse, October 25, 1960, for a traffic hearing. The hearing was to show cause why a 12-month suspended sentence should not be revoked because of King's part in a sit-down demonstration in an Atlanta department store. (AP/Wide World Photos)

Receiving the Nobel Peace Prize from Gunnar Jahn, chairman of the Nobel Committee, in Oslo, Norway, December 10, 1964. At that time, the 35-year-old King was the youngest man ever to receive the prize and the 12th American and the 3rd black to be awarded the Nobel. After receiving the honor, King increasingly adopted a global perspective on issues such as race, poverty, and violence. (AP/Wide World Photos)

Leading a protest march to the courthouse in Montgomery, AL, on March 17, 1965. From left are Rev. Ralph Abernathy, James Foreman, Martin Luther King, Jr., Rev. S. L. Douglas, and John Lewis. Abernathy, a high-ranking member of King's Southern Christian Leadership Conference, was a close friend of King's since the Montgomery Bus Boycott and was frequently at King's side, including the moment he was assassinated. (AP/Wide World Photos)

Addressing a public gathering in the riot-torn area of Los Angeles, on August 18, 1965. King attended many meetings in an attempt to solve the problems connected with the uprising. At left is King's close aide, Bayard Rustin, who helped influence King's turn to nonviolence during the Montgomery Bus Boycott. (AP/Wide World Photos)

CHILDREN ARE NOT
BORN TO BURN

NOW!

Dr. Benjamin Spock, left, King, center, and Monsignor Charles O. Rice, right, link arms as they march in an anti-Vietnam War rally in New York's Central Park on April 15, 1967. Although King's outspokenness on Vietnam was consistent with his philosophy of nonviolence, it cost him backing among both black and white supporters of the Civil Rights Movement. (AP/Wide World Photos)

With his wife, Coretta, and three of their four children in their Atlanta, GA, home, From left are: Martin Luther King III, 5, Dexter Scott, 2, and Yolanda Denise, 7. King spent far more time on the road than at home with his wife and children. (AP/Wide World Photos)

At his last public appearance at the Mason Temple in Memphis, TN, on April 3, 1968, in support of a sanitation workers strike. Although King did not want to make an address that evening, his emotional "Mountaintop" speech eerily foreshadowed his own death, which happened the very next day when he was assassinated on his motel balcony. (AP/Wide World Photos)

CHAPTER 6

From "Mike" to the "Moral Leader of Our Nation"

> Being a Negro in America means trying to smile when you want to cry. It means trying to hold on to physical life amid psychological death. It means the pain of watching your children grow up with clouds of inferiority in their mental skies. It means having your legs cut off, and then being condemned for being a cripple. It means seeing your mother and father spiritually murdered by the slings and arrows of daily exploitation, and then being hated for being an orphan.
>
> —Martin Luther King, Jr., *Where Do We Go from Here: Chaos or Community?* 1967

This chapter traces Martin Luther King, Jr.'s personal background: his childhood and early adult influences and the experiences he had that helped mold him into the man he became. King was exposed to dramatic events that left indelible marks on his personality. King had his share of peak experiences, but most of them flowed from the same currents of segregation that oppressed blacks throughout the South. In the segregated South, blacks were oppressed as a matter of law and too frequently through the use of violence, such as beatings and lynchings. This hostile environment subjected blacks to immense pressures in their day-to-day lives. It placed insurmountable obstacles in the path of promising young black talent, denied blacks opportunities and robbed them of their futures. To be black in the segregated South was to live a life walled in by hostility and surrounded by constant reminders that blacks were treated as second-class citizens. They felt the stress and burden of segregation every minute of every day, which constantly reminded them that many places—even public parks—were off limits to them and their children simply because of their skin color. The late tennis star Arthur Ashe once said that being black in the United States was so stressful it was like trying to hold down two full-time jobs. Perhaps Lerone Bennett, Jr. (1968), one of King's most eloquent biographers, captured it best when he described the stresses of being a "token" black in privileged sectors of white society:

> The problem here was not crass and vulgar bigotry but the day-by-day pinpricks, the stares, the frowns, the little snubs and meannesses that make the "token" Negro's life a guerrilla warfare on an undeclared battlefield. (44)

Martin Luther King, Jr. was born on January 15, 1929, and as a young boy he vowed to hate all white people. Later he learned to abide by St. Augustine's maxim to "hate the sin but love the sinner." Segregation was a system that instituted oppression of blacks on a daily basis and in all areas of life. King's "experience of segregation" will be considered as a singular milestone that left a profound influence on him.

A "PRIVILEGED" NEGRO BOY IN THE SEGREGATED SOUTH

King did not have an extraordinary childhood that foreshadowed his future as one of the 20th century's most extraordinary figures (Lincoln 1984, ix). Initially, he was called "Mike" after his father, but "Daddy King" eventually changed both his and his son's name to Martin Luther, thus bestowing on the young boy a rather demanding legacy. But Martin Jr. came from a nurturing home environment that was advantaged in comparison to the prevailing economic standards of most blacks in the South. Despite the obstacles and humiliations segregation posed for blacks in the South, Martin Luther King, Jr. was born into a relatively privileged life in Atlanta, Georgia. He was born just a few months before the onset of the Great Depression, the economic deprivations of which hit many blacks in the South particularly hard. Nevertheless, during that time of austerity, the King household was comfortably middle class. King's was not a life of luxury and idleness, but he did not know deprivation and destitution the way Atlanta's poor black community did. King often felt guilty about that, as if he had not worked for and hence did not deserve the relative comfort of his home surroundings. To alleviate that guilt, King took jobs that involved heavy manual labor so that he could be among the less privileged, learn about them, and understand their ways. One summer, King worked at the Railway Express Company unloading trucks and trains. Another summer, he worked at the Southern Spring Bed Mattress Company as a stockroom helper. It was tough work, if only for a summer, yet King found it purposeful, especially since he could have found much less demanding work through his father's extensive connections in Atlanta's black business community.

King was a hardy child. He was short and somewhat chubby; he only grew to a height of five feet, seven inches. He was athletic and liked to play sports. He usually excelled at neighborhood competitions. Young King was a good wrestler and no stranger to brawling (Oates 1982, 16). He became well-known for suggesting "let's go to the grass" to neighborhood pals in order to settle playground disputes (Bennett 1968, 21). But King was not a brute. Even at a young age he had a gift with words and preferred to use them more than not: "Almost from the beginning . . . young Martin made words and symbols central to his orientation to life" (Bennett 1968, 17). Impressed by the rhetorical skills of some of the adults around him, King remarked that one day he was going to get some "big words" for himself. No small wonder for the son and grandson of well-known preachers, whose spot at the pulpit every Sunday exposed King to the rich rhetorical flourishes of the black Baptist tradition.

King could also be an emotional, even dour boy. He even made a couple of halfhearted attempts at suicide. The occasion both times involved his beloved grandmother. On the first, when his grandmother was accidentally knocked unconscious, King thought she was dead and he leaped from the house's second story, in an apparently grief-stricken moment of suicidality. He survived that "attempt," just as he did when he leaped again from the second-story window upon learning of his grandmother's death (Bennett 1968, 18–19). On both occasions, it appears unclear what King's motives were and whether he actually understood what he was doing. Nevertheless, King—like Gandhi regarding his father—felt tremendous guilt for not being home when his grandmother died. Ten years later he said her death had a "tremendous effect" on his religious development as a child (Branch 1988, 57).

King was not born to nonviolence. Even after he learned about Gandhi's nonviolent resistance, King was not convinced that it would work in disputes between large groups, particularly in the U.S. context. While a nonviolent, turn-the-other-cheek philosophy might work in interpersonal conflicts, King felt it would not work in the struggle between entire racial or economic groups. He became increasingly convinced of this while studying German philosopher Friedrich Nietzsche's stinging attack on Christianity. Nietzsche argued that Christianity's emphasis on love, forgiveness, and pity were "harmful" practices, because they renounced humankind's natural inclinations, which were governed by the pursuit of power (Ansbro 1982, 1–2). As a result, Nietzsche argued, Christianity perpetuated human weakness among its adherents. But King was only temporarily convinced of Nietzsche's philosophy. As I will show, Nietzsche's appeal could not withstand the other influences in King's life, especially those of his professors who convinced him that Christian faith and works could be a source of great power.

In his youth, King had several milestone experiences that involved race and segregation, some of which left him, in his innocence, confused and bewildered, while others embittered him. One such incident involved two of King's closest friends, two white boys, sons of the neighborhood grocer. King grew up playing with these two boys, but when they all reached school age, King had to attend one school while the white boys went to another. One day, after school, King went across the street to meet the boys and discuss their new schools, but the boys' mother told him they could not play with him anymore, finally admitting to a confused King that black boys his age could not play with white boys. This was one of King's earliest experiences with the humiliation of segregation (Oates 1982, 10). Hurt and dejected, King made the trek back home and, like many young black boys his age, asked his mother for an explanation. While wiping young Martin's tears, his mother tried to explain to the boy, in terms he might understand, the history of race in America: slavery, segregation, Jim Crow Laws, beatings, and lynchings: "Don't let [this] make you feel you are not as good as white people. You are as good as anyone else, and don't you forget it" (Bennett 1968, 19).

King had another profound experience with segregation when he was eight years old. His father took him to a shoe store where the clerk insisted the two move to the rear of the store before they tried on any shoes. Martin Sr. refused and left the store, fuming— and without any new shoes. In his own recollection of the incident King said:

It was probably the first time I had seen Daddy so furious, and I guess I was hurt for the first time too. Daddy has always been an emotional man, and I can remember him muttering: "I don't care how long I have to live with this system [of segregation]. I'm never going to accept it. I'll oppose it to the day I die." (Bennett 1968, 20)

Yet another experience, again while at his father's side, illustrates the daily humiliations blacks had to endure in the segregated South and how such humiliations left their mark on young Martin. One time, Martin Sr. was stopped by a police officer who called Martin Sr. "boy" as he demanded his driver's license. Pointing to young Martin, Martin Sr. replied forcefully, "that's a *boy* there. I'm a *man*. I'm Reverend King" (Cone 1993, 24). These types of experiences introduced King to the injustices of segregation and racism: they left their mark. But they also planted the seeds of resistance in young King as he witnessed his father's dignified, forceful, and nonviolent opposition to daily humiliations.

King's school years were riddled with humiliations at the hands of segregationists. In his last year of high school, King performed exceptionally well in the school's public speaking contest: he was fast fulfilling his childhood vow to get some "big words" of his own. He made such an impressive speech about blacks and the U.S. Constitution that he was awarded a trip to Valdosta, Georgia, to perform in a statewide competition. However, as King and his teacher returned from the Valdosta contest, King was reminded of his race's second-class status in the segregated South. After having already entered the bus and taking the first available seats, the bus driver later ordered King and his teacher to vacate their seats when more whites entered the bus. When King refused, the bus driver became enraged by his defiance and called him and his teacher "black sons of bitches." As the situation threatened to spin out of control, King's teacher suggested it would be best if they moved. Although King protested, he obeyed his teacher's pleas. There he was, a bright young high school student, full of hope and expectation, forced to go to the back of the bus and stand with his teacher for the 90-mile ride back to Atlanta. King was infuriated and later said that "it was a night I'll never forget. I don't think I have ever been so deeply angry in my life" (Cone 1993, 25).

King suffered other humiliations on public transport that shaped his views. After spending considerable time in the North working and going to university, King came to enjoy the North's absence of overt segregation. He grew accustomed to dining in restaurants of his choice, to sitting anywhere on public transport, and to the generally less oppressive atmosphere that prevailed between blacks and whites. However, after a summer of working on a farm in the North, King was given a bitter reminder of segregation's oppressive shroud while taking a train ride home to the South. King was having a meal in the dining car when the train approached the Mason–Dixon Line, the old division between the North and the South. At that point, the dining car porters placed a curtain around King in order to segregate and exclude him from view of the white diners. King later remarked that he felt as if a curtain had been "dropped on my selfhood" (Cone 1993, 26). This humiliation was particularly galling for King since he had grown accustomed to the comparatively relaxed attitudes of northerners toward racial integration in public facilities.

To be sure, the accumulation of so many humiliations must, at last, have a deleterious affect. At one point young Martin vowed to hate all white people for the system of racial segregation that some whites had imposed on him and his race. After learning what it really meant to be black in America, with all the stress and burden brought on by the daily humiliations of racism, King said he was "determined to hate every white person. . . . How can I love a race of people who hate me?" (Cone 1993, 23). However, this attitude loosened considerably after King matured and met many whites and engaged them from a position of equality. Ironically, it was not his God-fearing, churchgoing parents, who initially taught King about a loving and forgiving Christ that loosened his attitude toward whites. Rather, it was his higher education that exposed him to new ideas and to whites of goodwill. Before that, he experienced a wrenching tension, between what his parents taught him about loving all God's children and the increasingly oppressive weight of segregation and white hatred expressed toward him, his family, and other blacks (Oates 1982, 11).

A STRONG FAMILY'S INFLUENCE

From both sides of the family, the King children learned to respect and love themselves and others (Oates 1982, 7–8), no matter what humiliations segregation had in store for them. From King's mother's side came a history of intellectual and academic pursuits. From his father's side came a tradition of hard work, masculinity, and athleticism as well as an aggressive will to fight against racial prejudice. From both sides came a tradition of ministerial work.

King's maternal grandfather was a well-known Baptist preacher in Atlanta and King's father, Martin Sr., was also a successful preacher.

Martin Sr. was a strong-willed and determined man. He was unsatisfied with the difficult and exploited life his father had as a sharecropper, forced to live in virtual servitude on a white-owned plantation. So he set out for Atlanta, dreaming of success and vowing to one day own a brick house of his own, instead of having to pay rent to a white landlord. That he did and then some. He achieved success in Atlanta's business community as well as in the church and became well respected among Atlanta's black elite. Martin Sr. was a self-made man who wanted to ensure that his children did not have to know the deprivation and hardship he had while growing up. Martin Sr. was a good, if stern, provider for his family. He worked long, hard days and studied at night. He put himself through high school and then Morehouse College. He became a Baptist pastor for two small churches in Atlanta and became active in the local fight for civil rights for blacks (Bennett 1968, 9).

King was a stubborn son and did not give in easily. Although Martin Jr. had disagreements with his father the way most sons do, he was able to combine "filibuster, charm, and stubbornness" to stand up to his father and deflect his father's forcefulness better than his siblings were. Unlike his older sister, Christine, who usually submitted to her father's impositions and unlike his younger brother, A.D., who usually rebelled against his father's dictates, Martin Jr. would usually listen to what his father had to say and then simply did whatever he wanted to (Bennett 1968, 24). Sometimes, Martin Jr. would simply say, "Aw, Dad," which was no answer at all, neither submitting to his father, nor openly defying him. But, with the "Aw, Dad" comment, Martin Jr. was able to show respect for his father while still charting his own course, defying "Daddy King" when Martin considered it in his own best interests to do so. King's biographers assert that this "skill"—one that brother A.D. apparently did not possess and that therefore led to strained and stressful relations between Martin Sr. and A.D.—also served King well when he became the leader of the Civil Rights Movement. His father remembered a kind of determination even when young Martin was being beaten: "He was the most peculiar child whenever you whipped him. He'd stand there, and the tears would run down, and he'd never cry [out loud]" (Bennett 1968, 24). King, who was no stranger to his father's beatings, said that "whippings must not be so bad, for I received them until I was 15" (Oates 1982, 181). Even as an increasingly famous preacher and civil rights leader, King had to contend with his sometimes overbearing father. For instance, when King was leading the Montgomery Bus Boycott, he began receiving death threats. One night, Martin Sr. showed up at his son's door, demanding that Martin Jr. return with him to Atlanta where it was safer. King listened to what his father had to say, but he firmly refused to give in to his father's demands (Oates 1982, 95).

King's mother, Alberta Williams, also came from a strong religious background. Alberta's father, Adam Williams, was a leading pastor in Atlanta's black community. He was also active in the civil rights struggle as a leader in the Atlanta branch of the National Association for the Advancement of Colored People (NAACP), the oldest civil rights organization in the United States. As a young married couple, Alberta and Martin Sr. developed a close relationship with Alberta's parents, living in their home while Martin Sr. joined Adam Williams as co-pastor at Williams's church. Alberta attended Spelman Seminary and Hampton Institute and worked as a teacher until her first child was born—Martin Jr.'s older sister, Christine. While Martin Sr. was strong-willed, opinionated, and emotional, Alberta was calm, cool, and slow to anger. Both personalities were apparent in King who once described himself as an "ambivert," part introvert and part extrovert (Bennett 1968, 18).

Through his family, King was also heavily influenced by the church, a not uncommon phenomenon for American blacks, especially those growing up in the segregated South. The church was a vital institution for the black community's lifeblood. The church, in effect, became a sanctuary where blacks could congregate and more fully be themselves, absent the racism and oppression that engulfed them in their daily lives in the South. The church provided a haven, not only for the expression of faith, but also for the expression of hope. The church gave blacks hope that there would be a better tomorrow, either in this world or the next.

A GROWING STUDENT WITH AN EXCEPTIONAL EDUCATION

From early childhood, King showed signs of superior intellect. He skipped the ninth grade altogether and actually graduated from high school at the age of 15. Still, he was not an excellent student— he remained bad at spelling and grammar and once admitted to having the reading level of an eighth grader upon graduation from high school (Branch 1988, 60). In 1944, he enrolled in Morehouse

College to study sociology. Even though he followed in his father's footsteps by attending Morehouse, King did not want to follow his father into the ministry, despite his father's exhortations. He objected to the image of the hand-clapping Baptist preacher, crying "Amen" and "Hallelujah." He felt becoming a minister was neither a proper intellectual pursuit, nor one through which he could make a significant impact on the world.

Morehouse College

Of course, King changed his mind about becoming a minister, but not by virtue of his father's influence. Rather, it was the result of his education at Morehouse and the people he was exposed to there. While at Morehouse, he attended lectures by professors and guest speakers who pushed him into loosening his hostility to the religious traditions and the church. He began to see that there was more to the church than emotionalism and that the church could be a force for social action leading to positive social change (Oates 1982, 15).

This is ironic, since it was also at Morehouse where King's doubts about religion began to surface and where they found expression (Cone 1993, 26–27). At first, faith and religion could not withstand the rigors of the scientific method and liberal education he was receiving. But Benjamin Mays, then president of Morehouse and one of King's intellectual role models, convinced King that religion in general and the ministry in particular could be an excellent place from which to fight for civil rights. King came to accept Mays's assertion that the "ministry could be a respectable force for ideas [and] even for social protest" (Oates 1982, 20). So, early in his college career and at the age of 17, King set out to join the ministry in order to pursue socially relevant works. He would follow in his father's and grandfather's footsteps after all.

King was not an outstanding student at Morehouse, although he did graduate in four years, at the age of 19, with a B.A. in sociology. While at Morehouse, King was introduced to the literary work of Henry David Thoreau, whose essay on civil disobedience had earlier influenced Gandhi. Ironically, Thoreau was influenced by Indian philosophy and scripture, such as the Bhagavad Gita. King was attracted to Thoreau's views on courting jail sentences as proper conduct for people concerned with honesty, justice, and social progress: "Under a government which imprisons any unjustly, the true place for a just man is also a prison" (Thoreau 1990, 34).

King was also impressed by Thoreau's opposition to slavery and by what he said even one person could do about it: "If one thousand men, if one hundred men, if ten honest men, ay, if one man, refusing to pay taxes . . . it would be the end of slavery" (Thoreau 1990, 34). Thoreau not only refused to partake in what he considered a government's evil acts, but he also argued that it was every moral and decent man's duty to disobey a dishonest government.

Crozer Theological Seminary

After King graduated from Morehouse College, he entered Crozer Theological Seminary in 1948, a small divinity school in Chester, Pennsylvania. With a student population of only about 100—perhaps one-fourth of whom were black—Crozer Theological was known for its liberal views (Frady 2002, 19). King's time at Crozer was one of great intellectual and personal ferment for him. On the personal side, King fell in love with a white woman, the daughter of a woman who worked at Crozer. When the Reverend Joseph Pius Barbour, a close friend of the King family who was looking out for King when King was in Chester, learned of King's intention to marry the woman, he urged King to reconsider. Barbour told King that if he returned to the South with a white bride, it would create severe problems in both the white and the black communities (Garrow 1986, 40). Even King's closest friends, all of whom liked the young woman, agreed with Barbour and advised him to abandon his marital plans. After a six-month involvement, the couple heeded the advice and ended the relationship. Barbour said King's heart was broken and "he never recovered" (Garrow 1986, 41). Ironically, King's action reflected the racial prohibitions against which he fought so hard (Jones n.d.).

Unlike his time at Morehouse, King threw himself into his studies at Crozer, where he excelled academically: he maintained an A average during his three years there, won several academic awards and scholarships, and was elected president of his senior class. He also graduated at the top of his class, winning valedictory honors. Like his time at Morehouse College, his studies at Crozer were a time of great intellectual and moral discovery. He read many authors, including Karl Marx, Martin Heidegger, and Jean-Paul Sartre. Many influenced King but three philosophers in particular had a profound effect on him.

The first was G. W. F. Hegel (1770-1831), the German philosopher who wrote about what is called the "dialectical process."

According to Hegel, social progress occurs when opposing forces struggle against one another. The struggle usually forces a collision between the opposing forces that produces something better than either of the two opposing forces could have produced separately. Out of this painful clash, between what is called "thesis" and "antithesis," emerges the "synthesis." Synthesis represents the merging of the best parts of the thesis and the antithesis. This process leads to growth and progress for society. King was impressed by Hegel's ideas about this dialectical process. He found agreement in it with how he already felt about many things. The Hegelian dialectic provided King with an intellectual tool for making sense of a world that seemed to contradict itself at every turn. Blacks and whites were ostensibly equal under the Constitution, yet everywhere blacks were woefully unequal to whites. Christianity taught a forgiving love for others, yet King found it hard to love those who oppressed him. King also saw the dialectic working in capitalism with its "islands of poverty amidst oceans of prosperity."

Hegel's philosophies convinced King that his struggles, however risky and painful, were worthwhile because they would result in progress. Hegel helped King remain committed to his faith and the belief that "the universe bends toward justice," which is a phrase he used in his speeches. Hegel also freed King from having to make "either-or" choices (Oates 1982, 39). The dialectical process enabled King to avoid rejecting one side or another and instead combine the best of each side: this is what he did with capitalism and communism when he synthesized the two and called for a form of democratic socialism in the United States. When he compared communism with capitalism, King found good and bad points of both (King 1963, 93–100). King made a careful study of communism. He liked communism's emphasis on equability and admired the communist concern for the economically and socially downtrodden. But he criticized the doctrine for failing to see the truth and benefits of individual enterprise. And as an aspiring man of the cloth, he criticized communism for its atheism and hostile approach to religion. King said communism failed to see life as personal and spiritual and condemned it as a "Christian heresy" because it placed too much emphasis on materialism and disdained spiritualism. Furthermore, King could not accept communist ideology that saw war and violent conflict as acceptable, even desirable, behavior for bringing about change. King rejected the communist dictum that the ends justify the means.

Despite its positive qualities, King ultimately rejected not only communist theory but also communism in practice, citing the less-than-impressive records of communist regimes in the Soviet Union and the People's Republic of China. Although communist theory predicts that a "workers' paradise" will emerge and that the coercive state-governing structure will whither and disappear, King saw neither of those predictions fulfilled in the Soviet or Chinese cases. Rather, the Soviet and Chinese states grew stronger and more oppressive than their monarchical predecessors against which the communists revolted.

And while King admired capitalism for rewarding individual initiative, he criticized its failure to more fully reward good collective works because, for King, capitalism failed to see that life was best when it was social and when people gathered in groups with the intention of creating a better society. If unchecked, capitalism was an excessively harsh system that could grind up weaker and less-competitive individuals. For King, therefore, it would be best to synthesize these opposing forces and reap the benefits each had to offer. That is why he proposed a hybrid system that would combine the benefits of both capitalism and communism. King's idea was for capitalism to be retained in the United States but with a guaranteed national minimum income grafted onto it, thereby ensuring that everyone in the country had the resources necessary to meet their basic needs.

Hegelian thought influenced King in other areas as well. In his Ph.D. dissertation, for example, King applied the Hegelian technique to the study of two disparate religious thinkers: Paul Tillich and Henry Nelson Weiman and by joining two "indispensable elements of Christianity, faith and works" (Herman 1998, 125). In his church sermons, he spoke about how the soul must grapple with its contradictory tendencies toward good and evil and how the painful tension between these polar opposites could ultimately produce a good Christian. King argued that people were capable of both good and evil and that people constantly fought a personal war between these two tendencies.

King also relied on Hegel in his speeches and in his activism regarding racial justice. King saw Jim Crow Laws and the entire system of racial segregation as the thesis of southern white privilege. Opposed to the segregationists were civil rights leaders and (sometimes) federal government officials. Their efforts at desegregation are the antithesis. Segregation meant the forceful separation of blacks from whites in public facilities, a separation imposed on them against their will and without their consent. Desegregation meant the lawful and, if necessary, forceful end to segregation (the

National Guard was called out on occasion to enforce desegregation orders coming down from the federal government or the U.S. Supreme Court).

King, however, wanted neither the thesis of segregation, nor the antithesis of desegregation. Rather, he saw that the painful clash of these two opposing forces could produce a positive synthesis, in this case integration, which involved the voluntary mixing of the races, based on a desired, peaceful, and harmonious interaction between them. Integration was more than breaking the physical boundaries of segregation; it was creating a transcendent psychological bond between blacks and whites in addition to merely allowing blacks to use the same drinking fountains as whites. In true Hegelian fashion, therefore, King sought to use the tension created by segregationist and desegregationist forces in a creative, nonviolent way to fashion his beloved community.

In addition to Hegel, Walter Rauschenbusch (1861–1918), a deaf professor of church history at Rochester Theological Seminary, heavily influenced King. Rauschenbusch wrote about the social gospel in his *Christianity and the Social Crisis* (1907). Rauschenbusch condemned capitalism as the source of modern poverty and squalor in the United States. He argued that capitalism was based on a system of competition, greed, avarice, and plunder where good people would engage in sinful behavior due to this evil system of capitalism, which preached, above all, profit and personal gain. In response, Rauschenbusch called on Christians to eradicate capitalism and to socialize vital resources so they could be more equitably distributed throughout society (Oates 1982, 25). King was especially moved by how Rauschenbusch interpreted and applied Jesus Christ's social principles to contemporary problems. After reading Rauschenbusch, King believed that "the church should take a direct, active role in the struggle for social justice" (Bennett 1968, 36–37). He also took from Rauschenbusch an optimism in the progressive nature of humanity, believing possible the "moral reconstruction of society" (Frady 2002, 20). Although he did not accept everything Rauschenbusch had to say about capitalism and individuality, King was deeply struck by Rauschenbusch's theories. He heard an explanation for the poverty of blacks—capitalism's negative effects also had a racist tinge to it. Moreover, in Rauschenbusch, King found the sort of Christian-based social activism he longed for (Oates 1982, 26).

Third, Reinhold Niebuhr (1892–1971), a Protestant minister, also had a strong influence on King. Niebuhr is the theologian who most shaped King's ideas regarding sin (Cone 1993, 30). Niebuhr gave King a way to explain and understand the depth of evil and sinfulness to which individuals—especially acting in groups— could steep. Niebuhr's realism about the starkness of human behavior sometimes "saved King from the trap of illusory optimism about the capacity of man for good" (Oates 1982, 35). Niebuhr attacked liberal philosophy's "false optimism" about man's essential goodness and questioned the liberal notion of inevitable progress, arguing that people were essentially evil and capable of incredible acts of sin, especially when they come together in group behavior. Niebuhr also condemned pacifism as simplistic and unrealistic (Oates 1982, 34).

Niebuhr's influence on King posed a direct challenge to the ideas King got from Rauschenbusch. However, in his comparison of Rauschenbusch and Niebuhr, King again applied the Hegelian critique, which saved him from having to choose one over the other. King felt Rauschenbusch was too optimistic in his assessment of the human condition. But King felt Niebuhr was too pessimistic because he overemphasized humanity's evil nature and the hopeless situation in which humanity found itself. He also questioned Niebuhr's pessimistic argument that humanity was incapable of change and improvement. King insisted this attitude was "inadequate, both for the church and life" (Oates 1982, 39). He said Niebuhr did not fully understand the nature of nonviolent political resistance, arguing that Niebuhr erroneously equated nonviolent political resistance with "nonresistance" altogether, a distortion of the methods used by Gandhi and other nonviolent political resisters. In contrast to Niebuhr, King (1958) said:

> True pacifism is not unrealistic submission to evil. . . . It is rather a courageous confrontation of evil by the power of love, in the faith that it is better to be the recipient of violence than the inflicter of it, since the latter only multiplies the existence of violence and bitterness . . . while the former may develop a sense of shame in the opponent, and thereby bring about a transformation and change of heart. (99)

Although King had heard of India and Gandhi's nonviolent struggle against the British while he was growing up, his first real intellectual encounter with Gandhi occurred at Crozer. In 1949, King attended a lecture by the well-known pacifist A. J. Muste. In 1950, only two years after Gandhi's death, King listened to a speech by Mordechai Johnson, president of Howard University, a predominantly black college. Johnson spoke of his recent journey to India and about how Gandhian-style tactics of nonviolent resistance and redemption could be used successfully to overcome racial inequality in the United States. When King heard Johnson's impassioned speech (Johnson was himself a Baptist preacher), he became so "spellbound" and "electrified," that he went out and bought several books on Gandhi (Cone 1993, 29). He learned about Gandhi's technique of satyagraha and how Gandhi combined self-suffering, self-sacrifice, and a steely determination to win independence for India and attempt to transform Indian society. He may also have seen some parallels with his own life: both were people of color struggling with a white power structure, both had experienced humiliating treatment at the hands of whites on public transport, and both were committed to a life of service. However, King's conversion to Gandhian nonviolence was not immediate because he was not convinced that Gandhi's ideas and tactics would work well in the American South. King noticed that Gandhi's struggle against whites in India was from a position of being in the majority, where the white Europeans were seen as colonial interlopers, masters in another's house. But whites in America were in the majority and few considered them a "colonial" power (although, in his later, more radical years, King referred to the horrible poverty in America's inner cities as a form of "internal colonialism"). While at Crozer, King remained skeptical of pacifism and the power of nonviolence, despite the fact that George W. Davis, King's faculty adviser from whom he took nearly one-third of his courses, was a strict pacifist and an admirer of Gandhi (Branch 1988, 74). After Muste's speech, King got into a heated argument with him (Garrow 1986, 41). Not until the Montgomery Bus Boycott and his discussions with nonviolent activists, such as Bayard Rustin and later James Lawson, did King make his turn toward nonviolence. Rustin was an internationally renowned peace activist and a master nonviolent strategist. Lawson had lived and worked in India and was heavily steeped in Gandhian ideals.

Boston University

After graduating from Crozer Theological Seminary with a Bachelor of Divinity in the spring of 1951, King enrolled the following fall in Boston University's Ph.D. program in systematic theology. King was becoming a refined, classically educated young scholar. He was impressed with European culture and civilization. Moreover, he was becoming socially astute and politically active. While studying at Boston University, King became well-known among the black student intelligentsia in Boston. He shared an apartment with some other black intellectuals and they hosted frequent gatherings where many of Boston's young black academic minds would attend and discuss the prevailing philosophical and political questions of the day.

As with his educational pursuits at Crozer, King was an academic standout at Boston University. Several professors there had a significant influence on King, including L. Harold DeWolf and Edgar Brightman, two of the main authors of a philosophy called "Personalism." King took many courses from these two professors. According to the so-called Boston Personalists, altruism was an essential component of Christian belief because it created a bond between all individuals who could then retain their dignity and realize their full potential (Ansbro 1982, 17). Personalism holds that all individuals have value, not so much because of what their skills or qualifications are, but because everyone is a child of God, loved by Him and therefore deserving of love by others. Personalism grounded King in the belief that there existed a deeply personal God and that all human personality possessed dignity and worth because all people are made in God's image and should be loved because God loves them.

King was also active in the dating scene in Boston, having numerous female companions. He showed no sign of settling down until he became attracted to a promising young music student at Boston's New England Conservatory of Music. Coretta Scott had career aspirations as an operatic soprano. Although reluctant at first, Miss Coretta agreed to let a friend give King her phone number. They spoke on the phone for quite a while; actually Coretta remembers that it was Martin who did most of the talking (Bennett 1968, 46–47). Nevertheless, or perhaps because of this, Coretta, who was nearly two years older than King, was impressed by him and agreed to see him for a date.

Miss Coretta was surprised to hear King say at the end of their first date that she was everything he was looking for in a wife. Soon, they were seen everywhere together. It was clear that they were in love. But some of her friends cautioned her against marrying a would-be preacher from the South, warning her that her music career would suffer. But Miss Coretta had fallen in love with young Martin and they were married on June 18, 1953, in her parents' home in her hometown of Heiberger, Alabama. Although Coretta Scott King finished her music studies and graduated from the New England Conservatory—Martin even became the dutiful househusband as Coretta went through the final, grueling rounds of her studies—she never did have the chance to launch her music career. The spirit of the times, or zeitgeist, as King liked to call it, would not let her.

While King was finishing his doctoral thesis at Boston University, he considered his career options. Two in particular stood out: academia and the church. He considered these options partially against the backdrop of debts he felt he had to repay: debts to his parents and the church, both of which nourished and supported him, and debts to his college and theology professors who wanted him to join them in the academy. King was talented and gifted for a career in either field. So, he decided that, first, he would be a Baptist minister for a while and then, second, join the faculty at a university where he could pursue a cloistered intellectual life. Torn between a career in academia and the ministry, King resolved the situation in classic Hegelian fashion by synthesizing the two disparate careers when he accepted a position as a minister in a church whose congregation had strong ties to academia. King accepted an offer as minister at the Dexter Avenue Baptist Church in Montgomery, Alabama, because its congregation consisted of upper-income blacks who were connected to the all-black Alabama State College and dedicated to community service among Montgomery's black population. Dexter's congregation was, therefore, cut from the same academic and intellectual cloth as King and this would thus enable him to maintain his contacts with academia, while simultaneously ministering. Furthermore, King was encouraged by the fact that Dexter frowned on the emotionalism and Amen-ing of the more traditional black Baptist churches in the South (Bennett 1968, 49). Finally, King chose a southern church over several others in the North because he was from the South and he felt he could render the greatest service there. What is interesting—and ironic—about King's appointment is the way he forcefully asserted his authority over the congregation upon his arrival. He issued a statement that said in part that leadership of a church "never ascends from the pew to the pulpit, but it invariably descends from the pulpit to the pew" (Branch 1988, 115). This expresses a sentiment that is directly contradictory to Gene Sharp's view of nonviolent power and authority originating with masses and being conveyed upward toward the leader (see Chapter 1).

YOUNG AND FAMOUS

Significant influences on King did not cease after he left the bosom of his family or even after he left the halls of academe and the seminary. He had several peak experiences during the early years when he was just starting out as a young husband, father, Doctor of Philosophy, and minister. It appears that some of his most profound milestones occurred during the period just after he arrived in Montgomery. His intimate moment with God while kneeling and praying in his kitchen, his exposure to Bayard Rustin and later James Lawson, and his pilgrimage to India all occurred in the mid- to late 1950s when King was still in his twenties.

During the Montgomery Bus Boycott (see Chapter 8 for a detailed account of this nonviolent campaign), King was exposed to many new ideas and people, all of which created a groundswell of emotional and intellectual experiences that placed him irrevocably on the path of nonviolence. During a sleepless night early in the Montgomery Bus Boycott (January 27, 1956), King was pacing in his home, fretting about the anonymous death threats his family was receiving, the internal bickering and feuding between other black leaders and followers, and whether he even knew what he was doing. In recollecting this moment later, King said he knelt down in the kitchen and prayed for advice and heard an "inner voice" calming him and reassuring him. He later said that all fear melted away at that point. During that peak experience, King said it was as if he could hear that voice saying "Stand up for righteousness, stand up for truth; and God will be at your side forever" (Ansbro 1982, 53). From that point on, King's fears, self-doubt, and uncertainty vanished and were replaced by an inner calm and peacefulness that remained with him, providing him with an unending reserve of strength. That experience enabled King to react calmly to the crowd of blacks that had gathered outside his home after his house was firebombed. The crowd was angry and itching for revenge, but King spoke calmly, telling them that "we must love our white brothers," even if they do us harm. His words mollified the crowd and the potential for violence receded.

As King was making what he refers to as his "pilgrimage to nonviolence," Rustin spent a significant amount of time with King discussing the finer points of religion and nonviolent philosophy. Rustin was a veteran, yet controversial, civil rights organizer. He was a Quaker and brilliant peace activist with ties to many progressive religious and civil rights organizations such as the Fellowship of Reconciliation and the Congress of Racial Equality. He was the main organizer of the famous 1963 March on Washington. He was also openly homosexual—which was both rare and risky in the mid-20th century—and a one-time member of the communist party in his youth. He later quit the party and condemned its actions, but his past membership in the communist party and his sexual orientation made his association with Martin Luther King, Jr. problematic.

Rustin also introduced King to New York attorney Stanley Levison, who either provided or helped raise funds for King's organization. Levison was a socialist who had, despite his leftist politics, grown rich off of capitalist endeavors such as real estate investments and car sales. Like Rustin, Levison also had a keen mind for strategy and together they would help King with his speeches and books and consult with King about the best ways to fight integration using nonviolence. Although King grew to rely on Levison's business acumen, Levison was, above all, King's closest white friend and most reliable colleague, who made no demands of him, which was something King found increasingly rare as he grew increasingly famous (Branch 1988, 208–212, 226).

Early in the Montgomery Bus Boycott, King was not committed to nonviolence as a way of life. But Rustin and later the Reverend Glen E. Smiley, a white peace activist from the Fellowship of Reconciliation and a close friend of Rustin's, found in King an eager pupil who increasingly possessed a Gandhi-like view, but who had not yet fully incorporated nonviolence into his philosophical operational code (Garrow 1986, 68, 72). For instance, at the inception of the Montgomery Bus Boycott, King kept a gun under his pillow for the purpose of "self-defense." He also allowed guards to carry weapons. When Rustin spotted the gun on a chair one night, he reproached King for behaving hypocritically. They stayed up late at night discussing the matter. Rustin ultimately convinced King that the presence of weapons in King's home contradicted what he preached at the pulpit, what he said to the boycotters, and how he appeared to whites in Montgomery (Garrow 1986, 73). Rustin's arguments convinced King of the inefficacy of weapons. So, he got rid of the gun under his pillow and ordered his colleagues, some of whom were charged with protecting him, to also get rid of their guns while they were in his house. From then on, King would face all conflicts, violent or otherwise, based on his faith in God, the power of love, and his commitment to nonviolence (Oates 1982, 91).

King's experience in and personal growth from the Montgomery Bus Boycott crystallized his commitment to nonviolence. After his immersion in Gandhi's ideals and after practicing his own version of nonviolent resistance in Montgomery, King changed his mind about the potential of applying Christ's nonviolent love-ethic to political conflict. In his sermons and other speeches, he urged his followers to adhere to it in social relations. King saw Gandhi as the first person to ever recreate the love-ethic of Jesus into a force for positive, moral social change (Oates 1982, 32). King was now convinced that such a love-ethic could be effective, not just in individual conflicts and relationships, but in group conflicts as well, including black Americans' struggle for equal rights in the United States. King wrote:

> It was in this Gandhian emphasis of love and nonviolence that I discovered the method for social reform that I had been seeking. . . . I came to feel that this was the only morally and practically sound method open to oppressed people in their struggle for freedom. (Dalton 1993, 182)

Shortly after Montgomery, King had another milestone experience when he and Coretta visited India to observe firsthand Gandhi's legacy. Although King never met Gandhi, he certainly felt the Mahatma's presence during his trip to India in February 1959. King was a young man, having just turned 30, and was still new to the Civil Rights Movement. More important, his remained an open mind, searching for new ideas and answers to profound questions about God, faith, love, and justice. By this time, King acknowledged Gandhi's significant influence on him. He liked to say that Christ furnished the spirit and Gandhi provided the technique for his nonviolent approach to racial injustice. King recognized the compelling nature of his India visit when he said that although he might travel to other countries as a tourist, he came to India as a pilgrim. He also remarked that the trip, for him, was akin to encountering famous American Revolution heroes such as George Washington, John Adams, Thomas Jefferson, and Thomas Paine (Miller 1984, 63). King's trip to India deepened his commitment to nonviolence and his admiration for both India and Gandhi. Gandhi's capacity for self-criticism, his dispossession of material items, and his intense self-discipline in both private and public life impressed King. King was inspired by all these elements of Gandhi's life and tried to emulate them in his own life, although he had much less success at this than did Gandhi.

King toured Delhi wearing a Gandhi cap, met with dignitaries and officials, and gave several speeches and guest lectures. In some of his speaking engagements, King expressed admiration for how the Indians and their former colonizers, the British, lived together in friendship and equality (Oates 1982, 144). He marveled at what he considered the significant progress India's leaders seemed to be making in promoting the well-being of India's downtrodden class, its Untouchables. He congratulated Indians on their success in eliminating caste discrimination. He believed that India—its leaders as well as its general populace—was far more committed to and successful in combating caste discrimination than was the United States in combating racial discrimination.

King was also struck by the immense poverty and deprivation he observed in India; more than once he suggested that U.S. surplus food production should be used to feed India's hungry (Oates 1982, 142–143). But King was impressed with the legacy of change Gandhi left on India. While both India and the United States had laws against discrimination, King observed that only India's leaders actually backed their policy declarations with moral and forceful actions dedicated to uplifting India's Untouchables. After seeing all the help India's government was providing her Untouchables, King made special U.S. federal government aid to blacks one of his cardinal demands. King wished that U.S. leaders, such as President Dwight D. Eisenhower and President Lyndon B. Johnson, had the moral courage and commitment to work on blacks' behalf the way he observed India's leaders uplifting her Untouchables (Oates 1982, 142–144). Instead, King lamented the paltry response from Washington's leaders after Alabama Governor George Wallace stood up, proclaimed "Segregation now and segregation forever," and then physically blocked black college students from entering Alabama State University. Worse, King was disheartened at the equally tepid response by U.S. leaders after white terrorists bombed an Alabama church and killed four little black girls in attendance. Decades passed before the last perpetrator of that act of terrorism was finally charged and convicted.

But King's optimistic take on Indian society was a polite exaggeration made by an ingratiated guest of honor. Despite the reform-minded policies the Indian government implemented, India even today remains gripped by a tense conflict between the castes. In March 1999, for instance, violence broke out in a rural part of India where a mob went on a rampage and murdered several Untouchables. In addition, Indian society retains a persistent and stubborn type of de facto segregation between Untouchables and upper-caste Hindus.

King's trip to India altered his worldview. He adopted a more global perspective in his approach to racial conflict. He began to see a connection between people of color all over the world, struggling for basic human rights (Oates 1982, 142–144). He came to see that the struggles of blacks, Latinos, and the poor in America were inextricably linked to the struggles of Africans, Asians, and other people around the world, all fighting for freedom, dignity, and justice. He also developed a view of the interconnectedness of all people throughout the world. During his trip to India, he gave a memorable speech on world politics, declaring that the choices facing humanity in the midst of the Cold War and the Nuclear Age were no longer between violence and nonviolence, but between nonviolence and nonexistence (Miller 1984, 63). Such was King's newfound commitment to the philosophy of nonviolence. King even went so far as to suggest that India, in keeping with its Gandhian legacy, declare unilateral disarmament and demonstrate to the rest of the world that an independent country can survive and thrive without a massive military arsenal (Branch 1988, 254). However, few Indians took such a suggestion seriously—many were even put off by it—and by 1998 India had openly declared itself a nuclear weapons power.

King said his trip to India was one of the most eye-opening experiences of his life (Washington 1986, 24). Not only did the trip deepen his understanding of India and nonviolence, it also transformed him as well insofar as he tried to adopt a Gandhian lifestyle, albeit with only limited success. He tried fasting, meditation, and material dispossession. Coretta felt the changes King was going through in the early 1960s. Even though he had been very self-conscious about dressing well, he grew less concerned with clothes and his overall personal appearance. He began to exhibit an increased sense of selflessness. He spoke increasingly of ridding himself of possessions, including a fine home. This caused tension in the family since Coretta and the children did not share these sentiments. For a long time, he resisted his wife's entreaties to move from their small home into something bigger and nicer that would accommodate their growing family. Visitors were stunned to see the Kings' modest home and run-down old car. Even when he won the Nobel Peace Prize in 1964, which carried a cash award of $54,000—a considerable amount in those days—King did not live extravagantly. Against Coretta's objections, he donated the prize money to organizations in the struggle for civil rights.

King's trip to India "consummated his conversion to nonviolence" (Washington 1986, 31). His principles were solidifying. Now King was a bonafide advocate of nonviolence, philosophically committed to the method in his life and in his civil rights activism. He wrote that "the way of violence leads to bitterness in the survivors and brutality of the destroyers. But the way of nonviolence leads to redemption and the creation of the beloved community" (Washington 1986, 25).

CHAPTER 7

Kingian Principles of Nonviolence

If we are to have peace on earth, our loyalties must become ecumenical rather than sectional. Our loyalties must transcend our race, our tribe, our class and our nation; and this means we must develop a world perspective. . . . We are all caught in an inescapable network of mutuality, tied into a single garment of destiny. . . . If we are to have peace in the world, men and nations must embrace the nonviolent affirmation that ends and means must cohere.

—Martin Luther King, Jr., Christmas Eve speech, 1967

Nonviolence was not a way of life for King exactly the way it was for Gandhi. King's philosophical commitment to nonviolence did not extend to vegetarianism. King confessed to a weakness for barbecue. Additionally, although he made several attempts, King did not conduct fasts as a method of political resistance to the same extent that Gandhi did. More important, King's brand of nonviolence did not mimic Gandhi's insofar as Gandhi designed his nonviolent resistance to turn the Indian masses entirely against the British government to end British rule in India. King, by contrast, advocated use of nonviolent tactics to win rights for blacks and not to undermine the American government (Bennett 1984, 36).

Nevertheless, both King and Gandhi shared an unswerving belief that using nonviolent means to resolve social and political conflict was the only way to create a just outcome. King said that oppressed people could respond to their oppression in three ways:

1. They can acquiesce in their oppression and simply take it;
2. They can resist their oppression using violence; and
3. They can resist nonviolently.

Acquiescence was unacceptable for King because it reduced the oppressed to passive coconspirators in their own domination. Violent resistance was unacceptable because it only leads to temporary success. Nonviolent resistance was the best alternative because not only did it prove effective in creating long-term solutions, but it also fit King's moral disposition. Nonviolent resistance was "nothing less than Christianity in action . . . the Christian way of life in solving problems of human relations" (Washington 1986, 86). Later in his career, King was as devoted to the nonviolent creed as ever when he wrote in *Where Do We Go From Here?*:

> Through violence, you may murder the liar, but you cannot murder the lie, nor establish truth. . . . Darkness cannot drive out darkness: only light can do that. Hate cannot drive out hate: only love can do that. The beauty of nonviolence is that, in its own way and in its own time, it seeks to break the chain reaction of evil. (King, 1967, 62–63)

To be sure, King's philosophical views span a vast range of ideas and situations. He was a preacher with a Ph.D. after all and as such held forth on many different subjects. This chapter cannot chronicle all of King's views, so it will be confined to analyzing King's philosophical views as they pertain to nonviolence. But first, brief mention will be made of how King's views on social and economic relations became increasingly radicalized by the mid-1960s. Few in politics or the media make note of this during the annual celebration of Martin Luther King, Jr. Day, but King began calling for a kind of "democratic socialism" to be instituted in the United States to eradicate all forms of poverty in the country.

In 1967, an increasingly outspoken King called for a "revolution in values" to fight what he saw as the interconnected "triple evils" of racism, economic exploitation, and militarism (Garrow 1986, 564). Of course, he insisted that this revolution be carried out using only nonviolence. King would accept assistance from "whatever quarter" as long as they accepted nonviolence (Fairclough

1984, 234). King wanted the revolution in values centered on changing society from a materialistically obsessed, or "thing-oriented," society to a "person-oriented" society (King 1967, 186). According to King,

> One of the great problems of mankind is that we suffer from a poverty of the spirit which stands in glaring contrast to our scientific and technological abundance. The richer we have become materially, the poorer we have become morally and spiritually. . . . So much of modern life can be summarized in that great phrase from Henry David Thoreau: "improved means to an unimproved end." (171)

In conjunction with his call for a revolution in values, King increased his criticism of capitalist society because of what he felt capitalism did to the human personality, especially for people of color. In focusing his critique on two of the most basic tenets of capitalism, King said the U.S. economy was too profit-centered and too property-centered and not person-centered enough (Garrow 1986, 581). King felt there was something terribly wrong with capitalism, as if it were the common denominator linking racism, economic exploitation, and militarism (Fairclough 1984, 238). King disparaged an economic system that contributed to the creation of "islands of poverty" amid "oceans of plenty." But King's critique of capitalism did not make him out to be a Marxist, as many of his detractors, including FBI Director J. Edgar Hoover, claimed. King's increasing concern for the poor and his growing hostility toward what he considered the negative hallmarks of capitalist society, such as racism, exploitation, and materialism, owed more to the influences of the social gospel rather than to any Marxist interpretation to which he may have been exposed (Fairclough 1984, 239).

Toward the end of his life, King became increasingly critical of privileged groups, calling on them to give up some of their wealth. By the end of 1966, just over one year before his assassination, King began remarking that a majority of whites were racists and only a minority of them genuinely wanted authentic equality (Fairclough 1984, 235). King became exasperated with whites, who seemed more interested in protecting their privileged position than in helping fulfill America's dream for all its citizens:

> Why do white people seem to find it so difficult to understand that the Negro is sick and tired of having reluctantly parceled out

to him those rights and privileges which all others receive upon birth or entry in America? I never cease to wonder at the amazing presumption of much of white society, assuming that they have the right to bargain with the Negro for his freedom. (Oates 1982, 302)

King's call for a "revolution in values" and "democratic socialism" was met with intense criticism by his detractors as un-American. It earned him special attention from FBI Director J. Edgar Hoover, who had King's phones wiretapped wherever he went. However, King pointed out that the United States already had a kind of socialism, but only for the rich, in the form of corporate subsidies and tax breaks (Fairclough 1984, 241). To achieve his revolution in values, King called for a nonviolent "Poor Peoples' Campaign," in which whites from Appalachia, blacks from the South, and Native Americans from the West would join together and gather in Washington, DC, and bring government operations to a halt with massive marches, protests, and sit-ins. King planned to launch a massive nonviolent civil disobedience campaign that would channel the poor peoples' frustration away from looting and burning and toward something more constructive. To do that, King said, "We've got to find a method that will disrupt our cities if necessary, create the crisis that will force the nation to look at the situation . . . and yet at the same time not destroy life or property" (Garrow 1986, 580). Alas, King was assassinated before his plans for the Poor Peoples' Campaign reached fruition.

KING'S PHILOSOPHICAL VIEWS ON NONVIOLENCE

In his acceptance speech for the Nobel Peace Prize, King said that "nonviolence is the answer to the crucial political and moral questions of our time" (King 1964). Toward that end, he tried to fashion his philosophical commitment to nonviolence into a practical strategy of action that would not only be effective, but also appeal to a broad cross section of people. Toward that end, he developed a basic five-point program of nonviolence that combined his philosophical beliefs with the desire to put forth a workable strategy. First, King argued that nonviolence was not for cowards. To be sure, it took great courage to place oneself, unarmed and seemingly defenseless, in front of a gang of armed white racists or heavily armed, horse-mounted police officers and state troopers wielding billy clubs and truncheons. Second, King insisted that nonviolence was not to be used to defeat or humiliate opponents but rather to win their friendship and understanding. King understood that converting opponents to his cause was far more effective than defeating them because defeated opponents would only seethe in defeat and bide their time until they could mount a vengeful counterattack. Third, and in conjunction with the above, King counseled that nonviolence should be used to fight evil and not the person caught up in those evil forces. King was an eternal optimist about human personality and believed that all people were redeemable and that nonviolence was the catalyst for that redemption. Fourth, nonviolence was beneficial because it avoided the "external" or physical harm that violence inflicted on the body and also because it avoided "internal" or psychological harm to the spirit. Finally, King argued for a nonviolent remedy because the forces of the universe bend toward justice. Equipped with this knowledge, nonviolent activists would be able to accept pain and suffering without retaliating because they knew their efforts would ultimately be rewarded (Herman 1998, 129–130).

King did not acquire his philosophical views on nonviolence haphazardly. Rather, his views on the subject were the result of a careful, deliberative study and practice that occurred throughout the course of his adult life. King's was not a static, closed mind. His views on society and nonviolence's place in it were flexible, developmental, and adaptive. However, that is not to say that his commitment to nonviolence was fickle. It was not. King's belief in and emphasis on nonviolence was unequivocal. And nonviolence did not mean nonresistance, as it was so often misrepresented in the media and even in educational programs. According to King, nonviolence "is not passive resistance to evil; it is active nonviolent resistance to evil" (Oates 1982, 78).

King's philosophical views on nonviolence centered on several key elements: the beloved community, the principle of agape, justice and just laws, civil disobedience and self-suffering, and means and ends. This chapter will now discuss each of these concepts in detail, followed by a brief section on King's views of nonviolence in world politics and his response to his black critics who called for "black power" instead of love. The choice, as he liked to put it, was not between violence and nonviolence but between nonviolence and nonexistence. "We still have a choice," King said, "between nonviolent coexistence or violent co-annihilation" (King 1967, 191).

The Beloved Community

King encouraged people to commit themselves to creating a "thou-centered" society or one that values the other as much as, if not more than, the self. This was the crux of King's greatest dream, attaining the beloved community. King's beloved community is a "community" because the people are commonly invested with shared vows, creeds, dogmas, and beliefs. And it is "beloved" because this sharing is based on a genuine commitment to loving one another (Herman 1998, 116).

For King, the beloved community could only be achieved through a peaceful and harmonious integration of whites and blacks, poor and rich, Jews and gentiles, and so forth. The beloved community and the true peace that it would bring is not achieved simply by eliminating the presence of a negative, evil force such as segregation. Rather, this must be accompanied by the presence of a positive force, one that would ensure justice, goodwill, and brotherhood. The key to creating this beloved community was integration, which was far more than merely ending segregation.

King believed that simply ending segregation or even achieving desegregation, would not go far enough toward building his beloved community. In typical Hegelian fashion, King saw the thesis of segregation placed in opposition to the antithesis of desegregation and called instead for integration. Integration not only fit King's Hegelian approach to social conflict, it also fit his Christian teaching and belief. Integration was a much greater and positive social force than desegregation because the former indicated a positive acceptance of blacks and welcoming them as full equals in the total range of human activities in American society, including voting, higher education, and advanced employment (Herman 1998, 140). According to King, integration is creative, profound, and positive because it means the open and willful acceptance of blacks and not just the grudging acquiescence to their inclusion that desegregation implies. Segregation is an evil system that is diametrically opposed to the human personality because it substitutes an "I–it" relationship between people for an "I–thou" one. This reduces blacks to the condition of "things," such as a pet, rather than raises them up to the level of human or person and everything that implies. This denies blacks more than their freedom; it denies them their very lives.

Although desegregation is a good, it is a "negative" good that is not enough because all it does is eliminate the evil system of segregation. Desegregation merely ends segregation's lawful practice of racial exclusion but does nothing to replace it with its positive counterpart. If desegregation is all that occurs, then we are left with only a hollow shell of a beloved community because the emptiness and shallowness will remain; there will be physical proximity only between whites and blacks and no spiritual affinity. According to King, all desegregation does is bring "elbows together," while keeping "hearts apart" (Washington 1986, 118). Integration, on the other hand, "unchains the spirit" and recognizes the connection between all people (Washington 1986, 121). According to King, "Men often hate each other because they fear each other; they fear each other because they do not know each other; they do not know each other because they cannot communicate; they cannot communicate because they are separated" (Cone 1993, 36). According to James Cone, this statement represents the heart of King's integrationist philosophy.

King's emphasis on a thou-centered society frequently found expression in his speeches and sermons when he would say that he could not be everything he ought to be unless "thou" (or you) are able to become everything "thou" ought to be. For King, all humanity was bound up in an inescapable web of mutuality—he liked to call it a "single garment of destiny"—in which all people must live together and ensure the healing and growth of everyone else. King referred to this as the solidarity of the human family (Herman 1999, 138). He liked to express his concern for thou in a sermon he gave regarding the Good Samaritan. While traveling the dangerous and treacherous road between Jerusalem and Jericho, the Good Samaritan happened upon a man who had been beaten and robbed. King admired the Good Samaritan for stopping and aiding the wounded man, asking not "If I stop to help this man, what will happen to me?" but rather, "If I do not stop to help this man, what will happen to him?" King called this "dangerous altruism," which is risking your own life to save another (King 1963, 19–20).

Only full racial integration can actually uplift all human personalities and lead to creation of the beloved community. And the only way to achieve this beloved community, the only way to uphold and nurture this human family, the only way to achieve harmonious integration of the human family is through nonviolence. To be sure, the beloved community could not be obtained using violent means since that would be the very negation of the concept. Nonviolence and concern for the other is at the core of King's beloved community because they were critical elements for resolving conflicts and for repairing any rupture that might tear at the fabric of society. Not only was nonviolence a healthy method for expressing discontent, it also helped foster the beloved community because it saved people from letting their anger degenerate into

> morbid bitterness and hatred which distorts the personality and scars the soul. The beauty of nonviolence is that you can struggle without hating and it can re-establish the broken community. . . . We adopt nonviolence because our end is a community at peace with itself. (Washington 1986, 102–103)

King's desire for and vision of the beloved community was most powerfully expressed with his famous "I Have a Dream" speech during the March on Washington in August 1963. The March on Washington brought together 250,000 people, one-third of whom were white, to the nation's capital to peacefully march for freedom, jobs, equality, and racial justice. It was the largest and most peaceful integrated gathering of people in Washington, DC. The March itself was not King's brainchild, nor was King's organization, the Southern Christian Leadership Conference, central to the March's organization. Rather, Asa Philip Randolph, who King referred to as the "Dean" of Negro leaders, had the idea for such a march years before it actually occurred. And Bayard Rustin was the prime organizer of the event. But King's presence as the keynote speaker at the foot of the Lincoln Memorial cemented King's role as the moral and spiritual leader of the Civil Rights Movement. And, after the eloquent speech King gave that day, he was established as one of American history's greatest orators.

The "Dream" speech is rich with metaphors. For instance, King said that the authors of the Declaration of Independence and the U.S. Constitution had issued a "promissory note" of freedom and liberty for all Americans but when blacks had tried to cash their note, it came back marked "insufficient funds." He insisted that "now is the time" for speedy action on behalf of black civil rights and warned against accepting "the tranquilizing drug of gradualism." He cautioned supporters not to

> satisfy our thirst for freedom by drinking from the cup of bitterness and hatred. We must forever conduct our struggle on the high plane of dignity and discipline. We must not allow our creative protest to degenerate into physical violence. Again and again, we must rise to the majestic heights of meeting physical force with soul force. (Carson 1998, 224)

But the driving theme of King's speech was the "dream," of which he spoke so eloquently and which so marvelously illustrated his vision of the beloved community. Using alliteration, cadence, rhythm, and anaphora (repeating the same word or phrase over and over) that many black preachers were known for, King made an impassioned plea not only for black–white integration, but also for the fellowship of all humanity. King put down his prepared speech and began to ad lib and drum home a theme he had spoken of previously:

> I have a dream that one day this nation will rise up and live out the true meaning of its creed . . . that all men are created equal. I have a dream that one day on the red hills of Georgia the sons of former slaves and the sons of former slave owners will be able to sit down together at the table of brotherhood. I have a dream that one day even the State of Mississippi . . . will be transformed into an oasis of freedom and justice. I have a dream today! I have a dream that . . . one day right there in Alabama little black boys and little black girls will be able to join hands with little white boys and white girls as sisters and brothers. I have a dream that my four little children will one day live in a nation where they will not be judged by the color of their skin but by the content of their character. I have a dream today! (Carson 1998, 226)

King concluded his speech by calling on all Americans to come together and fulfill his vision of the beloved community. Again, using the cadences and anaphora of black preachers, King proclaimed:

> Let freedom ring from the mighty mountains of New York. Let freedom ring from the heightening Alleghenies of Pennsylvania. Let freedom ring from the snow-capped Rockies of Colorado. Let freedom ring from the curvaceous slopes of California. But not only that. Let freedom ring from Lookout Mountain of Georgia. Let freedom ring from every hill and molehill of Mississippi, from every mountainside, let freedom ring! And when this happens, when we allow freedom to ring, when we let it ring from every village and every hamlet, from every state and every city, we will be able to speed up that day when all of God's children, black men and white men, Jews and Gentiles, Protestants and Catholics, will be able to join hands and sing in the words of the old Negro Spiritual, "Free at last, free at last. Thank God Almighty, we are free at last!" (Carson 1998, 227)

The Principle of Agape

King adopted the idea of 'agape,' a Greek word meaning love. But agape did not mean love in the romantic, intimate way. Nor did it mean love in the way family members feel toward each other.

Rather, for King, agape meant a kind of disinterested love for all: "It is a love that seeks nothing in return" (King 1957). Agape is a realization and recognition that all peoples' lives are fully intertwined with one another as part of God's way and as part of a single process binding all of humanity. For King, agape did not mean that we must like our enemies or those who oppress us. He often said it was pretty hard to like some of the white segregationists in the South. Rather, agape was a way to forgiveness and restoration of the beloved community involving harmonious relationships with all God's children (Oates 1982, 33). He encouraged his followers to have agape for all people, even those who beat or otherwise oppress them because he was convinced of its redemptive power to repair a broken community: "*Agape* is an understanding, creative, redemptive goodwill toward all men. It enables us to love every man not because we like him or because his ways appeal to us but because God loves him" (Ansbro 1982, 8). King put it well when he said in a sermon that agape is when "you love those who don't move you. You love those that you don't like. You love those whose ways are distasteful to you. You love every man because God loves him!" (Branch 1988, 774).

King would exhort his followers to "hate the sin, but love the sinner." King asked his followers to remember that, even though they may not actually like their white oppressors, all people had value and must be loved. Moreover, even in victory, such as when Montgomery, Alabama, was ordered to desegregate its buses after a yearlong nonviolent bus boycott and court battle, King urged people to think of the result not as a defeat of whites or even as a "victory for 50,000 negroes in Montgomery" or "16 million negroes of America." Rather, he said, "That was a victory for justice and goodwill" (*The Speeches of Martin Luther King* 1988). Here, agape insists that it is not people whose defeat is sought. Rather, it is injustice, which breaks the society and separates people, that is the target for defeat. Again, his Personalist beliefs about the worth and dignity of all human personality precluded him from seeking to defeat people: they were all redeemable. King preached that even in the people who hate you the most, "there is some good there" (King 1957).

In a famous speech King gave after the victory in Montgomery, he insisted that nonviolent resistance in Montgomery was not based on winning rights for blacks, but for achieving friendship with those denying those rights (Oates 1982, 116). For King, it was not just important to give the appearance of being magnanimous in victory; it was vital to distinguish between men and the evil acts that an evil system might compel them to commit. For King, an evil, or sinful, act did not make a person evil; it was the evil and injustice that needed to be defeated, not the men and women who committed the acts, for they, like all people, were capable of redemption and should be treated thusly.

According to King's understanding of agape, when you love others, that gives your personality value and when others love you that gives them value. But agape is not love based on romance, kinship, or friendship. Rather, agape is "understanding [and] creative, redemptive, goodwill to all men. . . . A love which seeks nothing in return . . . the love of God operating in the human heart" (Washington 1986, 46). Ultimately, a man possessed of agape loves others not because he likes them and not because that person's ways appeal to him and not even because that person can help or protect him in some way. A person loves others not only because God loves them, but also because it is the only way to build a peaceful society. In his Nobel speech, King said,

> If [peace] is to be achieved, man must evolve for all human conflict a method which rejects revenge, aggression and retaliation. The foundation of such a method is love. (King 1964)

Justice and Just Laws

King believed that justice was critical to any country's growth and stability. Without justice, the door will always remain open for potentially violent conflicts to erupt. King argued that nonviolence thrives best in a climate of justice, but the potential for violence will grow to the extent that injustice prevails in a community. The more injustice in a community, the greater the potential for violence. "If a person's pentup emotions are not released nonviolently," King said, "history shows they'll be violently released" (Washington 1986, 362–363). King also warned of the increased possibility of a violent explosion if blacks, especially those residing in the inner cities, continued to live in horrendous poverty amid an incredibly affluent society: "No nation can suffer any greater tragedy than to cause millions of its citizens to feel that they have no stake in their own society" (Washington 1986, 360).

King questioned why whites were more interested in maintaining order than in achieving justice (Garrow 1986, 476). He cautioned that "injustice anywhere is a threat to justice everywhere," implying that order and justice were two sides of the same coin. In a thinly veiled reference to white moderates and liberals, he said, "Too many others have been more cautious than courageous" (King 1964, 94). During negotiations regarding demonstrations in Chicago for better housing, King stunned his audience with a bold and beautiful statement about how important achieving justice was to the black community:

> The basic thing is justice. We want justice. . . . Our humble marches have revealed a cancer. We have not used rocks. We have not used bottles [as did King's opponents]. And no one today, no one who has spoken, has condemned those that have used violence. . . . Maybe we should begin condemning the robber, and not the robbed. . . . No one here has talked about the beauty of our marches, the love of our marches [or] the hatred we're absorbing. Let's hear more about the people who perpetrated the violence. (Garrow 1986, 513)

King's words were so compassionate and stunning that those in the meeting fell into a shameful silence. Moreover, in a *Meet the Press* television interview, King said nonviolent demonstrations do not solve any social problems but can dramatize and call attention to the existence of a social ill that would otherwise be easily ignored (Washington 1986, 386). King was showing that one of the main strengths of nonviolent resistance was its ability to expose an injustice and bring it to the surface, despite efforts by those who would try to conceal the injustice.

Like Gandhi, Thoreau, and many others, King believed that people of conscience had a duty to actively undermine unjust laws because if they did not, they were then collaborators in perpetuating the injustice. But how is one to know which laws are unjust and which are not? Is it really wise to declare that we shall obey some laws and violate others? Couldn't anyone break the law and then justify the crime by claiming the law was unjust? Couldn't criminal behavior be rationalized in the name of nonviolence and civil disobedience? In short, didn't King open himself up to criticism that he was an anarchist because he advocated breaking laws, lawlessness in fact?

These were strong criticisms leveled against King and others who advocated civil disobedience. But King made powerful and convincing arguments in his defense of breaking unjust laws. Once, while in Chicago protesting against overpriced and unsanitary housing for inner city blacks, King collected all the tenants' rents in a housing project he had moved into and refused to turn the money over to the landlords. King argued that withholding the tenants' rents—in effect breaking the law—was a "moral" issue of justice for the tenants that outweighed the "legal" issue of the landlords who deserved to be paid rent for their properties (Garrow 1986, 476).

Moreover, in the single most eloquent and influential statement to come out of the Civil Rights Movement, King delivered an amazing and powerful answer to his critics—and from inside the confines of a Birmingham jail cell no less. King's famous "Letter from Birmingham Jail" is one of the most profound statements ever written by an unjustly imprisoned man. Interestingly, the letter was penned over several days in the margins of newspapers, legal pads, and other scraps of paper given to King by sympathetic inmates as well as those visiting him. King's aides smuggled the bits of paper out of his jail cell after each visit. Clarence Jones, King's attorney in Birmingham, thought at first that King had lost his grip on reality: over several days, all King kept telling Jones was "I need more paper" (Frady 2002, 111). But his aides quickly realized that they were ferrying a seminal and historical document.

In the "Letter," King invoked some old and some new themes to weave a complex and brilliant web of religious, political, and philosophical arguments that explained his views about justice and breaking unjust laws. He invoked great philosophers, such as Socrates, and great religious figures, such as St. Thomas Aquinas, to defend his civil disobedience. He argued that the Civil Rights Movement was an essential expression of the American Dream because the treatment and condition of blacks in America was tied directly to America's destiny (Bosmajian 1984, 132–135).

In responding to several white clergymen in Alabama, who had published a joint letter accusing King of being an "outsider" and an "extremist," King defended his actions in Birmingham. To the charge of being an outsider, he responded that he was invited there, that he was an American and thus had the right to come to Birmingham, and that, like Paul the Apostle, he was, as a man of the cloth, called to a place where injustice existed. To the charge of being an extremist, he argued that the "question is not whether we will be extremists, but what kind of extremists we will be. Will we be extremists for hate or for love?" (King 1964b, 88). King acknowledged that he held extreme views and advocated extreme change in America's South, but he likened his extremism to that of Christ and said, like Christ, he resisted from a position of nonviolence and love, which placed him on solid moral ground.

The white clergymen blamed King for all the trouble in Birmingham, but King said blaming him for resisting injustice was like blaming a victim for being robbed. King said, "[W]e who engage in nonviolent direct action are not the creators of tension. We merely bring to the surface the hidden tension that is already alive" (King 1964b, 88). He also said:

> Our nonviolent direct action program has as its objective not the creation of tension, but the *surfacing* of tension already present. We set out to precipitate a crisis situation that must open the door to negotiation. . . . Constructive crisis and tension are necessary for growth. (Washington 1986, 350)

King also responded to his critics who asserted that his civil disobedience undermined law and order. How could a society preserve order, they asked, if its religious and spiritual leaders advocate breaking the laws? Regardless of whether King advocated violence or nonviolence, they insisted, law-breaking posed a threat to public safety. King answered this attack by citing biblical exegesis as well as making other fine points. King's letter defended his advocacy of law-breaking by explaining that it was not The Rule of Law in general that he wished to undermine, but rather individual, unjust laws in particular that must be disobeyed in order to establish justice:

> The answer is to be found in two types of laws. There are *just* laws and there are *unjust* laws. I would agree with St. Augustine that an "unjust law is no law at all."
>   Now, what is the difference between the two? How does one determine whether a law is just or unjust? A just law is a man-made code that squares with the moral law or the law of God. An unjust law is a code that is out of harmony with the moral law. To put it in the terms of Saint Thomas Aquinas, an unjust law is a human law that is not rooted in eternal and natural law. Any law that uplifts human personality is just. Any law that degrades human personality is unjust. All segregation statutes are unjust because segregation distorts the soul and damages the personality. (Carson 1998, 93)

It was a brilliant argument that not only appealed to his critics' *religious* sense of right and wrong, but also to their sense of fairness. King went on to argue that unjust laws are those that are "inflicted" on a minority that had no part in creating that law. Since blacks were denied the chance to participate in the legislative process that yielded segregation laws, they should not feel bound by them.

Overall, the "Letter" was a masterful, yet sensitive, rebuke to King's fellow clergymen. On the one hand, King refuted—with eloquent prose and cogent arguments—the criticisms leveled against him. On the other hand, he used a bit of sardonic wit to chastise his fellow clergymen and remind them of their differing situations when he apologized for writing a letter

> that is much too long to take your precious time. I can assure you that it would have been much shorter if I had been writing from a comfortable desk, but what else is there to do when you are alone for days in the dull monotony of a narrow jail cell? (Washington 1986, 302)

Civil Disobedience and Self-Suffering

To fight injustice and to create a just society, King advocated civil disobedience against unjust laws. Recall that civil disobedience is the open and willful defiance of an unjust law while expressing fealty, or loyalty, to The Rule of Law. A civil disobedient does not break the law because he or she is opposed to laws in general; rather, he or she breaks only those laws deemed unjust while accepting punishment.

Self-suffering, the willingness to have pain inflicted on oneself and avoid inflicting pain on others, is what distinguishes the civil disobedient from the "outlaw." And that is the crux of King's civil disobedience: openly defying laws considered unjust and willingly accepting the punishment and the accompanying suffering. King wrote in his "Letter from Birmingham Jail":

> In no sense do I advocate evading or defying the law, as would the rabid segregationist. That would lead to anarchy. One who breaks an unjust law must do so openly, lovingly, and with a willingness to accept the penalty. I submit that an individual who breaks a law that conscience tells him is unjust, and who willingly accepts the penalty of imprisonment in order to arouse the conscience of the community over its injustice, is in reality expressing the highest respect for law. (Carson 1998, 194)

If a person breaks the law and seeks to do so undetected or seeks to avoid punishment, that is not civil disobedience, rather it is criminal behavior and that is not what King advocates. The nonviolent activist who commits civil disobedience knows and expects that punishment is coming. The very act of punishment for violating an unjust law plays right into the hands of the nonviolent resister because it draws dramatic attention to a disgraceful situation. This puts the civil resister in an advantageous position. If the government does not react to the law-breaking, its authority will be undermined, thus inviting other challenges. Yet, to throw a nonviolent activist in jail for disobeying an unjust law—one that does not "square" with God's moral code—is to expose the government as oppressive. It places the government in an awkward no-win situation.

King knew that going to jail was a necessary component of the Civil Rights Movement, despite the fact that he remained intimidated by the prospect of imprisonment (Frady 2002, 75). "Jail-going wasn't easy for him," said his wife Coretta, "because he never liked to be alone" (Phillips 1999, 107). But he knew jail-going was necessary because it signified the willingness to suffer for a cause and King believed in the redemptive power of unearned suffering (King 1963, 141). When people fight in a just cause and open themselves to unearned suffering, it not only has an empowering effect on the sufferer but also has a transforming effect on the person inflicting the suffering. It works on their mind, makes them wonder, raises curiosity about their commitment and fosters doubt about their own cruel behavior:

> [T]his willingness to suffer, and this refusal to hit back will soon cause the oppressor to be ashamed of his own methods and this will lead to that day when we in America can live together in Christian brotherhood. (Oates 1982, 106)

King even quoted Gandhi regarding the redemptive power of unearned suffering when he said that "rivers of blood may have to flow before we gain our freedom, but it must be our blood" (Oates 1982, 79). Furthermore, King said that "if physical death is the price that some must pay to free their children from a permanent life of psychological death, then nothing could be more Christian" (Washington 1986, 10).

Additionally, King distinguished his brand of civil disobedience from what he referred to as his racist opponents' practice of "uncivil disobedience," which was breaking the law in order to uphold the unjust system of segregation or otherwise deny blacks their rights. King advocated a form of civil disobedience whereby the civil resister openly accepts punishment for breaking the law. By contrast, King chastised his segregationist opponents who, in the name of civil disobedience and standing up for what they thought was "just," broke the law yet did so neither in the spirit of self-suffering nor in the spirit of openly and courageously accepting the punishment. Rather, when these "uncivil resisters" broke the law, they did so at another's expense like when they beat or murdered civil rights workers and thus did not invite the suffering on themselves. Moreover, they did not break laws in open defiance, welcoming the penalty; rather they "seek to defy, evade and circumvent the law and they are unwilling to accept the penalty" (Washington 1986, 165). Segregationists who broke laws were not practicing civil disobedience at all; they were merely criminals whose acts were not intended to awaken the conscience of the nation but rather to instill fear and panic in their opponents.

Means and Ends

King's often-repeated comment that the ends are preexistent in the means (Washington 1986, 45) sums up perfectly his views on using proper and pure means to create a just end. Like Gandhi, King was unwavering on this position, insisting that his followers adhere to a consistent principle of noninjury. Purity of means was essential to King's philosophical outlook because his ultimate goal was the beloved community as described earlier. King saw no way of creating the beloved community using violent, or even deceitful, means. The ultimate goal of the Civil Rights Movement extended far beyond ending segregation. The real goal was not to defeat the white man, but to "awaken a sense of shame within the oppressor and challenge his false sense of superiority. . . . The *end* is reconciliation; the *end* is redemption; the *end is the creation of the beloved community*" (Garrow 1986, 81). Much like Gandhi, this type of reasoning actually elevates purity of means to the same level of ends, thus rendering means and ends indistinguishable from one another.

King said, "I have tried to make clear that it is wrong to use immoral means to attain moral ends. But now I must affirm that it is just as wrong or perhaps even moreso, to use moral means to preserve immoral ends" (King 1964b, 98). King observed that his racist, segregationist opponents started advocating the same "nonviolent" means he was, but only to uphold and strengthen the system of segregation. This forced him to acknowledge that there was a flip side to his exhortations about using pure means to derive pure ends, namely, that pure means could, in fact, be used to preserve unjust ends. That is what he saw some of his segregationist opponents doing when they defended their use of nonviolent tactics, such as business boycotts, to pressure white-owned businesses not to accede to calls for integration. King had to modify his message to say that pure means do not automatically create pure ends.

NONVIOLENCE IN WORLD POLITICS

Early in his career, King was skeptical of using nonviolence in world politics. He felt that nonviolent resistance between individuals or small groups in the same community would be effective, but he was unconvinced of its utility on the world stage, say, for instance, in conflicts between countries. King had said that war could serve a "negative" good and he offered the American Revolution as an example. War, therefore, could be used in some instances to prevent the spread of an evil force and war might be preferable to surrendering to an evil, totalitarian system. However, King's views on this matter were not static. After King earned the Nobel Peace Prize and after his trips overseas and further introduction into world politics, he changed his mind about the utility of violence and nonviolence in world politics. King argued that with the advent of modern weapons, such as nuclear bombs, no war could ever be limited to stopping evil only. Wars in the modern age would instead cause far more harm than any possible good. As a result, King urged an end to all arms races and an end to war as an instrument of politics, arguing that war could never again serve even as a negative good. King used his stature to urge world leaders to find an alternative to war.

King's entry into world politics did not stop with general statements about the obsolescence of war. Rather, King spoke out early and often about his opposition to U.S. involvement in Vietnam. King was the most prominent civil rights figure to voice opposition to American involvement in the war (Mack 2003, 109). As a Christian preacher who believed his philosophical commitment to nonviolence could not stop at the water's edge, King condemned the U.S.

war in Vietnam. He saw a connection between the war, class, and race and saw war as an enemy of the poor, not just those in the United States, but in the world in general.

In criticizing the U.S. role in Vietnam, King said:

> I know that I could never again raise my voice against the violence of the oppressed in the ghettos without having first spoken clearly to the greatest purveyor of violence in the world today—my own government. (Frady 2002, 185–186)

This proved risky for King and his role in the Civil Rights Movement because President Johnson, whose Vietnam policy King was so vehemently attacking, had been sympathetic to blacks' struggles. King's advisers and many other prominent African Americans, such as the NAACP's Roy Wilkins, the Urban League's Whitney Young, and even Nobel Laureate Ralph Bunche, urged King to refrain from getting involved in attacking the government's Vietnam policy. They told him foreign policy was not his area of expertise and that criticizing the government could only hurt his standing with President Johnson, whose help he needed in the struggle against state and local politicians in the South.

He insisted that he could not ignore speaking out against injustice, no matter where he saw it. Moreover, King used an eloquent metaphor to refute his detractors who were urging him to stay out of the Vietnam morass. To those who urged him to stick to civil rights, he replied that he had fought too long and too hard against segregation in public facilities to segregate his own mind when it came to moral concerns. King saw it as hypocritical to remain silent on one injustice (Vietnam) while speaking out against another (segregation). King once told an old friend, "[W]hen I say [SCLC—the civil rights organization he headed] is nonviolent, I mean nonviolent all the way. . . . Never could I advocate nonviolence in this country and not advocate nonviolence for the whole world. . . . That's my philosophy . . . I don't believe in the death and killing on either side, no matter who's heading it up. . . . Nonviolence is my stand and I'll die for that stand" (Garrow 1986, 573).

King also felt there were links between colonialism and economic imperialism on the one hand and racism and segregation on the other hand, not least because they disrespected human dignity and distorted human personality. King drew parallels between the condition of blacks in the United States and blacks in South Africa where a small minority of whites oppressed and segregated the vast majority of blacks. As King's views evolved in the 1960s, not only did his social views become more radical—witness his call for "democratic socialism"—but he also came to believe in the interconnectedness of all people in a single "world house" (King 1967, 167). King equated the Civil Rights Movement of blacks in the United States with freedom movements worldwide, in Asia, Africa, and elsewhere. He began to sense how domestic issues and influences did not stop at the water's edge, but rather that events in one country had impacts on events in others. He recognized the importance, therefore, of transforming what he called a "worldwide neighborhood" into a "worldwide brotherhood" when he said to the world that "together we must learn to live like brothers or we will be forced to perish as fools" (King 1967, 171).

KING'S VIEWS ON BLACK POWER

Although King did not support the black nationalist philosophy, which came to be known as "Black Power," it is important to make brief mention of this concept and how King dealt with this very popular slogan. Black Power was coined by black nationalists and first used in the Civil Rights Movement as a rallying cry by black nationalist Stokely Carmichael and his Student Nonviolent Coordinating Committee (SNCC) while he and other young black activists from the SNCC were demonstrating alongside King and his more moderate SCLC. Carmichael's cry for Black Power was a militant call by black nationalists for blacks to take an aggressive, confrontational approach toward whites. Black Power was a radical rallying cry that proved divisive because it unsettled sympathetic whites who worked alongside blacks in the Civil Rights Movement. Moreover, when the cry for Black Power rang out, King was embarrassed because it gave the impression that he was condoning a demonstration with a slogan that contradicted his emphasis on the beloved community and integration.

King understood the popularity of Black Power and tried to explain, on the one hand, why it was so popular among so many young blacks and, on the other hand, why it was so completely wrong for what he was trying to achieve. In his book *Where Do We Go From Here?* (1967), King explained that Black Power was popular because it gave voice to the despair and frustration blacks felt in the face of America's broken promise of equality. Despite King's promises that it would not take long for blacks to attain their rights, blacks' economic and social condition was no better off some 10 years later. Blacks were growing impatient about the lack of real progress and King did accept responsibility for their restlessness. Second, King also recognized the appeal of Black Power because it sought remedies through black independence and self-sufficiency. Third, King understood Black Power's psychological appeal to so many young black males because it helped raise their sense of pride, manhood, and self-respect (King 1967, 32–36).

While King condemned the violence that black youths committed, he tried to explain why so many succumbed to this temptation. He cited their justification for rioting, which came from Franz Fanon, a famous African radical who wrote that violence can have a positive, cleansing effect on a victimized population. King acknowledged Fanon's thesis, admitting that violence could have a kind of orgiastic effect on the oppressed. But King countered that nonviolent resistance is actually better in this regard because it can produce the exact same cleansing effect, but without the destructive effects of violence (Washington 1986, 322). King also challenged the youths' argument that their rioting helped them overcome their fear of whites. King asserted that after all the rioting, blacks were just as afraid of the white power structure as they ever were, only now their own neighborhoods were in a shambles. "Black militancy," said King, "speaks more of fear than it does of confidence" (Washington 1986, 323).

King saw Black Power as a pessimistic, unhopeful philosophy born of despair and thus bound to lose. He decried Black Power for its negative, separatist connotations, which seemed to push the goal of black domination rather than black equality. King also condemned Black Power as self-contradicting because, on the one hand, Black Power rejects white culture and white values, yet, on the other hand, Black Power militants favored using tactics, such as force of arms, that represented the very worst white culture had to offer. Ultimately, King argued, blacks need whites and whites need blacks because "we are bound together in a single garment of destiny" (King 1967, 52). King suggested an alternative marching slogan, such as "Black Consciousness" or "Black Equality," which still emphasized pride and love of one's race but did not suggest the intention of black domination and possible violence that the phrase Black Power seemed to advocate.

Commensurate with his views on Black Power, King also addressed the Black Nationalist Movement's call for a return to Africa as the only way African Americans could achieve their full rights, dignity, and potential. But King was against this sentiment, arguing that returning to Africa was like running away from the problem and not confronting the injustice where it was occurring, in the United States: "we are American citizens, and we deserve our rights in this nation" (Oates 1982, 118). In a similar vein, King also argued that African Americans, since they were a product of two different worlds—the developed Western countries and the less-wealthy African continent—were in a unique position to act as a vital link, bridging the gaps between Western and African culture. Again, Hegel's influence on King is revealed by his desire to synthesize disparate cultures, regions, and languages. On the one hand, blacks identify with Africa and their African heritage. On the other hand, American blacks are fully American in their language, education, and attitudes "so, although in one sense we are neither, in another sense, we are both Americans and Africans. Our very bloodlines are a mixture" (Washington 1986, 318). King felt black Americans were in a unique position to serve as the catalyst for saving not only the soul of the United States, but the rest of the world as well.

NONVIOLENT STRATEGY

King had a philosophical commitment to nonviolence that encompassed his entire life. He said his experience during the Montgomery Bus Boycott (see Chapter 8) did more to clarify his views of nonviolence than all the books he had read:

> As the days unfolded, I became more and more convinced of [nonviolence's] power. Living through the actual experience of the protest, nonviolence became more than a method to which I gave intellectual assent, it became a way of life. (Phillips 1999, 56)

But this philosophical commitment was manifested in a strategy of political action that would help King accomplish his goals while remaining true to his principles. Toward that end, King recognized the importance of wielding power in political and social conflicts. But for King, power was not to be wielded through the barrel of a gun, but through the right and just exercise of nonviolent direct action: "nonviolence is power, but it is the right and good use of power" (King 1967, 62). Moreover, power was to be exercised with a loving hand because "power without love is reckless and love without power is sentimental" (Garrow 1986, 564). Further, King emphasized the power of love and its transforming and redemptive qualities: "I still believe that love is the most durable power in the world" (Washington 1986, 11). One of King's major mottoes during protests and marches was "freedom and justice through Love" (Washington 1986, 140).

In a 1960 *Progressive Magazine* article, King argued the appeal of nonviolence based on six basic premises. First, while nonviolent resistance demonstrated blacks' wish to change society, it showed no desire to use or tolerate the use of force. Second, nonviolence was appealing because it denied that vengeance for the oppression blacks suffered in the past was what motivated blacks in the Civil Rights Movement. Rather, nonviolence showed a new spirit of love, coupled with determination to win blacks' civil rights. Third, nonviolence was a powerful way to bring to action a great multitude in confronting the oppressive acts of the majority. Fourth, nonviolent resistance recognized the need to create discord and reveal pre-existing tensions that would lead to changes in the community but without destroying the community's fabric. Fifth, nonviolent resistance by blacks appealed to the emotional sensibilities of significant portions of the white community, not least of whom were the white liberals who sympathized with blacks' plight, but certainly opposed blacks using violent revolt to acquire their rights. Finally, nonviolent resistance in the face of violent attacks and oppression by the segregationists discredited the white power structure and cast doubt not only on their methods but also on their position, leaving them bewildered and panicky in the face of this new "marvelous" technique (Washington 1986, 97).

Many civil rights activists who came before King observed what Gandhi had accomplished using nonviolence in India and considered whether blacks in the United States could successfully adopt such a strategy. While many considered and then dismissed a nonviolent strategy for blacks as unworkable, others, such as Asa Philip Randolph and James Lawson, believed that a nonviolent strategy was exactly what was needed. Randolph was a well-known labor organizer who used the threat of a mass nonviolent march on Washington to successfully pressure President Franklin Roosevelt into integrating the nation's war industries in 1942 (Branch 1988, 699). Lawson was able to recruit hundreds of student volunteers by giving spellbinding speeches about love and nonviolence:

Love is the force by which God binds man to Himself and man to man. Such love goes to the extreme; it remains loving and forgiving even in the midst of hostility. It matches the capacity of evil to inflict suffering with an even more enduring capacity to absorb evil, all the while persisting in love. . . . We will accept the violence and the hate, absorb it without returning it. (Branch 1988, 291, 472)

King reinforced this rhetoric with a strong condemnation of violence. First, he said that violence would only bring a night of despair and a future of bitterness and chaos. Second, he opposed blacks using violence on practical grounds since blacks would be greatly outnumbered and easily defeated by a heavily armed opponent that was well trained for violent battle. In any violent confrontation, blacks could never prevail since whites were larger in force and better prepared. King said, "The limitation of riots, moral questions aside, is that they cannot win" and hence are inferior to the strategies of nonviolence that are "more radical in their possible effects" (Garrow 1986, 581).

King was always exhorting his people to refrain from responding to violence with violence because that was what so many white segregationists wanted and what they were best prepared to respond to. James Bevel, a high-ranking member of the SCLC and a master nonviolent organizer, said getting blacks to hit back "is just what [white segregationists] want you to do. Then they can call you a mob and beat you to death" (Oates 1982, 337). Besides, he argued, since the black civil rights struggle was about "getting in," and not "throwing out," the social changes sought by blacks lent themselves to using nonviolent tactics rather than violent ones: "if one is in search of a better job, it does not help to burn down the factory" (Washington 1986, 58). King argued that opponents of integration preferred that civil rights activists use violence because it would validate their own use of violence and give them an excuse to unleash the massive firepower at their disposal: "our enemies would prefer to deal with a small armed group rather than a huge, unarmed, but resolute mass of people" (Washington 1986, 33).

King argued that nonviolence was consistent with blacks' own religious precepts and served blacks' need to act independently. Nonviolence was the perfect way for blacks to act up and overcome their passivity while avoiding the degenerative effects of using violence (King 1964b, 14). Moreover, unlike violent action—which was essentially restricted to the physically and psychologically capable—nonviolent action enabled virtually all blacks to join in resisting segregation. As King liked to say, nonviolent resistance meant that the "Ph.D.'s and the no D's" could participate, the educated and the illiterate, the young and the old, the healthy and the infirm, the poor and the rich, the white and the black. A nonviolent "army" has a universal quality unlike armies of violence where there exists a hierarchy according to rank and where the lame and physically unfit cannot participate. This is not the case with a nonviolent army which "has room for everyone who wants to join up" (King 1964b, 29).

King's was an inclusive strategy that ennobled all people and transformed them into a strong yet loving force. This strategy also had ways of working on the opponent too: according to King (1964b), nonviolence has the "marvelous effect of changing the face of the enemy" (28). Only nonviolence could "deliver" blacks their rights because nonviolence disarms the opponent and "exposes his moral defenses, it weakens his morale and at the same time, it works on his conscience" (Washington 1986, 102). Eventually, the opponent is thrown off balance and begins to question his or her own actions.

Nonviolent marches and protests in Birmingham help illustrate this point. Throughout the Birmingham protest, police Commissioner Bull Connor ordered city firemen to turn their high-powered hoses on the marchers. However, as King predicted, the violent reaction by the firemen in the face of nonviolent resistance by the demonstrators, some of them children in their middle school years, began to take a toll on the firemen. After a while they actually refused to obey Connor's order. It was as if the firemen were saying, "I am trained to use this hose to put out fires, not to fire on peaceful marchers." Unlike Connor's police officers wielding their clubs from atop horses, nonviolence "is a powerful and just weapon . . . which cuts without wounding and ennobles the man who wields it" (King 1964b, 14).

Jail-Going

King knew that courting jail terms was an essential element of a nonviolent strategy. Filling the jails with nonviolent demonstrators and marchers who refused to respond to the violent provocations of the authorities and their cronies served King's strategic objectives. Jail-going under these circumstances not only won King more adherents to the Civil Rights Movement—many activists considered it a badge of courage to get arrested standing up for their rights—but it also helped convince many in the news media of the moral superiority of the marchers' position. Although he retained considerable unease about being locked up in a southern jail—for quite some time King resisted the admonishments of younger members of the movement to get arrested with him—King was proud to be a "criminal" for having violated what he considered an unjust law. He urged his followers to cheerfully accept their prison sentence with pride and dignity. King also knew that filling the jails with otherwise law-abiding citizens—the young, the old, the clergy, whites, and blacks—would touch the hearts and minds of many southerners who might not have been sympathetic to King's cause. Willingness to incur self-suffering is how a nonviolent movement gains converts to its cause.

Being arrested and thrown into jail is not something to be undertaken lightly, especially for a black man in the segregated South. Blacks knew of jails as miserable places where they were beaten, tortured, and even killed. King cautioned that filling the jails with nonviolent demonstrators meant that thousands would have to leave their jobs, put off responsibilities, and undergo "harrowing psychological experiences for which law-abiding people are not routinely prepared. [But] the miracle of nonviolence lies in the degree to which people will sacrifice" (King 1964b, 36).

Questions arose regarding whether young members of the movement should defy the segregation laws and subject themselves to arrest, punishment, and possibly worse. King was aware that if he allowed children to march, he opened himself to criticism that he was using the children and placing them in harm's way. King labored over this issue and eventually accepted youth participation on several grounds. First, during several critical junctures in some of the protests, the marchers' ranks were depleted by all the arrests and the youth were needed to replenish the ranks. Second, the youth themselves were eager to participate and showed courage in the face of repression. King realized that the youth's participation could not be denied them; they were likely to march with or without his guiding hand.

Third, King recognized the public relations bonanza the movement would reap when images of police arresting young schoolchildren and carting them off to jail in yellow school buses were splashed across the nation's television screens. King realized how vital positive media coverage was to his cause; at one point, he remarked that "without the presence of the press there might have been untold massacre in the South" (Oates 1982, 178). King realized that nonviolent resistance must be dramatic, compelling, and provocative in order to command national and worldwide media attention.

Questions also arose regarding whether white activists should participate in marches and jail-going. Some blacks, particularly the radical black nationalists, objected to white participation, arguing that if blacks were to achieve freedom, then it must be fought for and won by blacks without any help from whites. However, King and his aides believed that, in their cause to integrate the South, they could hardly exclude whites from their marches since that would send a contradictory message.

Role Playing and Training Drills

In time and after several blunders, King recognized that extensive preparation for engaging the segregationists on the battlefield was vital to the success of the movement. Any time you have to organize a mass of people to act in unison, you need to constantly prepare, organize, and train. King and his aides organized role-playing drills to help train demonstrators how to act and react in potentially dangerous confrontations. SCLC workers prepared the volunteers by playacting like the violent bigots who were expected to attack the marchers. By simulating what they had already experienced, SCLC activists would jump up in the face of a volunteer, calling him or her all sorts of dirty names. The SCLC also trained the marchers to react forcefully, yet peacefully, to the racial epithets and provocations the marchers were sure to encounter. This prepared them for what to expect.

Self-Improvement and Reforming Blacks

Much like Gandhi before him, King insisted that attaining black rights and achieving his beloved community actually began with reforming black culture and black behavior. He even invoked Gandhi's legacy of Indian self-improvement when he attempted to promote it in his own community. For blacks to win their rights, they had to improve their own community. He encouraged blacks, regardless of whether they were highly educated professionals or blue collar laborers, to take pride in their work. He told street sweepers to sweep like Michelangelo painted so that people would remark that here worked the greatest street sweeper that ever lived.

He admonished black preachers to refrain from whooping and hollering at the pulpit just to get "Amens" out of the congregation. He insisted that black doctors read more medical journals. King also blasted blacks for their dismal voter participation rates, calling their indifference, even hostility, to voter participation a shameful "form of moral and political suicide" (Oates 1982, 129).

Moreover, he criticized sinful behavior in the black community as a major obstacle to black aspirations. He condemned black-on-black crime and excessive alcohol consumption. He discouraged blacks from purchasing flashy cars, such as Cadillacs, when their budget really would not allow for such luxuries (Oates 1982, 126–127). King said he understood well the motivation blacks had for buying fancy cars: it gave them a chance to own something nice when so many other nice things in life were denied them. But he insisted that the family's more essential needs must take precedence.

Tactics and Goals

Any strategy, whether violent or nonviolent, must make tactical plans of action in accordance with accomplishing process, achievement, and ultimate goals. Writing for the *Saturday Review* in 1965 right after the Selma March (see Chapter 8), King listed the goals of nonviolent direct action. King said a nonviolent resistance campaign meets its goals when several events occur:

1. When nonviolent demonstrators can go into the streets and exercise their constitutional right to protest for rights;
2. When racists resist by unleashing violence, thus revealing their unsupportable behavior;
3. When Americans of conscience and in the name of decency join the nonviolent demonstrators and demand federal intervention and legislation guaranteeing equal rights for blacks; and
4. When the U.S. administration, under such heavy public pressure, initiates immediate intervention and legislation codifying these rights. (Washington 1986, 48)

Those can all be considered *achievement* goals, as described in Chapter 2. King achieved *process* goals each time he raised money for his organization, usually from fees for speaking engagements, and each time the SCLC's membership rolls grew. Without continually accomplishing these process goals, the SCLC would cease to exist. Of course, King's *ultimate* goal was attaining the beloved community.

Additionally, every plan of action has at its disposal several tools, weapons, and methods with which to launch their action. Accordingly, the Civil Rights Movement used many different nonviolent tactics to achieve its goals. These included freedom rides, sit-ins, boycotts, marches, and nonviolent protest marches. Nonviolent activists, mostly college student volunteers who were trained by preachers and others skilled in nonviolent techniques (Branch 1988, 275), used freedom rides to integrate transportation on interstate busing routes. Although the Supreme Court had long ago declared segregation on interstate busing unconstitutional, most interstate buses in the South remained segregated. To bring attention to this fact, black and white activists would board southbound interstate buses and sit together as the bus entered the South. In some cases, the so-called freedom riders were so violently attacked and beaten at bus stops that federal troops were called in to ensure their safety, just for trying to uphold a Supreme Court ruling. On at least one occasion, a mob of white rioters barricaded a bus's doors shut and then set it on fire, only to attack the choking activists once they broke free from the burning bus. In another instance, the Birmingham police agreed to give the Ku Klux Klan 15 minutes to beat the freedom riders before arresting the haggard activists (Branch 1988, 418–420).

Sit-ins occurred at lunch counters and other retail outlets throughout the South. Department stores, such as Woolworth's, had whites-only diners. Hundreds of black youths, together with a few whites, sat down at segregated counters, demanding either to be served or arrested. Many were severely beaten, sometimes even by the police, not just by angry white civilians. As with the freedom rides, lunch counter sit-ins proved to be a provocative nonviolent tactic for bringing to light the injustices blacks suffered in the segregated South. Ironically, whenever the activists were beaten by white mobs, the police almost invariably arrested the activists, as if their peaceful sit-in was to blame for the riotous mobs attacking them. The freedom rides and the sit-ins, which often took place without King's personal participation, were a great success insofar as they exposed the violent hatred of so many whites toward blacks. The violence the protesters endured, just for sitting on a bus or eating at a lunch counter, shocked the nation and convinced many of the evils of segregation.

Boycotts proved to be a very effective tool for pressuring businesses to hire and promote blacks. Sometimes only one store was singled out—to set an example—and sometimes entire neighborhoods or commercial districts were targeted. Of course, the most famous boycott, the Montgomery Bus Boycott, launched the modern Civil Rights Movement. The next chapter will discuss this boycott at length.

Marches and nonviolent protests occurred frequently throughout the South and the North. Hundreds, sometimes thousands, of whites and blacks would march peacefully, carrying signs calling for freedom and justice. Often times these marchers were subjected to violent responses by the local and state police who used tear gas, billy clubs, attack dogs, and high-powered water tanks in their attempts to waylay the marchers. Such protests and the graphic media coverage of them proved pivotal in focusing the nation's attention on the injustices visited upon blacks in the South and in the northern ghettoes. The Selma March, which will be discussed in detail in the following chapter, and the March on Washington were among the most famous marches. Marches dramatized evil and racist practices and mobilized forces of goodwill to generate pressure for peaceful change. However, as with boycotts, sit-ins, and other forms of nonviolent resistance, King said marches must be sustained for at least 30 to 45 days in order to produce inconvenience and thus command the media's attention (Washington 1986, 60).

As King turned his attention away from fighting segregation in the South to fighting poverty and racism in the North, he began to realize that new nonviolent tactics were called for. In the South, white racism against blacks was expressed overtly and manifested itself in blatant segregation laws. Few whites or blacks in the South had ever witnessed blacks standing firm in their struggle for equality: the mere sight of Alabama or Georgia blacks nonviolently demonstrating for equal rights was a severe form of rebellion in the South. And when southern segregation laws were overturned, blacks in the South could feel a real sense of accomplishment and progress.

In the North, however, racism occurred in more subtle forms such as discrimination in education, housing, and employment. These "structural" forms of racism kept northern blacks hemmed into crowded, squalid ghettoes where poverty and despair prevailed. King said that "in the North, there are brothers and sisters who are suffering discrimination that is even more agonizing, in a sense, than in the South. . . . In the South, at least the Negro can see progress, whereas in the North, all he sees is retrogression" (Cleghorn 1984, 122). Moreover, using nonviolent tactics to fight this more covert and entrenched form of racism was proving quite difficult for King in the North.

Amid the turmoil of northern city life, King's traditional forms of nonviolent resistance—the standard demonstrations and marches—went unnoticed because they were engulfed in the hustle and bustle of the city. As such, King turned toward more drastic tactics of nonviolent resistance, including more massive forms of civil disobedience that were designed to seriously disrupt a city's functioning and make it difficult for the government to quell (Garrow 1986, 574).

Strategic Errors

King was by no means a master strategist. He was bound to make mistakes along the way. Indeed, devising a plan for mass nonviolent resistance is fraught with peril. People must be properly trained to react nonviolently to many potentially violent situations. They must be prepared mentally and physically for harrowing, potentially life-threatening situations. Scarce resources must be allocated wisely and effectively. They must have the resources to sustain their defiance for the long haul. And process, achievement, and ultimate goals must be woven together using a seamless strategic approach that accomplishes all the movement's objectives. To be sure, King and other leaders of the Civil Rights Movement made some serious tactical errors. For instance, King ignored his own advice regarding remaining in jail as long as it takes to bring the weight of the nation's conscience to bear on the local authorities. At several vulnerable points during the movement, King was the only person who could raise money for the movement (by virtue of his paid speaking engagements throughout the country). But the longer King remained in jail, the less money he could raise. After some difficult soul searching, King posted bond and left jail to go on a speaking tour. This opened King up to attacks of hypocrisy. He later admitted that it was a "tactical" error for him to accept bail and leave jail during the Montgomery Bus Boycott because if he had stayed in prison, it would have "dramatized and deepened our movement" (Washington 1986, 344).

In the Albany, Georgia, nonviolent campaign (see Chapter 8), King made the tactical error of participating in a general citywide protest against all forms of segregation. By protesting segregation in general, the SCLC's resources in Albany were spread too thin and rendered ineffective. The movement in Albany failed to achieve any meaningful goals. Later, King acknowledged that he should have focused on a specific target, such as the downtown commercial district. Although these businesses upheld segregation practices, their dependence on black shoppers made them vulnerable to a boycott by black customers. A better strategy would have seen these businesses as a natural target for a concentrated nonviolent boycott.

Finally, according to King, the most pervasive strategic error he made "was in believing that, because our cause was just, we could be sure that the white ministers of the South, once their consciences were challenged, would rise to our aid" (Washington 1986, 344–345). However, much to King's heartbreak and frustration, this did not occur. He was unable to find a way to win them over.

Federal Involvement

Another aspect of King's strategy was to combine nonviolent political resistance with a legal and legislative strategy at the federal level. By engaging the federal government in the conflict in the South, King sought to use federal laws and court rulings to supersede and overrule the segregationist laws and rulings by state legislatures and courts. Legislatively, King worked hard to get the U.S. Congress to pass federal laws that would nullify the segregationist laws passed by state legislatures in the South. He combined this with a series of lawsuits that would eventually work their way up to the federal court system. This strategy proved fairly controversial because King's critics charged that he could not create a beloved community by "legislating morality." Further, they argued, using federal law and the federal courts to force desegregation on the South contradicted his philosophy of nonviolence since such legalistic methods would be coercive rather than conversion-oriented.

King responded to these critiques in typical eloquent fashion. First, he said that "direct [nonviolent] action is not a substitute for work in the courts and the halls of government. . . . Direct action and legal action complement one another" (King 1964b, 33). Here again, observe King's Hegelian tendencies when, instead of having to choose between the thesis (working within the system by going to court) and antithesis (working outside the system by challenging it with nonviolent protests), King opted instead for a Hegelian synthesis that combined the best aspects of both and, in King's mind, reinforced the efficacy of both.

Second, King also said that while it may be true that you cannot "legislate morality," behavior can be regulated. And while it may be true that the law cannot make whites love blacks, outlawing segregation can be seen as an achievement goal, paving the way toward accomplishing the ultimate goal of the beloved community. Desegregation can be written into the laws as a legal remedy to segregation, but integration must be "written on the heart" of men and women (Washington 1986, 123). King liked to say, "The law may not change the heart, but it can restrain the heartless" (Washington 1986, 100). King's overall approach to reaching the beloved community can be summed as the "Three Ls:" *love* (based on agape and nonviolence to win the heart of the opponent), *legislation* (actions by the U.S. Congress to end segregation and change behavior), and *lawsuits* (constitutional fights in the courts to settle the question of segregation once and for all).

CONCLUDING COMMENTS

King recognized both the moral and the practical imperative of using nonviolence in social conflict. The moral imperative was based on his philosophical beliefs and the practical imperative incorporated his desire to create a moral strategy. Thus, King believed that nonviolent resistance was both morally (philosophically) required and strategically (practically) effective. And again in Hegelian fashion, King tried to synthesize the philosophical and strategic components to come up with a new force, which he called "nonviolent direct action." He said that nonviolent resistance should not be used as a strategy just because it was expedient for the moment. If people use nonviolence only because they are afraid to use something else or because they lack other tools or methods, then they are not being truly nonviolent and, in fact, are violating the spirit of nonviolent direct action. Ultimately, nonviolence should be a way of life that men live by because of the sheer morality of its claim (Washington 1986, 17) and also because it is an effective and practical strategy for accomplishing objectives.

CHAPTER 8

King's Nonviolent
Resistance Campaigns

> No one can scorn nonviolent direct action or civil disobe-
> dience without canceling out American history.
> —Martin Luther King, Jr., Address to the
> American Jewish Committee, 1965

This chapter examines several of the most well-known nonviolent resistance campaigns associated with Martin Luther King, Jr. and his Southern Christian Leadership Conference. Some of them, such as the Selma March, achieved significant results, while others, such as the Albany, Georgia, campaign, were mostly failures. Still others, such as the Chicago Housing Project Campaign, resulted in a mixture of success and failure. In discussing each of these campaigns, this chapter presents a general background and then focuses on how nonviolent tactics and strategies succeeded or failed to accomplish goals. Even with failed campaigns, such as the one in Albany, King learned valuable lessons about how nonviolent resistance could be better utilized in other campaigns.

Note that King had significant help in organizing and carrying out these nonviolent campaigns. Notable figures who helped train the nonviolent activists included Bayard Rustin, Robert Gregg, and James Lawson. Note also that the nonviolent campaigns mentioned in this chapter do not depict the black civil rights struggle in its entirety. Many campaigns were carried out by other black leaders who were unsympathetic and even hostile to King and the SCLC's nonviolent movement. These leaders included Huey Newton and the radical Black Panther Movement, Malcolm X's Black Nationalist Movement in the Nation of Islam, and Stokely Carmichael's Black Power Movement in the Student Nonviolent Coordinating Committee. Malcolm X launched particularly vicious and convincing attacks on Martin Luther King, Jr.'s approach to civil rights. When King called on blacks to love their white "brothers" after they beat, lynched, or murdered blacks, Malcolm condemned it as a tepid, emasculating response to blatant aggression.

THE MONTGOMERY BUS BOYCOTT (1955–1956)

Background to Montgomery

In May 1954, King gave his first sermon at the Dexter Avenue Baptist Church in Montgomery, Alabama, as part of his application to become pastor there. King and his sermon were very well received by the congregation, and he became the official pastor in September 1954. He was only 25 years old and was still writing his doctoral thesis at Boston University. Ironically, the same month King gave his application sermon at Dexter, the U.S. Supreme Court declared racial segregation in public schools unconstitutional in its landmark *Brown* ruling.

Montgomery was the first capital of the Confederacy during the Civil War. It was still referred to as the "Cradle of the Confederacy" when King moved there in 1954. With a population of 130,000, Montgomery's approximately 50,000 blacks chafed under a system of segregation, from which they suffered daily indignities. Montgomery, like other southern towns, had city ordinances, which enforced racial segregation in public facilities and accommodations. For instance, blacks and whites were not allowed to play checkers together on public property (Branch 1988, 13). Blacks in Montgomery suffered humiliating, even violent, treatment on the buses. Even though 70 percent of the passengers were black, the bus company did not employ a single black bus driver. Bus drivers verbally abused blacks, called them names, and made them pay their fare at the front of the bus, then get off the bus and reenter through the rear entrance. Oftentimes, the bus driver would pull away after a black passenger had paid the fare, but before having the chance to reenter from the rear.

Blacks were forced to sit in the back of the bus, but not on a first-come, first-served basis. If there were no seats, white passengers made black passengers surrender their seats and force them to stand in the aisle. If a white person came on the bus and sat down next to a black person, the black person had to get up and either find another seat or stand for the remainder of the trip. Moreover, the first four rows of each bus were reserved for whites only. If the unreserved section of the bus was full and even if there were no whites in any of the reserved seats, no blacks could sit in them: they had to stand.

Blacks in Montgomery hated the bus system, considering it one of the worst insults they had to endure. But the indignities and humiliations blacks suffered on the Montgomery buses reached a head in December 1955 when Rosa Parks, a 42-year-old seamstress in a department store and a volunteer activist for the local NAACP office, politely refused to give up her seat to a white person. Even after the bus driver threatened to have her arrested, Ms. Parks simply uttered a quiet, yet forceful "no," and remained seated. Later, she claimed her stubbornness was not born of any desire to ignite the Civil Rights Movement (which she did) or to be hailed as a hero (which she was) but rather because her feet were tired and aching and she simply could not bear any more. In any event, Ms. Parks was duly arrested, brought down to the police station, and fingerprinted like a common criminal. Little did she, or King for that matter, realize that her simple act of defiance would help ignite a nationwide protest movement for justice and equality for blacks.

The Montgomery Campaign

In response to Ms. Parks's arrest and to the general wellspring of discontent that was rising among Montgomery's blacks, local leaders in the religious and business community founded the Montgomery Improvement Association (MIA), a name coined by another black preacher in Montgomery, the Reverend Ralph Abernathy. In later years, Abernathy became one of King's best friends during the Civil Rights Movement. The two of them seemed inseparable: time after time, they were seen marching and praying together, side by side, getting arrested, and opening themselves up to the flying bottles and bricks of violent segregationists.

The MIA opted to resist the city's bus segregation laws by launching a massive boycott of the bus company, which began on December 1, 1955. A bus boycott was not a new idea. The Congress of Racial Equality, a civil rights organization that used nonviolent resistance, advocated using nonviolent boycotts to pressure businesses and government as early as 1942. This was also the group that spearheaded the now-famous freedom rides in the 1960s. Moreover, a bus boycott had been tried before, in 1953 in Baton Rouge, Louisiana. And since 70 percent of Montgomery's bus passengers were black, a well-organized and sustained boycott that was adhered to by a significant portion of Montgomery's black population could be financially crippling to the bus company. Black leaders hoped that the lost revenue, which could be especially severe since the Christmas shopping season had arrived, would compel the bus company, as well as city officials, to address long-held black grievances. In May 1956, about six months after the boycott began, the beleaguered bus company declared an end to its segregated seating policy only to have an Alabama court overrule the company and order it to reinstate the policy (Oates 1982, 99).

The MIA issued three demands, which blacks had long been calling for, as preconditions for blacks returning to the buses. First, bus drivers were to treat blacks with courtesy and respect. Second, people would be allowed to sit on the bus on a first-come, first-seated basis with blacks seating themselves in the rear of the bus first and sitting forward only when rear seats were taken up. Third, the MIA demanded that the bus company hire black bus drivers on the predominantly black-populated bus routes.

In hindsight, these demands seem perfectly reasonable, even tepid. Interestingly, the MIA's demands made no mention of ending segregation on the buses. Rather, these demands were made within the confines of segregation laws. Ironically, these minimalist demands were actually calling not for an end to segregation, but for more humane treatment of blacks within the system of segregation. Early in the boycott, King even said, "[W]e are not asking for an end to segregation. That's a matter for the legislature and the courts. We feel we have a plan within the law" (Garrow 1986, 24). This shows that King's views on nonviolent resistance and civil disobedience were still crystallizing. Unlike his famous "Letter from Birmingham Jail," which he penned some seven years later and in which he explained the importance of disobeying unjust laws, King did not advocate breaking any laws during the Montgomery Bus Boycott. King's own account of his turn toward nonviolence and his philosophical commitment to a life entirely based on nonviolence was chronicled in the book he wrote on the Montgomery Bus Boycott, *Stride Toward Freedom* (1958). The chapter entitled "Pilgrimage to Nonviolence" gives an account of how King, early in the boycott, was

admittedly only vaguely familiar with Gandhi and real nonviolent resistance. King completed his "pilgrimage" after spending long hours
of discussion and reading with friends and advisers who were encouraged by his receptivity to Gandhian styles of resistance. As the
boycott continued, King came to see that the essence of nonviolence
was based on a refusal to retaliate against evil because retaliation
only created multiple evils (Garrow 1986, 68).

Even though he was young, an outsider, and new to Montgomery, King emerged as the preeminent choice to be the leader of
the MIA. He was chosen as the boycott's leader because he was well
educated and an articulate speaker—which appealed to Montgomery's black professionals—and also because he was a Baptist
minister—which appealed to Montgomery's largely Baptist churchgoing blacks (Garrow 1986, 20). He was also chosen because, as a
new member of the community, he was not embroiled in any of the
social and political rivalries of Montgomery's black elite. There is
also some speculation that black leaders in Montgomery wanted to
have an outsider as a scapegoat in case the boycott failed.

In what would prove to be a hallmark of King's public speaking skills, he gave a stirring speech early in the boycott in which
he invoked the Constitution, God, and Jesus Christ to defend the
boycott and urge its adherents to remain strong in their nonviolent resistance:

> If we are wrong the Supreme Court of this nation is wrong. If we
> are wrong the Constitution of the United States is wrong. If we are
> wrong, God Almighty is wrong. If we are wrong Jesus of Nazareth
> was merely a utopian dreamer. . . . If we are wrong justice is a lie.
> (King n.d.)

The boycott lasted just over a year, longer than anyone predicted. During that time, people boycotting the buses experienced
many hardships, not least of which was finding alternative transportation to their jobs. Blacks who owned their own automobiles
organized an elaborate carpool and taxi system that helped ferry
blacks to and from work.[1]

Media coverage of the boycott was extensive and frequently
portrayed the boycotters in a favorable light. Some media outlets

---

[1]The Montgomery Bus Boycott is dramatically portrayed in the cinematic
production *The Long Walk Home* (1991), starring Whoopi Goldberg and
Sissy Spacek.

drew parallels between the Montgomery Bus Boycott and Gandhi's nonviolent resistance campaigns in India. One *ABC News* commentator likened Montgomery's protesters to Gandhi and compared the city of Montgomery's bankrupt position to that of the Colonial British in India (Garrow 1986, 66).

Black preachers and their churches in Montgomery played an absolutely vital role in sustaining the boycott. Not only did the preachers provide important spiritual guidance, support, and encouragement to the boycotters, but the churches proved to be excellent meeting places for organizing meetings and deciding on important issues and strategies.

Despite the unity demonstrated by the black community, the white power structure had no intention of giving in to the boycotters, so they made many different attempts to break the boycott. They claimed the boycott was being run by outside agitators, but really the whites had no idea who was running the boycott, so ignorant were they of Montgomery's black community (Branch 1988, 154). They issued threats and used violence and other underhanded techniques in their attempts to break the boycott. At one point, the city began harassing and arresting carpoolers, charging them with operating an unlicensed taxi service. Authorities even tried arresting people for refusing to ride the buses, claiming that they were engaged in an illegal economic boycott. By November 1956, King and the MIA were finding it difficult to hold the boycott together. They were facing increasingly effective challenges in the local courts. In what appeared to be the boycott's most difficult hour, King sat in an Alabama courtroom awaiting a ruling that would effectively cripple the boycott, when a reporter approached him with a note that said the U.S. Supreme Court had just declared all of Alabama's segregated laws regarding buses unconstitutional. On December 21, 1956, the MIA voted to end the boycott after the Supreme Court's ruling was administratively enacted in the state of Alabama. King was just 27 years old.

Even though some people claimed the Supreme Court ruling actually ended segregation on Montgomery's buses, without the bus boycott and other actions by the MIA, the Supreme Court's ruling would never have been implemented as fast and completely as it was. It is not that it took a Supreme Court ruling to make the MIA's boycott a success, it is the boycott—and the nonviolent training and self-respect blacks obtained during it—that enabled the Supreme Court's ruling to be successfully implemented. The boycott actually proved to be good training for both blacks and whites as it prepared them for the day when bus segregation would become a thing of the past.

Results of Montgomery

After the 1956 Supreme Court ruling declared Alabama bus laws unconstitutional, King cautioned blacks in Montgomery to avoid declaring they had defeated the white man. Rather, he said that "the real victory was in the mass meeting, where thousands of black people stood revealed with a new sense of dignity and destiny" (Oates 1982, 72). King was referring to the fact that a new attitude was emerging among black southerners, one that demanded respect and equal treatment, one that showed blacks were no longer cowed into submission by the white bullwhip of repression and segregation. Although the boycott did little to convert the white citizens of Montgomery, it had a tremendous impact on Montgomery's black community (Oates 1982, 112). First, the boycott demonstrated that the black church, which was vital for the social and economic relations of blacks in the South, could also be a political force with great transforming power. Second, nonviolent resistance, on which the boycott was based, provided a weapon that the black masses could wield regardless of their age, gender, education, or income level.

Third, Montgomery helped "straighten the backs" of blacks throughout the South by empowering them and giving them self-respect. Montgomery demonstrated that blacks could successfully stand up for their rights. Montgomery gave blacks around the country hope that they could be bigger, stronger, and more courageous than they had thought before. Events in Montgomery also influenced the creation of King's Southern Christian Leadership Conference, which became a civil rights organization that supplemented the older NAACP. In addition to the mostly legal strategy pursued by the NAACP, the SCLC would adopt the "Montgomery Way," and organize nonviolent direct action campaigns through the black churches throughout the South (Oates 1982, 123). King was the lynchpin of that new effort. Ironically, before Montgomery, King's approach to struggling for civil rights adhered to the traditional methods employed by the NAACP: filing lawsuits in federal courts. But King's Montgomery experience radically altered his views on nonviolence. Personally, Montgomery made King a national figure, especially among blacks throughout the country. From then on, wherever he went, he was swarmed by flocks of admirers and curiosity seekers.

ALBANY, GEORGIA (1961–1962)

Background to Albany

Even though bus segregation ended officially when the Supreme Court declared it unconstitutional, it was the nonviolent direct action of the Montgomery Bus Boycott that set the stage for the newly born Civil Rights Movement in which Martin Luther King, Jr. would soon play a pivotal role. The combination of court action and nonviolent direct action would become the hallmark of King's strategy. However, if Montgomery represented a success for King's strategy, the Albany, Georgia, campaign represented a failure. As a former slave-trading center, Albany, with about half of its 56,000 population black, proved to be an inviting target for the civil rights struggle. Albany's laws segregated blacks in theaters, in parks, at lunch counters, and on buses. The city also used restrictive voter registration laws that were designed to exclude blacks from the democratic electoral process.

Whether a movement uses violent or nonviolent strategies, it can scarcely succeed when its members are not united. That was the problem in Albany even before King arrived. The discord, in fact, made King a reluctant participant. Several civil rights organizations, among them the SNCC and the NAACP, launched a voter-rights campaign in Albany, hoping to increase black voter registration in the area. But the SNCC, which was a newer, more radical group of blacks whose members were young college students, frequently clashed with the older, more "mature" members of the NAACP, who urged patience. While the SNCC wanted more marches and protests, the NAACP wanted more lawsuits. Moreover, the local black leaders in Albany resented these "outside" organizations coming into Albany because their own economic interests were indirectly threatened by the new arrivals (Branch 1988, 526–527). They began negotiating an independent deal with Albany's white power structure. The movement was floundering, so some activists wanted to invite King to Albany to jumpstart the movement.

It was amid this internal feuding, bickering, and poor organization that Martin Luther King, Jr. and his SCLC entered Albany's

fray, by invitation, in December 1961. King ovecame his reluctance to go to Albany because he had not had a victory in several
years. So he went to Albany and marched with the others to get
himself arrested in hopes of bringing attention to the situation of
blacks in Albany. But King's arrival in Albany only served to exacerbate the divisions that already existed among black activists
there. Worse, the whites reneged on the deal local black leaders
negotiated with them: Albany's facilities remained segregated
(Oates 1982, 190–192) or closed down entirely to keep them from
being desegregated.

The Albany Campaign

King and the SCLC entered Albany unprepared and inexperienced. The SCLC had no comprehensive plan upon its entry into
Albany (Phillips 1999, 83). King also misunderstood the internal
dynamics of the movement among blacks there. Even though King
sensed this, he felt he could not turn his back on Albany because
Albany was on the verge of becoming one of the earliest mass nonviolent protest movements (Garrow 1986, 184) and he hoped to engineer a mass nonviolent movement to prove to his critics that
nonviolence in Montgomery was not a fluke.

Having observed King's earlier success, Laurie Pritchett, Albany's police chief, was well prepared for the nonviolent demonstrations. Pritchett had devised a better strategy for handling the
protesters than the protesters had devised for resisting the city's
segregation laws. Pritchett knew that if he responded to the nonviolent protesters using violence and police brutality, he would instigate a national crisis that would bring national media and national
government attention to Albany, which was the last thing the
whites in Albany wanted. So Pritchett and his police force behaved
respectfully and peaceably toward the protesters. He had a "possumlike wiliness," which he used to great effect by "killin' 'em with
kindness" (Frady 2002, 88). When the protesters kneeled and
prayed, he bowed his head and prayed along with them. But when
they finished praying, Pritchett calmly and politely rounded up the
protesters and drove them off to jail. No beatings occurred for the
cameras to record. Nor did the police call the protesters names or
use racial slurs. Pritchett matched this strategy with an equally
masterful idea to detain the protesters in faraway jails, located in
adjacent counties whose sheriff's agreed to house them. Pritchett

had organized a makeshift fleet of vehicles to transport all the protesters to outlying county jails, some of which were infamous for their brutal treatment of blacks (Branch 1988, 536). Isolated in distant prison cells, the protesters were unable to draw attention to Albany's injustices. The extra jail space available to Pritchett also made it difficult for the protesters to create a crisis situation by filling the jail cells. As one protest organizer lamented, the movement ran out of protesters before Pritchett ran out of jail cells. Despite the fact that Albany experienced the greatest mass arrests to date—more than 750 (Branch 1988, 550)—the movement remained weak, divided, and in disarray. To make matters worse, Albany's black masses grew increasingly disinterested in the campaign, having experienced considerable hardship and sacrifice without observing any tangible gains.

King and Abernathy were convicted of leading a protest and given a 45-day prison sentence. Although they planned to serve the full term in order to draw attention to the situation, someone anonymously paid the fine to get them released from jail just two days after their term began. Although Pritchett implied that a local black had paid the fine, he and some of his white allies actually paid it (Branch 1988, 606) because Pritchett did not want the increasingly popular Reverend King languishing in one of his jail cells. Abernathy said it was the first time he was ever thrown *out* of jail.

Results of Albany

When the nonviolent campaign ended, Albany remained just as segregated as it always was. For that, the campaign can be considered a dismal failure. Several factors account for the failure in Albany (Garrow 1986, 217–218). First, Chief Pritchett's professionalism kept the public drama to a minimum. With little to film that was sensational, the media lost interest and the story slipped from the headlines. Second, the internal feuding among black activists hamstrung the movement and drained its momentum. King's tolerance for the petty bickering did not help matters.

Third, no help of any kind came from the federal government (Phillips 1999, 83). President John F. Kennedy turned out to be more interested in preserving order in Albany than in creating justice for Albany's blacks. As such, Kennedy and the federal government proved unhelpful and even insensitive to the blacks in

Albany. Moreover, the Kennedy administration praised Chief Pritchett for the way he handled the situation (Oates 1982, 200). Contrary to his campaign pledge to take the initiative on civil rights issues, President Kennedy's administration was far more reactive than active. Fourth, the movement adopted a faulty strategy, which focused on using political power to launch a general attack on the entire system of segregation in Albany. In its early stages, the Albany campaign issued many demands: desegregation of the bus and train stations, libraries, parks, and medical services and a halt to police brutality (Frady 2002, 87). King acknowledged that the campaign should have focused instead on using blacks' economic power in Albany, which was much more substantial than their political power. He realized that blacks could have used their considerable purchasing power to focus a specific attack on Albany's downtown white-owned businesses, which were vulnerable to black economic pressure. But at the time King did not understand how little political power blacks actually had in Albany because so few of them had obtained the right to vote (Garrow 1986, 226).

King's decision to obey a federal court order, which barred all forms of civil disobedience in Albany, also hurt the campaign (Garrow 1986, 194–199). King obeyed the court injunction because he did not want to anger the federal courts or federal government, which he saw as a badly needed ally in his fight against city and state politicians in the South. When King obeyed the injunction, the movement fizzled. Even though the injunction was overruled, it turned out to be too late since violence among the increasingly frustrated black population broke out. King was blamed for the violence and called off the remaining scheduled march for fear of more violence breaking out. "Did you see them nonviolent rocks?" Chief Pritchett drawled sarcastically (Branch 1988, 618). King called for a day of penance in response to the violence and went all over Albany preaching nonviolence, arguing that whites want blacks to be violent. In a desperate move to hold the campaign together, King courted a jail sentence, but the judge suspended his term. The movement was over and King suspended the demonstrations and went back to Atlanta, where he was headquartered (Oates 1982, 199).

Despite the fact that Albany remained as segregated as ever, King did make an attempt to claim some successes from the movement there. First, he said that blacks in Albany had gained self-esteem and self-confidence and therefore would be better prepared to handle injustices done to them. Second, King said he grew wise about how nonviolence works. He learned how to plan and devise future mass nonviolent resistance campaigns. King's nonviolent resistance campaign in Birmingham was devised based on lessons learned from Albany. Third, the number of blacks registered to vote in Albany more than doubled, although voter registration was not part of the campaign's original plans or demands (Frady 2002, 95). Moreover, Stanley Levison argued that the real victory was the suspension of King's jail sentence because it signified that, even in Albany, King's stature and influence was a force that could not be ignored (Branch 1988, 629).

BIRMINGHAM, ALABAMA (1963)

Background to Birmingham

In the early spring of 1963, King's SCLC, together with the Alabama Christian Movement for Human Rights, launched a nonviolent protest campaign—called Project C for "Confrontation"—for civil rights in Birmingham, a town that King considered ripe for a mass nonviolent campaign. Birmingham was arguably the most segregated city in the United States and King felt that if a campaign against segregation was successful in Birmingham, the bastion of racist segregation, then it could "break the back of segregation all over the nation" (King 1964b, 47). King said Birmingham was a city that had apparently never heard of Abraham Lincoln, Thomas Jefferson, or the U.S. Constitution (Phillips 1999, 156). In addition, local civil rights activists were agitating against segregation and had won some small victories, including promises from some of the businesses to desegregate their lunch counters. Birmingham, unlike Albany, had no significant organizational rivalries or petty jealousies to deal with in large measure because other organizations like the NAACP and the SNCC were not operating there. Moreover, although there were plenty of disagreements over timing and strategy, blacks in Birmingham were more united than they were in Albany. Ironically, it was the whites in Birmingham who were deeply divided: moderate businessmen clashed with rabid segregationists over Birmingham's international image.

Having learned from the Albany debacle, King and the SCLC were much better prepared for Birmingham. Now he insisted on being the one to choose when and where he would next fight. He wanted the SCLC to get in "on the ground floor" so that he could control the timing and pace of the campaign (Branch 1988, 632). Great care and planning went into formulating the strategy in Birmingham, which had several elements. First, they had to fill the jails with nonviolent protesters demonstrating against segregation. King was determined to recruit enough volunteers in order to overflow the jails with nonviolent offenders singing songs about freedom and justice.

Second, blacks would fight with their strengths. That meant utilizing their considerable economic power instead of their more limited political power. King felt that blacks in Birmingham possessed sufficient buying power such that if black consumers launched a boycott, many businesses would surely feel the pinch (King 1964b, 48–49). The protesters planned to target only a few key businesses clustered in Birmingham's downtown area where an economic boycott could be wielded effectively. King wanted to focus his efforts on only one aspect of segregation so he could utilize resources more effectively. That these businesses were clustered together in relative proximity also made them an inviting target. Moreover, the Easter season, which was the second busiest shopping season of the year, was fast approaching, so these businesses would definitely see a substantial drop in sales.

Third, the strategy had to be creative. Nonviolent training workshops were conducted to prepare the marchers for the risks that came with protesting in the segregated South. Seminars were conducted to teach demonstrators how to resist without rancor, how to take a beating without hitting back, how to stand up to being cursed without lashing out, and how to accept being spit on without responding in kind (Oates 1982, 218). Such preparation, so sorely lacking in Albany, demonstrated that King and his organization were improving their ability to organize a mass nonviolent movement. Moreover, and again reflecting lessons learned from Albany, this time King vowed to disobey any court order that declared marches illegal. In fact, a state court did issue an injunction against marching but, true to his word, King defied it.

A fourth and crucial element of the strategy was that the resistance had to be provocative as well as nonviolent. King sought to provoke the city's police commissioner, a rabid segregationist named Eugene "Bull" Connor, into brutally responding in order to expose the true nature of segregation. Bull Connor did not disappoint: his violent and clumsy response to the young demonstrators proved to be the perfect foil for King's nonviolent resistance.

Nonviolent resistance had to be provocative in order to precipitate the moment that King called "creative tension," which is that moment when the injustices prevalent in Birmingham would be brought to the surface. King believed that to cure injustice it must be brought out into the open and exposed before the light of human conscience. With this strategy, King sought to precipitate a crisis situation that would force open the door to negotiation. King sought to win support in the court of public opinion. Since he felt that federal intervention by the Kennedy administration was crucial to ending segregation, he wanted nonviolence in Birmingham to expose segregation as the brutal and hate-filled practice it was (Garrow 1986, 228). Although the Kennedy administration was sympathetic on civil rights, the White House repeatedly counseled King to wait. But King wanted to demonstrate to Washington, DC, and to the American public in general the urgent need for change in the South. He realized, again from his Albany experience, that the federal government was unlikely to intervene unless it was under severe pressure to do so.

The Birmingham Campaign

When the campaign was launched in April 1963, King issued the "Birmingham Manifesto," which demanded an end to segregation at lunch counters, in rest rooms, at drinking fountains, and in other public facilities. Blacks began staging protests, demonstrations, and sit-ins and were getting arrested in increasing numbers. At one point, the movement began to falter. Despite all the planning, the campaign still encountered severe obstacles: they were again running out of people to fill the jail cells and they were also losing media attention, which was diverted to civil rights problems in Mississippi (Branch 1988, 710–711). However, local black youths—college and high school students and even some of their little brothers and sisters in middle school—took up the call and volunteered to march and submit to arrest. At first King was reluctant to expose children so young to such a great risk, but in the end, he agreed to their participation because it could lead to a single, climactic confrontation that might end segregation in Birmingham once and for all. He also thought the spectacle of young children risking their lives marching for freedom and justice might finally awaken the entire country to what was happening in Birmingham (Oates 1982, 233). And when Bull Connor engaged the youths with high-powered fire hoses and attack dogs, the images of nonviolent young people being mauled by inhumane police tactics were transmitted to a shocked nation—and world.

The gambit worked. More than 1,000 youths—some as young as six—marched against segregation in Birmingham. On their first day, 500 of them were arrested (Frady 2002, 112). Since the police ran out of vehicles, the children were carted off to jail in school buses, during which, with television cameras rolling, they cheerfully sang songs of freedom. When some media outlets deplored the tactic of using children, King challenged the media to denounce the centuries of exploitation and abuse of black children by the white systems of slavery and segregation (King 1964b, 103). By employing the youth marches, the campaign's long-proclaimed desire to fill the jail cells became a reality (Garrow 1986, 250). This is an achievement goal in the nonviolent resistance strategy described in Chapter 2.

One of the most spectacular events of the entire campaign occurred when the true power of nonviolence was witnessed. On May 5, some 3,000 youths were marching when they approached a police barricade. The youths knelt down and prayed and one marcher said to the police officers and firefighters there, "How do you feel doing these things . . . ? Bring on your dogs. Turn on your hoses. We're not going to retreat." At that the protesters resumed their march, Bull Connor ordered the police and firefighters to turn on the hoses and arrest the demonstrators. However, no hoses were turned on. Instead, the police and firefighters, some with tears in their eyes, fell back and refused to obey Bull Connor. The marchers went peacefully right through their ranks as an enraged Connor was left powerless because his own people refused to obey him. As the marchers passed through the ranks, they cried "Hallelujah!" and conducted a prayer service nearby (Frady 2002, 103). Here, nonviolence worked exactly as its advocates claim it should: on the hearts and minds of the opponents as it sows wonder and doubt about their actions. King said "I saw there, I felt there, for the first time, the pride and power of nonviolence" (Oates 1982, 237).

Results of Birmingham

With the jails finally filling and with still more youths marching, King's hoped-for moment of creative tension had arrived and the business leaders finally agreed to serious negotiations with

King, which was yet another achievement goal accomplished. Ultimately, the demonstrations and masses of unrestrained black teenagers convinced the downtown businessmen that segregation was not worth the price they would have to pay (Garrow 1986, 264). On May 7, after several marathon negotiating sessions, agreement was reached on nearly all the demands made by the movement. It was a victory for nonviolent resistance to the extent that these demands were met; however, few white residents seemed converted to King's dream of a beloved community. Rather, the white businessmen appear to have agreed to the demands, not because they were converted to King's philosophy, but because they calculated that their concessions were the most expedient way to get back to business. It was not the conversion that King sought, but rather the result of coercion.

According to the agreement, within 90 days, lunch counters, rest rooms, fitting rooms, and drinking fountains in stores would be desegregated. Within 60 days, blacks were to be considered for employment as clerks, salespeople, and for other positions previously prohibited to them. Within two weeks, a biracial committee to improve communication between blacks and whites would be established (Oates 1982, 240). King did receive some criticism, however, insofar as the agreement did not specify the actual number of blacks to be hired—they could not resolve this, so they ignored it. Additionally, since progress in actually implementing the agreement was sluggish and only patchy, questions were raised about just how much nonviolent resistance had actually accomplished in Birmingham (Garrow 1986, 258). Nevertheless, King saw Birmingham as a great success for several reasons. First, he believed it would lead to protest movements aimed at dismantling segregation in public facilities throughout the South and he was right. Birmingham's success set off a whole slew of protests against segregated public accommodations across the South. The domino effect had begun. By one count, more than 700 demonstrations against segregation were sparked in nearly 200 cities and towns (Frady 2002, 119).

Second, the protests in Birmingham produced publicity regarding the injustices blacks had to endure in the South. Birmingham revealed to the nation that southern racism and segregation were far more vicious than most whites ever realized or were willing to admit (Garrow 1986, 264). According to David Garrow (1986), the "SCLC had succeeded in bringing the civil rights struggle to the forefront of the national consciousness [which] outweighed the narrower question of whether the settlement provided for speedy enough desegregation of Birmingham's stores" (264). Birmingham transformed many Americans—and people all over the world—from mere sympathizers into active participants in support of the Civil Rights Movement. Birmingham created such a powerful national impact that it contributed directly to the passage of the 1964 Civil Rights Act, which prohibited segregation in public facilities and outlawed discrimination in employment, education, and voting. Although the Kennedy White House had initially opposed new civil rights legislation, Birmingham forced the president to begin thinking about a new civil rights bill; he even made a surprising yet powerful speech on national television in favor of new legislation (Branch 1988, 808, 823). Third, Birmingham was a success because local blacks learned how to organize and work together against a determined, often violent opponent. Again, King's success can be seen in helping blacks straighten their backs in confronting white racists and segregationists. For King, there was another success, especially in light of the Albany failing: Birmingham proved he could organize and lead a mass nonviolent resistance campaign (Oates 1982, 243). Birmingham had thus become the first clear-cut victory for King's mass nonviolent direct action movement (Frady 2002, 118). Birmingham also transformed King into the "star of a swarming hive" of civil rights leaders and activists (Branch 1988, 806). King's campaign in Birmingham also created the momentum for the famous March on Washington, which further pressured the federal government into passing civil rights legislation.

Birmingham exposed, for the entire world to see, the city's vicious segregationists, who turned high-powered fire hoses on marching youths, who clubbed unarmed old ladies, and who used police dogs to attack nonviolent marchers. Each day the demonstrations grew stronger and each day the oafish Bull Connor could be counted on to do some outrageous act, which exposed segregation's brutal underpinnings. In response to the arrests, the attack dogs, and the brutal clubbings, King urged the demonstrators to remain steadfast and united in their nonviolence. He also declared to Bull Connor and the other segregationists:

> We will match your capacity to inflict suffering with our capacity to endure suffering. We will meet your physical force with soul force. We will not hate you. And yet, we cannot in good conscience obey your evil laws. Do to us what you will. Threaten our children and we will still love you. . . . Bomb our churches . . . and we will still

love you. We will wear you down by our capacity to suffer. In winning the victory, we will not only win our freedom, we will also appeal to your heart and conscience that we will win you in the
process. (Oates 1982, 236)

This statement reinforces the notion that King's ultimate goal was
not an end to segregation, but the creation of the beloved community. He sought not to coerce his opponents, but rather to convince
and convert them to his way of thinking. A difficult goal to achieve,
to be sure, especially considering that his opponents were devoted
segregationists who had no desire to join with King. Nevertheless,
it was a goal commensurate with a man who was philosophically
committed to nonviolence.

SELMA, ALABAMA (1965)

Background to Selma

After the success in Birmingham, Selma was a good choice for
King and the SCLC to broaden the struggle. In Selma, with more
than half of its 29,000 population black, the focus was not on department stores or buses, but the voting booths. King wanted to
win free voting rights for blacks in Selma the way he fought to wipe
out segregation in public facilities in Birmingham. About 50 miles
west of Montgomery, where King's earnest involvement in the Civil
Rights Movement began, Selma was another city of great symbolic
importance in the South. As the birthplace of Bull Connor, as a former slave-trading center, and as an important military depot during the Civil War, Selma's historical legacy of racism was of deep
significance to blacks. Selma was also where the first White Citizens' Council, whose members were adamantly, often violently, opposed to integration, was established. White Citizens' Councils in
the South were established to help enforce a "rigid racial caste system that kept blacks impoverished" (Oates 1982, 326).

King wanted to use Selma to challenge Alabama's restrictive
voter registration laws and to compel President Johnson to sponsor federal legislation regarding voting rights. King met with President Johnson in late 1964 and discussed with him the need for a
law guaranteeing blacks the right to vote. King had long argued
that unencumbered access to the ballot box for blacks was essential to guaranteeing their freedoms. Moreover, he felt that the tra-

ditional approach used to win blacks their constitutional right to vote—lawsuits on an individual case-by-case basis—were ineffective because they were taking too long and, hence, needed to be supplemented with more concrete legislative action at the federal level. But Johnson demurred, arguing that he would be unable to win enough support in Congress to get such a bill passed. He also argued that it would detract from his efforts to get other legislation passed that he felt had priority. King, who by now realized that the federal government was not quick to action, rather it was quick to reaction, left the White House determined to use nonviolence to again provoke a moment of creative tension, which would compel the federal government to act, much like it had with respect to Birmingham and the consequent Civil Rights Act. Selma proved to be his staging ground.

The Selma Campaign

By January 1965, King realized that matters in Selma were reaching the point of nonviolent struggle and confrontation. The SCLC, in conjunction with the SNCC, began organizing a nonviolent voting rights campaign to be waged in Selma. On February 1, King and more than 200 others were jailed for demonstrating in favor of voting rights in Selma. While King was jailed, he issued specific instructions to sustain the movement and to expand its reach. Thousands of blacks were being jailed, yet the marches continued as King urged them on. King's instructions, details, and exhortations from his jail cell in Selma were brilliant tactical moves as they ensured the movement's momentum and also increased favorable media attention for the marches.

King's moment of creative tension was fast approaching as several violent outbursts by whites opposing the nonviolent marchers ultimately compelled President Johnson to act. Three such outbursts stand out. First, on February 26, a black youth named Jimmie Lee Jackson died after police shot him while he was trying to stop them from beating his mother and grandfather. Second, on March 7, nonviolent marchers were attacked, tear-gassed, and beaten by police on the Edmund Pettus Bridge. Third, the March 11 beating death of a white Unitarian minister, Reverend James Reeb, ultimately forced President Johnson to take action.

In response to Jimmie Lee Jackson's death, King announced plans to conduct a nonviolent march from Selma to Montgomery where the marchers would call on Alabama Governor George Wallace to end police brutality and to remove all the obstacles that kept blacks from exercising their constitutional right to vote. The march began in King's absence because he was suddenly called out of town. However, like Bull Connor in Birmingham, Sheriff Bill Clark in Selma could be counted on to do some outrageous act that would demonstrate the true, brutal nature of segregation and white racism in the South. For instance, when black applicants approached the Selma courthouse to register to vote, Sheriff Clark was there to forcibly push them back. He even beat one woman with a billy club, pictures of which were splashed across newspapers throughout the country. The SCLC was, in a way, pleased with Clark's conduct, considering him another Bull Connor, who could be counted on to help expose the ugliest aspects of segregation in the South (Garrow 1986, 381).

As the marchers attempted to cross the Edmund Pettus Bridge into Sheriff Clark's jurisdiction, they were met by a large group of police officers equipped with antiriot gear. After declaring the march an unlawful gathering, horse-mounted police troopers moved in on the marchers to force their retreat back up the bridge. At first, the marchers stood still, remaining where they were. But as the police advanced, launching tear gas grenades and clubbing marchers, the bruised and bloodied demonstrators were forced to retreat to safety across the bridge. It was a shameful and bloody attack that was captured by the national news media and spurred many otherwise complacent people to action on behalf of the marchers.

King, who had long criticized America's white clergymen for too often being a "taillight" instead of a "headlight" in the struggle for civil rights, made plans to escalate his nonviolent direct action by calling on the nation's clergy to join him in what he called a "ministers' march to Montgomery." In response, more than 400 ministers, rabbis, priests, and nuns marched alongside King in Selma (Oates 1982, 349). It was a brilliant inspiration by King and a great symbolic success—a process goal—for the movement.

However, after Reverend Reeb was beaten and clubbed to death, President Johnson went on national television and explicitly endorsed the SCLC's efforts in Selma, comparing them to Lexington, Concord, and Appomattox (Garrow 1986, 385, 408). Johnson said the police acts in Selma denying American citizens the right to vote had aroused the conscience of the nation. In announcing his plans to submit a new voting rights bill to Congress, Johnson proclaimed that "the time for waiting is gone" and, in obvious identification with the Civil Rights Movement, he even recited the movement's slogan when he quoted the black spiritual song saying, "We *shall* overcome." While King welcomed Johnson's pledge to federal action, he was angry that no such public outcry occurred after Jimmie Lee Jackson was killed, but only after the white minister, Reverend Reeb, died (Oates 1982, 354).

Ten days after Reeb's death, the 54-mile march from Selma to Montgomery resumed. But this time, the marchers were protected from white violence during the entire three-day march by nearly 2,000 troops from the Alabama National Guard, who were placed under federal command by orders from President Johnson, something for which King had long been asking. A. L. Herman (1998, 134) compares this march to Gandhi's famous Salt March to the sea at Dandi (see Chapter 5) as the nation increasingly realized the march's significance and symbolic importance. After King and the other marchers arrived in Montgomery, the largest gathering of civil rights demonstrators in southern history (Oates 1982, 362) heard King's rousing "How Long? Not Long!" speech in which he expressed the hope and confidence that soon blacks would win their rights. By utilizing his now familiar use of anaphora, King's speech rang with the similar rhythmic, hypnotic cadences as his famous "I Have a Dream" speech:

> Let us . . . march to the realization of the American dream. Let us march on segregated housing. . . . Let us march on segregated schools. . . . Let us march on poverty. . . . Let us march on ballot boxes. . . . I know you are asking today "How long will it take?" I come to say to you this afternoon, however difficult the moment, however frustrating the hour, it will not be long, because truth pressed to earth will rise again. How long? Not long, because no lie can live forever. How long? Not long, because you still reap what you sow. How long? Not long, because the arm of the moral universe is long but it bends toward justice. How long? Not long! Not long because mine eyes have seen the glory of the coming of the Lord! (Carson 1998, 286)

But in that same speech, King predicted a "season of suffering" as civil rights activists confronted increasingly violent and virulent white opposition from the likes of Sheriff Clark and his notorious "possemen" and the White Citizens' Councils. Indeed, King's dire prediction was confirmed when a carload of Ku Klux Klan night riders gunned down Viola Gregg Liuzzo, a white Detroit housewife, as she was giving marchers a ride back to Selma from Montgomery.

Results of Selma

The Selma march was marked by many accomplishments. According to Stephen Oates (1982, 365), the Selma march was the Civil Rights Movement's and King's finest hour. Through his actions in Selma, King had done far more than prove himself as a leader: he had proved the power of nonviolent resistance, albeit ensured under the watchful eye of the National Guard. Selma was a watershed event for King, nonviolence, and the Civil Rights Movement because for the first time it energized otherwise inert adherents into becoming active fighters and participants in the struggle. Selma brought the ugly reality of racism right into peoples' living rooms. It finally spurred whites and blacks from all over the country, not just to express sympathy with the plight of blacks in the South, but to actually go down South themselves and march alongside King and the others. If Birmingham energized Americans to express support for the movement in their own hometowns, Selma spurred them to actually travel to the Deep South and risk their own safety and join the marchers (Oates 1982, 365). King must have seen the beginnings of his dream of the beloved community taking form right there in Selma.

Perhaps the greatest tangible success that stemmed from the Selma March was the August 1965 passage of the Voting Rights Act, which essentially killed the Jim Crow Laws (see the Introduction to this part). The Voting Rights Act opened the ballot booth to many blacks, giving them the right to vote. It had a profound impact on electoral politics in the South. Many local white officials, who openly supported segregation, were voted out of office. Other white politicians had to change their stance on segregation if they wished to remain in office. Ironically, even George Wallace, the rabid segregationist governor of Alabama who once stood on the steps of a state college campus to deny black students entry and said "segregation now and segregation forever," began courting black voters for fear of being voted out of office (Oates 1982, 371). Decades later, a bedraggled retired Governor Wallace, in constant pain from an assassination attempt that left him permanently disabled, was filmed making a laughable, feeble attempt at redemption. Director Spike Lee interviewed Wallace for Lee's documentary *Four Little Girls* (1997), about the murderous church bombing in Alabama. At one point, a decrepit Wallace called over his clearly reluctant black assistant to have the man affirm that Wallace and he were good friends.

In the glow of his successes in Selma, King announced the "Alabama Project," a three-pronged nonviolent strategy designed to turn up the pressure on Alabama and intensify the campaign for civil rights there. The Alabama Project's strategy included:

1. Asking that no company locate new plants in Alabama;
2. Calling on all private and public organizations to withhold funds and investments from the state of Alabama; and
3. Calling for all civil rights supporters to boycott all Alabama products.

Notice how, with each successive stage in this plan, the strategy escalates its nonviolent attack. As the chapters on Gandhi showed, this type of escalation is the hallmark of a well-planned nonviolent strategy. However, many opposed this plan, including some of King's closest advisers and friends in the SCLC who lost interest in the plan fairly quickly. Not much came of the Alabama Project as King began reorienting the SCLC's focus on other programs (Garrow 1986, 417). This is ironic since the NAACP today has called for a similar boycott of the state of South Carolina, protesting its use of the Confederate flag flying over its statehouse. Many businesses in South Carolina are, in part, responding to this type of pressure and calling openly for the flag's removal.

THE CHICAGO HOUSING PROJECT (1966)

Background to Chicago

By the mid-1960s, the Civil Rights Movement had struck many significant victories in the South; the most blatant forms of inequality for blacks, namely, segregation, were melting away. And the nonviolent direct action of King's SCLC accounted for many of those victories. Although the South was not a "finished product" in terms of equality and race relations, King began to turn his attention toward the North, where the situation for blacks was significantly different. In the South, blacks faced blatant forms of discrimination that were readily identified and targeted. However, conditions in the North were quite different.

Although northern blacks were not subjected to the racism of Jim Crow Laws, they faced an entirely different kind of racial discrimination that revolved around life in the crowded, dilapidated urban ghettoes. Joblessness and poor housing conditions in the ghettoes contributed to the frustration, despair, and hopelessness that many northern blacks felt. At times, this despair erupted in massive and horrible riots in urban centers, such as in the Watts section of Los Angeles in August 1965. As King was exposed to the conditions of blacks in the ghettoes, he became increasingly convinced of what some of his aides, such as Bayard Rustin, were telling him for a couple of years: that the most serious issues facing the Civil Rights Movement were economic problems of class rather than of race (Garrow 1986, 439–440). As early as 1964, King was emphasizing economic issues and calling on the federal government to do more in the way of government programs that would target poor people throughout the country, including poor whites, blacks, Latinos, and Native Americans. King's public rhetoric had an increasingly "sharp edge" to it as he referred to northern slums as "little more than a domestic colony." He decried "our vicious class system" and spoke of the need for major economic reform on behalf of the country's poor people (Garrow 1986, 455, 466). King saw that the severely depressed economic standards of blacks were a "structural part of the economy" and lamented that "[s]o often . . . I have had to watch my dream turn into a nightmare" (Garrow 1986, 434). The economic deprivation of America's northern slums seemed to fly in the face of the hopeful optimism King expressed in his famous "I Have a Dream" and "How Long? Not Long" speeches.

In conjunction with his concern for the economic injustices in the urban centers of the North, King began contemplating how new forms of nonviolent direct action might be utilized to expose the racism blacks faced in the North, which took more subtle and covert forms than in the South and, hence, were much more difficult to expose and combat. For example, blacks in the North faced substandard housing but often had to pay higher prices for it. Additionally, black entrepreneurs experienced severe obstacles to obtaining business loans. Along with discrimination in employment and higher education, these deeply embedded forms of racism were harder to eradicate.

In fighting for the rights of blacks in the North, King acknowledged that the situation was significantly different from the South:

> Constitutional rights was the subject of the fight in the South. In the North, human rights is more the question. So here [in the North], the concept of civil disobedience is different. There are fewer unjust laws. (Garrow 1986, 449)

Early in his career, King worked under the mistaken belief that victories for blacks in the South would have positive spin-off effects on blacks in the North (Oates 1982, 367). However, while southern blacks learned to fight for their rights and win victories, the misery of slum life in the northern ghettoes continued unabated. Ghetto blacks in the North were walled in by racist real estate practices, discriminatory bankers, and exploitative landlords (Oates 1982, 368). King was feeling guilty over the fact that he was fighting to get blacks a seat at the lunch counter only to realize belatedly that many blacks did not have the economic wherewithal to buy a meal at that counter. Moreover, the population of the urban centers was decreasing as middle-class Americans moved into the suburbs. This left the remaining poor and lower-class urbanites with a de- creased tax base, which meant there were fewer resources to fund badly needed infrastructural improvements in the cities' schools, parks, libraries, and so forth. King warned that these conditions left blacks in the ghettoes "seething with unarticulated fury and frustration" and that more riots, which he called "the language of the unheard," could occur unless more was done to alleviate the misery of the northern slums (Oates 1982, 368, 377).

By 1966, the appeal of nonviolence was waning since many blacks, 10 years removed from the Montgomery Bus Boycott, had seen little change. This worried King and galvanized him to make ef- forts to regenerate faith in nonviolent direct action. He chose to press the movement in the North and Chicago was his first effort. In July 1965, King was energized by a march on Chicago's City Hall, where he gave a speech before a crowd some 30,000 strong. King chose Chicago for several reasons. With a population of about 3.5 million, almost one-third of which was black, Chicago was one of the most "ghettoized" of the great northern cities (Oates 1982, 380) and thus presented a challenge for King and the SCLC. If they succeeded in Chicago, it might have a domino effect in the North similar to what happened in the South after the successes in Birmingham and Selma: "If we can break the system in Chicago, it can be broken anywhere in the country," King said (Frady 2002, 171). Also, King chose Chicago because it already had a vibrant, active Civil Rights Movement (Garrow 1986, 434). Besides, other northern cities, such as Philadelphia and New York, were considered and rejected. The SCLC faced unwelcoming hosts in New York, and in Philadelphia the local black leaders were embroiled in internal disputes.

But Chicago nevertheless presented a difficult challenge. King's nonviolent campaigns in the South were small compared to the effort that would be required in such a large metropolis. And Chicago's Mayor Richard Daley had an extremely powerful political machine, which many Chicago blacks supported and which could be counted on to block King's efforts at reform. Mayor Daley had his own plans for improving Chicago's ghettoes and he did not welcome King's efforts. Moreover, King likely could not expect too much assistance from the Johnson administration because King had begun intensifying his attacks on President Johnson's Vietnam War policy.

The Chicago Campaign

In January 1966, King announced commencement of the Chicago Campaign whose main achievement goal was to obtain relief for Chicago's slum dwellers in the form of improved housing (recall that King's ultimate goal was always creation of the beloved community). Some of the stated goals of the campaign included:

1. Demonstrating to slum-dwellers that all was not hopeless and that they could do something to improve their conditions;
2. Securing support from Americans nationwide for improved housing, education and social opportunities for blacks in the inner cities; and
3. Creating the beloved community by making *qualitative* changes in peoples' souls, like rejecting racism and discrimination and *quantitative* changes in the material conditions of blacks in the inner cities, like cleaner and better homes and schools. (Oates 1982, 387)

To dramatize the conditions of slum life in the ghetto, King and his family rented an apartment on Chicago's West Side. While living in the cramped, dilapidated quarters, he learned firsthand the conditions that prevailed in the ghetto: compared to white neighborhoods in Chicago, blacks were paying higher rents for smaller apartments that were in much worse condition (Oates 1982, 388). King observed a behavioral change in his children's personality while they lived in the cramped apartment. With fewer things to do and in a suffocating, closed-in space, King observed that his children screamed and fought with each other far more than they ever did before (Oates 1982, 408). King's residence in a West Side slum inspired the blacks living there, drew widespread media attention, and compelled the landlord in the building to finally make long-overdue repairs. Some observers joked that all King had to do was establish residence in each of Chicago's many slums in order to provoke improvements.

Although considerable planning went into the campaign, it was not well organized, no real long-term strategy emerged and its leadership suffered from internal bickering. The closest the activists came to devising a coherent strategy was a general list of activities that would be progressively interventionist. These included formation of a "slum dwellers union"; organizing and educating people about the conditions in the slums; carrying out demonstrations, rent strikes, and other boycotts; and planning for massive direct action to spark change across the country (Garrow 1986, 457; Oates 1982, 387). King's temporary absence—he was traveling in Europe—did not help matters since the activists in Chicago slowed their efforts, lost their focus, and accomplished few real tangible goals.

The campaign did not start off well because the organizers faced many obstacles and experienced many mishaps. First, it was perpetually short of funds, which hamstrung organizing efforts. Second, many blacks turned out to be uninterested in joining the proposed slum dwellers union; disunity on that score proved fatal to the union's prospects. Third, local black leaders, who were heavily influenced by King's rival Mayor Daley, were angry and unsupportive of his efforts regarding better housing in the slums; they wanted to focus on education. Fourth, Mayor Daley used his considerable financial resources to launch his own housing improvement project, which effectively neutralized King's efforts. Daley even suggested that King go back home to Georgia and several local black leaders echoed the sentiment (Oates 1982, 393–394).

Moreover, the campaign was distracted by the attempted assassination of James Meredith, a well-known civil rights worker in Mississippi. Consequently, King felt compelled to leave Chicago and go to Mississippi to help organize the "Meredith March for Peace in Mississippi" (it has also been referred to as the "Meredith March Against Fear"). Unfortunately, King's return to the South did not prove to be very much of a welcome respite from the problems he was facing in the Chicago Campaign. The Meredith March turned out to be unsuccessful as well. Not only did this march provoke some of the most violent police brutality to date, but King's call for federal intervention similar to Selma fell on deaf ears, perhaps because the Johnson administration was perturbed by King's increasingly vocal attacks on Johnson's Vietnam War policies (Oates 1982, 403).

Moreover, King was embarrassed at the Meredith March by some young black radicals, led by Stokely Carmichael from the SNCC, who did not want whites to join them in the march and who deliberately sought to provoke matters by shouting the black nationalist slogan "Black Power!" as they marched. King was forced to undertake delicate negotiations with some of the marchers to find a compromise where they could all continue together. Later, Carmichael acknowledged that he deliberately used the "Black Power!" slogan in public for the first time in King's presence to try to force King into taking a stand. King did take a stand, but not the one Carmichael wanted. King resisted the "Black Power!" slogan and said he would not join the march unless the SNCC pledged to refrain from shouting it. He also said that blacks would win nothing by chanting such slogans or resorting to violence. King denounced "Black Power!" and, in a speech to a Mississippi audience, he remained adamant in his condemnation of violence:

> I'm sick and tired of violence. I'm tired of the war in Vietnam. I'm tired of war and conflict in the world. I'm tired of hate. I'm tired of selfishness. I'm tired of evil. [But] I'm not going to use violence no matter who says it. (Frady 2002, 184)

The debacle in Mississippi made King all the more determined to score a victory for nonviolence in Chicago. Upon his return there, he announced plans for a massive rally at Chicago's Soldier Field on Sunday, July 10. "Freedom Sunday," as it was called, was designed to launch an all-out push to make Chicago an "open city" for housing. But, alas, King's plans for Chicago did not bear fruit. As he was canvassing Chicago neighborhoods—through church rallies and community centers—to win support for Freedom Sunday, King was booed by blacks in the audience, some of whom were vocal "Black Power!" advocates. King was startled and hurt by the booing: it was the first time that had ever happened to him. But he sympathized with the hecklers because

> for 12 years, I and others like me, had held out radiant promises of progress. I had preached to them about my dream. I had lectured to them about the not too distant day when they would have freedom. . . . Their hopes soared. They were now booing because they felt we were unable to deliver on our promises. (Oates 1982, 406)

Freedom Sunday arrived during one of Chicago's infamous heat waves, which lowered turnout for the event. Moreover, Mayor Daley refused to accept King's demands for improved housing, arguing that he had his own antislum program. In response, King vowed to conduct sit-ins, camp-ins, demonstrations, and boycotts and to otherwise provoke matters to expose racism in Chicago and force Daley to act. That is exactly what happened. King led a march of slum dwellers, including some gang members, through an all-white neighborhood. The whites there were so inflamed that they became violent and started a riot, which continued even after King and the other marchers had departed.

King was hit in the head with a rock and was almost stabbed during the riot. King remarked that he had never before seen a white crowd so hostile and hate-filled, including the white rage he saw in Selma and later in Mississippi. King was gratified, however, by the conduct of his own marchers, particularly the gang members who refused to hit back even as they were bloodied and broken by the flying bottles and debris, courtesy of the white rioters. To King, this was especially gratifying because he had worked hard in reaching out to gang members, convincing hundreds of them to put their guns and knives down and act as "marshals" once the marches began. Their behavior during the riot confirmed for King that "even very violent temperaments can be channeled through nonviolent discipline" (Oates 1982, 413).

Results of Chicago

Before the white riots on August 5, the riots that occurred in Chicago were mostly conducted by blacks who were enraged when city officials turned off the fire hydrants youths were using to keep cool during the heat wave. Although those riots embarrassed Mayor Daley—they showed that his antislum programs were not really working—it was the potential for more white riots that helped set the stage for the "Chicago Summit" between King, other black leaders, and city officials. As the marches continued in white neighborhoods, they exposed some of the ugliest forms of racism the Civil Rights Movement had ever seen. Some whites displayed Nazi swastikas and rebel flags while chanting white power slogans and "Hate! Hate! Hate!" King announced a huge interracial march, but Mayor Daley thwarted this effort by obtaining a court injunction against holding the march at the proposed sight.

Undaunted, King changed the venue of the march to Cicero, an all-white Chicago suburb that was a bastion of white racism and intolerance and in an area that lay outside the antimarching court order. Mayor Daley, horrified by King's planned march in Cicero and embarrassed by the ugliness the marches had already revealed in many white Chicagoans, finally agreed to meet with King (Oates 1982, 414–415).

By late August, they announced the "Summit Agreement," which contained many provisions that looked really good, at least on paper. First, the settlement called for intensified efforts at enforcing fair housing laws. Next, banks agreed to equality in loans and business leaders pledged to work for fair housing. Third, the settlement established the Council on Metropolitan Open Housing to investigate housing standards around the city and oversee open occupancy provisions, meaning housing could not be denied people based on race (Garrow 1986, 519; Oates 1982, 415).

Many blacks denounced the settlement as a sell-out, especially because it contained no concrete timetable for the proposed changes and little in the way of enforcement mechanisms. King was even booed and heckled by an audience as he tried to build support for the agreement. Nevertheless, others defended the settlement as the best they could hope to get from Mayor Daley's powerful political machine. For King, the settlement showed that nonviolence could force the white power structure in a northern city as large as Chicago into making significant concessions, which it had never done before. If Mayor Daley's powerful political machine could be moved by nonviolence in Chicago, then nonviolence could work in other northern cities. Others disputed this assessment. According to Louis Lomax (1984), for instance, Chicago was a failure, not for King, but for his "Christian nonviolent attack upon complex socio-economic problems" so deeply embedded in places like Chicago's ghettoes (171).

Ultimately King and the SCLC accomplished little of tangible consequence from their efforts in Chicago. Ghetto life changed little for the vast majority of blacks in Chicago's inner city. And the voter registration drive activists left behind also sputtered to a standstill; in all of Chicago, only a few hundred newly registered voters were added to the rolls (Garrow 1986, 544). The most successful aspect of King's efforts in Chicago was "Operation Breadbasket," a jobs creation program headed by a young, eager minister named Jesse Jackson, but which had little to do with King's original goals of improving housing for blacks. Modeled after a successful program in Atlanta, dozens of Chicago clergymen gathered employment data in industries—bakeries, milk companies, soft drink bottlers, and soup companies—suspected of job discrimination against blacks. These four industries were chosen because they were susceptible to black economic pressure since so much of their profits depended on black patronage. As such, threats of boycotts helped lead to the hiring of hundreds of blacks in positions in these industries from which they were previously excluded.

The Chicago Campaign was considered by many to be the northern equivalent of the failed Albany campaign. "There's no question," one of King's aides said, "King was beaten" in Chicago (Frady 2002, 178). One organizer even conceded that one of the movement's prime achievement goals—the unconditional surrender of the slum system—was unrealistic to begin with (Oates 1982, 428). King's nonviolent resistance in Chicago was effective in exposing the problems slum dwellers faced but it did not prove adept at eliminating the evil itself. King and his staff could raise and publicize the issues, they could dramatize and even provoke, but protests in Chicago did not eliminate the racism and injustices suffered by blacks in Chicago (Garrow 1986, 353). Chicago forced King to realize just how deeply entrenched racism and discrimination in America actually were. But for King, all that meant was that his nonviolence had to be more creative, more militant and more disciplined, all of which he planned for in the Poor Peoples' Campaign.

THE POOR PEOPLES' CAMPAIGN (1968)

Although King was unable to launch the Poor Peoples' Campaign—he was assassinated before he had a chance to complete preparations—it is still worth examining briefly because it sheds light on how King's approach to civil rights in America both remained the same and changed. His approach remained the same in at least two key ways. First, he was as committed to nonviolence and nonviolent direct action to agitate for social and economic change as he ever was before. Despite his failure in Chicago, his commitment to nonviolence never wavered; perhaps it even grew as he saw how little violence—in the form of riots—had actually accomplished. Second, despite being frequently dejected, King refused to give up on people, including whites, holding—until the very end—an optimistic hopefulness about the redemptive potential of all people.

However, despite these stable core beliefs, King was also going through some changes. His views about whites, American society, economics, and the U.S. government were changing considerably, becoming significantly more militant and radical. King began to acknowledge that only a small portion of whites, mostly college students, were truly committed to obtaining real equality and justice for blacks.

King's views about the American economy were becoming equally extreme. Observing the incredible wealth of a country right alongside horrifying destitution, King complained in 1966 that "something is wrong with the economy of our nation . . . something is wrong with capitalism" (Garrow 1986, 537). Although the legislative and constitutional changes the Civil Rights Movement had won for blacks represented an impressive accomplishment, King considered these only surface changes because the substantive conditions of blacks—particularly the many who lived in poverty—had not changed very much. Increasingly, King's rhetoric became more militant, changing from that of "reform" to that of "revolution," and his Poor Peoples' Campaign was to be the agent sparking that revolutionary change.

The Poor Peoples' Campaign had several major goals. King's vision of reform in America had now reached full blossom. He sought to bring a broad cross section of the nation's poor people—whites from Appalachia, blacks from the rural South and urban North, Lations from the Southwest, and Native Americans from the West—to the nation's capital to conduct civil disobedience campaigns so massive as to disrupt the normal functions of government. Herewith, the focus was going to be on economic issues of class, not political issues of race. He sought congressional passage of legislation that would guarantee:

1. A minimum annual income for all Americans;
2. A federal government commitment to achieve full employment; and
3. Production of at least half a million low-costing housing units per year. (Garrow 1986, 595–596)

Consistent with the Hegelian principle of synthesis, King wanted to combine the best of capitalism—with its emphasis on hard work and individual achievement—with the best of socialism—with its emphasis on caring for the weak and needy.

King hoped to achieve this economic revolution through nonviolent direct action that would combine massive civil disobedience with self-suffering in hopes of redeeming the oppressor and healing the rifts in American society. King planned to transform his nonviolence into a new, more mature level of civil disobedience to "compel unwilling authorities to yield to the mandates of justice" (Garrow 1986, 581). King was increasingly militant in his stance. He said nonviolence must now be "dislocative and disruptive" because "pressureless persuasion does not move the power structure" (Garrow 1986, 591). King was clear about his intentions for the nation's capital: "we're not going to Washington to beg . . . [but] to demand what is ours" (Garrow 1986, 592). He made plans to occupy the city's buildings with strategically placed demonstrations throughout the city, bringing Washington to a standstill until his demands were met.

Specifically, King's plans called for recruiting 3,000 poor people from 10 different cities and then training them in nonviolence for several months. Then they would be transported to Washington, DC, to engage in direct action designed to disrupt transportation and government operations in the capital until the country responded to the plight of the poor. Phase One called for the poor to encamp in plainly visible shantytowns in Washington and undertake brief, exploratory demonstrations. Phase Two called for the Poor Peoples' Army to dramatize the plight of the poor by disrupting government operations throughout the city and getting arrested. With this phase, King hoped to dramatize the vast gulf in economic standards that existed between America's poor and wealthy classes. Phase Three, if needed, involved a new, more drastic idea: nationwide boycotts of businesses and shopping centers if changes were not forthcoming (Oates 1982, 460–461).

King's course was bold and risky. The Poor Peoples' Campaign was subjected to near universal criticism, emanating from just about all quarters of American society, including within his own organization. James Bevel, a senior SCLC aide, urged King to abandon the Poor Peoples' Campaign and focus on ending American involvement in Vietnam instead (Mack 2003, 122). Worse, the SCLC might not have the financial or organizational resources to support such a campaign and there was still the prospect that King might not be able to assemble the broad, inclusive coalition of poor people for action (Oates 1982, 450). But King was determined to carry out his plan, even as he was increasingly isolated, depressed, and preoccupied with death. He had predicted that he would be assassinated in Washington during the campaign, but he was killed in Tennessee while supporting a garbage workers' strike in Memphis the day after giving a prophetic speech in which he hinted that he knew his own end was near. With King's memory looming large, the SCLC, which by then was engaged in a momentous struggle for its very survival, made a spirited attempt at carrying out King's Poor Peoples' Campaign, but it proved to be a small, inconsequential affair.

CONCLUDING COMMENTS

Martin Luther King, Jr.'s nonviolent direct action campaigns in the United States were designed not just to win black citizens the rights and freedoms that white citizens enjoyed by virtue of their birth in the country. They were also designed to help redeem the soul of a country whose lofty promises and creeds were not being upheld for vast portions of her population.

Toward that end, King's campaigns did not accomplish their ultimate goal of creating the beloved community, at least insofar as the entire nation is concerned. To be sure, King's actions, his words, and his own ultimate sacrifice changed the hearts and minds of many white—and black—Americans. More concretely, his campaigns did contribute directly to significant achievement goals, not least of which were the passage of two landmark pieces of legislation ultimately guaranteeing legal equality and rights for blacks and others. The direct political result of King's "Christian Satyagraha" was the Civil Rights Act of 1964, which was a direct outcome of the Birmingham Campaign and the Voting Rights Act of 1965, which was a direct outcome of the Selma March (Herman 1998, 134). In the early 1960s, President Kennedy resisted King's call for civil rights legislation, counseling African Americans to wait. King's refusal to wait resulted in the Birmingham Campaign and that moment of creative tension that sparks change in America. Then in the mid-1960s, President Johnson cautioned King that the time was not right for voting rights legislation: he too told African Americans to wait. The result this time was the Selma Campaign. Ultimately, King's greatest gift to blacks was that he "taught them how to confront those who oppressed them, how to take pride in their race and their history, [and] how to demand and win their constitutional rights as American citizens" (Oates 1982, 373). Surely no small accomplishment for a man who did not live to see his 40th birthday.

PART IV

Comparing Gandhi and King

CHAPTER 9

_____

A Comparative Analysis
of Gandhi and King

This chapter compares the similarities and differences between Gandhi and King. Although an entire book could be devoted to comparing these two great historical figures, this chapter will focus on their roles as political leaders, religious devotees, family men, and heroes.

AS POLITICAL LEADERS OF NONVIOLENT RESISTANCE MOVEMENTS

As Leaders Dealing within Their Own Movement

King's leadership style contrasts quite sharply with Gandhi's. King was not the administrator Gandhi was. Both were master fund-raisers and Gandhi kept scrupulous books and financial records while King did not have the attention to detail as did Gandhi. But King's closest aides, who followed him out of a true belief in nonviolence as a philosophy of life and accepted him as their leader, did not expect King to be a great administrator: that was not his role. He was a dreamer, an orator, and a holy man of faith. According to one aide:

> What else does he need to be? He's a symbol that there needs to be a moral voice in America talking about the injustice and the inequity. . . . He doesn't need to know how to answer a telephone. (Oates 1982, 286)

Unlike Gandhi, when it came to settling disputes between their respective staffs, King was conflict averse. He did not like to have to make personnel decisions, especially those involving someone's dismissal. He did not enjoy open, conflictual confrontations within his staff and sought to avoid them. King rarely lost his temper, but when he did, his aides were left stunned and paralyzed by the moment. He was also steadfastly loyal to close friends and advisers, such as Stanley Levison and Jack O'Dell. Levison was King's close friend. O'Dell, who helped run the SCLC's New York office and had an affinity for numbers, had built a substantial donor list. When the U.S. Justice Department admonished King to jettison Levison and O'Dell because they were thought to be communists, King balked, demanding to see proof of their communist affiliations. When the government failed to produce any shred of evidence, King demurred, his sense of loyalty to Levison and O'Dell trumping whatever political calculus the federal government was trying to get him to make. Eventually, however, pressure from President Kennedy and Attorney General Robert Kennedy compelled King to fire O'Dell, which was one of the most agonizing decisions he ever had to make. However, King maintained close contact with Levison—usually through indirect channels—despite the Kennedy brothers' entreaties.

While King was indifferent to staff discipline and reluctant to fire anyone for a serious transgression, Gandhi was not. Gandhi discovered a childhood friend, who was living with him in South Africa, in bed with a prostitute. Despite the debt of loyalty Gandhi once felt he owed this man, he immediately expelled him from his house and never welcomed him back again. By contrast, when King finally succumbed to intense pressure to force the resignation of his controversial aide, Bayard Rustin, he nevertheless maintained close contact with Rustin, so much so that the "firing" was official in name only. Additionally, although both men were very sensitive, King was far more reluctant to hurt peoples' feelings than was Gandhi, who was apparently more concerned with pursuing the truth, even if it meant offending those closest to him, including family members.

Gandhi was less averse to wading into the middle of difficult and controversial matters that arose within his movement. Although his was an "inclusive" type of leadership, Gandhi also had authoritarian (Dalton 1993, 96), even dictatorial, traits when it came to getting his way in the Congress Party. Gandhi knew how popular he was and how essential his participation in Congress was in order to get mass support for Congress policies. However, if Congress began to veer in a direction that Gandhi opposed, he would threaten to resign from his leadership position. Even though his official position in Congress was at times merely symbolic, his resignation, or threat thereto, would have serious negative consequences for the party's popularity. As such, Gandhi successfully used this personal power to force Congress into choosing one leader over another and to force Congress into adopting his satyagraha methods as official party platforms, even though many, if not most, of the Congress leaders did not share anything near his philosophical commitment to nonviolence. Despite their intense love for him, some leaders, especially Nehru, thought Gandhi's ideas about nonviolence, village spinning programs, and a simplistic life of labor without heavy industrialization were not only quaint or quirky, but downright dangerous to the security of an emerging independent Indian nation.

Neither was Gandhi reluctant to involve himself in the personal confrontations among his followers. A famous example of this is the feud between two of Congress's greatest leaders, Jawaharlal Nehru and Vallabhbhai Patel. Both men were headstrong and stubborn and possessed great force of personality and they disagreed on many policies and programs within the Congress Party, both before and after Indian independence. Their feud grew so bad at times that they could not even stand to talk to each other. After independence, both leaders would write to Gandhi offering to resign so that the other could assume unquestioned leadership over the Congress Party and the country's government (which were virtually one and the same thing just after independence). Yet Gandhi would have none of that, taking a very active role in urging them to work together to iron out their differences. Nor was Gandhi reluctant to take sides in these feuds, agreeing with one person (usually Patel) and opposing the other (usually Nehru).

In King's case, when differences such as these emerged, he often remained silent, seemingly aloof. He appears to have had no stomach for settling serious disputes between people in the movement. He often procrastinated when he was called on to make a difficult decision to settle such matters. He did not like to confront combative personalities among the black leadership. When it came to debating, arguing or otherwise doing battle within the movement, "he was at a loss," said trusted confidante Bayard Rustin (Garrow 1986, 343). Since Montgomery, King presented "an almost galactic remoteness" to those around him (Frady 2002, 46).

According to Garrow (1986), "[C]ombat with people outside the movement was one thing, but head-to-head unpleasantness was something King avoided consistently," adopting a passive stance (343). This is ironic when considered against the backdrop of King's very active approach to resisting segregation and also in light of his relentless and harsh self-criticism. King disliked speaking harshly of anyone and was reluctant to ask for anyone's resignation. In one case, even after determining that an aide was guilty of stealing from the SCLC's treasury, King resisted asking for the aide's resignation. Some saw King's passivity and gentleness amid rowdy office gatherings as a fault while others saw it as a valued blessing. He would quietly sit through raucous sessions and then, in true Hegelian fashion, he would try to reach a synthesis among all the different viewpoints, trying to appeal to everyone. Aides said he never got angry and demonstrated unusual patience (Garrow 1986, 464–465). Perhaps that is exactly the type of leader the Civil Rights Movement needed, given its many discordant voices.

It is interesting to note that neither King nor Gandhi sought the mantle of leadership: it was thrust upon them as if it sought them out. If not for Gandhi's rude exposure to white racism on a train in South Africa, he may not have ever tried to organize Indians there. Instead, he probably would have become South Africa's richest "colored" attorney. Moreover, upon his return to India after a 20-year absence, Gandhi was not initially a prime mover in Indian politics. Nor did he deliberately seek out injustices against which to launch satyagraha campaigns (Brown 1989, 108). Instead, he sought—through months of travel—to rediscover an India that he ceased to know while away for so long. The same can be said of King who was a reluctant leader at first (Phillips 1999, 41). Upon his return to the South after years away at northern schools and as pastor at the Dexter Avenue Baptist Church in Montgomery, King planned on having two professional careers, first as a pastor at some respectable middle-class church in the South and, second, as a professor in the hallowed halls of academe. Leading and organizing a mass, nonviolent resistance campaign for 13 years was not among his plans. Both Gandhi and King were outsiders to the movement whose leadership reins they assumed. Gandhi had only been in South Africa a very short while before he began organizing the Indians. Likewise, King had only been in Montgomery a short while before someone nominated him to head up the bus boycott effort. Perhaps it was this "outsider" status that initially made these two men appealing to their respective communities: neither was (yet) caught up in any petty internal squabbles, so each could approach the issues relatively unfettered and unencumbered by stifling internal politics.

As leaders and moral spokespersons, both felt strongly about people taking the initiative for their own self-improvement. Both were extremely self-critical and tried to meet a very high standard of self-improvement they set for themselves and then for others. Both used their leadership roles to reform their own people from within as much as they sought to confront oppression from without. King argued that blacks "must assume the primary responsibility" for making changes that would improve their status (Washington 1986, 148). If blacks believe that others will be more concerned about their rights than they themselves are, then they will contribute to their own victimization and marginalization in American society. In criticizing blacks for becoming cynical and disillusioned with American society, King said they "[h]ave so conditioned themselves to the system of segregation that they have lost that creative something called *initiative*. So many [blacks] use their oppression as an excuse for mediocrity" (Washington 1986, 150).

Gandhi believed that Indians' economic, political, and spiritual reform went hand in hand. Recall his three-part program for improving Indian society: weaving homespun cloth, attaining Hindu–Muslim unity, and ending untouchability. In each of these programs observe Gandhi's passionate desire to reform India. In constantly preaching khadi (homespun), Gandhi sought radical *economic* reform to revive each village and help make it self-sufficient. In preaching Hindu–Muslim unity, Gandhi sought *political* reform to help ensure the survival of a single "mother" India. And, in launching his controversial attack on untouchability, he sought *spiritual* reform in an effort to save Hinduism from internal self-decay. These issues were far more important to him than was political independence from Britain, for what was the point of changing political leadership in Delhi if village life remained so hopelessly destitute, if India was brutally divided, and if Hinduism remained a corrupt and oppressive system?

Toward the end of their lives, both Gandhi and King had experienced many failures and frustrations with their own people. Both acknowledged that their followers practiced nonviolence, not as a philosophy the way they did, but as an expedient. It was not from a philosophical conviction to nonviolence that most of their adherents launched boycotts or tax resistance. Rather, it was because of the practical utility of using nonviolent methods, including the fact that Gandhi's and King's popularity made it essential to have their support. If this meant adopting nonviolence as a pragmatic policy tool, so be it: Gandhi and King were under no illusions, both knew that they were being used. As the more radical Black Power Movement began to grow in popularity by the mid-1960s, King saw his appeal declining and he began to ruminate on whether history had passed him by. The same feelings of ineffectiveness plagued Gandhi at different points in his life, most notably during the mid- to late 1920s, right after his poorly planned satyagraha campaign led to disaster and then again in the 1940s as independence and partition degenerated into civil war (Dalton 1993, 185).

Nevertheless, neither Gandhi nor King hesitated to criticize those with whom they had philosophical disagreements. Of Malcolm X's aggressive rhetoric about using "any means necessary" in defense of black rights, King argued that such an approach was neither morally nor strategically sound. Of the white clergy who gave sympathetic lip service to black civil rights, King chastised them for too often being a "taillight" rather than a "headlight." Of the black activists in the Civil Rights Movement, King complained that it was populated with too many middle-class people and not enough activists from the grass roots in the rural South or the northern ghettoes (Garrow 1986, 540). Of the federal government, on which he relied so much in his confrontation with local and state governments in the South, King was critical of its snail-like pace in introducing civil rights legislation. King was also a vocal opponent of the federal government's foreign policy in Vietnam. For his part, Gandhi published articles criticizing the Congress leadership. He accused it of being corrupt and venal. He charged Congress with being more concerned with protecting its privilege of power than with helping India's destitute masses. He wrote forceful articles railing against ancient Hindu traditions, such as child marriages and untouchability, calling for an end to both.

One of the most important issues to discuss in this regard is the challenge both Gandhi and King faced in their attempt to mold their constituents into a unified front. Neither man was successful in this. The black community, as with the Indian, suffered from internal divisions, not least of which were those arising out of religious differences. Not all blacks in America are Christians, just as not all Indians are Hindus. Even though virtually all blacks and all Indians experienced the humiliation of white racism and white oppression, this shared experience proved to be an insufficient base on which Gandhi and King could build a lasting united front.

Interestingly, both were subjected to withering critiques from the Muslim leaders in their respective communities. To be sure, it must be a coincidence of history that both men—devout religious leaders that they were—confronted an increasingly hostile coethnic population that did not practice their faith, but instead practiced Islam.

The so-called Black Muslims in America, especially the Nation of Islam, through its gifted and powerful speaker Malcolm X, leveled scathing criticism against King and the nonviolent resisters. Most of Malcolm X's vitriol was reserved for whites, who he called "two-legged dogs," "blue-eyed devils," and "pale, sickly things." He used to rouse his black urban audiences in the North with fiery speeches, telling them, "Do you know why the white man really hates you? It's because every time he sees your face he sees a mirror of his own crime" (Frady 2002, 158). But Malcolm X was as unsparing in his attack on King's nonviolence. He proclaimed that King, with his nonviolent love-thy-oppressor philosophy, was speaking a language whites could not understand. Similarly, Mohammed Ali Jinnah, the powerful and charismatic leader of the Muslim League in India, had strong disagreements with Gandhi and blamed the Mahatma for some of the Hindu–Muslim problems. He became such a powerful force in Indian politics that he was able to thwart all of Gandhi's efforts to keep India united. This despite the fact that Malcolm X and Jinnah had great respect and admiration for King and Gandhi, respectively, and held them both in high regard.

There were times when Gandhi and King were well aware of their waning influence and the declining popularity of their message of nonviolence. Toward the end of his life and after observing the ghetto riots, a crestfallen King remarked that perhaps he should just allow the violence to take its course. Such feelings did not last long however, since he refused to stop speaking against violence and war no matter if he was the sole remaining person in the country speaking out thusly. Gandhi also knew that many of his "followers" tolerated him more than they adored him or believed in satyagraha.

As symbolic leaders of a popular movement, both Gandhi and King were beloved by the masses. But this is no small wonder since both so heavily identified themselves "downward" with the poor and disenfranchised. Despite coming from privilege (or perhaps because of it?), Gandhi and King had an intimate understanding of, and could implicitly relate to, the needs of the common folk (Oates 1982, 290). On marches, both drew throngs of people who just wanted to get a glimpse of them or to somehow participate in a historic moment. Like Gandhi, King was swarmed by onlookers trying to get closer to him, to touch him. Obviously, these throngs presented a security risk to King's person, but he did not fear that. A white reporter covering a march in Mississippi was astounded at the impact King had on the rural, uneducated blacks, even bringing tears to the faces of 5-year-old girls (Oates 1982, 399).

Both identified with the poor masses and worked tirelessly on their behalf. They lived like the poor, Gandhi in primitive rural huts, King in tenements in the Chicago ghetto. They traveled like the poor, Gandhi by third-class rail or by bare feet, King by bus or mule. They dressed like the poor, Gandhi in his simple white loincloth, King in his signature farmer's overalls. They worked like the poor, Gandhi toiling in the hot fields or at his spinning wheel, King bending down during the harvest with migrant farm laborers. Both saw that it was among their country's poorest that the most suffering occurred and, hence, that the most service needed to be rendered. They also recognized that it was among these multitudes that great reservoirs of untapped courage could be harnessed for nonviolent resistance. And both furnished these people with a potent weapon for removing their blinders, for overcoming their ignorance and illiteracy, and for giving them hope and a way to fight to end their despair (Oates 1982, 290).

As Leaders Confronting the Opponent

> There will be no rest, there will be no tranquility . . . until the nation comes to terms with our problem.
>
> Never let them rest.

The first quote, by King, indicates his relentless pursuit of justice for his people. His famous "We Will Never Be Satisfied" speech reinforces that image. The second quote, by Gandhi, is similar to King's. Both knew how to sustain a mass-oriented nonviolent resistance campaign. Even if they and their closest aides were jailed, there would be no let up among the rank-and-file nonviolent resisters. Civil disobedience and noncooperation would continue.

Although both the statements indicate a degree of relentlessness in confronting their opponents, both men sought to avoid taking advantage of their opponents' hardships. For instance, during a satyagraha campaign in South Africa, Gandhi suspended the campaign when white laborers on the railways went on strike. Gandhi thought it dishonorable and thus inconsistent with truth to take advantage of the opponent—the government—when it was weakened by the railway crisis. In suspending his own campaign while the government dealt with the white strikers, Gandhi was, in fact, letting them rest. King was sometimes convinced to delay a direct action campaign under similar circumstances. In one instance, he postponed a campaign until after Easter weekend. Ironically, Gandhi and King drove themselves mercilessly, rarely taking time to let themselves rest. Even into his late seventies, Gandhi was constantly on the move, sleeping only a few hours a night and walking miles and miles in his bare feet. King logged hundreds of thousands of miles each year as he traipsed around the country and the world preaching nonviolence, soliciting funds, and raising understanding of the Civil Rights Movement. Both Gandhi and King had exceptional fund-raising abilities, King through his eloquence and Gandhi through his persistent plodding. Gandhi was renowned for his ability to persuade his wealthy female visitors (and some men) to give him their expensive jewelry so he could donate it to various trust funds for the poor.

Recall earlier statements that nonviolence is not passive: it is active, creative, and provocative. While Gandhi and King may not have perfected nonviolent forms of resistance, they certainly helped the method progress in ways not seen before. One such way was provoking their opponents into arresting and jailing them. They knew that provoking their white opponents into arresting them would raise a groundswell of popular support. Imprisoning nonviolent resisters—with the cameras rolling—would only demonstrate to the world how desperate and morally bankrupt the governing authorities were. Indeed, the British government often refused to accept Gandhi's "invitation" to arrest him, knowing full well this would turn the people against it. King had similar experiences, such as when he was surprisingly bailed out of jail: he suspected this was the work of the very same sheriff (or his lackeys) who had arrested him in the first place.

Gandhi and King spoke eloquently of the experience of jail-going. King gave beautiful speeches about transforming a prison from a "dungeon of shame" into a "haven of freedom and human dignity." Gandhi made jail-going "the hallmark of integrity and national commitment rather than an experience of degradation and public shame" (Brown 1989, 17). While in jail, both would engage in extensive prayer and study. Each would also do considerable writing, King's "Letter from Birmingham Jail" being the most famous. Moreover, imprisonment served yet another purpose, especially for Gandhi. He had become so popular and beloved that he welcomed jail as the only way to get respite from the throngs of admirers who flocked around him wherever he went, just to glimpse him or touch his legs or feet. This glimpsing or touching is referred to as *darshan* in Hinduism: Hindus believe that obtaining a Mahatma's darshan is an important holy ritual. Of course, it often left Gandhi jostled, weary, and even bruised about his legs and shoulders. Sometimes he had to shout at the darshan seekers just to get them to back away enough so he could walk down the street unhampered.

In examining the confrontation with their opponent, several interesting comparisons between Gandhi and King come to light. First, both felt directly the sting of white racism. As youths, whites intimidated both of them, but as adults they fearlessly stood up to the white power structure. Second, both confronted a white power structure that was extremely resistant to change. Like many others, they saw the essential hypocrisy of the whites: on the one hand, whites proclaimed adherence to a noble philosophy based on liberty, equality, and democracy. On the other hand, whites denied these same rights to people of color. Despite the support and sympathies they received from many whites, Gandhi and King each realized that the white power structure would not share its power and privilege willingly. They knew it would take an extended struggle, with considerable suffering, to win for their own people the same rights and freedoms that whites had come to expect as a matter of their birthright.

Although they both faced white opponents, it is interesting to note that Gandhi faced his adversary from the position of being a member of the Indian majority (in India, not South Africa) while King faced whites as a member of a minority. The British were greatly outnumbered in India, yet only a few hundred thousand British were able to dominate more than 300 million Indians. The British came to India of their own free will, as a colonizing race. Blacks were brought to America against their free will, as a slave race.

Gandhi sought to overthrow his opponent's governing system, arguing that to cooperate with the British system of government in India was to cooperate with evil. Words like that, considered seditious by the authorities, earned Gandhi a prison sentence. By contrast, King did not seek to overthrow the system of government in the United States. Rather, by exposing its shameful conduct, he sought to compel it to live up to its declared creed "that all men are created equal" and enjoy the same "inalienable rights." He sought, to use a familiar cliché of the time, a "seat at the table." He did not seek to overturn the table. King believed in American society and the American system of government. He believed the United States was truly an exceptional country and wanted blacks to be able to freely and equally participate in the wide range of opportunities the country offered. Although his views of the U.S. economic system grew more harsh and critical toward the end of his life, he never sought to "overthrow" the United States, only to reform it.

AS RELIGIOUS DEVOTEES

In youth, both Gandhi and King were skeptical of organized religion. In rebelling against the Hinduism of his devout mother, young Gandhi secretly ate meat. He even said he was inclined toward atheism. He did not read the Hindu holy book the Bhagavad Gita until he was a law student in London. King disdained the emotionalism and showmanship characteristic of many of the black churches he attended: he vowed never to become a minister. But their attitudes toward religion, more specifically toward faith, changed dramatically in early adulthood.

Both Gandhi and King were driven the most by their strong faiths. These were not politicians trying to be holy men; these were holy men trying to be politicians. In both cases, observe that a spiritual man is entering politics because he feels his religious beliefs compel him to do so. Despite their moments of doubt, despite their bouts with depression, and despite the hatred, chaos, and violence swirling all around them, neither lost faith. As their careers progressed—through failures and successes—it appears that they grew even stronger in their respective faiths. According to C. Eric Lincoln (1984), "[T]he peculiar genius of Martin Luther King is that he was able to translate religious fervor into social action, thereby creating political leadership under the rubric of his religious ministry" (xiii). But these same words could just as easily be written about Mohandas Gandhi, especially since both translated that fervor while at great peril to themselves and for Gandhi during a life span that was twice as long as King's.

During their nonviolent resistance campaigns, God and religion were constantly invoked. For instance, during his early years in South Africa, Gandhi said to the satyagrahis, "God is with us and so long as our cause is good, I don't mind a bit what powers the government are given or how savagely those powers are used" (Tendulkar 1951, 1:88). King made similar proclamations about having God on his side. On many occasions, King not only invoked God through citing scriptures, but also Jesus Christ. During the Montgomery Bus Boycott, King used language strikingly similar to Gandhi's in proclaiming that the movement could not fail because "our cause is just and God is on our side." At other times, King would proclaim, in his best preacher's baritone voice, that "if we are wrong, Jesus Christ is wrong! If we are wrong, God Almighty is wrong!" Moreover, King cited a broad range of authoritative theologians to bolster his arguments. He did this with masterful effect in his "Letter from Birmingham Jail" when he cited both St. Augustine and St. Thomas Aquinas to argue that unjust laws must be disobeyed.

Both leaders put themselves and their movements on the side of a just and merciful God. Both invoked love as a preeminent pillar of their religious program. King's use of agape brought "Gandhi's spirit of inclusiveness into an American context more than any other aspect of King's philosophy" (Dalton 1993, 183). It is worth repeating here that King liked to say that Christ furnished the spirit—of love, justice, redemption, and bearing the cross of suffering—and Gandhi furnished the method—of nonviolent resistance characterized by steadfastness, self-suffering, and soul force.

As far as his commitment to nonviolence, Gandhi said that if presented with the hypothetical choice between violence and cowardice, he would choose violence because "at least we would have acted like men." Despite his obvious feminine qualities, Gandhi also had a streak of machismo running through him: he admired the courage of combat soldiers and sought to instill in his "army" of nonviolent satyagrahis that same bravery. King acknowledged that history did provide some examples, such as the American Revolution, where legitimate and just victories were won using violence. Later on however, King's commitment to nonviolence, even in world politics, was unwavering. He remained steadfast in his moral condemnation of violence in general terms, especially insofar as it concerned the "black revolution," which was not seeking independence and separation like the American colonists, but rather seeking integration and inclusion in the fullness of the American Dream (Washington 1986, 365).

Some of Gandhi's critics point out that his near fanatical devotion to God and truth, expressed primarily through his own Hindu faith, actually helped fan the flames of religious intolerance between Hindus and Muslims. A strong case can be made for this point of view. Despite his own Herculean efforts to attain Hindu–Muslim unity, Gandhi's constant emphasis on religion and religious piety actually contributed to an increase in religious intolerance, which was not so hard to do in the first place since Hindus and Muslims had a shaky relationship for decades. At first, Mohammed Ali Jinnah, leader of the Muslim League and "father" of Pakistan, was a powerful and influential member of Congress with staunch unionist sentiments. However, he turned away from Congress as he began to perceive that the party was becoming increasingly a *Hindu* nationalist party, as opposed to an *Indian* nationalist party. Jinnah blamed this evolution in part on Gandhi who was constantly emphasizing religion in his speeches and actions. Rightly or wrongly, Jinnah and many other Muslims feared that Gandhi's emphasis on religion in politics would harm the Muslim minority; they worried that the British Raj would be replaced by a "Hindu Raj." This despite, or perhaps because of, Gandhi's outspoken support for Muslim rights and religious tolerance. Gandhi's satyagraha campaign on behalf of Muslims right after World War I was designed to show Muslims—and Hindus—that he saw them as part of a single, unified India. However, this campaign raised the ire of Hindu extremists, who felt he should concentrate on Hindu concerns: after all, according to these extremists, Muslims did not deserve Gandhi's support since they were only converts to Islam and since Muslims ate the flesh of the Hindus' sacred animal, the cow. They began to work against Gandhi's program of Hindu–Muslim unity. Additionally, questions arose among some in the Muslim community as to Gandhi's motivations. Was he trying to usurp the leadership within their own community?

The religious devotions of Gandhi and King elicited very strong responses, both from people who adored them and from those who reviled them. To his followers, Gandhi was "Bapu," an endearing term that means father, or "Mahatma," which means "great soul," and is reserved for only those Hindus who attain the highest form of reverence. However, to his detractors, especially the Hindu extremists who feared he was giving away too much to the Muslims, Gandhi was not a Mahatma, nor even did they refer to him by his given name, Mohandas. Instead, they referred to him as "Mohammed" Gandhi, an alliterative play on the term Mahatma and meant as an insult to Gandhi, since Mohammed is a very popular name given to Muslims. To his intractable British adversary, Winston Churchill, Gandhi was nothing more than a "half-naked fakir." King's followers referred to him as "L.L.J." for "Little Lord Jesus" or just "Little Jesus." Upon his arrival somewhere, his admirers shouted, "King is King!" or "Hail to the King!" His black opponents in the SNCC, however, referred to him derisively as "Da Lawd" (Frady 2002, 96), and white racists referred to him as "Martin Luther Coon" or "Martin Loser King."

In comparing Gandhi and King against the backdrop of religion, it is also useful to point out a paradoxical combination of values they both possessed. In the first instance, each was a staunch nationalist. Gandhi was fiercely proud of India and its impressive civilization. He thought India, with its rich ancient history, had much to offer the world. After all, as the birthplace of two of the world's most widely practiced religions, India was considered The Holy Land to Hindus and Buddhists. He wanted India to be run by Indians, not by an alien power. Despite intense efforts by his European acquaintances to convert him to Christianity, Gandhi always remained a Hindu. He was very proud of the faith into which he was born and which itself was born of his beloved Mother India. Ironically, he could have converted thousands of Christians and Muslims to *his* faith, but he never sought to do so, insisting only that people should strive to be the best Muslim or Christian or Hindu they could be. As an Indian nationalist, Gandhi thought it was shameful that Indians conducted their meetings in English, not in a native Indian tongue. He urged his comrades to study a major Indian tongue, such as Hindi or Urdu, as well as their own local dialect.

Like Gandhi, King was a patriot, a quintessential American: he believed that America was ordained by God to be special, even unique, among all the other countries. This is called the Doctrine of American Exceptionalism and is shared by most American politicians. Like so many other Americans, King saw the United States as a "beacon on a hill," providing a guiding light for the rest of the world to follow. Even his opposition to the Johnson administration's policies in Southeast Asia were couched in patriotism: King said he opposed the U.S. war in Vietnam "because I love America." Furthermore, he believed that black Americans in particular could set a fine example for the rest of the world to follow. Because of their unique role in history, black Americans could teach the rest of the country and the world all about the transforming power of nonviolence. By "bearing the cross" of others' shame, by acting out their resistance using nonviolence and self-suffering, black Americans could redeem the soul of the entire nation, which would then serve as a shining example for the rest of the world to follow. Interestingly, Gandhi himself made reference to this in the 1930s when he said that "it may be through the Negroes [in the United States] that the unadulterated message of nonviolence will be delivered to the world" (Dalton 1993, 182). So, as lovers of their own countries, both Gandhi and King possessed a nationalist vision that was essentially exclusivist in its patriotic fervor. Ironically, Gandhi's Indian nationalism led him to demand independence from Britain and the *exclusion* of whites from Indian rule while King's American nationalism led him to demand the *inclusion* of blacks in the American Dream.

Yet, and in the second, paradoxical, instance, their exclusivist nationalistic sentiments were offset by their universalistic visions for humanity. Fueled by their deep religious convictions, each envisioned a kind of global inclusiveness that called for spiritual and human oneness, regardless of nationality. For Gandhi, everyone is a child of God and must be treated thusly. Each person is spiritually connected to everyone else: to hurt one person is to hurt oneself. For King, his philosophy of Personalism meant that every human being had worth and value and must be treated as part of a single, unified garment of human destiny. King's Personalist vision did not only apply to Americans, but to all of humanity. Since he believed that "injustice anywhere is a threat to justice everywhere," the whole world must be redeemed, not just white Americans. He increasingly came to believe that peoples' suffering around the world was connected to suffering in the United States. He developed a global vision that did not just include Americans or black Americans, but all people around the world who suffered. The Poor Peoples' Campaign that he was organizing when he was murdered is a good example of his inclusive vision for bringing justice to all who suffered, not just blacks.

As religious devotees, both men insisted on living the totality of their lives informed by a single, unifying creed, nonviolence. Gandhi's nonviolence was acquired through his deeply held Hindu beliefs and then leavened by European and American influences, such as Leo Tolstoy and Henry David Thoreau. King's was acquired through his deeply held Christian beliefs, then fortified by the influences of Gandhi, Rustin, and others. In both cases, their religiously based adherence to nonviolence was a singular unifying theme, a common thread woven through all their public and private actions. All aspects of their lives were filtered through the demanding prism of nonviolence. As such, both refused to divide their lives into separate compartments, even though that would have been the easy thing to do. In Gandhi's case, everything he did was essentially political, just as it was religious (Brown 1989, 297). Everything was out in the open, nothing was done in secret. All his political acts, all his religious acts, all his experiments with diet, celibacy, and nonpossession and even his maddeningly frequent about-faces on issues were all conducted under the unifying rubric of satyagraha, which had as its most important endeavor the desire to see God through the pursuit of truth. For King, his faith dictated not only his nonviolent actions with respect to the Civil Rights Movement, but also regarding other heady public policy issues, especially his concerns about widespread poverty in America and in his opposition to U.S. policy in Vietnam. His opposition to the war alienated the Johnson administration, cost him considerable financial support among white liberals, and angered many black leaders who turned their backs on him. But King's concern for uplifting all people all over the world, not just American blacks, demonstrates his inclusivist vision, which became increasingly evident after he won the Nobel Peace Prize in 1964.

While both were men of deeply held religious convictions, their faith was not confined to the cloister. They may have been idealistic dreamers, but Gandhi and King were also men of action, believing that their faith demanded their presence at the ramparts of an epic historical struggle. Both were keen at taking the best moral and spiritual tenets of their faiths and turning them into political action that was high-minded. Such action was thus so deeply symbolic that it struck the peoples' deepest psychological chords and transformed many of them into sympathetic adherents if not active resisters. This is what Robert King (2001) calls "engaged spirituality." Gandhi, for instance, used the fast to demonstrate to Hindus the extent he was willing to suffer for his principles. King used not only the symbol of the cross, but also Negro spirituals to fuse political action with a holy message:

> The spirituals did for the Civil Rights Movement what Gandhi's fasts did for his own reform movement: they brought people together and gave them the courage to resist oppression, while also affecting the consciences of the people outside the movement. (King 2001, 158)

AS MEN

Before they were men, both Gandhi and King had relatively privileged youths at least by comparison to their coethnics, other Indians for Gandhi and other blacks for King. Although both were deeply scarred by the racism and discriminatory policies of their white oppressors, both were fortunate to come from stable families that were, again, relatively economically secure and even relatively insulated from the worst that white racists had to offer. Both of their fathers were "strong and ample providers who exercised considerable influence within their respective communities" (Dalton 1993, 177). Gandhi's grandfather, then father, then brother, all had nice positions in the local government. King's father was a self-made business entrepreneur and preacher. His family was solid middle class. As young boys, however, Gandhi and King did have strikingly different personalities. Young King was athletic and liked to play rough games. Although he did not like to fight, he was willing to settle playground disputes with his fists by suggesting to his opponent "let's go to the grass." Few childhood rivals accepted King's offer. King was short and stocky and very physical: he could give a hit as well as take one. By his own recollection Gandhi, who was much more slender, even by Indian standards, did not have much interest in athletics at all. There are few, if any, accounts of Gandhi brawling as a youngster.

Although both had expensive, high-powered educations that brought them into direct contact with their white adversaries, Gandhi was not much of a student compared to King. Although Gandhi eventually became a lawyer, which was unusual for an Indian from his village, his schooling, from early childhood through law school in London, was not marked by any significant or outstanding academic achievements. King, by contrast, was an exceptional graduate student and later a well-respected and promising young scholar. Perhaps King's academic rise was due to the post–World War II need to fill the schools and colleges. However, it is unlikely that this alone, especially in the segregated Deep South of the 1940s and 1950s, would have been enough to propel an African American all the way through to his Ph.D. King was, indeed, an intellectual, trained in the Classics (Greek, Roman, and early Christian writers). To be sure, both Gandhi and King were well read; Gandhi's numerous jail terms afforded him the opportunity of reading a diverse set of authors.

What is paradoxical about King's obvious intellect is the plagiarism he committed in writing his dissertation at Boston University. If King was an intellectual lightweight, it would have been easily discovered in the classroom or at the many salons he and his housemates hosted in Boston. Few doubt King's academic genius, which was evident from early childhood, so why did he plagiarize parts of his doctoral thesis? Did he cut corners in his haste to finish? Was he becoming academically lazy? Or was it simply an outgrowth of the common and widely accepted practice among black preachers to borrow material from one another without giving attribution?

Unlike King, Gandhi was painfully shy. As a young barrister, Gandhi had difficulty mustering the courage to speak up in a court case, even though it was his turn and everyone was waiting for him to speak. By contrast, King won a debating contest while he was in high school and was already accomplished at the pulpit before he graduated from college. King's impressive speech-making ability has been the subject of numerous studies by communications scholars. Neither was King shy in his pursuit of women. He was quite the ladies' man while Gandhi hardly even understood the impact of his childhood marriage to Kasturbai. King was a galavanter while Gandhi sought to achieve celibacy at a much earlier age than is traditionally expected of Hindu males. Even some of Coretta's friends in Boston warned her about young Martin's reputation as a womanizer.

What they both did share, however, was a strong moral center. As a little boy, King seemed to know instinctively that something was immoral about how his best friend's parents no longer allowed their son to play with Martin because of his skin color. And King was outraged by having to give up his seat to a white person on an overnight train ride. For his part, young Gandhi refused to obey his teacher's instructions to copy off of another pupil's exam so that a visiting school official could see that the teacher's students had all achieved a 100 percent mark. Even in his rebelliousness, Gandhi's moral center eventually overrode his youthful impulses. After stealing and lying, the young Mahatma-to-be could not overcome the sense of guilt and shame he felt and thus confessed his sin to his father. And once Gandhi made a promise—as a young law student in London or an accomplished barrister in South Africa—there was absolutely no going back on it.

Neither Gandhi nor King can be considered excellent role models as a family man, at least in the traditional sense. Unlike the conventional father and husband, Gandhi's attachment to and love of family did not supercede his love of others. Gandhi made no distinctions as to how he treated people, whether they were blood relations or not. Gandhi virtually disowned his eldest son, Harilal, when the son strayed from the path that the father expected him to follow. After Gandhi learned of Harilal's drinking, his cavorting, and his public conversion to Islam, Gandhi no longer considered him a son. Gandhi would instruct other family members not to share anything with Harilal. Is this the proper approach a votary of love and nonviolence takes with another human being, whether born as a son or not? Gandhi thought so, since it was conduct, not blood, that determined what was right or wrong. Whether they were Christians, Jews, Hindus, or Muslims, Gandhi referred to those who lived at his ashrams and practiced ahimsa as "son," "daughter," "brother," or "sister." Furthermore, in correspondence with family members, Gandhi was harsh, refusing to send them money, proclaiming that all his resources were devoted to his social uplift programs and that family relations did not deserve his largesse just because they were kin. He insisted that if his relatives joined him at the ashram, or in various satyagraha campaigns, then they could expect as much love and support from him as he gave to other people, no more and no less.

Gandhi was strict with Kasturbai too, rarely giving in to her wishes. For instance, he forbade her to keep gifts, even though she argued that the gifts she wished to keep were meant for her, not for him or the ashram. He also dictated to doctors what medicines she could have in times of illness. That is not to say that Gandhi did not love his wife, because he did. It is just that his love for her transcended conventional notions of spousal fealty.

And King loved Coretta too, but he also was strict with her. Right at the end of their first date, King surprised and shocked Coretta by expressing his desire to marry her. But this proposal was conditioned on Coretta's willingness to accept the traditional role of housewife who would keep the home and raise the children. Despite her considerable prospects as a professional singer, King insisted that Coretta remain home. Once they were married, he even forbade her from partaking in nonviolent resistance campaigns. Coretta once said, "I've never been on the scene when we've marched. . . . I'm usually at home because my husband says, 'you have to take care of the children'" (Garrow 1986, 308). Moreover, King was by today's standards an absentee father, not seeing his children for weeks at a time. King, also, was unfaithful to his wife (more on this to come).

Gandhi and King shared similarities and differences in how they tried to cope with human passions, including their materialist, carnal, and culinary desires. Despite the objections of their spouses, Gandhi and King both sought to overcome what many consider a natural human desire, to acquire material possessions. In Gandhi's case, he gave up virtually all worldly possessions, save a pair of spectacles, a walking stick, a few articles of clothing, some writing implements, and some crude dining ware. He liked to joke that his wealthy benefactors had to spend a fortune just to keep him in poverty. At a very early age and much to the consternation of his wife, Gandhi began divesting himself of his—and his family's—possessions, putting them in trust for the poor or investing them in his ashrams or other public welfare programs. King also tried to shed his desire for material things, although he was less successful at this than was Gandhi. For the longest time, he resisted Coretta's pleas and delayed buying a new car and a new home, despite the fact that the family had clearly outgrown the old ones. He felt that he did not deserve to keep the money that was awarded with his Nobel Peace Prize while Coretta argued that he should (he won that argument). Although King's taste for fine suits seems to have stayed with him, by his last days, he was increasingly turning to the idea of complete denial of material possessions.

When it came to the palate, Gandhi and King diverged considerably. Judging that he must overcome all desires in order to see God face to face, Gandhi engaged in a lifelong experiment to conquer his palate. He was, of course, a strict vegetarian by his London days. In later life, he conducted nutrition experiments in order to see not only what was the most healthy diet for his constitution, but also to determine how little he could eat in order to cause as little harm as possible to other living things. Gandhi's repeated fasts were also tied to his desire to conquer his palate. For his part, King does not appear to have had any interest in conquering his palate. A little bit overweight, King was a meat eater who definitely enjoyed a good meal.

Regarding their sexuality, Gandhi and King show differences as well as similarities. On the one hand, both were nearly consumed by their preoccupation with sex. On the other hand, they came to terms with this preoccupation through sharply contradictory practices. Despite his guilt and self-loathing, King repeatedly succumbed to his sexual appetites. This weakness, perhaps coupled with his loneliness due to being away from home so much, led King to break his marital vows on numerous occasions. According to Ralph Abernathy's book *And the Walls Came Tumbling Down* (1989)—written long after King died—King engaged in more than one sexual liaison even on the night before he was assassinated. By contrast, Gandhi achieved celibacy at a very young age (37), albeit after several failed attempts. Yet, despite finally keeping his vow of celibacy for more than four decades, Gandhi remained preoccupied with his sexuality until his death. He clearly enjoyed the company of young women, writing to one: "The sexual sense is hardest to overcome in my case" (Wolpert 2001, 186). To be absolutely sure of his celibacy, Gandhi conducted a controversial experiment, by sleeping naked alongside young women. Despite the intense resistance with which the ashramites greeted this experiment, Gandhi felt strongly that he needed to demonstrate that he had conquered any lingering sexual desires. Interestingly, Gandhi and King both felt immense guilt about their sexuality: King was haunted by his infidelities while Gandhi never fully recovered from the shame of running off to his wife's bed just as his father was about to die.

Perhaps it was because of Gandhi's mother's lasting influence on him, but Mohandas Gandhi was far more in touch with his feminine side than was King. In writing to a friend, who was trying to dissuade him from undertaking one of his fasts, Gandhi said, "I know you have not missed the woman in me." He credited his feminine qualities "of heart and soul" with his resolve to choose a way of life that demanded such great sacrifice (Wolpert 2001, 167). After all, since his father died when Gandhi was still in his mid-teens, he grew into adulthood with only his mother as the prime example to emulate. Although King was much more traditionally masculine than Gandhi, King was gentle and sensitive to others.

However, when it came to women's issues, Gandhi was far ahead of his time while King was arguably behind his. Although he started out as a young male chauvinist in the first years of his marriage, Gandhi ended up calling for an end to child marriages because of the heavy burden it placed on young girls. It is important to note that Gandhi was born in 1869, during the Victorian Age and only four years after the American Civil War ended. Yet, notwithstanding the era into which he was born, Gandhi wanted to liberate women from their social shackles. He called for an end to purdah (enforced seclusion) because women must exercise their right and duty to serve outside the home as well as inside it (Brown 1989, 210). He called for equal treatment of women and insisted that men share in the housework at his ashrams. He even called on women to join the men in the nonviolent satyagraha campaigns. He felt women had a special strength of character and a great capacity for self-sacrifice and nonviolence. He also believed that women were perfectly situated to help him carry out his major reform programs, including spinning, ending untouchability, improving home hygiene, and even building friendships across communal boundaries (Brown 1989, 59). In South Africa, the women's fortitude and eagerness to serve impressed Gandhi. He also quickly recognized the considerable publicity value of women's public suffering and imprisonment during a satyagraha campaign (Brown 1989, 59).

By contrast, King insisted that Coretta's place was in the home, taking care of the children. According to James Lawson, a high-ranking member of the Civil Rights Movement, "Martin had real problems with having women in a high position" (Garrow 1986, 141). This despite the fact that women played a prominent role and were very much the backbone of the Civil Rights Movement (Dalton 1993, 178). Rosa Parks, whose famous "no" sparked the Montgomery Bus Boycott, has already been discussed. But other women made significant contributions to the Civil Rights Movement. For instance, despite King's resistance and open objections to having a woman in a position of leadership, he acquiesced in naming Ella Baker to an important leadership post in the SCLC, but only if it was made clear that this was a temporary position. King looked down on professional women and did not think that women could be effective leaders (Branch 1988, 232). Because of her exceptional organizational skills, Baker turned out to be an excellent choice as she brought the SCLC back from the brink of administrative collapse. In addition, Diane Nash turned out to be a critical organizer for the freedom rides at a time when the riders themselves were faltering in their commitment in the face of so many beatings and bombings. But against the wishes of the mostly male—and mostly older—civil rights leaders, she insisted on continuing with the freedom rides because "[i]f they stop us with violence, then the movement is dead" (Branch 1988, 430). Her courage and leadership during that time was instrumental in not only keeping the movement alive, but also keeping it nonviolent.

Some of the comments King made about women while he was in graduate school are sexist. Even at the height of the Civil Rights Movement, King's views about liberty, freedom, and equality did not extend to women. In the late 1950s, King wrote a column for *Ebony* magazine called "Advice for Living." In this column, he wrote that the "primary obligation of the woman is motherhood" (Garrow 1986, 99). In one column, a woman wrote in asking for advice about her cheating husband. Rather than hold the husband responsible for his behavior—an amazing irony given his own overwhelming guilt for committing the same misdeeds—King suggested that it was the wife's fault. He asked her to consider what the other woman had to offer her husband that she did not: "Do you nag?" he asked (Garrow 1986, 104). While King's traditionalist views of women may have been similar to some other men of his time, they certainly clashed with the major theme of his movement: that people should be free to determine their own fate and be welcomed to take part in the full spectrum of what America has to offer, without others placing obstacles in their path. Moreover, the Women's Liberation Movement was in full swing during King's last years, so he must have been fully cognizant of women's issues.

AS HEROES

As heroes, these two men do not belong just to their respective countries, nor do they belong solely to the era in which they lived. These men belong to the entire world and to all the ages. But what makes someone a hero? If a hero is someone who, knowing the danger, commits selfless acts of bravery, then surely Gandhi and King are heroes. But what specific traits of courage are evident in them?

King defined courage as the power of the mind to overcome fear (Phillips 1999, 306). To be sure, both King and Gandhi demonstrated fearlessness in the face of repeated death threats and several assassination attempts. King was spat upon, jailed, beaten, hit with bricks, bombed, and stabbed, yet he retained the courage to continue struggling for his beliefs (Phillips 1999, 287). In seminary school, a white racist pulled a gun on King and threatened to kill him. King calmed him with his words. Later, the student admitted he was wrong and publicly apologized to King (Oates 1982, 30). In handling the incident in such a levelheaded way, King became the most popular student at Crozer Theological Seminary. At a book signing ceremony for his first book *Stride Toward Freedom* (1958), a crazed woman stabbed King in the chest. Once while King was giving a speech, a white supremacist rushed the stage and punched him in the face and then began to pummel him. When King lowered his arms and looked calmly at his attacker, one person who witnessed King's response to the attack said that she never again doubted King's complete philosophical commitment to nonviolence (Branch 1988, 654). King's house was firebombed and he and his family were constantly receiving death threats. Yet he remained eerily calm amid this maelstrom. After the firebombing, King rushed home and confronted an angry black mob that wanted revenge. King calmed them, saying "[W]e must love our white brothers, even if they kill us." When hooded Ku Klux Klansmen rode through his neighborhood trying to terrorize him, he went out on his doorstep (along with many others) and calmly remained there until the horsemen left. In the closing words of his last speech, King expressed this fearlessness eloquently:

> Well, I don't know what will happen now. We've got some difficult days ahead. But it doesn't matter with me now. . . . Like anybody, I would like to live a long life. Longevity has its place. But I'm not concerned about that now . . . [because] I've seen the promised land. I may not get there with you. But I want you to know tonight, that we, as a people, will get to the promised land. And I'm happy, tonight! *I'm not worried about anything! I'm not fearing any man!* Mine eyes have seen the glory of the coming of the Lord! (American Federation of State, County, and Municipal Employees n.d.; emphasis added).

On another occasion when King was obsessing about his own mortality, he gave his famous "Drum Major for Justice" speech about how he wanted to be remembered after he died:

> Tell them not to mention that I have a Nobel Prize. Tell them not to mention that I have three or four hundred other awards. . . . Tell them not to mention where I went to school. [Instead,] I'd like for somebody to mention that day that Martin Luther King, Jr. tried to give his life serving others. . . . That Martin Luther King, Jr. tried to love somebody . . . that I did try to feed the hungry . . . that I tried to love and serve humanity . . . that I was a drum major for justice . . . for peace . . . for righteousness. (Oates 1982, 458)

Somebody did mention those things about King at his funeral: that somebody was King himself when his widow, Coretta, had the funeral organizers play a tape recording of King's own "Drum Major" speech.

For his part, Gandhi received many death threats and in fact experienced several close calls. In South Africa, Gandhi was almost beaten to death by an angry crowd of whites. He refused to press charges against any of the perpetrators. After a burly Indian threatened to kill him, Gandhi showed no fear and even wrote in his newspaper that to do die by the hand of a fellow countryman would be a high honor, especially if he was able to have God's name on his lips while he fell. During the communal riots in Calcutta, Gandhi deliberately waded into the thicket of violence, residing in the abandoned house of Muslims. An angry mob of Hindus broke into the compound, demanding that he leave at once. They trashed the place, swinging clubs and sticks. Gandhi was almost hit in the head with a brick. Gandhi's life was in immediate danger, yet despite the violence directed at him, he remained calm and eventually talked the crowd into putting down their weapons and going home. On another occasion, a bomb exploded near the dais where he was conducting his prayer meeting. This was a failed attempt on Gandhi's life, conducted by members of the same group who would in fact succeed the next day, this time with three bullets to the chest. When the grenade exploded, Gandhi alone remained calm, soothing the crowd by resuming his prayer session. True to his wish, when Gandhi was shot by the Hindu extremists the next day, he said "Hey Ram" (Oh, God) two or three times and then fell to the ground.

Although neither man feared death, both seemed to be preoccupied with it. When King witnessed President Kennedy's assassination unfold on television, he grew quiet and told his wife that "this is what is going to happen to me" (Frady 2002, 120). Both were physically attacked on more than one occasion and each time both displayed a remarkable calmness in the face of their assailants. Both knew their lives were in danger, yet instead of having a "normal" fear of this, they seemed to exude a calming peacefulness, one that transformed not only their own personalities, but those close to them as well. Gandhi often talked about his wish to live 125 years. At other times, when he was saddened by the madness all around him, Gandhi exclaimed that life was not worth living. During some of his fasts, Gandhi was so consumed by his belief that he was about to die that he made arrangements for his funeral and other things. For his part, Martin Luther King, Jr. fully expected to be assassinated. After Malcolm X was gunned down in 1965, a chastened King remarked that he too would not live to see his 40th birthday. He died at the age of 39.

It is no small irony that Gandhi and King were assassinated by an individual(s) who came from the group each sought most to reform. In Gandhi's case, coreligionist extremist Hindus assassinated him: it was Hindus Gandhi most sought to reform and redeem. King was murdered by a white man, again a member of the group of people he most sought to reform.[1] Sadly, news of both

---

[1]Although convicted for it, James Earl Ray later denied his involvement and the surviving King family agrees, believing Martin's assassination was the product of a much wider conspiracy that may have involved the government.

men's assassination led to pockets of riotous violence. Still, Gandhi's assassination "more than any other single event, served to stop the communal violence surrounding [India's] partition" (Dalton 1993, 167).

Gandhi and King are also heroes not just because of the way they fearlessly confronted their impending deaths, but also because of how they lived their lives in the service of others. Not only does their courage in the face of death threats make them heroic, but so too does their concern for others. Although both could have been rich and successful as private citizens, both chose instead to sacrifice great career potential—and the comfort it would bring them and their families—for a life of service to others. Both men willingly gave up promising and lucrative careers for a life of voluntary poverty. And they did this while suffering the torment of personal demons. Each was tormented by his own sexuality, each went through bouts of sadness and possibly clinical depression and each was excruciatingly self-critical, in Gandhi's case publicly so. He even shared his nighttime involuntary discharge with the whole world when he wrote about it in his newspaper. Yet both confronted injustice with humanity and humility, with strength of character and courage. Both had a good sense of humor, both exhibited tenderness and gentleness toward others. Indeed, both were far more concerned with caring for and serving others than they were for themselves.

Both were men of vision, who dreamed of a world united by its common threads, not torn asunder by its "jangling discords," as King would say. Both were provocateurs, not for hate and violence, but for love and nonviolence. Both were men of prophecy, making startlingly accurate and dire predictions about the nature of violence in the coming years.

Both were master communicators, King seemingly born to the bully pulpit while Gandhi had to learn to overcome his shyness in front of large groups. Both became highly accomplished public speakers, able to use rhetoric and metaphor with great effect. For instance, King would say "The cloud is dark, but the sun is shining on the other side" (Cleghorn 1984, 117). He accused his fellow clerics of being more "more cautious than courageous" and for remaining silent "behind the anesthetizing security of stained glass" (King 1986, 299). Gandhi would say, "through darkness, only light persists." Both had a knack for dramatizing, in stark and vivid imagery, the injustices that their people suffered and both had a flair for the theatrical drama necessary to lead a mass nonviolent movement. They were able to harness important religious, political, and cultural symbols that resonated deeply among their country folk.

Above all, both were men of action with a gift for illustrating high-minded, idealistic principles of love, truth, justice, peace, and redemption through steadfast and courageous acts of nonviolent defiance. For Gandhi it was his use of Hindu symbols and British democratic values. For King it was his use of Christian imagery and the U.S. Constitution. Both had an uncanny knack for demonstrating their deeply held beliefs through mass, nonviolent action. Both were able to activate large swaths of their populaces, especially the common folks who found appeal in their message. Both reinterpreted and reapplied values deeply embedded in their cultures to great advantage for the cause of justice and nonviolence.

CHAPTER 10

Legacies for the 21st Century

On September 11, 2001, 19 terrorists hijacked four fuel-laden civilian aircraft and crashed two of them into the World Trade Center in New York City and a third into the Pentagon just outside Washington, DC, killing all on board and thousands more on the ground. The fourth hijacked plane crashed in the Pennsylvania countryside, again killing all on board. Not just Americans were killed, but people from dozens of countries. Americans and people all over the world were simultaneously fearful, hurt, confused, and enraged by this act of murderous violence. Calls went out for justice and revenge. People debated what caused the attack and what were the best means by which to deal with such naked violence. Should the United States and its allies lash out in violent response and bomb the suspected perpetrators wherever they were thought to be? Should such action take into consideration the likely death of innocent civilians? Would such violent retaliation even produce the desired outcome? Would it produce more suicide bombers? Would abstaining from violent reprisals produce the desired goals? Would abstention invite more attacks?

This terrorist event presents a clear challenge to the legacies of Mohandas Gandhi and Martin Luther King, Jr. They lived and died using nonviolent means to achieve justice, yet at the dawn of the 21st century and against the backdrop of the worst terrorist attack on the United States in its history, is there anything from Gandhi's and King's lives and works that can inform us about how to deal with the problems of modern-day civilization? Did they bequeath

us a workable blueprint for resolving future conflicts? Can Gandhian or Kingian nonviolence be applied in addressing today's incredible challenges of poverty, illiteracy, hunger, racism, inequality,
and, yes, terrorism?

Consider how some of King's words from decades ago resonate
against the backdrop of this hateful act:

> If we are to have peace on earth, our loyalties must become ecu-
> menical rather than sectional. Our loyalties must transcend our
> race, our tribe, our class and our nation; and this means we must
> develop a world perspective. . . . Now the judgment of God is upon
> us and we must either learn to live together as brothers or we are
> all going to perish together as fools. (King 1967, 68)

Surely, these sentiments reverberate across the decades and echo
in our mind's eye.

PACIFISM AND THE CHALLENGE OF VIOLENCE

Amid the madness of India's violent partition in 1947, a dis-
consolate Gandhi remarked that nonviolence is "on trial." Amid the
riots and white violence King witnessed, he despaired to Ralph
Bunche, a dear friend,

> maybe we just have to admit that the day of violence is here and
> maybe we have to just give up and let violence take its course. The
> nation won't listen to our voice. Maybe it'll heed the voice of vio-
> lence. (Garrow 1986, 617)

To be sure, after the suicide plane crashes in the United States,
nonviolence is indeed on trial, perhaps now more than ever. In the
immediate aftermath of the attacks, the overwhelming majority of
Americans were far from thinking about a nonviolent response.
Most supported a military reprisal and, by so doing, declared their
wish to, in King's prophetic words, "heed the voice of violence."
Most newspaper editorials called for counterattacks. Those advocating a nonviolent alternative solution were shouted down, condemned as unpatriotic, or labeled hopeless and naïve idealists.
Opinion writers were nearly united in calling for military action; the
main difference was in how much military action should be taken
and not whether violence should be used in the first place. Newspapers were not the only media outlets beating the war drum: cable

television news stations, with their need to fill a 24-hour news cycle, were incessant in hyping the call to arms. For instance, before any congressional declaration of war and before any retaliatory U.S. military action was launched, CNN's coverage of the event was headlined as "America's New War," thus begging the questions, What "war"? Who is the enemy in this war? And, if this is a "new" war, what "old" war did it replace?

One columnist's opinion piece in the *Washington Post* was titled "To War!" Others tried to silence the voices of what they referred to as "pacifism." They condemned pacifists for being soft and for playing into the hands of the terrorists. A *Washington Post* columnist, in an opinion headlined "Pacifist Claptrap," even went so far as to call pacifists "evil" and to equate pacifism with terrorism when he reasoned that "[t]he American pacifists, therefore, are on the side of future mass murders of Americans. They are objectively pro-terrorist" (Kelly 2001, A25). The columnist also referred to many pacifists as "liars," "frauds," and "hypocrites." One wonders if the author might include "pacifists" such as Gandhi and King in his list of "liars," and, if so, can one imagine a worse insult to the likes of Gandhi, who held truth as the highest goal of his entire life's work? But what of Gandhi and King? What of their response to violence, including terrorism? How might they react to the murderous attacks of September 11? How would they react to the violence of 19 suicidal mass murderers? King would not advocate lashing out against the terrorists by using more violence because violence never gets at the root causes of a situation. Violence to King could never truly solve a conflict. King told his staff in a speech he gave to them at one of their retreats:

> Violence may murder the murderer, but it doesn't murder murder. Violence may murder the liar, but doesn't murder lie; it doesn't establish truth. Violence may even murder the dishonest man, but it doesn't murder dishonesty. Violence may go to the point of murdering the hater, but it doesn't murder hate. It may increase hate. It is always a descending spiral leading nowhere. This is the ultimate weakness of violence: It multiplies evil and violence in the universe. It doesn't solve any problems. (Cone 1993, 270)

King's words, written decades ago, echo the sentiments of His Holiness the Dalai Lama, who is the spiritual leader of Tibetan Buddhists and a staunch advocate of nonviolence. Writing in his "Message on the Commemoration of the 1st Anniversary of September 11" the Dalai Lama said:

> How to respond to such an attack is a very difficult question to an-
> swer. . . . [R]etaliation that involves the use of further violence may
> not be the best solution in the long run. . . . Terrorism cannot be
> overcome by the use of force because [using force] does not address
> the complex underlying problems. In fact, the use of force . . . may
> exacerbate [them]. (Government of Tibet in Exile 2002)

Later in the same commemoration, the Dalai Lama pointed out that
conflicts must be resolved by getting at their root causes. Violent
responses to violent attacks do not resolve anything; they only
drive the conflict deeper, thus making real conflict resolution even
more remote:

> Human conflicts do not arise out of the blue. . . . [I]t is important
> to take necessary preventive measures before the situation gets
> out of hand. Once the causes and conditions that lead to violent
> clashes have fully ripened and erupted, it is very difficult to con-
> trol them and restore peace. Violence undoubtedly breeds more vi-
> olence. If we instinctively retaliate when violence is done to us,
> what can we expect other than that our opponent to also feel jus-
> tified [in] retaliating. This is how violence escalates. (Government
> of Tibet in Exile 2002)

Gandhi lived in India during a time when terrorism was commonplace. He wrote about it often and responded to his militant
critics who felt that his nonviolence was only prolonging British
rule. One of Gandhi's more famous sayings was based on the Old
Testament notion of punishing evildoers by inflicting the same
harm on them that they inflicted on others, but Gandhi summed
up the futility of this tit-for-tat reasoning by saying simply "An eye
for an eye leaves the whole world blind." Gandhi's book *Hind
Swaraj*, which was discussed at length in Chapter 4, is an eloquent
response to those who would use violence and terrorism to gain
their freedom.

King condemned the use of violence in any form—riots, terror,
war, and the like. As I have shown, King's condemnation was based
on both moral and practical considerations. King used Christ's
teachings to argue that violence was morally wrong, no matter
what outrage a person suffered. Violent retaliation only drives the
conflict further down and cannot perform the necessary healing
function, thus condemning those in the conflict to an endless cycle
of violent tit for tat. Practically, King argued that if blacks resorted
to violence, like some black nationalists advocated, they would be

annihilated by the more numerous, better-armed, and better-trained white opponents, who would now have an excuse to unleash all their tools of violence with an awesome fury. In an article published in *Look* magazine just after his assassination, King argued that "there was less loss of life in ten years of Southern [nonviolent] protest than in ten days of Northern riots" (Washington 1986, 64). He went on to say that not only was violence by blacks morally wrong, but strategically weak because it served to intensify whites' fears, relieve their guilt, and open the door to even more repression at the hands of the white power structure. In his book *The Trumpet of Conscience* (1968), King said:

> The limitation of riots, moral questions aside, is that they cannot win and their participants know it. Hence, rioting is not revolutionary, but reactionary because it invites defeat. It involves an emotional catharsis, but must be followed by a sense of futility. (15)

Similarly, what would Gandhi or King have to offer in the face of the September 11, 2001, terror attacks, which were apparently not the work of a sovereign nation, but of a dangerous individual and his network of supporters? Above all, neither would find all of a sudden an excuse to renounce nonviolence and say that it is no longer useful and thus make a turn toward the gun. When both were repeatedly threatened with violence, they did not chuck their creeds out the window. Both became stronger because of their deep philosophical commitment to nonviolence. Gandhi welcomed the bullet with God's name on his lips. King refused to hit back when his home was firebombed; he encouraged his supporters that "we must love our white brothers," even those who hate us and do despicable deeds. He also discarded the firearm he kept under his pillow at the beginning of the Montgomery Bus Boycott. So, terrorism and other forms of violence occurred a lot in Gandhi's and King's lifetimes, yet both remained fully committed to a life of nonviolence. It was especially in times of violence and crisis that their commitment to nonviolence was heightened. They demonstrated the courage to remain nonviolent not only as an active strategy against injustice but also as a reactive response to hatred and violence. Both did not fear what they expected: their assassinations. Their lives were repeatedly placed in mortal danger, yet their counsel of nonviolence remained resolute.

A country adopting Gandhian or Kingian nonviolence finds its answers in the nature of nonviolence's preventive qualities. A country that bases its foreign policy on Gandhi's ahimsa or King's beloved community rests on the assumption that it eliminates the incentive for others to attack in the first place. And if the opponent is committed to destroying you regardless of your approach, then it is better to die without having broken your vows than to renounce them and become like your opponent. As the Dutch theologian and humanist Erasmus said some 500 years ago:

> Try to help your enemy by overcoming him with kindness and meekness. If this does not help, then it is better that one perish than both of you. It is better that you be enriched with the advantage of patience than to render evil for evil. . . . The greater your position, the more ready you ought to be to forgive another's crime. (Merton 1996, 48)

In other words, one must be prepared to die. This illustrates the idea that nonviolent alternatives to violent confrontations define the conflict and one's goals in that conflict differently and thus define success differently. Success, in this regard, is not defeat of the opponent by any means necessary. Rather, success is, first, remaining nonviolent yourself, thus reducing the overall level of violence and destruction in the world. Second, success means conquering the conflicts that separate people and not the people themselves. Success does not mean destroying or holding onto territory, it does not mean seizing someone else's financial assets, it does not mean having bigger and better weapons of mass destruction, it does not mean launching economic sanctions to starve the opponent into submission: success in Gandhian and Kingian terms means clearing the forest of not only the branches and leaves of a conflict, but of its roots as well. It also means replanting the forest with the seeds of peace. So, if Gandhi or King, or others, were to be killed by virtue of conducting a conflict on this moral plane of conflict resolution, then so be it. After all, Gandhi used to say that if he died like that, perhaps his killer(s) would benefit from it by seeing the error of their violent ways. That is the root of nonviolence's transformative powers and the rock on which Gandhi and King built their foundations.

On another level, however, some wonder if such an approach might leave a country open to attack by unscrupulous and tyrannical foes. Perhaps, but there is evidence to the contrary. For example, Costa Rica is a neutral country with no national military defense. Located in Central America, unarmed Costa Rica exists in a tough neighborhood. During the 1980s, several bloody wars were being fought in nearby countries like El Salvador and Nicaragua. Yet, through all that, Costa Rica remained unarmed and virtually unscathed. Perhaps Costa Rica's unarmed neutrality made it unthreatening to others. Now consider the converse: history is replete with examples of one nation launching an attack on another because it feared the other nation's growing military capability, for example, Athens and Sparta, Japan and the United States, and the United States and Iraq.

To be sure, both Gandhi and King lived and practiced what they preached about meeting violence with love and about meeting brute force with soul force. This commitment to nonviolence was not only based on interpersonal or domestic conflicts. Gandhi and King were committed to nonviolence in international relations as well although it is at this level of conflict where advocates of nonviolent resistance meet their greatest challenge and have the most difficulty coming up with a response. How does one respond nonviolently to someone like Adolf Hitler or Osama bin Laden? Doesn't nonviolent resistance only open the door to even more abuse? Doesn't nonviolent resistance actually enable ruthless dictators to work their tyranny more easily? According to the critics, the answer is yes. After Hitler's 1939 invasion of Poland made clear his militaristic and territorial desires in Europe, a famous Protestant theologian and pacifist, Rienhold Niebuhr, changed his mind about pacifism in international relations when he came out in favor of a military response to stop Hitler (Fahey and Armstrong 1992, 198).

Gandhi suggested that Jews in Europe use nonviolent resistance to counter Hitler, since Hitler was only one man and other Germans could be appealed to. But Jews pointed out that Gandhi's British opponents in India were nothing like their opponent in Germany. Gandhi responded by essentially saying that nonviolent resistance, like violent resistance, would take a lot of suffering and pain. Later, in 1947, Gandhi told one of his biographers that it would have been better for the Jews to commit mass suicide rather than succumb to the Nazis (Dalton 1993, 137). Needless to say, many Jews were outraged and offended by this remark. Perhaps it shows that Gandhi had no real effective nonviolent response to Hitler, but that does not invalidate the technique of nonviolence. It only means that nonviolent resistance has not yet reached its full development.

Scholars have examined the question of whether nonviolent resistance can work at the international level, even against ruthless tyrants. For instance, citizens of Norway used nonviolence to successfully resist Hitler during the Nazi occupation of their country (Jameson and Sharp 1963, 156–186). In addition, non-violent political resistance has worked against other tyrants and despots. Consider the People Power Revolt that brought down the dictatorship of Ferdinand Marcos in the Philippines in the 1980s (Kessler 1991, 194–217). Starting with Poland in the late 1980s, communist regimes in eastern Europe fell more as a result of non-violent civilian mass uprisings than anything else. One scholar argues that it is now a matter of historical record that the most effective form of resistance against communist tyranny turned out not to be violence, but nonviolence (Piekalkiewicz 1991, 136–161). And it is the same type of resistance Nobel Peace Prize winner Aung San Suu Kyi uses to confront the military dictatorship in Myanmar (Burma).

Even Gandhi and King were met with intense criticism by prominent members of their own community. Tagore, India's popular poet laureate and also an admirer of the Mahatma, nevertheless argued that Gandhi's nonviolence only emasculated Indians and made it easier for the British to suppress them. Tagore also criticized Gandhi's nationalistic stances, calling nationalism a "great menace" to international peace (Dalton 1993, 71). Gandhi's response to Tagore was the same as it was to others: he remained steadfast in his commitment to nonviolence. Gandhi also defended his advocacy of nationalism, arguing that Indian nationalism in particular was "health-giving" and "humanitarian" (Dalton 1993, 71). Recall that one of King's most vocal—and vicious—critics was Malcolm X of the Nation of Islam. He launched scathing attacks on King's nonviolence, arguing that it was a "cowardice-producing narcotic" (Cone 1993, 176).

Gandhi and King transformed nonviolent direct action into a respectable form of resistance because they showed how powerful a weapon it could be. Furthermore, they proved that people can live their lives—even in modern society—in accordance with high-minded morals and rules, yet not be stunted by them. They demonstrated to the world that people of different faiths, races, and cultures could harness this "marvelous new militancy" as King called it. They showed that nonviolent direct action is not just some pie-in-the-sky method that only granola-eating tree huggers use. It is for serious people who want to effectuate change without harming others. Gandhi is referred to as a "gentle revolutionary" (King 2001, 156) because he fought for radical change but only through peaceful means. And King's genius lay in his tireless efforts at reconciling seemingly irreconcilable positions.

Nonviolent resistance enabled blacks and Indians to straighten their backs and stand up for themselves. They literally lost their fear. According to Nehru, "The essence of [Gandhi's] teaching was fearlessness and truth, and action allied to these." Nehru asserted that Gandhi found an "all-pervading fear" in India and raised against it his "quiet and determined voice: be not afraid" (Gifford 1982, 78). Nehru believed that one of Gandhi's greatest achievements was his ability to instill his countrymen with courage (Aung San 1991, 184). Nehru also said, "As fear is a close companion to falsehood, so truth follows fearlessness" (Dalton 1993, 66–67). Perhaps that is why Gandhi had so little fear and why he counseled so many to bid good-bye to fear. Showing courage and fearlessness was a hallmark of both men and remains one of their greatest legacies. It was as if both men said: "behold what can be done in the absence of fear!" According to Arne Naess (1965), "Fear is deep-seated; it possesses us, and it is mainly the force of fear itself that prevents its removal. Fear cannot be fought, it has to be replaced" and it can only be replaced, as Gandhi said, by putting trust in its place (50).

One of Gandhi's greatest accomplishments was that he could take great ideas such as swaraj and satyagraha and translate them into mass action that helped repair Indians' self-esteem, helped restore their courage, and helped in recruiting a whole new constituency of activists: "his combination of vision and action gave him enduring significance" long beyond his own life span and far beyond the specific issues with which he struggled (Brown 1989, 197). Gandhi's great appeal "never lay merely in his evocation of the great ideals of freedom and quality, truth and nonviolence. His impact came from a singular ability to express these ideas in actions" (Dalton 1993, 62). Indeed, the 20th century produced few great leaders who could marry their lofty ideals with direct action: Gandhi and King will go down as two of the century's greatest leaders in that regard. Their work empowered those who had never before felt that their voices were heard or that they could make a difference. Gandhi said that "real *swaraj* will come not by the acquisition of authority by a few, but by the acquisition of the capacity by all to resist authority when abused . . . by educating the masses to a sense of their capacity to regulate and control authority" (Dalton 1993, 194).

As King liked to say, no man can ride your back if it is not bent over. Moreover, nonviolent resistance proved quite effective in forcing change, especially when compared to the lack of change

wrought in the wake of violence. For instance, King's nonviolent resistance campaigns led directly to passage of the Civil Rights and
Voting Rights Acts, even after President Johnson and others who
proclaimed, at least rhetorically, their support for equality advised
King to wait.

GANDHIAN AND KINGIAN RESPONSES TO
SOCIOECONOMIC ISSUES

In my senior seminar on nonviolence, I like to ask my students
who they think made the following statement and when they think
it was made:

> We have created an atmosphere in which violence and hatred have
> become popular pastimes. . . . By our silence, by our willingness to
> compromise principle; by our . . . readiness to allow arms to be
> purchased at will and fired at whim; by allowing our movie and
> television screens to teach our children that the hero is the one
> who masters the art of shooting and the technique of killing; by al-
> lowing all of these developments we have created an atmosphere
> in which violence and hatred have become pastimes. . . . This
> virus of hate that has seeped into the veins of our nation, if
> unchecked, will lead inevitably to our moral and spiritual doom.

Few students guess correctly that this statement was made by King
in a speech just after the assassination of President Kennedy in
1963. Sadly, King's dour observations about American culture ring
true today. His warning about the dangerous combination of hatred and guns in American popular culture is just as applicable
today as it was more than 40 years ago.

But terrorism—like the assassination of a president or the suicide bombing of the World Trade Center—is not the only kind of violence with which Gandhi and King concerned themselves. Their
legacy for the 21st century extends to broader social and economic
issues. Gandhi and King worked tirelessly for social justice: in
Gandhi's case, it was his unique reform-minded brand of swaraj,
and for King, it was the beloved community. Their ideas and methods do have relevance today and their positions and recommendations on only a few issues will be examined here. Over a half
century of political and religious activism, Gandhi was prolific in
promulgating his views on just about every issue imaginable. In addition to the religious and political issues covered in this book,

Gandhi also wrote and spoke at length about health care, social welfare, diet, hygiene, education, agriculture, and the military, to name just some topics. To discuss how all his views on these matters may apply to the 21st century is certainly beyond the scope of this book. However, focus shall be on the following significant issues in examining both men's legacy for the 21st century: poverty because both were primarily concerned with this and since so much of the world's population still lives in economic destitution; agriculture because so much of the world's population remains tied to the land as a form of sustenance; and education because so many believe that education can rectify many of the world's ills.

To be sure, much of the world's population is still mired in a grinding cycle of poverty: according to the United Nations, more than one-fifth of the planet's population is forced to survive on just one dollar a day. Even in the United States, one of out five children lives in poverty. So, how can Gandhi and King inform us about poverty in the 21st century? They both argued that poverty was one of the worst forms of violence. Even Gandhi took the United States to task for its exploitation of the poor and weak as a form of "veiled violence" (Dalton 1993, 197–198). Each proposed their own version of nonviolence to combat poverty. For instance, Gandhi declared his support for democracy and individual freedoms, but not the unfettered, selfish individuality that seems so prevalent in the United States today. He called for freedom, but with a social conscience, he called for individuality, but with social restraints (Dalton 1993, 198). In a clever reapplication of Christianity's Seven Deadly Sins,[1] Gandhi compiled his own list:

1. Politics without principles;
2. Wealth without work;
3. Pleasure without conscience;
4. Knowledge without character;
5. Commerce without morality;
6. Worship without sacrifice; and
7. Science and technology without humanity.

Also, recall that Gandhi proposed many other ideas for alleviating India's teeming poverty. Swadeshi and homespun have already been discussed at length as has his village-life prescription: Each

---

[1]In Christianity, the Seven Deadly Sins are pride, greed, sloth, lust, covetousness, envy, and gluttony.

village was to be self-sufficient, sustaining itself on its own home-spun labors and that of nearby locales. In addition, machines and other products of modern-day industrialization were to be avoided if they denied people the chance to perform meaningful manual labor. Gandhi preferred the spinning wheel, not the spinning turbine. But he did not oppose all modern machinery: he recommended adoption of the Singer sewing machine.

Gandhi also had specific recommendations for agricultural reform, recommendations that if followed, might have created an India with less hunger and more agricultural self-sufficiency than is presently the case. Gandhi believed the best way to handle India's persistent under- and unemployment was to revive Indian villagers' agricultural skills in such a way that they could cultivate the land and care for themselves. So, agricultural reform played a central role in Gandhi's vision of Indian swaraj. However, India's modern agricultural policies have created the exact opposite effect:

> [I]f India had adopted Gandhian economics, there would be far less heavy industry there, but there would also be far fewer urban slums and far healthier rural life. The prosperous middle class would be smaller, but the desperately poor would also be far less numerous. (Pinto 1998, 21)

Since swadeshi was critical to Gandhi's reform plan for India, it follows that his position on agricultural issues would dovetail with that. The place of agriculture was critical in this vision: he wanted men to work in the open air, not only to be able to be self-sufficient but for moral and political reasons. Agriculture was the ideal form of social and economic activity, it was a vocation "in the context of community which led to freedom" (Pinto 1998, 37, 39). Agriculture and cultivation constituted the bulk of the work performed by members of Gandhi's ashrams in South Africa and India. This is also why Gandhi emphasized swadeshi so much: it gave the idle peasants a skill to perform, it gave them the ability to be self-sufficient, and it also gave them a degree of pride and satisfaction with their day's labors.

When juxtaposed against the current agricultural situation in India today—despite advanced technology, India is no longer self-sufficient in foodstuffs—Gandhi's views on linking agricultural production to the other aspects of his nonviolent social reform program resonate deeply. If India's agricultural planners adopt Gandhi's ideas on community-service-oriented agriculture, India's starving millions might no longer go hungry. This may or may not be the case, but the point here is that Gandhi's views on agriculture, which views are more than 50 years old, are still relevant today: they can still offer suggestions for reform and improvement of India's dismal food production industry. According to Gandhi, "[F]rom the very beginning it has been my firm conviction that agriculture provides the only unfailing and perennial support to the people of this country" (Pinto 1998, 92). Yet, as India's agricultural industry modernizes—perhaps a more appropriate term might be *mechanizes*—many poor, rural Indians remain unemployed and malnourished: "The harrowing results of India's oft-trumpeted 'Green Revolution' have left ample lesson to show what happens when growth without morality and ethics is given precedence" (Pinto 1998, 120). Perhaps there is no greater argument than this to take a closer look at Gandhi's recommendations for agriculture, which involve a complete socioeconomic overhaul based on Gandhi's ideas of nonviolence, truth, love, self-sufficiency, manual labor, nonpossession, and service toward others. The key to achieving this transformation is to "persistently subvert selfish worldly pursuits with ethical livelihood," no small task in a modern society dominated by mass consumer behavior (Pinto 1998, 162).

If Gandhi's ideas on agriculture were unconventional, so too were his plans for education. Even in the 1930s, Gandhi's ideas on education were provocative. His plan to radically overhaul India's educational system (this plan, which did not succeed, called, in part, for mass resignations of Indian teachers and boycotts by students) generated much talk and controversy and dominated the Congress Party's agenda for a time (Brown 1989, 303). But are Gandhi's ideas on education relevant today? Gandhi recognized the importance of a nationwide system of education as a prerequisite to Indian independence (Morarji 2001, 1). However, Gandhi did not wish to copy the British system that was imposed on India, a system he believed was used more to condition Indians into accepting British rule and authority than to actually teach Indians how to be self-sufficient. Gandhi felt the British system of education taught little of use to Indians, especially those in rural India who needed practical training, particularly in cultivation. Instead, the real strength of Gandhi's vision of education for today is that he

> makes the connection between the need for ideals and action. The social responsibility of the educated individual is to act for the good of all. Education must therefore inspire and empower individuals to

act morally not only through spiritual training, but through constant relevance to local cultural knowledge and daily practices,
such as agricultural work. (Morarji 2001, 11)

Gandhi sought an educational system that helped create "economic
freedom" while at the same time strengthened bonds between the
people and their local cultures. He was concerned that the Western-style educational system was creating an Indian population
with contradictions: people were "educating" themselves into un-
employability while at the same time becoming beguiled by Western-style mass consumerism, the passions and desires for which
required Indians to abandon their own cultural attachments and
bonds. Arguably, his concerns have been borne out in India today
as a recent education study done in India suggests:

> Mothers . . . see that education takes away their children from the
> land and village without providing the dream desk-jobs in the
> cities. . . . [They preferred training in traditional occupations] be-
> cause it was more stable and less dependent on external market
> conditions. . . . They wish that schools would teach them the kind
> of traditional livelihood skills which Gandhi advocated. (Morarji
> 2001, 13)

As for King, he did not widely discuss manual labor or simple (vil-
lage-style) agriculture as a panacea for American social development
or reform. This differing focus of Gandhi and King can be explained
by the fact that while Gandhi's India was still largely agrarian, King's
America was highly industrialized and even beginning to take its first
awkward steps toward a postindustrial age characterized by mass
telecommunications and high-technology industries. But King did
identify closely with sharecroppers: his grandfather was one and he
often wore blue overalls to show his solidarity and identification with
the plight of common folks. He said, "All labor that uplifts humanity
has dignity and worth" (King 1967, 127–128).

Of course, King did emphasize the importance of education in
his social programs. As a formidable intellectual and scholar, King
recognized the importance of a good education as a necessary component of his program to uplift all human personality. He saw education as a vehicle through which blacks could progress and cited
the Jewish people as an example to emulate: "The Jewish family
enthroned education and sacrificed to get it" (King 1967, 154). He
fought for the desegregation of public schools and called on school
districts to level the playing field by spending as much money per

black pupil in the cities as they were spending on white pupils in the suburbs. He called for the construction of massive "education parks," which would bring many students of diverse backgrounds from a large geographic area into one place. He believed such parks would create economies of scale and lead to greater integration. He called for a greater federal role in education, which would buck the historical trend of local control. He also demanded that schools provide more real-world, on-the-job training and put less emphasis on requiring students to obtain various certificates, which only served as exclusionary devices.

But above all, King's desires were dominated by ending poverty in America. He found it unconscionable that a country as rich as the United States still had so many people living in extreme economic deprivation. He called poverty a "curse" that had no justification in the modern age. He criticized the American economic system for its merciless drive for profits and possessions. He said the U.S. economic system was characterized by a form of "internal colonialism," with rich outer rings of upper-class suburban life surrounding poor inner cities. He condemned a system that produced a rich country filled with slums that leave their inhabitants "dominated politically" and "exploited economically" (Frady 2002, 172).

But how to relieve poverty in America? When he first started out, King believed that the only thing that was necessary was reform of the existing institutions in American society. However, in his last years, King wanted to reconstruct the entire society (Frady 2002, 192). He called for a "revolution in values" in the United States that would shift it from a "thing-oriented" society to a "person-oriented" society. He said, "When machines and computers, profit motives and property rights are considered more important than people, the giant triplets of racism, materialism and militarism are incapable of being conquered" (King 1967, 186). He criticized "typical" antipoverty programs in housing, education, and family counseling as failures because they were spasmodic and fragmented. Instead, he argued that problems in housing and education would recede only when poverty itself was first abolished. And he said, "The solution to poverty is to abolish it directly" by the government guaranteeing a minimum national income for all Americans. He called for a "Marshall Plan" for the inner cities.[2] He suggested nationalizing important sectors of the U.S. economy in order

---

[2] The Marshall Plan was a multibillion dollar American investment program designed to rebuild Europe after it was destroyed in World War II.

to guarantee that the U.S. government would see to the needs of the poor. He wanted the guaranteed national income to be pegged to the median income and he wanted it to increase along with total social income. He wanted the program to apply to all the poor, two-thirds of which, he hastened to add, were white. He also tried to defend this idea—which would be considered as radical today as it was then—by arguing that two disparate groups already enjoyed a guaranteed income: the wealthy, by virtue of the returns on their investment securities, and the poor, by virtue of their welfare benefit. Overall, his nonviolent revolution in values planned a "massive assault upon slums, inferior education, inadequate medical care . . . the entire culture of poverty" (Frady 2002, 168).

King could never accept communism because of its atheism, but he also rejected capitalism as too cutthroat. But King's radicalism evolved into what can be referred to as "Christian socialism" or "democratic socialism." He said, "If we are to achieve real equality, the United States will have to adopt a modified form of socialism" (Frady 2002, 25). To King this meant blending strong government action with the spiritual teachings of Christ in order to ensure justice, freedom, and equality for everyone. At its core, King's Christian socialism was concerned with alleviating the destitution of the "other" by the sacrifice of the "self." During his last years, especially, he tried to put these lofty ideals into practice.

INDIA AND THE UNITED STATES TODAY

Does today's India reflect Gandhi's vision? In short, the answer is mostly no. Overall, since Gandhi did not prevail on the issues that mattered to him—Hindu–Muslim unity, homespun, and ending untouchability—there is little to suggest that Gandhi is the father of contemporary India (Brown 1989, 389). Contrary to what Gandhi wished, India evolved into a modern country with a centralized government, a sophisticated military, and heavy industrial and agricultural sectors. India today more closely resembles Nehru's vision than Gandhi's. Nehru wanted to mold India into a powerful, democratic, secular state with a strong central government and modern weapons and industries. Nehru's vision for India is a product of British and Western influences, something that Gandhi rejected. India has evolved in ways that Gandhi would have opposed, not least of which in the military/defensive sphere. Gandhi's desire to see India's military melt away has not occurred.

India has a large military and devotes a large portion of its national resources to its military sector, an almost obscene amount given its widespread poverty. In 1998, India (and then rival Pakistan immediately thereafter) tested and exploded nuclear bombs, thus becoming only the sixth (and seventh) countries to openly declare their nuclear weapons status. Gandhi would surely have opposed this. India's national security is not based on Gandhi's revolutionary ideas of self-suffering, ahimsa, and satyagraha, but rather on the traditional military sciences.

Nor has India's economy evolved the way Gandhi envisioned. Gandhi wanted Indians to live simply and in their local villages. Neither has India's political complexion emerged as Gandhi wished. The subcontinent remains divided between India and Pakistan, archenemies who have fought three major wars and engaged in numerous border skirmishes. With the election of the staunch Hindu Nationalist Party in the late 1990s and India and Pakistan again moving to the brink of war in 2002, Gandhi's hopes for Hindu–Muslim unity are more remote now than before. Ironically, now that both countries are nuclear-armed, a Gandhian-style nonviolent resolution to the conflicts that separate Pakistan and India is more urgent now than ever before.

Perhaps Gandhi's greatest tangible legacy lies in the advances for so-called Untouchables. His work on their behalf seems to have borne fruit. Today, it is illegal to discriminate based on a person's birth station (caste). Outcastes are specifically mentioned in India's Constitution, which delineates special protections for them. However, despite these legal protections, Gandhi's Harijan remain severely oppressed in many parts of India, particularly in some hard-to-reach rural areas, where violent acts by upper-caste Hindus are committed against them with some regularity. There is a sad irony to this, given Gandhi's optimistic views on life in rural India.

It is also ironic, given that King was so impressed with the efforts India's national government was making in the 1950s to reform treatment of its discriminated minority populations. Which begs the questions, Does the United States of today reflect King's vision? Has segregation been replaced by true integration? Has King's dream of a beloved community been realized? Is a person today judged by the content of his character and not the color of his skin? In short, the answer here, as with Gandhi, is also mostly no. Although there has been considerable progress in ending segregation, King's beloved community still remains a dream. At the turn of the century, America's urban centers were experiencing racial resegregation, both voluntary and involuntary on the part of blacks. Racial profiling of blacks on the streets, on the highways, in the malls, and in the restaurants still exists (so, too, does it for other groups, such as Arab and Muslim Americans). Indeed, just a few short weeks after King gave his famous "I Have a Dream" speech on the steps of the Lincoln Memorial, he sadly proclaimed that he saw that dream degenerate into a nightmare when four "beautiful, unoffending, innocent Negro girls were murdered in a church in Birmingham" (Washington 1986, 257). It was decades before even one of the perpetrators responsible for that particularly hideous act of terror was brought to justice (another suspect died of old age before he was arrested and another was declared legally incompetent to stand trial).

That is not to say that King's dream is irrelevant for today. It is as poignant now as it was 40 years ago. Signs of significant progress help keep the dream alive. Although the black community's average socioeconomic status remains far less than the national average, some improvements have been made, for instance, in higher education. Further, Martin Luther King Jr. Day, a national holiday celebrated in January of every year, helps keep that dream alive. Its celebration is cause for seminars, essays, and speeches commemorating King's life and for calling on Americans to renew their commitment to the beloved community.

Another legacy of these men is found in their near-universal appeal, not just within their particular groups, but on a broader plane. King's philosophy of nonviolence, so well portrayed in his eloquent speeches and leavened by his direct action campaigns, resonated with whites as well as blacks. King appealed to blacks as a Baptist preacher who beautifully captured and portrayed the essence of blacks' experiences and dreams. King was able to turn blacks' faith in the church into a form of political and social action that drew on images of Christ, the Negro preacher, and even Gandhi. This type of outreach to blacks "bypassed the cerebral centers and exploded in the well of the Negro psyche" (Bennett 1984, 25). But King also appealed to whites through his use of the symbols of Christianity and democracy and by invoking nonviolence, love, and redemption, which not only reassured whites but also gave them something they could identify with (Meier 1984, 147).

The same goes for Gandhi, about whom British schoolchildren wrote essays. Even millworkers in Lancashire, England, who suffered considerable hardships because of Gandhi's boycott of British cloth, embraced Gandhi when he visited them. Such is the legacy of a man who, having launched a massive nonviolent boycott campaign, embarked on a visit to see the people who were the target of his boycott efforts.

Neither Gandhi nor King wished to be remembered for their political achievements. To them, their legacy was not their accomplishments in the political sphere or their public awards and accolades. As mentioned earlier, King did not want those achievements mentioned at his funeral, but instead he wanted to be remembered as someone who tried to "love somebody" and who tried to "feed the hungry." For his part, Gandhi saw himself as a seeker after truth and wished to be remembered for his creative experiments in trying to find the truth, rather than for his political achievements (Brown 1989, 74). With no official title, no political position, no great scientific achievement, no wondrous invention, and with virtually no personal property of his own, Gandhi's legacy is one of a detached, relentless search after the truth in order to see God face to face. His *The Story of My Experiments with Truth*, as his 1957 autobiography is subtitled, indicate a reformist mentality, one unafraid of trying new things and discarding others that do not reveal the truth. Gandhi once said that "experience convinces me that permanent good can never be the outcome of untruth and violence." Sound and wise counsel for any age and time. Upon Gandhi's death, Albert Einstein said, "In our time of utter moral decadence, he was the only statesman to stand for a higher human relationship in the political sphere"; and U.S. Senator Arthur H. Vandenberg said Gandhi "made humility and simple truth more powerful than empires" (Fischer 1950, 10–11).

Ironically, despite their humility, both men became somewhat obsessed with their own place in history. Gandhi brooded about his uselessness in the face of Hindu–Muslim ravages. He admitted that he was unable to find a nonviolent solution to many of India's problems and wrote as late as 1944 that he "was still groping" for a solution and later said "I tried and failed" (Brown 1989, 344). But to Gandhi that did not mean the method was flawed, it only meant that people, and him especially, were not sufficiently good at practicing ahimsa. It was not ahimsa that had failed, but something else, something he had mistakenly believed was true ahimsa, but what he came to call the "passive resistance of the weak." He believed that real nonviolence, what he called "the nonviolence of the strong," had yet to be discovered (Brown 1989, 375).

Similarly, King possessed the same strange mix of despair and hopefulness. The hopefulness came from his dream and the vision he had for the promise of America. The despair arose from the almost unfathomable level of stress that burdened his psyche. Consider just some of the sources of stress with which King had to cope on a daily basis:

1. FBI and CIA surveillance and wiretaps, including phony recordings FBI Director J. Edgar Hoover used trying to discredit King;
2. Constant physical and verbal abuse;
3. Repeated death threats directed not only at him, but also his family;
4. Internal dissension within the SCLC;
5. Dissension between the SCLC and other civil rights organizations, like the NAACP and the SNCC;
6. Constant financial woes, which forced him to give several speeches a day just to raise enough funds to keep the SCLC afloat;
7. Traveling hundreds of thousands of miles each year and sleeping only four hours a night in strange place after strange place;
8. Rarely seeing his family;
9. Guilt and remorse over his personal weaknesses and sins; and
10. Frequent bouts of self-doubt over whether he had made a positive influence on society.

He questioned not only his leadership but the very essence of his nonviolent philosophy. But at the same time, he never gave up on his nonviolence. When a colleague suggested putting a person on the staff who held no commitment to nonviolence, King insisted, "No one should be on our payroll that accepts violence as a means of social change. The only way to have a world at peace is through nonviolence" (Garrow 1986, 622). King was merely echoing Gandhi's sentiments when Gandhi said that violence cannot ultimately resolve conflicts and that only the light of love can eliminate the darkness of hatred. For both men, it is important to note that while their expectations for their people went up and down, their hope and faith in nonviolence never waned. According to Gandhi, "My faith is as strong as ever. It is quite possible that my technique is faulty. . . . *Ahimsa* is always infallible. When, therefore, it appears to have failed, the failure is due to the inaptitude of the votary," or practitioner of the technique (Merton 1996, 172–173).

Therefore, it is the man, not the method, that needs to be fixed. Perhaps one student of Gandhi said it best:

> Whether we may think he succeeded or failed, Gandhi never ceased to believe in the possibility of a love of truth so strong and so pure that it would leave an "indelible impression" upon the most recalcitrant enemy, and awaken in him a response of love and truth. (Merton 1996, 60)

We cannot understand this belief as a matter of pragmatism; it is in fact a severe article of faith, a core belief for both Gandhi and King. And they remained undaunted by the naysayers who declared that what they were trying to achieve was impossible. Gandhi liked to remind people of all the things once thought impossible that were achieved.

There is evidence all around of Gandhi's and King's enduring legacies in the 21st century. Both men are the subject of numerous studies and books, both men have many Web sites dedicated to their memory and teaching. Both men are the subject of numerous international conferences and symposia that study their lives and work. Both men have been the subject of numerous film documentaries and cinematic movie productions. Both men have memorials and museums dedicated to them. Both men have national holidays honoring them. Both men have left behind a wealth of admirers and followers who today carry on their work all over the world. Both men have their words reproduced and replayed countless times in countless venues. Indeed, both men are more than historical figures—theirs is a legacy of timeless applicability and boundless potential, one for all the ages.

So it is that Gandhi's and King's greatest gift to us is their enduring spirits. They are testaments to what one person can do in the fight against injustice. It was not King's administrative skills or his organizational genius that led millions to pledge their loyalty to him—he was limited in these areas. Nor was it Gandhi's broad shoulders, sturdy frame, or thunderous speaking voice that aroused the Indian multitudes—he had none of these qualities. Rather, it was their ability to inspire people, especially the common folk who may not have been able to articulate their despair as eloquently as Gandhi or King but who knew a special spirit when they saw one and who knew when the grace of God had reached down from the heavens and touched one of His own.

Bibliography

Albert, David. (1985). *People power: Applying nonviolence theory.* Philadelphia: New Society Publishers.

American Federation of State, County, and Municipal Employees. (n.d.). *Memphis: We remember: I've been to the mountaintop.* Retrieved September 18, 2002, from http://www.afscme.org/about/kingspch.htm.

Ansbro, John J. (1982). *Martin Luther King, Jr.: The making of a mind.* Maryknoll, NY: Orbis Books.

Aung San Suu Kyi. (1991). *Freedom from fear and other writings* (Foreword by Vaclav Havel; edited with an introduction by Michael Aris). New York: Penguin Books.

Bennett, Lerone. (1968). *What manner of man: A biography of Martin Luther King, Jr. with an introduction by Benjamin E. Mays.* Chicago: Johnson Publishing.

Bennett, Lerone. (1984). When the man and the hour met. In C. Eric Lincoln (Ed.), *Martin Luther King, Jr.: A profile* (Rev. ed.; pp. 7–39). New York: Hill and Wang.

Bond, Douglas G. (1988). The nature and meaning of nonviolent direct action: An exploratory study. *Journal of Peace Research,* 25, no.1, 86–87.

Bondurant, Joan V. (1971). The search for a theory of conflict. In Joan V. Bondurant (Ed., in association with Margaret Fisher), *Conflict: Violence and nonviolence* (pp. 1–25). Chicago: Aldine–Atherton.

Bondurant, Joan V. (1988). *Conquest of violence: The Gandhian philosophy of conflict* (2nd ed.). Princeton, NJ: Princeton University Press.

Boserup, Anders, and Mack, Andrew. (1975). *War without weapons: Nonviolence in national defense.* New York: Schocken Books.

Bosmajian, Haig. (1984). The letter from Birmingham jail. In C. Eric Lincoln (Ed.), *Martin Luther King, Jr.: A profile* (Rev. ed.; 128–143). New York: Hill and Wang.

Boulding, Kenneth. (1962). *Conflict and defense: A general theory.* New York: Harper and Brothers.

Branch, Taylor. (1988). *Parting the waters: America in the King years, 1954–63.* New York: Simon and Schuster.

Brown, Judith. (1989). *Gandhi: Prisoner of hope.* New Haven, CT Yale University Press.

Carson, Clayboren E. (Ed.). (1998). *The autobiography of Martin Luther King, Jr.* New York: Warner Books.

Chadha, Yogesh. (1997). *Gandhi: A life.* New York: Wiley.

Chapple, Christopher Key. (1998). Jainism and nonviolence. In Daniel L. Smith-Christopher (Ed.), *Subverting hatred: The challenge of nonviolence in religious traditions* (pp. 13–24). Cambridge, MA: Boston Research Center for the 21st Century.

Cleghorn, Reese. (1984). Crowned with crises. In C. Eric Lincoln (Ed.), *Martin Luther King, Jr.: A profile* (Rev. ed.; pp. 113–127). New York: Hill and Wang.

Cone, James H. (1993). *Martin and Malcolm and America: A dream or a nightmare?* Maryknoll, NY: Orbis Books.

Cox, Gray. *The ways of peace: A philosophy of peace as action.* New York: Paulist Press.

Crespigny, Anthony de. (n.d.). *The nature and methods of nonviolent coercion.* Jerusalem: Mennonite Peace Library.

Dajani, Souad. (1991). *Strategic issues in the Palestinian Intifadah.* Paper presented at the Conference of the Middle East Studies Association, Washington, DC, November 23–26.

Dalton, Dennis. (1993). *Mahatma Gandhi: Nonviolent power in action.* New York: Columbia University Press.

Dugger, Celia W. (1999, May 2). In India, lower-caste women turn village rule upside down. *New York Times,* p. A1.

Erikson, Erik H. (1969). *Gandhi's truth: On the origins of militant nonviolence.* New York: Norton.

Fahey, Joseph J., and Armstrong, Richard. (Eds.). (1992). *A peace reader: Essential writings on war, justice, nonviolence, and world order* (Rev. ed). New York: Paulist Press.

Fairclough, Adam. (1984). Was Martin Luther King a Marxist? In C. Eric Lincoln (Ed.), *Martin Luther King, Jr.: A profile* (Rev. ed.; pp. 228–242). New York: Hill and Wang.

Fischer, Louis. (1950). *The life of Mahatma Gandhi.* New York: Harper.

Fischer, Louis. (1954). *Gandhi: His life and message for the world.* New York: New American Library.

Frady, Marshall. (2002). *Martin Luther King, Jr.* New York: Penguin Books.

Galtung, Johan. (1959). Pacifism from a sociological point of view. *Journal of Conflict Resolution,* 3, 67–84.

Galtung, Johan. (1969). Violence, peace, and peace research. *Journal of Peace Research*, 6, no. 2, 167–191.

Galtung, Johan. (1989). *Nonviolence and Israel/Palestine.* Honolulu: University of Hawai'i, Institute for Peace.

Gandhi, Mohandas K. (1922). *Indian home rule* (2nd improved ed.). Madras, India: S. Ganesan.

Gandhi, Mohandas K. (1951). *Nonviolent resistance (satyagraha).* New York: Schocken Books.

Gandhi, Mohandas K. (1957). *Gandhi: An autobiography. The story of my experiments with truth* (Mahadev Desai, Trans.). Boston: Beacon Press.

Gandhi, Mohandas K. (1990). On satyagraha. In Robert L. Holmes (Ed.), *Nonviolence in theory and practice.* Belmont, CA: Wadsworth Publishing.

Garrow, David J. (1986). *Bearing the cross: Martin Luther King, Jr., and the Southern Christian Leadership Conference.* New York: Morrow.

Gert, Bernard. (1966, October 22). Justifying violence. *Journal of Philosophy*, 66, 616–628.

Gifford, Henry. (1982). *Tolstoy.* Oxford, UK: Oxford University Press.

Government of Tibet in Exile. (2002). *His Holiness the Dalai Lama's message on the commemoration of the 1st anniversary of September 11, 2001.* Retrieved January 21, 2004, from www.tibet.com/newsroom/message1.htm.

Grant, Philip. (1990). Nonviolent political struggle in the occupied territories. In Ralph E. Crow, Philip Grant, and Saad E. Ibrahim (Eds.), *Arab nonviolent political struggle in the Middle East* (pp. 75–90). Boulder, CO: Lynne Rienner Publishers.

Gregg, Richard B. (1934). *The power of nonviolence.* London: James Clarke.

Herman, A. L. (1998). *Community, violence, and peace: Aldo Leopold, Mohandas K. Gandhi, Martin Luther King Jr., and Gautama the Buddha in the twenty-first century.* Albany: State University of New York Press.

Hettne, Bjorne. (1976). The vitality of the Gandhian tradition. *Journal of Peace Research*, 13, no. 3, 227–245.

Howard, Michael. (1977, July). Ethics and power. *International Affairs*, 53, no. 3, 364–376.

Jameson, A. K., and Sharp, Gene. (1963). Nonviolent resistance and the Nazis: The case of Norway. In Mulford Q. Sibley (Ed.), *The quiet battle: Writings on the theory and practice of nonviolent resistance* (pp. 156–186). Boston: Beacon Press.

Jones, Kirk Byron. (n.d.). King had a mentor in Chester. Retrieved August 20, 2002, from http://www.oldchesterpa.com/famous_king_jr_martin_luther.htm.

Kanithar, V. P. (Hemant), and Cole, Owen W. (1995). *Hinduism.* Chicago: NTC/Contemporary Publishing.

Kelly, Michael. (2001, September 26). Pacifist claptrap. *Washington Post*, p. A25.

Kessler, Richard J. (1991). The Philippines: The making of a "people power" revolution. In Jack A. Goldstone, Ted Robert Gurr, and Farrokh Moshiri (Eds.), *Revolutions of the late twentieth century* (pp. 194–217). Boulder, CO: Westview Press.

King, Martin Luther, Jr. (1957, November 17). *Loving your enemies.* Retrieved November 18, 2001, from http://www.mlkonline.com.

King, Martin Luther, Jr. (1958). *Stride toward freedom: The Montgomery story.* New York: Harper.

King, Martin Luther, Jr. (1963). *Strength to love.* New York: Harper and Row.

King, Martin Luther, Jr. (1964a). *Nobel Prize acceptance speech.* Retrieved January 21, 2004, from www.nobelprizeo.com/nobel/peace/MLK-Nobel.html.

King, Martin Luther, Jr. (1964b). *Why we can't wait.* New York: New American Library.

King, Martin Luther, Jr. (1967). *Where do we go from here: Chaos or community?* New York: Harper and Row.

King, Martin Luther, Jr. (1968). *The trumpet of conscience.* New York: Harper and Row.

King, Martin Luther, Jr. (1986). Letter from Birmingham city jail. In James M. Washington (Ed.), *A testament of hope: The essential writings and speeches of Martin Luther King, Jr.* (pp. 289–302). San Francisco: HarperCollins.

King, Martin Luther, Jr. (n.d.). *MIA mass meeting speech.* Retrieved February 12, 2004, from http://www.stanford.edu/group/King/publications/speeches/MIA_mass_meeting_at_holt_street.html.

King, Robert H. (2001). *Thomas Merton and Thich Nhat Hanh: Engaged spirituality in an age of Globalization.* New York: Coninuum.

Lakey, George. (1987). *Powerful peacemaking: A strategy for a living revolution.* Philadelphia: New Society Publishers.

Lincoln, C. Eric. (Ed.). (1984). *Martin Luther King, Jr.: A profile* (Rev. ed.). New York: Hill and Wang.

Lipsitz, Lewis, and Kritzer, Herbert M. (1975, December). Unconventional approaches to conflict resolution: Erikson and Sharp on nonviolence. *Journal of Conflict Resolution,* 19, no. 4, 713–733.

Lomax, Louis. (1984). When nonviolence meets black power. In C. Eric Lincoln (Ed.), *Martin Luther King, Jr.: A profile* (Rev. ed.; pp. 157–180). New York: Hill and Wang.

Mack, Adam. (2003). No "illusion of separation": James L. Bevel, the civil rights movement, and the Vietnam war. *Peace and Change,* 28, no. 1, 108–133.

Martin, Brian. (1989). Gene Sharp's theory of power. *Journal of Peace Research,* 26, no. 2, 213–222.

McCarthy, Ronald M. (1990). Appendix B: The techniques of nonviolent action: Some principles of its nature, use, and effects. In Ralph E.

Crow, Philip Grant, and Saad E. Ibrahim (Eds.), *Arab nonviolent political struggle in the Middle East* (pp. 107–120). Boulder, CO: Lynne Rienner Publishers.

McGuinness, Kate. (1993). Gene Sharp's theory of power: A feminist critique of consent. *Journal of Peace Research,* 30, no. 1, 101–115.

McReynolds, David. (n.d.a). Philosophy of nonviolence: Part two. Retrieved January 26, 2004, from http://www.nonviolence.org/issues/philo-nv2.php.

McReynolds, David. (n.d.b). Philosophy of nonviolence: Part four. Retrieved January 26, 2004, from http://www.nonviolence.org/issues/philo-nv4.php.

McReynolds, David. (n.d.c). Philosophy of nonviolence: Part seven. Retrieved January 26, 2004, from http://www.nonviolence.org/issues/philo-nv7.php.

Meier, August. (1984). The conservative militant. In C. Eric Lincoln (Ed.), *Martin Luther King, Jr.: A profile* (Rev. ed.; pp. 144–156). New York: Hill and Wang.

Merton, Thomas. (Ed.). (1996). *Gandhi on nonviolence: Selected texts from Mohandas K. Gandhi's nonviolence in peace and war.* Boston: Shambhala.

Miller, William Robert. (1984). The broadening horizons. In C. Eric Lincoln (Ed.), *Martin Luther King, Jr.: A profile* (Rev. ed.; pp. 40–71). New York: Hill and Wang.

Morarji, Karuna. (2001, Summer). The continuing relevance of Gandhi's views on education in India and beyond. *COPRED Peace Chronicle,* 25, no. 4, 1+.

Naess, Arne. (1965). *Gandhi and the nuclear age.* Totowa, NJ: Bedminster Press.

Nagler, Michael. (1986). Nonviolence. In Ervin Laszlo and Jung Youl Yoo (Eds.), *World encyclopedia of peace* (vol. 2; pp. 72–78). New York: Pergamon Press.

Nakhre, Amrut. (1982). *Social psychology of nonviolent action: A study of three satyagrahas.* Delhi, India: Chanakya Publications.

Oates, Stephen B. (1982). *Let the trumpet sound: The life of Martin Luther King, Jr.* New York: Harper and Row.

Page, Kirby. (1963). Is coercion ever justified? In Mulford Q. Sibley (Ed.), *The quiet battle: Writings on the theory and practice of nonviolent resistance* (pp. 52–54). Boston: Beacon Press.

Phillips, Donald T. (1999). *Martin Luther King, Jr. on leadership: Inspiration and wisdom for challenging times.* New York: Warner Books.

Piekalkiewicz, Jaroslaw. (1991). Poland: Nonviolent revolution in a socialist state. In Jack A. Goldstone, Ted Robert Gurr, and Farrokh Moshiri (Eds.), *Revolutions of the late twentieth century* (pp. 136–161). Boulder, CO: Westview Press.

Pinto, Vivek. (1998). *Gandhi's vision and values: The moral quest for change in Indian agriculture.* New Delhi, India: Sage Publications.

Pontara, Guiliano. (1965). Rejection of violence in Gandhian ethics of conflict resolution. *Journal of Peace Research,* 2, no. 3, 197–215.

Pontara, Guiliano. (1978). The concept of violence. *Journal of Peace Research,* 15, no. 1, 19–31.

Rawls, John. (1971). *A theory of justice.* Oxford, UK: Oxford University Press.

Salmon, Jack D. (1988, March). Can nonviolence be combined with military means of national defense? *Journal of Peace Research,* 25, no. 1, 69–80.

Satha-Anand, Chaiwat. (1986). *Exploring myths on nonviolence.* Paper presented at the Conference on Nonviolent Political Struggle, Amman, Jordan, November 15–18.

Schell, Jonathan. (1985). Introduction. In Adam Michnik, *Letters from prison and other essays* (Maya Latynski, Trans.). Berkeley: University of California Press.

Sharp, Gene. (1959, March). The meanings of nonviolence: A typology (revised). *Journal of Conflict Resolution,* 3, no. 1, 41–66.

Sharp, Gene. (1973a). *The politics of nonviolent action. Part one: Power and struggle.* Boston: Porter Sargent Publishers.

Sharp, Gene. (1973b). *The politics of nonviolent action. Part two: The dynamics of nonviolent action.* Boston: Porter Sargent Publishers.

Sharp, Gene. (1990). *The role of power in nonviolent struggle.* Cambridge, MA: Albert Einstein Institution.

Shashtri, Sunanda Y., and Shastri, Yajneshwar S. (1998). *Ahimsa* and the unity of all things: A Hindu view of nonviolence. In Daniel L. Smith-Christopher (Ed.), *Subverting hatred: The challenge of nonviolence in religious traditions* (pp. 67–84). Cambridge, MA: Boston Research Center for the 21st Century.

Smith-Christopher, Daniel L. (1998). Political atheism and radical faith: The challenge of Christian nonviolence in the third millennium. In Daniel L. Smith-Christopher (Ed.), *Subverting hatred: The challenge of nonviolence in religious traditions* (pp. 141–165). Cambridge, MA: Boston Research Center for the 21st Century.

Speeches of Martin Luther King. (1988). Videotape produced by Darrell Moore. Oak Forest, IL: MPI Home Video.

Tendulkar, D. G. (1951). *Mahatma: Life of Mohandas Koramchand Gandhi* (vols. 1 and 3). New Delhi, India: Publications Division, Ministry of Information and Broadcasting, Government of India.

Thoreau, Henry David. (1990). Civil disobedience. In Robert L. Holmes (Ed.), *Nonviolence in theory and practice* (pp. 29–40). Belmont, CA: Wadsworth Publishing.

Washington, James Melvin. (Ed.). (1986). *A testament of hope: The essential writings and speeches of Martin Luther King, Jr.* San Francisco: HarperCollins.

Wink, Walter. (1987). *Violence and nonviolence in South Africa: Jesus' third way.* Philadelphia: New Society Publishers, in cooperation with the Fellowship of Reconciliation.

Woito, Robert S. (1982). *To end war: A new approach to international conflict.* New York: Pilgrim Press.

Wolpert, Stanley. (2001). *Gandhi's passion: The life and legacy of Mahatma Gandhi.* New York: Oxford University Press.

Index

Note: Gandhi has been abbreviated as G and King as K.

ABOUT THE AUTHOR

MICHAEL J. NOJEIM is Associate Professor of Political Science at Ohio University-Eastern, St. Clairsville. He teaches courses on nonviolence and has trained inmates in Ohio's prisons to resolve their conflicts using nonviolent means.